KT-526-233

Haskell

The Craft of Functional Programming

Simon Thompson

University of Kent at Canterbury

PARK LEARNING CENTRE
UNIVERSITY OF GLOUCESTERSHIRE
PO Box 220, The Park
Cheltenham GL50 2RH
Tel: 01242 714333

ADDISON-WESLEY

HARLOW, ENGLAND • READING, MASSACHUSETTS • MENLO PARK, CALIFORNIA • NEW YORK
DON MILLS, ONTARIO • AMSTERDAM • BONN • SYDNEY • SINGAPORE
TOKYO • MADRID • SAN JUAN • MILAN • MEXICO CITY • SEOUL • TAIPEI

© Addison Wesley Longman 1996

Addison Wesley Longman Limited
Edinburgh Gate
Harlow
Essex
CM20 2JE
England

and Associated Companies throughout the world.

The right of Simon Thompson to be identified as author of this Work has been asserted by him in accordance with the Copyright, Designs and Patents Act 1988.

All rights reserved. No part of this publication may be reproduced, stored in a retrieval system, or transmitted in any form or by any means, electronic, mechanical, photocopying, recording or otherwise, without prior written permission of the publisher or a licence permitting restricted copying in the United Kingdom issued by the Copyright Licensing Agency Ltd, 90 Tottenham Court Road, London W1P 9HE.

The programs in this book have been included for their instructional value. They have been tested with care but are not guaranteed for any particular purpose. The publisher does not offer any warranties or representations nor does it accept any liabilities with respect to the programs.

Many of the designations used by manufacturers and sellers to distinguish their products are claimed as trademarks. Addison Wesley Longman has made every attempt to supply trademark information about manufacturers and their products mentioned in this book. A list of the trademark designations and their owners appears below.

Cover designed by Designers & Partners of Oxford.
Typeset by CRB Associates, Norwich.
Printed and bound in the United States of America.

First printed 1996

ISBN 0-201-40357-9

British Library Cataloguing-in-Publication Data
A catalogue record for this book is available from the British Library.

Library of Congress Cataloging-in-Publication Data is available

Trademark Notice
Miranda is a trademark of Research Software Limited
Unix is a registered trademark of Novell Inc.

To Alice
and Rory

Preface

Over the last fifteen years, functional programming has come of age. It has been used successfully on a number of substantial projects. A variety of robust and efficient implementations of functional languages have been developed. A functional language is taught as the first programming language in many university computing courses, and at a later stage in most others. Before examining the reasons for its popularity, we give a short overview of functional programming.

What is functional programming?

Functional programming is based on the simplest of models, namely that of finding the value of an expression. This we meet in our first years at school, when we learn to work out expressions like 8+(3-2) by evaluating the two halves, 8 and (3-2), and adding the results together. Functional programming consists of our defining for ourselves functions like + which we can then use to form expressions.

We define these functions by means of equations, like

```
addD a b = 2*(a+b)                                    (1)
```

which we use to calculate the value of an expression like addD 2 (addD 3 4). We evaluate this using (1) to replace applications of addD with their values, so that we can write down a calculation of the value of the expression thus:

```
addD 2 (addD 3 4)
= 2*(2 + (addD 3 4))
= 2*(2 + 2*(3 + 4))
= 32
```

As well as using (1) to calculate, we can read it as a logical description of how the function addD behaves on any values a and b; on the basis of this we can reason about how it behaves. For instance, for any values a and b,

```
addD a b = 2*(a+b) = 2*(b+a) = addD b a
```

This equation holds for *all* possible input values, in contrast to the information we gain from testing a function at a selection of inputs.

On top of this simple model we can build a variety of facilities, which give the functional approach its distinctive flavour. These include higher-order functions, whose arguments and results are themselves functions; polymorphism, which allows a single definition to apply simultaneously to a collection of types; and infinite data structures which are used to model a variety of data objects.

The Haskell language also has support for larger-scale programming, including user-defined algebraic types, such as lists, trees and so on; abstract data types; type classes and modules. These contribute to separating complex tasks into smaller sub-tasks, making the components of systems independent of each other, as well as supporting software re-use.

Why learn functional programming?

As a vehicle for learning programming principles a functional language like Haskell has many advantages. As we have seen, it is based on a simple model which allows us both to perform evaluation by hand, animating our understanding, and to reason about how the programs behave. In this text, both calculation and reasoning have a central part.

The language is higher-level than most. For example, in Haskell the type of lists is defined directly as a recursive type, and so there is no need to examine its implementation by pointers; indeed the functional language can be used as a design language for an imperative implementation. A second instance is provided by polymorphism; generic definitions are introduced with almost no overhead, in contrast to object-oriented languages such as Modula-3 and C++. Haskell also allows, through its type classes, over-loading of names to mean similar things at different types. Moreover, the language supports larger-scale programming by means of its abstract data type and module mechanisms.

For these reasons we see Haskell as providing a sound introduction to programming principles, which can be complemented later by learning an imperative language. Equally valuable is to learn Haskell after using a more traditional language, since it can broaden our view of the programming process as well as illustrating many software engineering techniques of general worth.

Haskell, Hugs and Gofer

The Haskell programming language is set out in the language definition (Hudak *et al.*, 1992; Peterson *et al.*, 1996) and the programs in this book conform to that definition.[1] Haskell 1.3 is broadly similar to version 1.2; the most notable changes lie in the input/output mechanism, and the way in which libraries are organized.

The finalization of the Haskell 1.3 definition has been going on during the final editing of the book, and changes in the definition have been tracked to the best of the author's ability. As the definition is in advance of available implementations, the code available for the programs in the text will be available in Haskell 1.2 and 1.3 forms, for Gofer, Hugs and other implementations of the standard. The pertinent differences are documented in the code, which can be obtained as described on page xi.

Haskell is an advanced programming language, intended for real-world applications, and so it contains a multitude of features. In this introductory text we cannot hope to cover the whole language, although we do aim to include brief descriptions of some of the features we omit, as well as pointers to the literature. Among the topics omitted are constructor classes, the do notation for monads, the `array` library and records.

Beginning students of a language benefit from using as simple an implementation as possible. For this reason we describe the Hugs and Gofer interpreters as we go. Gofer is a Haskell-like language, whose major difference from Haskell is in its type class mechanism, whereas Hugs (for Haskell Users' Gofer System) is an implementation of Haskell.[2] The Haskell programs we give also work in Gofer, with the exception of some of the more advanced class-based functions. We have also implemented the programs containing modules using the Glasgow Haskell compiler; for details of this and other implementations of Haskell see Appendix F.

The approach

The material is grouped into three parts. In the first, we build a foundation, focusing on programming over basic types and lists, using first-order, non-polymorphic programs. Only when readers are fluent with the basics of functions, types and program construction do we look at the three ideas of higher-order functions, polymorphism and type classes, which together give modern functional programming its distinctive flavour and power. Based on this, in the final part we look at larger-scale programming, supported also

---

[1] This is with the exception of the abstract data types of Chapter 12, which use the approach found in Gofer and Hugs. However, a full explanation of the Haskell mechanism is also provided in that chapter.

[2] Apart from the fact that the current release does not implement the module system.

by an exploration of user-defined types, modules, input/output and lazy evaluation, and concluding with an analysis of program efficiency.

As we saw at the beginning of the preface, we can write down calculations of expressions which use our defined functions, and also give proofs of various of their properties; both aspects are emphasized in the text, although it can be read independently of the material on proof.

The crucial test of any programming text is whether it helps the reader to write programs. The book is called 'The *Craft* of Functional Programming' because it aims to give readers help with design of programs right from the start. At each stage we give advice on how functions, types or modules can be designed; in many cases we give a series of steps which aim to simplify the problem by breaking it down into smaller parts.

Software of any importance will be modified during its lifetime; modification and re-use are emphasized when we discuss design, and in the final part of the book we look in particular at how libraries of polymorphic higher-order functions can be re-used in many different contexts.

The advice on design is supplemented by examples and case studies of varying size and complexity. Some, like the Huffman coding example, are free-standing; others, such as the library database, are re-visited a number of times to illustrate how new techniques can be applied to solve existing problems in different ways. This is important in linking together the different parts of the text, and in showing the variety of ways that any problem can be solved in Haskell.

Finally, other case studies are introduced step-by-step. We first see the simulation example when we design algebraic data types in Chapter 10; next it provides realistic examples of abstract data types in Chapter 12, and finally we look at its top level in Chapter 13. Each aspect is separate; together they provide a substantial case study. Other aspects of our approach are:

- Throughout the text, whenever a function is defined we give its type explicitly; the type forms the first and most important piece of documentation for any definition.

- Material is included on how to find proofs by induction; a template to help with setting down the precise goals of an induction proof is included, as is a discussion of how to search for proofs about functions defined by equations.

- Appendices contain support material of various kinds. In one we give pointers to sites from which implementations of Haskell and Gofer can be obtained. Common errors and error messages are collected in a second; a glossary of programming terms commonly used in another. A fourth appendix gives functions from parts of the Haskell standard preludes, a fifth examines how functional and imperative programming are linked and a sixth gives references for further reading. Finally, we give an overview of how to understand an unfamiliar function definition in Haskell.

- Over four hundred exercises of varying difficulty are included.

- Further support material, including the code for all the definitions in the text and support material for teachers, can be found on the World Wide Web page

```
http://www.ukc.ac.uk/computer_science/Haskell_craft/
```

Outline

The material is presented in three parts.

Part I. Basic functional programming

The aim of Part I is to introduce the basic tools of functional programming, and to give detailed guidance about how to *build* programs to solve particular problems.

The technical material covers the basic types of Haskell: numbers, both integers and floating-point, characters and Booleans, and the structured types of tuples and lists. Readers are introduced to function definitions involving guards, pattern matching and local definitions through a sequence of examples and sections.

Throughout the introduction, details are given about how particular problems can be approached, to encourage students to develop their own solutions. Divide-and-conquer methods and top-down design are encouraged, and illustrated by means of examples including a small database, the production of supermarket bills, text processing and the solution of various sorts of algebraic equation.

To animate the programs, calculations of many examples are given, and readers are encouraged to try definitions out using these rewriting sequences. Integrated into this and the other parts of the book are proofs of program properties. These are shown to be written to a template, in the cases of proof over numbers and lists, and many examples of graded difficulty are presented. More traditional approaches to software testing are also discussed and encouraged.

The material in this part is all first-order and non-polymorphic, deliberately. The aim of the part is to give students a firm grounding on which they can make the abstractions which are the subject of the next part. The approach in this part of the book is purposely slow and intended to reinforce ideas through examples; we indicate which sections may be omitted to make a 'fast track' in the notes for the teacher below.

Part II. Abstraction

This part forms the bridge between the material on basic functional programming, and the larger-scale programs of the final part. The distinctive features of languages like Haskell are that they are *higher-order*, allowing functions as arguments to and results of other functions; they are *polymorphic*, with definitions applying to, for instance, all types of list rather than to lists of a single type; and finally they contain *classes*, which give a mechanism for overloading names to mean similar things at different types. Classes also support an object-oriented style which we touch on in Part III.

Higher-order and polymorphic functions are shown in this part to be generalizations or abstractions of definitions familiar from the first part: an example is the map function which applies an operation to every member of a list, irrespective of the operation (which becomes a parameter) and the type of the list.

The simplest example of an overloaded function is equality, ==, which uses different methods at different types to check the equality of two elements. We say that types with an equality function belong to the equality class Eq, and in general a type belongs to a class if the functions in the class definition are defined over that particular type.

These technical ideas are introduced, and many of the examples of Part I are re-examined to show the general higher-order functions they exemplify or use. Libraries of general functions are developed, particularly over the polymorphic list type.

The consequences of these ideas for software design and engineering are also examined: polymorphic higher-order functions are ideal candidates for re-use, and this is illustrated in the examples.

The most technical chapter of the book is the final one of this part, where type checking is presented. This is necessary fully to exploit the features of the language, and also to understand the error messages which result when type checking fails.

Program verification is a continuing theme here, and it is argued that theorems about general functions are re-usable in the same way as the functions themselves.

Part III. Larger-scale programming

The final part of the book brings in aspects of the language which support larger-scale programming: user defined concrete (or algebraic) types; modules; abstract data types. In introducing each of these, examples are given, together with general principles for design of systems which contain algebraic and abstract data types, as well as how systems are built top-down and bottom-up using modules.

Among the examples we look at are the design and use of Huffman codes, the simulation of multiple queues (as might be found in a bank), finding the difference between two files, simple interactive programs and aspects of a simple arithmetic calculator.

Lazy evaluation is also discussed here. After showing precisely what it means and how it works, the consequences it has for program development are explored. These include data-directed solutions, infinite data structures and interactive streams of input and output.

For more complex interactions we show how a *monadic* approach to I/O is useful, and we also introduce an example of a monadic program in a general programming setting. Design principles for interactive programs are explored, and verification is addressed.

The book concludes with an analysis of program behaviour, including the time taken and spaced used during evaluation. Examples from the text are re-visited, and various strategies for optimizing program performance are introduced.

Appendices, bibliography and index

The appendices consist of: a comparison of functional and imperative programming; a glossary of commonly used and technical terms; sources for further reading; a discussion of common error messages, and their possible sources; an annotated listing of some of the built-in functions from the standard preludes and a reminder of the ways that unfamiliar definitions can be understood. We also give pointers to sites from which implementations of Haskell can be obtained.

Who should read this book?

This text is intended as an introduction to functional programming for computer science and other students, principally at university level. It can be used by beginners to computer science, or more experienced students who are learning functional programming for the first time; either group will find the material is new, challenging and interesting.

The book can also be used for self-study by programmers, software engineers and others interested in gaining a grounding in functional programming.

The text is intended to be self-contained, but some elementary knowledge of commands, files and so on would be needed to use any of the implementations of Haskell. Some logical notation is introduced in the text; this is explained as it appears. In the final chapter it would be helpful to have an understanding of the graphs of the $\log$, n^2 and 2^n functions.

To the teacher

Depending upon a teacher's preferences and the context in which the course is taught, different routes through the book exist. The ordering of the text roughly corresponds to the first year course at the University of Kent, although the material here is much expanded from that given to our students.

The book follows a linear progression, and it makes sense to follow it from Chapter 1 to Chapter 15; if time does not permit, a coherent course on smaller-scale programming is given by the first part; together with the second, students will gain an additional grounding in the novelties of functional programming, while more advanced techniques are introduced in Part III. For a 'fast track' through Part I, one can omit Sections 2.9, 2.13, the exercise in 2.14, 4.7, 4.8 and 5.4.

In Part III it is possible to pick and choose chapters and sections, rather than following the material page-by-page. The case studies illustrate the material, but a teacher could use his or her own examples rather than those of Huffman coding or relations and graphs, for instance. The calculator and simulation examples are distributed through Part III; another approach would be to delay them until all the supporting material has been studied.

Integral to this course is reasoning about programs, but the material on proof in this text stands independently, and so a proof-free course could be given by omitting Chapters 3 and 5, and Sections 7.8, 10.7 and 13.9. It would also be feasible to give the proof material rather later than it appears in the text. Also standing alone is the material on program behaviour; this could be omitted if so desired.

It is impossible to exclude some more technical sections from the book, but some of this material could be deferred, mentioned in passing or given an informal gloss. In the first two parts, Sections 5.4, 8.4 and 9.3 are potential candidates.

Students should be encouraged to use the information in the appendices. Depending upon their backgrounds, the comparison of functional and imperative programming can be illuminating in both directions; at the University of Kent we find that linking the treatment of lists in a functional and an imperative language is very helpful for students who are learning the intricacies of pointer-based linked lists

Also to be recommended to students is the glossary; both for beginners to programming, and to those familiar with other programming paradigms, some of the terminology of functional programming is either new or consists of common terms used in a slightly different way from the norm. In either case, students should be encouraged to look up words they are unsure about. Also in the appendices are a full treatment of common errors, a reminder of the different ways to understand an unfamiliar function and sources for further reading.

Resources for teachers, including the program text for all the definitions in the book (in both Haskell and Gofer) and a teachers' guide are available on-line from the World Wide Web page mentioned above.

Acknowledgements

I am very grateful indeed to Roy Dyckhoff and Ham Richards, whose refereeing of the manuscript has brought to light numerous errors and slips of the finger. Equally importantly, they have been able to suggest many ways of improving the presentation of the ideas in the book. Olaf Chitil, Steve Hill, Tom Locke and Dan Russell have performed a similar service for the material on type classes and monads.

I have used Hugs and Gofer in writing the text, and I therefore very much appreciate the efforts of Mark Jones in building these excellent systems. Many of the programs here were translated into Haskell; this was made much easier by the `mira2hs` program written by Denis Howe.

The staff at Addison Wesley Longman have smoothed the way of the book at every stage. Particular thanks are due to Simon Plumtree, Stephen Bishop and Dylan Reisenberger for editing and production in the UK, as well as Ari Davidow in the USA for World Wide Web support and CRB Associates for typesetting. At the University of Kent, Sally Fincher, Louise Heery and Richard Hesketh have endured my novice's questions about the Web with great good humour.

Jane, Alice and Rory have again come up trumps, making space and providing support while I was writing the book; thank you all very much.

Simon Thompson
Canterbury, April 1996

Contents

Part I

Basic Functional Programming

Introducing functional programming

This chapter introduces the fundamental ideas of functional programming in Haskell, including how to write, test and use functional programs. We also discuss how to use the Hugs and Gofer systems which give implementations of Haskell suitable for use with this book; other implementations of Haskell are discussed in Appendix F.

1.1   What is functional programming?

This section introduces the fundamental ideas behind functional programming, some of which are familiar from our first introduction to arithmetic at school. It also brings in some of the terminology we will be using throughout the book.

Computer programs

Computers are machines to perform tasks which can be automated; some of these are jobs which we could do if we so wished, like calculating the total cost of a basket of shopping at the supermarket, while others, like producing accurate weather forecasts, are only possible because of the speed at which present-day computers operate.

    Common to all these systems is the **program**, which describes how the system is to behave. We can describe programs to each other in ordinary language:

```
Take a number, subtract three, double it and add six.

Take the total cost of the items in the bill, then add
VAT at the standard rate.

Lay out the words of the book so that each line of the
book is of length exactly eighty letters.
```

Although these programs appear clear, they are ambiguous. We can interpret what should be done in more than one way: do we round up or down in the VAT calculation; what do we do with lines at the end of a paragraph? Even if we were able to *write* our programs in English, present-day computers would be unable to interpret what we had written; instead we have to use a computer **programming language**.

    Programming languages are formal languages which are used for describing programs. This book describes **functional** programming, in the programming language Haskell. During the short history of computing, languages have become more **high-level**: the first languages were simply a shorthand for operations on the hardware of the computer; since then the trend has been to make languages which directly express ideas at a level closer to the way we think. Functional languages are among the highest-level languages in present-day use.

    Since programming languages are precisely defined there is no possibility of the ambiguities we saw with English. To anticipate a little, we could re-write our first program in Haskell thus

```
((n - 3) * 2) + 6
```

where the n stands for the unknown number over which this program works.

Functions

Despite their variety, computer programs can all be seen to be behaving in a similar way. Programs take **input** data, and transform them into **output** data. A functional program *describes* directly how the data are analysed, manipulated and re-assembled. The most common way of describing a transformation is as a **function**. A function is something which will return an output which depends upon one or more inputs (Figure 1.1).

We will often use the term **result** for the output, and the terms **arguments** or **parameters** for the inputs. Examples of functions include

- A function giving the distance by road (*output*) between two cities (*inputs*).

- A supermarket checkout program, which calculates the bill (*output*) from a list of bar codes scanned in (*input*).

- Mathematical functions, like *sin*, *cos*, $\sqrt{}$ and so on, whose inputs and outputs are numbers.

- A text formatting program, such as the one used to prepare this book. The input is the unformatted text, together with instructions about how exactly it is to be processed; the output consists of the appropriate printing instructions.

- A database system, which gives a reply (*output*) to a question concerning the information it contains (*input*).

- A process controller, which controls valves in a chemical plant. Its inputs are the information from sensors, and its output the signals sent to the valve actuators.

- An interactive program returns a sequence of responses (*output*) in reply to a sequence of commands (*input*).

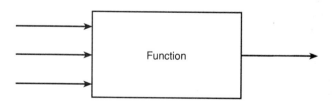

Figure 1.1   A function.

Calculation

When we first start at school, we learn how to **calculate** the value of **expressions** like ((7 - 3) * 2). Every expression like this has a **value** which is a number. To work out the value of ((7 - 3) * 2) we need to multiply together the left- and right-hand sides. The latter is a number, 2, but the left-hand side needs to be calculated itself. This gives 4, and so the whole expression gives 8. A larger example can be written

```
((7 - 3) * 2) + 6
= (4 * 2) + 6
= 8 + 6
= 14
```

For many expressions, there is more than one way to calculate their value; the order in which we calculate does not affect the result we produce. For instance,

```
(7-3) * (4+2)          (7-3) * (4+2)
= 4* (4+2)            =  (7-3) *6
= 4*6                 = 4*6
= 24                  = 24
```

To help us with arithmetic we can use a calculator; we key in an expression such as (7-3)*(4+2), which involves numbers and the operations +, −, *, to get the result 24.

Functional programming

Functional programming is based on the idea of calculation. We define for ourselves the functions to be used, and the implementation will calculate the values of expressions which use these functions, just as a traditional calculator will calculate arithmetical expressions like those given above.

A functional program, or **script** as it is called in Haskell, consists of a number of definitions of functions and other values such as numbers and pairs. As an example, suppose assessment marks need to be analysed. Functions in a script could include ones to:

- give the total of a collection of marks;
- sort a list of student names or of numbers;
- calculate the most common value in a sequence of marks; and so on.

Using these functions we can, for instance, produce

- the total marks awarded to a particular student over a given year,
- the list of students sorted according to their average mark for the term.

In summary, functional programming consists of defining functions and other values. An implementation of a functional language will calculate the value of any expression using the defined functions.

Appendix A contains a comparison of functional and imperative programming in languages like `Pascal` and `C`.

Types

The examples we discussed earlier cover many different areas; data include 2, 1, 3.145, "A piece of text", "Another piece of text", *January*, *July* and so on. We do not expect all these data to be treated in the same way, and they can be grouped into *types* of similar data. Informally,

- 2, 1, 3.145 are numbers, 2, 1 being whole numbers or **integers**, while 3.145 is a floating point number with a fractional part;
- "A piece of text" is an example of a text string; and
- *January*, *July* are months

Once we have divided the data into types, we can see that the functions we define will expect certain types of data. For example, +, −, *, / expect numbers and return numbers; the function giving the number of days in a month expects an argument which is a month, and returns an integer. It makes no sense to add together two months, or to ask for the number of days in a bar code.

This informal idea of type is formalized in Haskell (as it is in nearly every programming language in common use). Every object has a type, and the system will, for instance, check that functions are applied only to objects of the appropriate input type. These and other **type constraints** apply to the expressions and definitions which we write, and are enforced by the Haskell system.

In the chapters to come we shall explore the types in detail; here we briefly introduce the type `Bool` of Boolean values which is mentioned in the following section. The Booleans, named after George Boole who was one of the founders of modern logic, are the two values `True` and `False` which we can think of as the two results of a logical test, such as 'Is this number greater than that number?'. For instance, 2>1 will have the value `True` whereas 2>11 has the value `False`. These values, sometimes called **truth values**, can be combined by the operators '*and*', && '*or*', || and '*not*', not. A test t_1 && t_2 will be True only if both the tests t_1 and t_2 give True, for instance.

1.2   Haskell

In this section we introduce Haskell programming, and show how to make calculations using Haskell functions.

An example script

Figure 1.2 gives an example Haskell script. A script contains a number of definitions. Each definition associates a name, like answer or square, with a value, which may be of any type. The script also contains **comments** which are added to a script to make it easier to read, both for the person who has written it, and anyone else. The symbol -- makes the part of the line to its right a comment. The comments at the start of the script indicate its general purpose; those which follow comment on the purpose of the individual definitions.

We now discuss the definitions in the script one by one.

```
answer :: Int
answer = 42
```

The first line **declares** the type of a name. The notation '::' is read as '*is of type*', and so the first line says that answer is of type Int, the Haskell type of integers or whole numbers. The next line gives the value of 42 to answer. The symbol '=' is used to make a definition.

```
newline :: Char
newline = '\n'
```

Here newline is defined to be the newline character, belonging to the type Char; a full description of this type and special characters such as newline is to be found in the following chapter.

```
yes :: Bool
yes = True

greater :: Bool
greater = (answer>71)
```

Here two Boolean values are defined. First yes is given the value True; then greater is given the value False, since 42 fails to be larger than 71. The

```
-----------------------------------------------------------------
--                                                             --
--      example.hs                                             --
--                                                             --
--      Some example definitions to illustrate the form        --
--      of Haskell scripts.                                    --
--                                                             --
-----------------------------------------------------------------

answer :: Int               -- An integer constant
answer = 42

newline :: Char
newline = '\n'

yes :: Bool                 -- The answer yes is represented
yes = True                  -- by the Boolean value True.

greater :: Bool             -- Uses the value of answer
greater = (answer>71)


-----------------------------------------------------------------
--      To square a whole number                               --
-----------------------------------------------------------------

square :: Int -> Int
square x = x*x


-----------------------------------------------------------------
--      Are three whole numbers equal?                         --
-----------------------------------------------------------------

allEqual :: Int -> Int -> Int -> Bool
allEqual n m p = (n==m) && (m==p)


-----------------------------------------------------------------
--      The maximum of two integers                            --
-----------------------------------------------------------------

maxi :: Int -> Int -> Int
maxi n m
  | n>=m            = n
  | otherwise       = m
```

Figure 1.2 An example script.

definition of `greater` uses one of the other definitions, `answer`. In Haskell any definition may use any other definition in the same script; in particular it can use a definition which occurs after it in the script.

In this script each definition is preceded by a declaration of its type. The type of a definition is the most important piece of documentation we can supply. It tells us how a definition can be used: we can only use `yes` where a Boolean value is expected, for example. Because of this, we always give type declarations at the same time as our definitions, even though it is not compulsory in Haskell.

Scripts can also contain function definitions.

```
square :: Int -> Int
square x = x*x
```

The type declaration says that `square` is a function from integers to integers, since `Int -> Int` is the type of functions from `Int` to `Int`. We can read '`->`' as 'to', so the declaration of the type of `square` reads 'square is of type `Int` to `Int`'.

The definition itself is an **equation**. It gives the result, `x*x`, of applying `square` to `x`. `x` is a **variable**, which stands for the input of the function. The output is defined, using this input, on the right-hand side of the defining equation.

It is worth stressing the syntax here: to apply a function `f` to the arguments `a`, `b` and `c`, we write `f` next to the arguments, thus

```
f a b c
```

This way of writing function application is called **juxtaposition**.

```
allEqual :: Int -> Int -> Int -> Bool
allEqual n m p = (n==m) && (m==p)
```

`allEqual` is a function which takes three numbers to a Boolean. Formally it has the type `Int -> Int -> Int -> Bool`. Its value, when applied to the three numbers n, m and p is a combination of two tests: the test that n equals m, given by n==m, and the test that m equals p. The result will be `True` if both tests give `True`, and will be `False` if not. A final example is given by

```
maxi :: Int -> Int -> Int
maxi n m
  | n>=m        = n
  | otherwise   = m
```

The function `maxi` is to return the maximum of its two integer arguments. In deciding the answer, we make a *test* of which is larger. Tests or **guards** are

Boolean expressions which lie between the bar, | and the equals, =, 'guarding' which option is to be chosen.

If n is bigger than or equal to m, the output is n; if not we try the next guard. Here it is otherwise, signalling that in all other circumstances (that is when m is larger than n) the result is m.

We call a definition like this a **conditional equation**, since it states that

```
maxi n m = n
```

if the condition or guard n>=m has the value True; otherwise the equation

```
maxi n m = m
```

will hold. The two alternatives given in the definition are called its **clauses**.

The full details of scripts and the syntax of definitions will be covered in later chapters.

Calculation in Haskell

We explained that functional programming was like calculation or evaluation in arithmetic, except that we use our own functions and other definitions. How is evaluation done with the definitions we saw in Figure 1.2?

The definition of answer is clear: answer has the value 42, so in evaluation we can replace it by 42. Function definitions can be interpreted similarly. We can, for example, read the definition

```
allEqual n m p = (n==m) && (m==p)
```

as giving the value of allEqual n m p for any values of n, m and p. We get *particular* values of allEqual by replacing, or **substituting** for, the variables with the values in the defining equation, thus:

```
allEqual 2 3 3            allEqual 5 5 5
= (2==3) && (3==3)        = (5==5) && (5==5)
```

We continue the calculations by working out the component Boolean values, and then combine them using &&.

```
allEqual 2 3 3            allEqual 5 5 5
= (2==3) && (3==3)        = (5==5) && (5==5)
= False && True           = True && True
= False                   = True
```

Examples can involve more than one definition:

```
allEqual (square 3) answer (square 2)
= ((square 3) == answer) && (answer == (square 2))
= ((3*3) == 42) && (42 == (2*2))
= (9 == 42) && (42 == 4)
= False && False
= False
```

The definition of `maxi` contains two cases, given by the two clauses of the conditional equation:

```
maxi n m
  | n>=m        = n
  | otherwise   = m
```

To work out which of the values to use, we have to work out the values of the guards one by one from top to bottom until one is found which gives the value `True`. In writing out the calculation, '??' is used to signal the calculation of a guard. For instance

```
maxi 3 1
  ??  3>=1 = True
= 3
```

Here we have to judge whether 3>=1 holds to tell which clause applies. Since 3 is greater than 1, the first clause is used; on the other hand,

```
maxi 3 4
  ??  3>=4 = False
  ??  otherwise = True
= 4
```

As 3>=4 is `False`, the second clause is examined. This is an `otherwise` clause which always applies if it is reached. A more complicated example of evaluation is now given:

```
allEqual (maxi 1 5) 5 (maxi 4 2)
= ((maxi 1 5) == 5) && (5 == (maxi 4 2))
  ??  1>=5 = False
  ??  otherwise = True
= (5 == 5) && (5 == (maxi 4 2))
  ??  4>=2 = True
= (5 == 5) && (5 == 4)
= True && False
= False
```

When we perform a calculation, we can choose to evaluate things in a different order. It is most important that *this will not change the final answer we produce*, although it may mean that no answer is found; this is explored in detail in Chapter 13. For instance,

```
allEqual (maxi 1 5) 5 (maxi 4 2)
= ((maxi 1 5) == 5) && (5 == (maxi 4 2))
    ??  4>=2 = True
= ((maxi 1 5) == 5) && (5 == 4)
    ??  1>=5 = False
    ??  otherwise = True
= (5 == 5) && (5 == 4)
= True && False
= False
```

It can be helpful to show in a calculation which part of the expression we are going to evaluate next. We do this for the previous example now, by underlining at each stage the part of the expression to be evaluated next.

```
allEqual (maxi 1 5) 5 (maxi 4 2)
= ((maxi 1 5) == 5) && (5 == (maxi 4 2))
    ??  4>=2 = True
= ((maxi 1 5) == 5) && (5 == 4)
    ??  1>=5 = False
    ??  otherwise = True
= (5 == 5) && (5 == 4)
= True && False
= False
```

The two cases of underlining in (5 == 5) & (5 == 4) show that we have really done two steps in one here, by evaluating both sides of the '&&' at once.

1.3   Gofer and Hugs

Haskell is the programming language of this text. It has numerous implementations, detailed in Appendix F. The programs we provide will be usable in any implementation, but to aid beginners we also describe how to use one of the simpler systems. Gofer is a functional programming environment which has been available for some years for PCs, Macintoshes and various Unix machines. Gofer is close to Haskell but not identical, whereas Hugs (short for Haskell Users' Gofer System) is a subset of full Haskell. The programs in this book will work for either system, apart from some of the examples involving classes; see Chapter 8 for details.

Gofer and Hugs are invoked by typing `gofer` or `hugs`. In either case we get back the prompt:

```
?
```

after an initial message giving the name of the system and of the file of standard functions, called the **prelude**, and so on. Invoking Gofer or Hugs begins what is called a **session** which continues until the system is quit.

The systems act like a calculator; the prompt indicates that the system is ready to read an expression. The expression is evaluated, and then its value is printed. This behaviour, which is shared by many computer systems, is often called a 'read-evaluate-print loop'. An example interaction might look like

```
? 2+3
5
? (1*6)==(3 'div' 5)
False
    . . .
```

where the user's input is shown underlined. (We just make this distinction in this introductory section, as generally underlining is distracting.)

Haskell scripts are stored in *files*, carrying the suffixes '.g' or '.hs'. Suppose that the script from the previous section is stored in the file example.hs. This can be loaded into the system in two ways. During a session, it is loaded by typing

```
? :l example.hs
```

or it can be loaded when the system is started up by typing

```
gofer example.hs   hugs example.hs
```

instead of the command on its own. Once loaded, the definitions given in the file can be used in the expressions to be evaluated.

```
? maxi (square 2) 1
4
? allEqual answer 3 $$
False
```

In the second example $$ is used as shorthand for the last expression evaluated, in this case `maxi (square 2) 1`.

Typing an expression after ':type' will give its type.

```
? :type 2+answer
Int
? :type maxi
Int -> Int -> Int
```

Instead of typing an expression, one of a number of *commands* can be issued. The most important commands include

:e	Invoke the built in editor on the current script.
:e parrot.g	Edit the file parrot.g.
:l rabbit.hs	Load the script rabbit.hs (clears other loaded files).
:a hare.hs	Load the script hare.hs, without clearing other files.
:?	Display a list of commands.
:q	Quit the session.
!blah	Escape to perform the Unix command blah.

There is extensive documentation on the Gofer and Hugs systems, available in machine-readable form; consult your local system manager for details of where this might be.

Examples from this book and other backup resources are to be found on the World Wide Web at

```
http://www.ukc.ac.uk/computer_science/Haskell_craft/
```

where further details can be found about how to access particular items.

1.4   Practical work

Learning a programming language is like learning any other craft; you can learn part of the skill by reading about it, but you only learn fully by *doing* it. Each chapter of the book contains exercises of various sorts, together with hints about how to do some of them, and advice about functional programming in general.

Using Gofer and Hugs

Section 1.3 gave an introduction to the Gofer and Hugs systems. To see them in practice, begin a session by typing gofer or hugs and then type the following expressions. Before you type an expression in, write down what result you expect.

```
(2+3)
$$-1      $$  -|
5-4-3
7/3
7 'div' 3
4 'div' $$
7 'mod' 3
True || False
not False && False
```

Now make a new file by typing

```
:e myExample.hs
```

which will take you into the editor on the file myExample.hs. Type in the definitions from the file example.hs (excluding the comments if you wish) and then type

```
answer + 42
greater
square answer
square $$
allEqual 2 3 3
allEqual 5 5 5
allEqual (square 5) answer (maxi (-4) 2)
```

Gofer and Hugs errors

Any system cannot guarantee that what you type is sensible; if something is wrong, you will receive an **error message**. Try typing

```
2+(3+4
2+(3+4))
```

These errors are in the **syntax**, and are like sentences in English which do not have the correct grammatical structure, such as 'Fishcake our camel'. The first expression has too few parentheses, the second too many. After the '4', a closing parenthesis is expected, to match with the opening parenthesis before '3'. The error messages reflect this by saying that what follows '4' is unexpected:

```
ERROR: Syntax error in expression (unexpected end of input)
ERROR: Syntax error in input (unexpected ')')
```

Now try the following expression.

```
maxi 2 True
```

This gives a **type** error, since `maxi` is applied to a Boolean value, rather than an integer:

```
ERROR: Type error in application
*** expression     : maxi 2 True
*** term           : True
*** type           : Bool
*** does not match : Int
```

The message indicates that something of type `Int` was expected, but something of type `Bool` was present instead. Here `maxi` expects something of type `Int` for both arguments, but `True` of type `Bool` is found in the place of the second argument.

When you get an error message like the one above you need to look at how the *term*, in this case `True` of type `Bool`, does not match the *context* in which it is used: the context is given in the second line (`maxi 2 True`) and the type required by the context, `Int`, is given in the final line.

Type errors do not always give rise to such well-structured error messages. Typing either `4 && True` or `4 5` will give rise to a message like

```
ERROR: Cannot construct instance .... in expression
```

We will explore the technical details behind these messages in a later chapter; for now it is sufficient to read these as 'type error!'.

The last kind of error we will see are **program** errors. Try the expression

```
4 `div` (3*2-6)
```

We cannot divide by zero (what would the result be?) and so we get the message

```
Program error: {primDivInt 4 0}
```

indicating that a division of 4 by 0 has occurred. More details about the error messages produced by the Gofer and Hugs systems can be found in Appendix G.

Writing scripts

One of the first tasks you will be asked to do is write new programs, or in the Haskell terminology, scripts. When you are starting to program (or indeed when you have more experience) it is often useful to ask what you can build on. There are three ways you can do this.

First, you can build on what you have already written or seen. Suppose you are asked to write a function

```
allFourEqual :: Int -> Int -> Int -> Int -> Bool
```

which gives the answer True if its four arguments are all equal to each other. We have already written a similar function, allEqual, and you could modify that definition to get the new function definition.

Second, you could think of solving a *simpler* problem first. Suppose you are asked to write a function

```
howManyEqual :: Int -> Int -> Int -> Int
```

which when given three numbers returns how many of them are equal to each other; the answers will be 1, 2 and 3. Instead of solving that problem, ask yourself how you could simplify it. An obvious simplification would be to write instead

```
howManyOfTwoEqual :: Int -> Int -> Int
```

which when given *two* numbers returns how many of them are equal. Once you have solved this, you have a model to work on for defining howManyEqual.

Third, and last, you could *use* a function already defined. You could, if asked to write a function to cube a number, use the function you know for finding the square of a number.

```
cube :: Int -> Int
cube x = x * square x
```

Testing

Once you have written a function which does not cause any syntax or type errors, you need to assure yourself that it has the required effect. One way you can find that it does *not* do what it should is to test it with representative test data.

Suppose you have to write a function allEqual to check whether three numbers are equal. What would be suitable test data? You need to think about the different kinds of input you could give to a function like this. It splits three ways, to start with:

- all three inputs are equal;
- two of the inputs are equal;
- all three inputs are different.

You should test each of these different kinds of input. You might stop there, or decide that the ordering of the inputs might matter, so you could test the three different numbers in different orders. Again, you might want to check zero and negative numbers separately, or make even more different cases.

If you have the definition of the function allEqual in the file eq.hs, to test it you need to load the file into Gofer or Hugs as explained above and then evaluate the test expressions:

```
allEqual 3 3 3
allEqual 3 4 3
allEqual 4 3 5
```

It is a useful property of an interpreter like Gofer or Hugs that we can evaluate expressions one after another interactively, and so test functions in the way we have seen here.

Whatever the approach you take to testing, you can never test *all* the possible inputs, and errors can slip through quite thorough tests. One way out of this problem is to take a different approach and to **prove** that a function behaves as it ought to on all its inputs. This we address in Chapter 3.

EXERCISES

1.1   Give a definition of the function allFourEqual of type

```
Int -> Int -> Int -> Int -> Bool
```

which gives the result True if its four arguments are equal.

1.2   Can you give a definition of allFourEqual which *uses* the function allEqual?

1.3   Give definitions of the functions

```
howManyEqual :: Int -> Int -> Int -> Int
```

and

```
howManyOfTwoEqual :: Int -> Int -> Int
```

which count how many of their arguments are equal.

1.4 Give a definition of a function

```
allDifferent :: Int -> Int -> Int -> Bool
```

which gives the value True if the three arguments are all different. You might
need to use the function '/=' with the property that m /= n is True if m and n are
not equal.

1.5 Design test data for the function allDifferent.

1.6 What is wrong with the following definition of allDifferent?

```
allDifferent n m p = ( (n /= m) && (m /= p) )
```

Does this definition pass your test data?

1.7 Give a definition of howManyEqual which *uses* the functions allEqual and
allDifferent.

1.8 Give a definition of the function

```
fourPower :: Int -> Int
```

which returns its argument to the power four. Give a definition which uses the
function square.

1.9 Design what you consider to be adequate test data for the function allEqual.
Consider the function

```
tester :: Int -> Int -> Int -> Int Bool
tester n m p = ((n+m+p) == 3*p)
```

Does it behave in exactly the same way as the allEqual function does for your
test data? What do you think this conclusion implies for testing in general?

1.10 Write down calculations of the following expressions

```
maxi ((2+3)-7) (4+(1-3))
howManyOfTwoEqual 3 3
howManyEqual 3 4 3
```

Your answers should use underlining to show the next expression to be evaluated,
and should show tests being calculated.

1.11 Perform calculations of the following expressions

```
allFourEqual 5 6 4 5
howManyOfTwoEqual 3 4
```

Your answers should show tests being calculated.

SUMMARY

This chapter has laid the foundations for the rest of the book. We have seen the fundamental ideas behind functional programming:

- a function is an object which transforms input(s) to an output;
- a script is a collection of definitions;
- a type is a collection of objects of similar sort, such as the whole numbers (or integers), or the calendar months;
- every object has a clearly defined type, and we state this type on making a definition;
- functions defined in scripts are used in writing expressions to be evaluated by the implementation; and
- the values can be found by performing calculation by hand.

We have also seen how definitions are written in Haskell, and how the system is used to perform calculations involving them. Finally, we saw various ways to solve problems by modifying solutions to similar problems or by using functions already defined; we concluded by showing how to test the definitions we make.

2 Basic types and simple programs

This chapter explores the basic types of Haskell – numbers, Boolean values, characters, strings and tuples – and straightforward forms of function definition. The basic types are common to almost all programming languages.

2.1 The numbers: integers

The Haskell type Int contains the integers. The integers are the whole numbers, used for counting; they are written thus:

```
0
45
-3452
2147483647
```

The last value here is the maximum integer maxInt in the Int type, since these numbers are represented in a fixed amount of space. For the majority of calculations these fixed size numbers are suitable, but if full accuracy is needed the Integer type can be used.[1] We perform arithmetic on integers using the following operators and functions:

+, *	Add, multiply two integers
^	Raise to the power; 2^3 is 8
-	Subtract one integer from another, when infix: a-b; change the sign of an integer, when prefix: -a
div	Whole number division; for example div 14 3 is 4. This can also be written 14 `div` 3
mod	The remainder from whole number division; for example mod 14 3 (or 14 `mod` 3) is 2
abs	The absolute value of an integer; remove the sign
negate	The function to change the sign of an integer

Note that `mod` is written between its two arguments, and so is an **infix** version of the function mod. Any function can be made infix in this way.

NB. A common pitfall occurs with negative numbers. For example the number minus twelve is written as -12, but the prefix '-' can often get confused with the infix operator to subtract one number from another and can lead to unforeseen and confusing type error messages like

```
ERROR: Cannot construct instance Num (a -> a) in
expression
```

or

```
ERROR: Type error in application
```

[1] We choose to work with Int here for two reasons. The main reason is that various standard Haskell functions which we introduce later in the chapter use the Int type. Also, Int is the only integer type in Gofer.

If in any doubt, you should enclose negative numbers in parentheses, thus: (-12).

There are ordering and (in)equality relations over the integers, as there are over all basic types. These functions take two integers as input, and return a Bool. The relations are

>	greater than (and not equal to)
>=	greater than or equal to
==	equal to
/=	not equal to
<=	less than or equal to
<	less than (and not equal to)

In what follows we will use the term the **natural numbers** for the non-negative integers: 0, 1, 2, ...

2.2   Programming with integers

We begin to look at programming with integers by looking at some examples. Suppose we are given a function

```
sales :: Int -> Int
```

which gives the weekly sales from a shop, where weeks are numbered in sequence 0, 1, 2, ... We are asked to find out the following information:

- total sales for the period week 0 to week n;
- the maximum weekly sale during weeks 0 to n;
- the week in which the maximum sale took place;
- whether there is a week between week 0 and week n in which no sales took place;
- a week between week 0 and week n in which no sales took place (if there is such a week).

How should we begin? If we were asked, for instance, for the total sales for the period week 0 to week 2, we could simply write

```
sales 0 + sales 1 + sales 2
```

However, we have to give the answer for each possible value of n. In other words, we need to write a *function* whose input is n and whose output is the total sales for the period up to week n. To solve the other problems we will also need to write functions.

If we are asked to write a function, the first thing we should do is to choose a name for it and to write down its type. Here we have

```
totalSales :: Int -> Int
```

as we take as input a week number n and give as the output the total of the sales during the period up to and including week n. How does the definition look? It can be split into two cases.

- The sales up to week 0 are going to be just `sales 0`.

- What about the case of week n when n>0? The total will be

    ```
    sales 0 + sales 1 + ... + sales (n-1) + sales n
    ```

    where the underlined part is the total sales up to week (n-1). We therefore get the total we seek by adding this underlined value, `totalSales (n-1)`, to the sales in week n.

The definition in Haskell is then going to be

```
totalSales n
  | n==0       = sales 0
  | otherwise  = totalSales (n-1) + sales n
```

Suppose that the sales in weeks 0, 1 and 2 are 7, 2 and 5. The definition gives

```
totalSales 2
= totalSales 1 + sales 2
= (totalSales 0 + sales 1) + sales 2
= (sales 0 + sales 1) + sales 2
= (7 + 2) + 5
= 14
```

We can tackle the problem of finding the maximum sales in weeks 0 to n in a similar way. The function will have type

```
maxSales :: Int -> Int
```

and again we can make two cases in the definition.

- The maximum in the weeks up to week 0 must be `sales 0`.

- In the case when n>0 the maximum can occur in one of two places. It can either be in the weeks up to (and including) week (n-1), or it can be week n itself. The maximum for the weeks up to (n-1) is maxSales (n-1), and this has to be compared to sales n.

The Haskell definition of the function is

```
maxSales n
  | n==0                         = sales 0
  | maxSales (n-1) >= sales n   = maxSales (n-1)
  | otherwise                    = sales n
```

There is, in fact, a neater solution of the problem. In the general case, what we have to do is find the maximum of maxSales (n-1) and sales n. We can therefore use the function maxi defined in the previous chapter, thus:

```
maxSales n
  | n==0        = sales 0
  | otherwise   = maxi (maxSales (n-1)) (sales n)
```

Why is this solution preferable?

- The two cases of n being 0 and being greater than 0 are clearer in this solution.

- Finding the maximum of two values is a separate calculation, and so the program should make it a separate function definition. Any problem is made easier to solve if it is split into two problems which can be solved separately. This is sometimes called the 'divide and conquer' principle.

- Because of this separation, the solution is easier to read and understand.

The solutions to the other problems follow a similar pattern, which is a pattern which we shall see repeated throughout this book. To define a function (call it fun) over 0, 1, 2, ... we should

- Give the value fun 0. This is the **base case** or starting value;
- Give the value fun n using the value of fun at (n-1). This is the **recursive** case.

This form of definition is called **primitive recursion**.

As this explanation makes clear, functions defined this way work over the natural numbers. If we apply `totalSales` to a negative number, what will happen?

```
totalSales (-2)
  = totalSales (-3) + sales (-2)
  = (totalSales (-4) + sales (-3)) + sales (-2)
  = ...
```

The calculation will carry on forever, or at least until the system had exhausted its available resources, signalled by `ERROR: Control stack overflow`.

It would be better to check for a negative argument and to return the result 0, say, in that case.

```
totalSales n
  | n==0       = sales 0
  | n>0        = totalSales (n-1) + sales n
  | otherwise  = 0
```

As can be seen from the example above, calculation of this function works just as we saw in Chapter 1.

To summarize this section, we have now seen three ways of defining functions on numbers.

- In Chapter 1 we saw a direct definition of the square function, by a single equation.

  ```
  square x = x*x
  ```

- In the same chapter we saw the definition of `maxi` which used two clauses in the conditional equation:

  ```
  maxi n m
    | n>=m       = n
    | otherwise  = m
  ```

- In this chapter we have seen the use of the function at a smaller value, e.g. `totalSales (n-1)`, in defining the value `totalSales n`. If we want to use this principle in defining a function, we should ask the question: 'How could I solve the problem for n if I had already solved it for n-1?'.

  An example of this is in defining the factorial function, which takes n to the product $1*2*...*(n-1)*n$. If we have factorial n-1, that is $1*2*...*(n-1)$, we only have to multiply it by n to get factorial n.

EXERCISES

2.1 Add a check for the argument being positive to the `maxSales` function defined above.

2.2 Define a function to find the week in which maximum sales occur during weeks 0 to n. What does your solution do in the case that the maximum value happens in more than one week? On the basis of the answer to this question, give a more precise description of your function.

2.3 Define a function to find a week in which there are zero sales in weeks 0 to n. Your function should return (n+1) if there is no week in weeks 0 to n with zero sales.

2.4 Define a function which returns the number of weeks during the period week 0 to week n in which there are zero sales.

2.5 Using your answer to Exercise 2.4 as a guide, define a function which when given a number s and a week number n returns the number of weeks during the period week 0 to week n in which there are sales of s.

2.6 How would you use your answer to Exercise 2.5 to solve Exercise 2.4?

2.7 To test the functions which use `sales` use the definition

```
sales n = n 'mod' 2 + (n+1) 'mod' 3
```

Design test data for the functions using this `sales` function. Your answers should explain how the test data have been selected.

2.8 The functions defined so far operate over the period 0 to n. Generalize them so they work over the period week m to week n, where you can assume n is greater than or equal to m. You should first write down the types of the new functions, and then give their definitions.

2.9 The factorial of a positive integer n is the product $1*2*\ldots*(n-1)*n$, and the factorial of 0 is usually defined to be 1. Give a Haskell definition of the factorial function.

2.10 Give a definition of the function of m and n which returns the product $m*(m+1)*\ldots*(n-1)*n$.

2.11 The Fibonacci numbers are the sequence 0, 1, 1, 2, 3, 5, ... whose first two values are 0 and 1, and whose subsequent values are calculated by adding together the previous two values (0+1=1, 1+1=2, 1+2=3, ...).

Write a definition of a Haskell function `fib` so that `fib n` is the nth number in the sequence.

2.12 Suppose you are given a function

```
stock :: Int -> Int
```

which gives the flow of stock in and out of a warehouse week-by-week. A positive number is a flow out of the warehouse, a negative one a flow in. Write functions which find the total outflow and inflow over the period of weeks 0 to n: the outflow function finds the total of the positive values, and the inflow function the total of the negative values.

2.13 Give a definition of the function

```
power :: Int -> Int -> Int
```

so that `power k n` is k to the power n. You can assume that n is positive.

2.14 Using the facts that

```
power k (2*n)   = square (power k n)
power k (2*n+1) = square (power k n) * k
```

write an alternative definition of the `power` function.

2.3 Syntax

The syntax of a language describes the properly formed programs. This section looks at various aspects of the syntax of Haskell, and stresses especially those which might seem unusual or unfamiliar at first sight.

Definitions and layout

A script contains a series of definitions, one after another. How is it clear when one definition ends and another begins? In writing English, the end of a sentence is signalled by a full stop, '.'. In Haskell the **layout** of the program is used to say where one definition ends and the next begins.

Formally, a definition is ended by the first piece of text which lies at the same level or to the left of the start of the definition.

When we write a definition, its first character opens up a box which will hold the definition, thus

```
square x = x*x
```

Whatever is typed in the box forms part of the definition...

```
square x = x*x
         +x
                   +2
```

...until something is found which is by the line (or to the left of that). This closes the box, thus

```
square x = x*x
         +x
                   +2
cube x = ...
```

In writing a sequence of definitions, it is therefore sensible to give them all the same level of indentation, and in our scripts we shall always write top-level definitions starting at the left-hand side of the page.

This rule for layout is called the **offside rule** because it is reminiscent of the idea of being 'offside' in soccer. The rule also works for conditional equations (such as maxi) which consist of more than one clause.

There is, in fact, a mechanism in Haskell for giving an explicit end to part of a definition, just as '.' does in English: the Haskell 'end' symbol is ';'. We can, for instance, use ';' if we wish to write more than one definition on a single line, thus:

```
answer = 42 ;   newline = '\n'
```

We see error messages involving ';' even if we have not used it ourselves. If we break the offside rule thus:

```
funny x = x+
1
```

we receive an error message like

```
ERROR .... : Syntax error in expression (unexpected ';')
```

since internally to the system a ';' is placed before the 1 to mark the end of the definition, which does indeed come at an unexpected point.

Recommended layout

The offside rule permits various different styles of layout. In this book for definitions of any size we use the form

```
fun v₁ v₂ ... vₙ
  | g₁        = e₁
  | g₂        = e₂
  ...
  | otherwise = eᵣ      (or   | gᵣ       = eᵣ)
```

with each clause starting on a new line, and the guards and results lined up. If any of the expressions e_i or guards g_i is particularly long, then the guard can appear on a line (or lines) of its own, like this:

```
fun v₁ v₂ ... vₙ
  | a long guard which may
    go over a number of lines
        = very long expression which goes
          over a number of lines
  | g₂      = e₂
  ...
```

Names in Haskell

Thus far in the book we have seen a variety of uses of names in definitions and expressions. In a definition like

```
type Pair = (Int,Int)


addTwo :: Pair -> Int
addTwo (first,second) = first+second
```

the names or **identifiers** Pair, addTwo and first are used to name a type, a function and a variable. Identifiers in Haskell must begin with a letter – small or capital – which is followed by an optional sequence of letters, digits, underscores '_' and acute accents.

The names used in definitions of values begin with a small letter, as do variables and type variables, which are introduced in Part II of the text. On the other hand, capital letters are used to begin type names, such as Pair; type constructors, such as True and False; and also the names of modules and type classes, which we shall encounter below.

An attempt to give a function a name which begins with a capital letter, such as

```
Fun x = x+1
```

gives the error message 'Undefined constructor function "Fun"'.

There are some restrictions on how identifiers can be chosen. There is a small collection of **reserved words** which cannot be used; these are

```
case class data default deriving else hiding if import in
infix infixl infixr instance interface let module of
renaming then to type where
```

The same identifier can be used to name both a function and a variable, or both a type and a type constructor; we recommend strongly that this is *not* done, as it can only lead to confusion.

Comments

Comments are the name given to explanatory text which is included in a script. Among the information we might supply are brief descriptions of the behaviour of functions, including assumptions about the sort of arguments which they expect: a function to give the square root of a number would expect a non-negative number, for instance. We often also include 'housekeeping' information such as the date that the file was created, when it was last modified, and the number and nature of the modifications made.

We have already seen one form of comment. Any text to the right of the symbol -- forms a comment. Longer comments can be written on multiple lines by beginning each line with the symbol --, but another mechanism is provided in the language.

The symbols {- and -} enclose a *nested* comment, which can extend over multiple lines. Moreover, a nested comment can include other nested comments, hence the name. These comment symbols work like parentheses, and just as for parentheses, it is an error if the opening and closing comment symbols do not match up.

Nested comments are particularly useful for **commenting out** parts of a script. Suppose we want to try an alternative definition for a particular function; we enclose the original definition between {- and -} and add the new definition to the script.

EXERCISES

2.15 Rewrite your solutions to the earlier exercises to use the recommended layout.

2.16 Given the definitions

```
funny x = x+x
  peculiar y = y
```

explain what happens when you remove the space in front of the `peculiar`.

2.4 Operators

The Haskell language contains various operators, such as +, ++ and so on. Operators are **infix**, so that they are written between their arguments. In principle it is possible to write all applications of an operator with enclosing parentheses, thus

```
(((4+8)*3)+2)
```

but expressions rapidly become difficult to read. Instead two extra properties of operators allow us to write expressions uncluttered by parentheses.

Associativity

If we wish to add the three numbers 4, 8 and 99 we can write either 4+(8+99) or (4+8)+99. The result is the same whichever we write, a property we call the **associativity** of addition. Because of this, we can write

```
4+8+99
```

for the sum, unambiguously. Not every operator is associative, however; what happens when we write

```
4-2-1
```

for instance? The two different ways of inserting parentheses give

```
(4-2)-1 = 2-1 = 1          left associative
4-(2-1) = 4-1 = 3          right associative
```

In Haskell each non-associative operator is classified as either left or right associative. If left associative, any double occurrences of the operator will be bracketed to the left, if right associative, to the right. The choice is arbitrary, but follows custom as much as possible.

Binding powers

The way in which an operator associates allows us to resolve expressions such as

    2^3^2

where the same operator occurs twice, but what is done when two different operators occur, as in the following expressions?

    2+3*4
    3^4*2

For this purpose the 'stickiness' or **binding power** of the operators need to be compared. * has binding power 7 while + has 6, so that in 2+3*4 the 3 sticks to the 4 rather than the 2, giving

    2+3*4 = 2+(3*4)

In a similar way, ^ with binding power 8 binds more tightly than *, so

    3^4*2 = (3^4)*2

A full table of the associativities and binding powers of the predefined Haskell operators is given in Appendix E. In the section 'Do-it-yourself operators' below we discuss how operators are defined in scripts and also how their associativity and binding power can be set or changed by declarations.

A pitfall – function application

The tightest binding is function application, which is given by writing the name of the function in front of its argument(s) thus: $f\ v_1\ v_2\ \ldots\ v_n$. This binds more tightly than any other operator, so that f n+1 is interpreted as f n added to 1, rather than f applied to n+1. If in doubt, it is sensible to parenthesize each argument to a function application.

Similarly, as '–' is both an infix and a prefix operator, there is scope for confusion. f -12 will be interpreted as 12 subtracted from f, rather than f applied to -12; the solution again is to bracket the argument.

Operators and functions

Operators can be converted to functions, which *precede* their arguments, by enclosing the operator in parentheses. We therefore have, for example, `(+)` as a function of type `Int -> Int -> Int` so that

```
(+) 2 3 = 2 + 3
```

We can also convert functions into operators by enclosing the function name in back quotes, thus `` `name` ``. We therefore have, using the maximum function defined earlier,

```
2 `maxi` 3 = maxi 2 3
```

Do-it-yourself operators

The Haskell language allows us to define operators in exactly the same way as functions. Operator names are built from the operator symbols:

```
! # $ % & * + . / < = > ? @ \ ^ | : - ~
```

with some restrictions explained in Appendix E.

To define the operator `&&&` as an integer maximum function, we write

```
(&&&) :: Int -> Int -> Int
a &&& b
  | a > b       = a
  | otherwise   = b
```

The associativity and binding power of the operator can be changed; for details see Appendix E.

2.5   Definitions: patterns

The function definitions we have seen so far have consisted of a single equation or a conditional equation containing more than one clause. At the start of the definition we have

```
fun v₁ v₂ ... vₙ
```

the function name `fun` applied to the **variables** v_1 to v_n.

Instead of a single conditional equation, we can supply two or more such equations. These describe how the function behaves when it is applied to **patterns** rather than variables. The simplest patterns are variables and **constants**. As a first example, the definition of `totalSales` from Section 2.2 can be rewritten to be

```
totalSales 0 = sales 0
totalSales n = totalSales (n-1) + sales n
```

The first equation applies to the 0 case; the second equation will apply in all other cases. This is the general behaviour when a function is defined using more than one equation. In finding the value of the function on a particular input, we use the *first* equation for which the input matches the pattern on the left-hand side.

The argument a matches the pattern p if

- p is a constant and a is equal to p, or
- p is a variable.

There is a third form of pattern which we introduce now. Suppose we are to check whether an integer is zero or not. We can write

```
isZero :: Int -> Bool
isZero 0 = True
isZero _ = False
```

In the final equation we use the **wild card** pattern '_' which matches any value. We cannot use the value it matches on this right-hand side, however, so we use _ when we will not need the matched value on the right-hand side. To the definition of pattern matching we add a clause to explain wild card patterns

- a matches the pattern _, for any value a.

A final example using pattern matching is the sequence of Fibonacci numbers 0, 1, 1, 2, 3, 5, ... whose first two values are 0 and 1, and whose subsequent values are calculated by adding together the previous two values.

```
fib :: Int -> Int

fib 0 = 0
fib 1 = 1
fib n
  | n>1       = fib (n-2) + fib (n-1)
  | otherwise = 0
```

We add the guard in the final conditional equation so that on a negative input the result is defined (and 0), rather than undefined, going into an infinite loop.

EXERCISES

2.17 Give a definition using pattern matching of the maxSales function from Section 2.2.

2.18 The factorial function returns the product of 1 to n for a positive integer n, and has value 1 at 0. Give a definition of the factorial function using pattern matching.

2.6 Programming with Booleans

The Boolean values True and False represent the results of tests, which might, for instance, compare two numbers for equality, or might check whether the first is smaller than the second. The Boolean type in Haskell is called Bool.

The Boolean operators provided in the language are.

&&	and
||	or
not	not

We can explain the behaviour of the operators by truth tables

t_1	t_2	t_1 && t_2	t_1 || t_2	t_1	not t_1
T	T	T	T	T	F
T	F	F	T	F	T
F	T	F	T		
F	F	F	F		

Booleans can be arguments to, or results of, functions. We now look at some examples. Exclusive or is the function which returns True if one of its arguments has the value True and the other False; exclusive or is like the 'or' of a restaurant menu: you may have chicken or fish as your main course, but not both! The built-in or is 'inclusive' because it returns True if one or both of its arguments are True.

```
exOr :: Bool -> Bool -> Bool
exOr x y = (x || y) && not (x && y)
```

We can use the constants `True` and `False` as arguments, in defining 'not' for ourselves.

```
myNot :: Bool -> Bool
myNot True  = False
myNot False = True
```

We can also use a combination of constants and variables to re-define `exOr`.

```
exOr True  x = not x
exOr False x = x
```

Section 2.2 has examples which analyse weekly sales from a shop, where the function `sales :: Int -> Int` records the sales.

One further question we can ask is whether there are zero sales in a particular week. We make this test in week n by writing `(sales n == 0)`. We can write a function which does this test now:

```
isZeroWeek :: Int -> Bool

isZeroWeek n = (sales n == 0)
```

On the right-hand side is the Boolean expression, so that the value for week 0, say, will be given by `(sales 0 == 0)`.

One of the original tasks in Section 2.2 was to decide

- whether there is a week between week 0 and week n in which no sales took place.

The function to make this decision will have the type

```
zeroInPeriod :: Int -> Bool
```

so that `zeroInPeriod n` has the value `True` if there are zero sales in one of the weeks `0,...,n`.

Once we know the type of a function, how do we start to write its definition? We can do it in stages.

- First design the left-hand side. We decide on what the arguments should be: are they to be variables, or general patterns? If they are patterns, what exactly should they be? To do this we need to think about the cases the definition will divide into.

- Once we have decided the left-hand side, we can fill in the details on the right. In filling in these details we may choose to write or use some other functions.

The `zeroInPeriod` function will have two cases, depending on whether the argument is zero or positive, so the left-hand sides will look like

```
zeroInPeriod 0 =
zeroInPeriod n =
```

Now to look at the right-hand sides. In the first case, the only week we are looking at is week 0, so we have to check whether sales that week are zero:

```
zeroInPeriod 0 = isZeroWeek 0
```

In the case of n non-zero we can find a zero in either of two places

sales 0	sales 1	$\cdots$	sales $(n-1)$	sales n

$$\triangleleft \;\ldots\ldots\; \texttt{zeroInPeriod } (n-1) \;\ldots\ldots\; \triangleright$$

It can be in the weeks up to n-1, which is tested by `zeroInPeriod (n-1)`, or it can be in week n, tested by `isZeroWeek n`. This gives the full definition.

```
zeroInPeriod :: Int -> Bool

zeroInPeriod 0 = isZeroWeek 0
zeroInPeriod n = zeroInPeriod (n-1) || isZeroWeek n
```

Pitfalls

It is not hard to find yourself writing definitions like

```
isZeroWeek n
  | sales n == 0    = True
  | otherwise       = False
```

where the Boolean expression is placed in a guard.

When the expression `sales n == 0` has the value `True`, the function has value `True`, and when the expression has the value `False`, the function has value `False`. Instead of doing this, we should simply write

```
isZeroWeek n = (sales n == 0)
```

just as we did earlier. In a similar way, we could have defined the `zeroInPeriod` function thus:

```
zeroInPeriod 0
  = isZeroWeek 0
zeroInPeriod n
  | isZeroWeek n     = True
  | otherwise        = zeroInPeriod (n-1)
```

but it is clearer to use the 'or' operator, '||', to combine the two. We can read off how the function behaves from the original definition: there is a zero in weeks 0 to n if there is a zero in weeks 0 to n-1 *or* if week n is itself zero. This is not so clear from the definition given here.

EXERCISES

2.19 Give a definition of the nAnd function

```
nAnd :: Bool -> Bool -> Bool
```

which gives the result True except when its two arguments are both True.

2.20 Give a definition of the function allZeroPeriod so that allZeroPeriod n tests whether the sales for every week in the period 0 to n are zero.

2.21 Give definitions of functions

```
isAbovePeriod  :: Int -> Int -> Bool
allAbovePeriod :: Int -> Int -> Bool
```

so that isAbovePeriod target n is True if at least one of the sales in weeks 0 to n exceeds the value target. allAbovePeriod checks whether sales exceed the target in all the appropriate weeks.

2.22 Design test data for these functions, using your own definition of the sales function. You can define the function to have the values you choose thus:

```
sales :: Int -> Int
sales 0 = 345
sales 1 = 32
sales 2 = 0
  ...
```

Explain for each of the functions why you have defined the sales function and chosen the test data in the way you have.

2.23 Using your own definition of sales, give calculations of zeroInPeriod n for two values of n, one leading to the value True and the other to False.

2.24 Define the function

```
numEqualMax :: Int -> Int -> Int -> Int
```

so that `numEqualMax n m p` is the number of n, m and p which are equal to the maximum of the three. For instance,

```
numEqualMax 1 1 1 = 3
```

This is an exercise in defining guards properly; you need to be careful to cover all cases.

2.25 Give test data for the function `numEqualMax`, explaining how you made your choices.

2.26 How could you simplify this definition to one with a single clause?

```
funny x y z
  | x>z        = True
  | y>=x       = False
  | otherwise  = True
```

2.7 Characters and strings

People and computers communicate using keyboard input and screen output, which are based on sequences of **characters**, that is letters, digits, and 'special' characters like space, tab, newline and end-of-file. Haskell contains a built-in type of characters, called `Char`.

Individual characters are written inside single quotes, thus: `'d'` is the Haskell representative of the character d. Similarly `'3'` is the character three. Some special characters are represented as follows:

tab	`'\t'`
newline	`'\n'`
backslash (\)	`'\\'`
single quote (')	`'\''`
double quote (")	`'\"'`

There is a standard coding for characters as integers, called the ASCII coding. The capital letters `'A'` to `'Z'` have the sequence of codes from 65 to 90, and the small letters `'a'` to `'z'` the codes 97 to 122. The character with code 34, for example, is written '\34'. There are also the conversion functions

```
toEnum :: Int -> Char
fromEnum :: Char -> Int
```

which convert an integer into a character, and vice versa. We shall also use the names `chr` and `ord` for these two functions, in deference to programming tradition.

The coding functions can be used in defining functions over `Char`. To convert a small letter to a capital an offset needs to be added to its code:

```
offset = ord 'A' - ord 'a'

capitalize :: Char -> Char
capitalize ch = chr (ord ch + offset)
```

Note that the `offset` is defined as a constant. This is standard practice, making the program both easier to read and to modify. To change the offset value, we just need to change the definition of `offset`, rather than having to change the function (or functions) which use it.

Characters can be compared using the ordering on their codes. So, since the digits 0 to 9 occupy codes 48 to 57, we can check whether a character is a digit, thus:

```
isDigit :: Char -> Bool
isDigit ch = ('0' <= ch) && (ch <= '9')
```

Strings of characters belong to the type

```
String
```

and are enclosed in double quotes, thus:

```
"baboon"
""
"\99a\116"
"gorilla\nhippo\nibex"
"1\t23\t456"
```

Try evaluating these strings in Hugs. On screen you will see the strings without the quotes, and with the special characters expanded out, as follows.

```
baboon

cat
gorilla
hippo
ibex
1     23        456
```

Strings can be joined together using ++, so that `"cat"++"\n"++"fish"` prints as

```
cat
fish
```

Haskell allows us to name types: to give them **synonyms** in other words. Built into the standard prelude of Haskell is the synonym

```
type String = [Char]
```

which expresses the fact that strings in Haskell are just lists of characters. Values of many types can be converted to strings by means of the function `show`; in particular, `show` can be applied to numbers, Booleans, and other types built from these which are introduced below.

As we said, strings are lists of characters; in Chapter 4 many more operations on lists are given and all these are available for manipulating strings. In particular, `length` will give the length of a string.

A pitfall

It is easy to confuse a, 'a' and "a". To summarize the difference:

a	is a name or a variable, if defined it may have any type whatever;
'a'	is a character;
"a"	is a string, which just happens to consist of a single character.

Similarly, there is a difference between

emu	a Haskell name or variable;
"emu"	a string.

EXERCISES

2.27 Define a function to convert small letters to capitals which returns unchanged characters which are not small letters.

2.28 Define the function

```
charToNum :: Char -> Int
```

which converts a digit like '8' to its value, 8. The value of non-digits should be taken to be 0.

2.29 Define a function

```
printDigit :: Char -> String
```

which converts a digit to its representation in English, so at '6' it will have the value "Six", for instance.

2.30 Define a function

```
romanDigit :: Char -> String
```

which converts a digit to its representation in Roman numerals, so at '7' it will have the value "VII" and so on.

2.31 Define a function

```
onThreeLines :: String -> String -> String -> String
```

which takes three strings and returns a single string which when printed shows the three strings on separate lines.

2.32 Give a function

```
duplicate :: String -> Int -> String
```

which takes a string and a natural number, n. The result is n copies of the string joined together. If n is 0, the result should be the empty string, "", and if n is 1, the result will be the string itself.

2.33 Using the previous answer, or otherwise, give a function

```
makeSpaces :: Int -> String
```

so that makeSpaces n is a string of n spaces.

2.34 Using the previous answer, give a function

```
pushRight :: String -> String
```

which takes a string and forms a string of length `linelength` by putting spaces at the front of the string. If `linelength` were 12 then `pushRight "crocodile"` would be `"   crocodile"`.

2.35 Can you criticize the way the previous function is specified? Look for a case in which it is not defined what it should do – it is an exceptional case.

2.8 Floating point numbers

In Section 2.1 we introduced the Haskell type `Int` of integers. In calculating we also want to use **fractions**, which are represented in Haskell by the **floating point** numbers which make up the type `Float`.

Internally to the Haskell system there is a fixed amount of space allocated to representing each `Float`. This has the effect that not all fractions can be represented by floating point numbers, and arithmetic over them will not always be accurate. It is possible to use the type of double-precision floating point numbers, `Double` for greater accuracy, or for full-precision integer arithmetic to use `Integer`; as this is a programming tutorial we restrict our attention to the types `Int` and `Float`.

Fractions in Haskell can be given by decimal numbers, such as

```
0.31426
-23.12
567.347
4523.0
```

The numbers are called floating point because the position of the decimal point is not the same for all `Float`s; depending upon the particular number, more of the space can be used to store the integer or the fractional part.

Haskell also allows numbers in **scientific notation**. These take the form below, where their values are given in the right-hand column of the table

`231.61e7`	231.61×10^{7}
`231.6e-2`	$231.61 \times 10^{-2} = 2.3161$
`-3.412e03`	$-3.412 \times 10^{3} = -3412$

This representation allows larger and smaller numbers than the decimals above. Consider the number 2.1^{444}. This will need well over a hundred digits before the decimal point, and this would not be possible in decimal notation of limited size (usually 20 digits at most). In scientific notation, it will be written as `1.162433e+143`.

+ - *	Float -> Float -> Float	Add, subtract, multiply.
/	Float -> Float -> Float	Fractional division.
^	Float -> Int -> Float	Exponentiation $x\hat{\ }n = x^n$ for a natural number n.
**	Float -> Float -> Float	Exponentiation $x**y = x^y$.
==, /=, <, >, <=, >=	Float -> Float -> Bool	Equality and ordering operations.
abs	Float -> Float	Absolute value.
acos, asin, atan	Float -> Float	The inverse of cosine, sine and tangent.
ceiling floor round	Float -> Int	Convert a fraction to an integer by rounding up, down, or to the closest integer.
cos, sin, tan	Float -> Float	Cosine, sine and tangent.
exp	Float -> Float	Powers of e.
fromInt	Int -> Float	Convert an Int to a Float (Haskell).
fromInteger	Int -> Float	Convert an Int to a Float (Gofer).
log	Float -> Float	Logarithm to base e.
logBase	Float -> Float -> Float	Logarithm to arbitrary base, provided as first argument.
negate	Float -> Float	Change the sign of a number.
read	String -> Float	Converts a string representing a Float to its value.
pi	Float	The constant pi.
show	Float -> String	Convert a number to a string.
signum	Float -> Int	1, 0 or -1 according to whether the argument is positive, zero or negative.
sqrt	Float -> Float	(Positive) square root.

Figure 2.1   Floating point operations and functions.

Haskell provides a range of operators and functions over Float in the standard prelude. The table in Figure 2.1 gives their name, type and a brief description of their behaviour. Included are the

- standard mathematical operations: square root, exponential, logarithm and trigonometric functions;

- printing and reading functions: `show`, `read`;
- functions to convert integers to floating point numbers: `fromInt`, `fromInteger`, and vice versa: `ceiling`, `floor` and `round`.

Haskell can be used as a numeric calculator. Try typing the expression which follows to the `hugs` prompt:

```
sin (pi/4) * sqrt 2
```

In Gofer we receive error messages on typing in this expression. We need to show explicitly that the numbers 4 and 2 are floats. This we can do by typing

```
sin (pi/4.0) * sqrt 2.0
```

This conversion is not necessary in Haskell since the numbers 4 and 2 belong to both `Int` and `Float`; they are **overloaded**. This is also true of some of the numeric functions; addition, for instance, has both the types

```
Int -> Int -> Int
Float -> Float -> Float
```

We shall explore this idea of overloading in more detail when we discuss type classes below (see Chapter 8).

In general if we wish to add an integer quantity, like `floor 5.6` to a float, like `6.7`, we will receive an error message if we type

```
(floor 5.6) + 6.7
```

since we are trying to add quantities of two different types. We have to convert the `Int` to a `Float` to perform the addition, thus:

```
fromInt(floor 5.6) + 6.7
```

where `fromInt`[2] takes an `Int` to the corresponding `Float`.

EXERCISES

2.36 Give a function

```
averageSales :: Int -> Float
```

so that `averageSales n` is the average of the values `sales 0` to `sales n`.

---

[2] Note that in Gofer the conversion function is called `fromInteger`.

2.37 Define a function

```
salesExceed :: Float -> Int -> Int
```

so that `salesExceed val n` gives the number of weeks in the period 0 to n in which sales exceed `val`.

2.38 Define a function

```
aboveAverageSales :: Int -> Int
```

which returns the number of weeks 0 to n in which sales exceed the average for that period. Do you see how you can use the answers to the two preceding questions?

2.9 Programming with numbers and strings

This section covers a longer example, that of giving sales information in a readable form, using the functions `totalSales`, `averageSales` and so on. The sales are to be printed in a table, with summary information (total and average sales) appearing at the bottom.

Suppose that the sales for weeks 0, 1 and 2 are 12, 14 and 15; the output from `printTable 2` should look like

```
    Week        Sales
       0          12
       1          14
       2          15

    Total         41
    Average   13.6667
```

Top-down

We begin by working through the solution **top-down**, that is by defining the auxiliary functions we need as we go along. At the top level, we have to define

```
printTable :: Int -> String
```

which outputs the whole table. The table itself has four parts: the heading, the week-by-week values, the total and the average. The solution also has these parts, which are joined together by ++.

```
printTable n
  = heading ++ printWeeks n
    ++ printTotal n ++ printAverage n
```

The heading has an immediate definition

```
heading :: String
heading = "      Week      Sales\n"
```

To print the values for the weeks 0 to n we have to print the line for each week. We therefore need to define a function

```
printWeek :: Int -> String
```

which is used in defining printWeeks using recursion much as we have done before.

```
printWeeks :: Int -> String

printWeeks 0 = printWeek 0
printWeeks n = printWeeks (n-1) ++ printWeek n
```

The top-down approach has now reduced the problem to one of defining the functions printWeek, printTotal and printAverage.

Bottom-up

Now we look to building the functions printWeek and printAverage from their parts. In doing this we use some of the Haskell built-in functions, such as show.

We will also need a function to help with positioning text; in particular we need a function which can place text to the right-hand side of a column:

```
rJustify :: Int -> String -> String
```

so that for example,

```
rJustify 12 "elephant" = "    elephant"
```

If the text is longer than the given length, the function returns it unchanged; it is *not* cut to fit the space.

Given this we can write the function to print a week's values:

```
printWeek n
  = rJustify offset (show n) ++
    rJustify offset (show (sales n)) ++ "\n"
```

where

```
offset :: Int
offset = 10
```

In the definition, we twice use `show` followed by `rJustify`. A clearer solution makes this into a function, and *uses* the function twice:

```
rPrintInt :: Int -> String
rPrintInt n = rJustify offset (show n)

printWeek n
  = rPrintInt n ++ rPrintInt (sales n) ++ "\n"
```

The final task is to define the last lines of the table. The weeks have the numbers printed in columns of width ten; to align the average with the sales figures, we define

```
printAverage :: Int -> String
```

in a similar way to printing a week:

```
printAverage n
  = "\n      Average " ++
    rJustify offset (show (averageSales n))
```

where again we can make the definition clearer by defining an auxiliary function `rPrintFloat` which prints a floating point number with a given width. This gives the definition

```
printAverage n
  = "\n      Average " ++ rPrintFloat (averageSales n)
```

The system is complete once `rPrintFloat`, `rJustify` and `printTotal` are defined. We leave these as exercises, since they are variants of what we have already done.

The full solution can be seen in Figure 2.2. The development of the solution here is typical of many. A top-down solution takes us from the original problem `printTable` to smaller problems like `printWeeks` and

```
printTable :: Int -> String
printTable n
  = heading ++ printWeeks n
    ++ printTotal n ++ printAverage n

heading :: String
heading = "     Week      Sales\n"

printWeeks :: Int -> String
printWeeks 0 = printWeek 0
printWeeks n = printWeeks (n-1) ++ printWeek n

printWeek :: Int -> String
printWeek n
  = rPrintInt n ++ rPrintInt (sales n) ++ "\n"

offset :: Int
offset = 10

rPrintInt :: Int -> String
rPrintInt n = rJustify offset (show n)

printAverage :: Int -> String
printAverage n
  = "\n    Average " ++ rPrintFloat (averageSales n)

rPrintFloat :: Float -> String
rJustify    :: Int -> String -> String
printTotal  :: Int -> String
```

Figure 2.2 Printing sales information.

printAverage. These in turn can either be solved directly, like heading, or give rise to other problems, like printWeek. Once we get closer to a solution, it is worth asking ourselves how we can use what we already have in predefined functions to build a solution bottom-up. In particular here we used the built-in facilities for printing numbers.

Another important step in the strategy was to recognize parts of the solution which could be themselves described by functions, making the solution easier to read and understand, as well as making it easier to modify, if this were needed. In this solution, we made printing an integer in a space of ten characters a separate function, rPrintInt, after seeing it used twice in defining printWeek.

EXERCISES

2.39 Define the functions `rPrintFloat` and `printTotal` specified in the example.

2.40 Define a function

```
spaces :: Int -> String
```

so that `spaces` n is a string of n spaces. You might like to think of a definition of the form

```
spaces 0 = ""
spaces n =
```

[Hint: remember that you can use ++ to join together two strings.]

2.41 Using the `spaces` function, or otherwise, define the function `rJustify` used in the example.

2.42 Show how to modify the table so that

- the number of weeks of zero sales is listed;
- the number of weeks of above average sales is listed;
- (*harder*) each week with above average sales has its entry marked by a star.

2.43 Give a definition of a function

```
factorialTable :: Int -> Int -> String
```

so that `factorialTable` m n tabulates the values of factorial from m to n inclusive. You should make sure that your answer outputs something sensible if either of m or n is not a natural number, or if m is larger than n.

2.10 Data structures: tuples

In writing programs, we model items in the real world by values of particular types. We can represent a temperature by a number, a telephone number by a string (why not a number?), a person's name by a string, and so forth. The types we have seen so far just contain single values, while real-world objects can be complex. Many real-world objects can be modelled by a collection of data items; for instance, a person in a mailing list may be specified by their name, telephone number and age.

Haskell provides composite types, called **tuple types**,[3] which are built up from components of simpler types. The type

$$(t_1, t_2, \ldots, t_n)$$

consists of tuples of values

$$(v_1, v_2, \ldots, v_n)$$

in which $v_1 :: t_1, \ldots, v_n :: t_n$. In other words, each component v_i of the tuple has to have the type t_i given in the corresponding position in the type.

We can model our type of people in the mailing list by the type

```
(String,String,Int)
```

whose members include

```
("Joe Grundy","0000-000000",73)
```

To record that we want to think of this type as representing people, we can give the following type definition or **type synonym** in Haskell

```
type Person = (String,String,Int)
```

Definitions like this are treated as shorthand in Haskell – wherever a name like Person is used, it has exactly the same effect as if (String,String,Int) had been written.

Other examples include

```
mary :: Person
mary =  ("Mary Poppins","0800-000-000",68)

intP :: (Int,Int)
intP =  (34,32)
```

As part of the development of programs, we often have to choose between different types to represent the objects we have to model. Tuples are often used to group data together; some representative examples follow.

---

[3] The reason for the name is that these objects are usually called pairs, triples, quadruples, quintuples, sextuples and so on. The general word for them is therefore 'tuple'. In other programming languages, these types are called records or structures; see Appendix A for a more detailed comparison.

- A function to return both the minimum and maximum of three numbers can return a pair, and therefore has the type

```
minNmax :: Int -> Int -> Int -> (Int,Int)
```

- A person's name can be represented in many ways. In the example above we used a single string, but it could also be represented by a type of pairs, (String,String), of first and last names.

- When returning a week in which sales are zero, there is a possibility that there may be no such week. One way of dealing with this is for the function to return an (Int,Bool) pair. If the Boolean part is False, this signals that no zero week was found; if it is like (4,True), it signals that week 4 was such a week.

Functions over tuples are defined by pattern matching. Instead of writing a variable for an argument of type (Int,Int), say, a *pattern*, (x,y) is used.

```
addPair :: (Int,Int) -> Int
addPair (x,y) = x+y
```

On application the components of the pattern are matched by the corresponding components of the argument, so that

```
addPair intP
  = addPair (34,32)
  = 34 + 32
  = 66
```

Patterns can contain constants, and nested patterns:

```
shift :: ((Int,Int),Int) -> (Int,(Int,Int))
shift ((a,b),c) = (a,(b,c))
```

Functions which pick out particular parts of a tuple can be defined by pattern matching. For the Person type, the definitions might be

```
name  :: Person -> String
phone :: Person -> String
age   :: Person -> Int

name  (n,p,a) = n
phone (n,p,a) = p
age   (n,p,a) = a
```

name mary is "Mary Poppins", for instance. Haskell has these functions on pairs built in. They are

```
fst (x,y) = x
snd (x,y) = y
```

Each element of a given type of tuples will contain the same number and type of components: two Strings and an Int in the case of Person, for example. Types of lists, which are discussed later, contain lists with differing numbers of elements, all of which must have the same type.

A pitfall

It is important to distinguish between the functions

```
addPair :: (Int,Int) -> Int
addPair (a,b) = a+b

addTwo :: Int -> Int -> Int
addTwo a b = a+b
```

addPair has a single argument which is a pair of numbers: it returns the sum of the two parts. addTwo has two arguments, each of which is a number, and returns their sum. We shall see later that the second function can be used in a more flexible way than the first; for the moment it is important to realize that there is a difference, and that type errors will result if we confuse the two, thus

```
addPair 3 4
addTwo (2,3)
```

EXERCISES

2.44 Define the function minNmax which returns both the minimum and maximum of two numbers.

2.45 Give a definition of the function

```
maxOccurs :: Int -> Int -> (Int,Int)
```

which returns the maximum of two numbers, together with the number of times it occurs. Using this, or otherwise, define the function

```
maxThreeOccurs :: Int -> Int -> Int -> (Int,Int)
```

which does a similar thing for three arguments.

2.46 Give a definition of a function

```
orderTriple :: (Int,Int,Int) -> (Int,Int,Int)
```

which puts the elements of a triple of three numbers into ascending order. You might like to solve the simpler problem for pairs first.

2.47 Redefine the function which finds a week of zero `sales` value, so that it has type

```
Int -> (Int,Bool)
```

and behaves as described above.

2.48 Design test data for the preceding exercises; explain the choices you have made in each case. Give a sample evaluation of each of your functions.

2.11 Function definitions

The definitions of functions we have seen so far consist of a number of equations or conditional equations, each of which can have multiple clauses. In this section we see how local definitions can be attached to each equation or conditional equation. To recap, the definitions resemble:

```
fun p₁ p₂ ... pₙ
  | g₁           = e₁
  | g₂           = e₂
  ...
  | otherwise    = eᵣ

f q₁ q₂ ... qₖ
  | h₁           = f₁
  ...
  | hₛ           = fₛ

  ...
```

Here p_1, q_1, ... are patterns; g_1, h_1, ... are Boolean expressions called guards and e_1, f_1, ... are the expressions which give the results of the function in the different cases.

In the following we shall often say 'equation' to mean 'equation or conditional equation'.

An example definition is given by the function which gives the highest common factor (hcf) of two positive integers

```
hcf :: Int -> Int -> Int
hcf n m
  | m == n      = n
  | m > n       = hcf m n
  | otherwise   = hcf (n-m) m
```

Local definitions

There is one more feature of definitions which we introduce now. Each (conditional) equation can be followed by a list of definitions which are **local** to the function or other object being defined. These definitions are written after the keyword where. A simple example is given by a function which is to return the sum of squares of two numbers.

```
sumSquares :: Int -> Int -> Int
```

The result of the function will be the sum of two values, sqN and sqM, so that

```
sumSquares n m
  = sqN + sqM
```

The definition of these two values can be done in the where clause which follows the equation, thus

```
sumSquares n m
  = sqN + sqM
    where
    sqN = n*n
    sqM = m*m
```

In such a simple example, it is perhaps hard to see the point of making the local definitions, but if a more complicated function of the two numbers is required, the definition is made much clearer. An example of this is the function printAverage, developed in Section 2.9.

```
printAverage :: Int -> String

printAverage n
  = text ++ averageVal
    where
    text      = "\n    Average "
    averageVal = rPrintFloat (averageSales n)
```

At the top level we see that two strings are joined together; we can then look at each of the two separately. The definition also reflects how it might have been written: first we decide that we print a piece of text saying that the average is being written, then we give the value of the average.

In each case, the layout of the definition is important. The offside rule is used by the system to determine the end of each definition in the `where` clause.

The `where` clause must be found in the definition to which it belongs, so that the `where` must occur somewhere to the right of the start of the definition. Inside the `where` clause, the same rules apply as at the top level: it is therefore important that the definitions are aligned vertically. If not an error will result. Our recommended layout is therefore

```
f p₁ p₂ ... pₖ
  | g₁          = e₁
  ...
  | otherwise   = eᵣ
    where
    v₁  a₁ ... aₙ = r₁
    v₂ = r₂
    ....
```

This example also shows that the local definitions can include functions – here v_1 is an example of a local function definition. We have given type declarations for all top-level definitions; it is also possible to give type declarations for `where`-defined objects in Haskell. In cases where the type is not obvious, a declaration should be included. An example of this is given by the `maxsq` function included in the next section.

Let expressions

It is also possible to make definitions local to an expression. For instance, we can write

```
let x = 3+2 in x^2 + 2*x - 4
```

giving the result 31. If more than one definition is included in one line they need to be separated by semicolons, thus:

```
let x = 3+2 ; y = 5-1 in x^2 + 2*x - y
```

We shall find that we only use this form occasionally.

Scopes

A Haskell script consists of a sequence of definitions. The *scope* of a definition is that part of the program in which the definition can be used. All definitions at the top-level in Haskell have the whole script they are defined in as their scope: that is, they can be used in all the definitions the script contains. In particular they can be used in definitions which occur before theirs in the script, as in

```
isOdd, isEven :: Int -> Bool

isOdd 0  = False
isOdd n  = isEven (n-1)

isEven 0 = True
isEven n = isOdd (n-1)
```

Local definitions, given by where clauses, are not intended to be 'visible' in the whole of the script, but rather just in the (conditional) equation in which they appear. The same is true of the variables in a function definition, their scope is the whole of the conditional equation in which they appear. Specifically, in the example which follows, the scope of the definitions of sqx, sqy and sq and of the variables x and y is given by the large box; the smaller box gives the scope of the variable z.

```
maxsq x y
 ┌─────────────────────────────┐
 │  | sqx > sqy      = sqx      │
 │  | otherwise      = sqy      │
 │      where                   │
 │      sqx  =  sq x            │
 │      sqy  =  sq y            │
 │      sq :: Int -> Int        │
 │      sq z =  ┌─────┐          │
 │             │ z*z │          │
 └─────────────└─────┘──────────┘
```

In particular it is important to see that

- the variables appearing on the left-hand side of the function definition – x and y in this case – can be used in the local definitions; here they are used in sqx and sqy;
- local definitions can be used before they are defined: sq is used in sqx here;
- local definitions can be used in results and in guards as well as in other local definitions.

It is possible for a script to have two definitions or variables with the same name. In the example, the variable x appears twice. Which definition is in force at each point? The *most local* is the one which is used.

```
maxsq x y
  | sq x > sq y     = sq x
  | otherwise       = sq y
      where
        sq x =     x*x
```

In the example, we can think of the inner box *cutting a hole* in the outer, so that the scope of the outer x will exclude the right-hand side of the definition of sq. When one definition is contained inside another the best advice is that different variables and names should be used for the inner definitions unless there is a very good reason for using the same name twice.

2.12 Programming with local definitions

We explore in this section how local definitions in where clauses are used in programming and how calculations are extended to handle local definitions.

Program development

Here we give a sample program which uses where clauses during its development. The problem is to define

```
    maxThreeOccurs :: Int -> Int -> Int -> (Int,Int)
```

which returns the maximum of three integers paired with the number of times it occurs among the three.

A natural solution first finds the maximum, and then investigates how often it occurs among the three:

```
maxThreeOccurs n m p
  = (max,eqCount)
    where
    max     = maxiThree n m p
    eqCount = equalCount max n m p
```

Note that max is used twice: in the final answer (max,eqCount) and in the call of the function equalCount. Working top down, we have used the function `equalCount` which counts how many of its final three arguments are equal to the first.

Now we have to define `equalCount`. We want to 'score' one for each of n, m and p equal to the number sought. We could say

```
equalCount val n m p
  = isN + isM + isP
    where
    isN = if n==val then 1 else 0
    isM = if m==val then 1 else 0
    isP = if p==val then 1 else 0
```

The right-hand sides here use the `if .. then .. else ..` construct. The expression

```
if c then e₁ else e₂
```

has the value e_1 if the condition c is `True` and e_2 if c is `False`.

The definition of `equalCount` above seems repetitive: we compare each value with the value `val`; we can make this comparison into a function, and then call the function three times:

```
equalCount val n m p
  = isVal n  + isVal m + isVal p
    where
    isVal :: Int -> Int
    isVal x = if x==val then 1 else 0
```

Observe that the function `isVal` uses the value `val` in its definition, and also that we have included a declaration of the type of `isVal` in the `where` clause.

Calculation

Calculations can be extended to deal with `where` clauses. The `sumSquares` function in the previous section gives, for example

```
sumSquares 4 3
= sqN + sqM
  where
  sqN = 4*4 = 16
  sqM = 3*3 = 9
= 16 + 9
= 25
```

```
      maxThreeOccurs 2 1 2
    = (max,eqCount)
      where
      max = maxiThree 2 1 2
          = maxi (maxi 2 1) 2
            ??  2>=1 = True
          = maxi 2 2
            ??  2>=2 = True
          = 2
    = (2,eqCount)
      where
      eqCount = equalCount 2 2 1 2
              = isVal 2 + isVal 1 + isVal 2
                where
                isVal 2 = if 2==2 then 1 else 0
                        = if True then 1 else 0
                        = 1
              = 1 + isVal 1 + isVal 2
              ...
              = 1 + 0 + 1
              = 2
    = (2,2)
```

Figure 2.3 Calculation of `maxThreeOccurs 2 1 2`.

The values of the local definitions are calculated beneath the `where` if their values are needed. All local evaluation is indented below the `where`. To follow the top-level value, we just have to look at the calculation at the left-hand side.

A longer example is given by Figure 2.3, which shows the calculation of `maxThreeOccurs 2 1 2`, where we assume that `maxiThree` is given by

```
maxiThree a b c = maxi (maxi a b) c
```

In the calculation of Figure 2.3, we also explicitly calculate the values of guards, using '??' to signal that a guard is being calculated. We also omit some steps of the calculation, signalled by '. . .'.

The vertical lines which appear are used to link the successive steps of the calculations when these have intermediate `where` calculations. The lines can be omitted.

EXERCISES

2.49 Compare the definition of `maxThreeOccurs` used here with your earlier solution, which does not use `where` clauses.

2.50 Calculate the values of the expressions

```
maxThreeOccurs 1 2 1
equalCount 4 2 1 3
```

2.51 Define the function

```
cJustify :: Int -> String -> String
```

so that `cJustify n st` gives a string of length n by adding spaces to both ends of st to centre it in the answer. You should think about what to do when the length of st is greater than n; and also about what to do when n is not a positive integer.

2.52 Define a function

```
stars :: Int -> String
```

so that, for example, `stars 3` is `"***"`. How do you deal with negative numbers?

2.53 Give a table of the `sales` function, so that if sales in weeks 0, 1 and 2 are 7, 5 and 9, the table will be

```
0   *******
1   *****
2   *********
```

2.54 Look at some of the exercises from earlier sections, and your solutions to them. How can they be made easier to read and understand by using `where` clauses?

2.13 Example: quadratic equations

The example in this section draws on many of the features introduced so far: numbers, strings, local definitions, pattern matching and guards.

It explores how a larger program is built from smaller components, and how problems can be broken down into separate sections.

The problem

A quadratic equation, like

```
a*X² + b*X + c = 0.0
```

generally has

- two roots, if $b^2 > 4.0 \ast a \ast c$;
- one root, if $b^2 == 4.0 \ast a \ast c$; and
- no roots, if $b^2 < 4.0 \ast a \ast c$.

This assumes that a is non-zero – the case which we call **non-degenerate**. In the degenerate case, there are three sub-cases:

- one root, if b /= 0.0;
- no roots, if b == 0.0 and c /= 0.0;
- every number a root, if b == 0.0 and c == 0.0.

Suppose for the moment that we only have to look at non-degenerate cases. We seek a program which when given the coefficients 1.0, 5.0 and 6.0 will print

```
The quadratic equation

    1.0*X^2 + 5.0*X + 6.0 = 0.0

has two roots: -2.0 -3.0
```

The formula for the roots is

$$\frac{-b \pm \sqrt{b^2 - 4ac}}{2a}$$

The solution

The solution splits naturally into two parts: finding the roots (if any) and printing the outcome. The roots are given by

```
oneRoot :: Float -> Float -> Float -> Float
oneRoot a b c = -b/(2.0*a)
```

and

```
twoRoots :: Float -> Float -> Float -> (Float,Float)

twoRoots a b c
  = (d-e,d+e)
    where
    d = -b/(2.0*a)
    e = sqrt(b^2-4.0*a*c)/(2.0*a)
```

Note the choice of types: the twoRoots function returns a value which is a pair of numbers, while the oneRoot function returns a single value.

The output consists of two parts; there is a header common to the three cases, while the values printed differ in those three. We make two separate definitions therefore

```
quadAnalyse :: Float -> Float -> Float -> String

quadAnalyse a b c
  = header a b c ++ roots a b c
```

The header of the output is given by

```
header :: Float -> Float -> Float -> String

header a b c
  = "The quadratic equation\n\n\t" ++
    show a ++ "*X^2 + " ++
    show b ++ "*X + " ++
    show c ++ " = 0" ++ "\n\nhas "
```

while the roots are printed by

```
roots :: Float -> Float -> Float -> String

roots a b c
  | b^2 > 4.0*a*c
        = "two roots: " ++ show f ++ " " ++ show s
  | b^2 == 4.0*a*c
        = "one root: " ++ show (oneRoot a b c)
  | otherwise
        = "no roots"
    where
    (f,s) = twoRoots a b c
```

One new feature is introduced here. The function `twoRoots` returns a pair when applied to a, b and c. We want to print the two halves of the pair. One way to obtain them is to use `fst` and `snd`, but we can also use the **conformal pattern match** of the result of the function to the pattern `(f,s)`. This means that f names the first half of that value, and s the second. The definition is called conformal, as for it to be effective, the value on the right needs to *conform* to or match the pattern on the left.

Error cases

In writing a function like `oneRoot`, an assumption is made that it is not to be called with a equal to 0. If `oneRoot` is called with a equal to 0, the system will give a run time error, that there has been an attempt to divide by zero.

It is possible to add to the definition a dummy value in that case – often the choice is 0 – or to make the function return an explicit error message and halt evaluation. This is done using the function `error` thus:

```
oneRoot a b c
  | (a /= 0.0)  = -b/(2.0*a)
  | otherwise   = error "oneRoot called with a==0"
```

If the `otherwise` case is reached, evaluation of the expression stops and the error message given, `"oneRoot called with a==0"`, is printed instead of the value of the expression. This gives a guide about where the problem has occurred.

EXERCISES

2.55 By modifying the function `roots`, add the three degenerate cases to the analysis.

2.56 An alternative, better structured, way of adding the degenerate cases is to define a separate function

```
degen :: Float -> Float -> Float -> String
```

which plays the same role as the `roots` function. A case analysis can be added to the top-level function `quadAnalyse` to decide which of the functions `roots`, `degen` is to be used.

2.57 Extend the definition of `twoRoots` so that it returns an error message if it is called in either the 'one root' or the 'no roots' cases.

2.58 In the case that (b^2-4.0*a*c) is negative, it is possible to say that there are two *complex* roots. Modify the functions so the complex roots are returned in this situation, rather than the 'no roots' message.

2.14 Design

Defining a function requires us to think about the particular combination of language features which will best fit what we wish to do. The points which follow offer some guidance on function design.

- In solving a problem it can help to look at similar problems, or simpler problems. A solution to a similar problem might be adapted; a solution to a simpler problem might be generalized to give a solution or be used as a part of the larger solution.

- In looking at a problem area, we need to decide the types to represent the data of the area. For instance, we might decide to represent telephone numbers as strings rather than as numbers because a leading zero in a telephone number like 0171... is part of the sequence of digits dialled, but is not significant in representing an integer.

- The first decision to make about a particular definition is the *type* of the object being defined; without being sure about this, it is not possible to make any further progress. A function which takes arguments of type $t_1, \ldots, t_n$ and gives a result of type t has type $t_1 \rightarrow t_2 \rightarrow \ldots \rightarrow t_n \rightarrow t$.

- Many problems are solved by breaking the problem into a number of parts, with each part having a simpler, separate, solution. This happened in the example of analysing quadratic equations, where finding the solutions and displaying them were identified as separate activities.

- Many other problems are amenable to solutions which are recursive: the solution to a 'smaller' case is used in solving the problem in the 'larger' case. For instance, the total sales for weeks 0 to n are the sum of the total sales for weeks 0 to (n-1) and the sales for week n, for example.

- Once the breakdown of the problem is decided, we can see the cases into which the problem breaks. This helps to design the patterns on the left-hand side of the equations, which we can do before thinking about the clauses which make up each conditional equation.

- In designing the clauses, there are decisions to make about using `where` clauses. These can help in developing the solution; if we need two strings in the solution we can say

    ```
    ... = front ++ back
    ```

    and then decide the values of `front` and `back` separately. This is another case where breaking the problem down into smaller parts makes it easier to see where the solution is going. The use of `where` clauses also makes it easier to read and modify the final solution.

- If we use a particular sort of expression more than once, it is a candidate for a function definition. We saw this with the script to give a formatted table of sales figures, when we made a definition of a function to print a number at the right-hand end of a block of space.

- A final, slightly different, approach is to work bottom-up. If we know that we have to solve problems to do with a particular area, like lines in geometry or supermarket bills, we might begin by building a *library* of useful functions which handle, for instance, line intersections or pricing items according to bar codes.

A Haskell script is intended to look like a sequence of conditional equations which define functions and other items such as numbers, tuples and so forth. The syntax of the language is designed to be straightforward, but there are some traps for the beginner.

- The layout of the script is significant; we give a recommended layout which makes it easy to read definitions, and to modify them without introducing syntax errors.

- There is a distinction between names beginning with small letters: `name1` etc., and those beginning with capitals: `Name1`. The former are used for defined functions, the latter for some basic and defined types and type constructors, which we come to below.

- The precedence of operators: `*` binding more tightly than `+`, and function application binding most tightly, can cause problems. If in doubt, brackets should be put into expressions to make their purpose clear. In particular, negative numbers like `(-12)` should be parenthesized when they are arguments to functions.

- There is a distinction between the name `a`, the character `'a'` and the string `"a"`. Confusing these can give errors stating that a name is undefined, or type errors.

The chapter contains many exercises. Doing practical work is the only way to become familiar with the craft of programming in Haskell.

EXERCISES

The sequence of exercises which follows leads up to a solution of the problem of whether two lines on a flat surface intersect. An application of this is in the layout of printed circuit boards, or canals, when lines which do not intersect need to be drawn.

A point is given by two coordinates, and a line by the two points at its ends. We can therefore define

```
type Point = (Float,Float)
type Line  = (Point,Point)
```

A line could be represented in two different ways, depending upon the order in which the two points specifying it are given. A line in our system $((x_1,y_1),(x_2,y_2))$ is called **sensible** if $x_1 <= x_2$.

2.59 Define functions which return the x (first) and y (second) coordinates of a point.

2.60 Define a function which decides whether a line is vertical.

2.61 If a line is $((x_1,y_1),(x_2,y_2))$, its equation is given by

$$\frac{y - y_1}{x - x_1} = \frac{y_2 - y_1}{x_2 - x_1}$$

Define a function

```
yValue :: Float -> Line -> Float
```

which when given an x-coordinate and a line gives the corresponding y value on the line. You may assume that the line is not vertical, or include a test for this if you wish: why is this necessary?

2.62 Define a function which makes any line into a sensible one by swapping the end points if necessary.

2.63 If the two sensible lines $((x_1,y_1),(x_2,y_2))$ and $((x_3,y_3),(x_4,y_4))$ are known to be either horizontal or vertical, the following test is sufficient to see whether they intersect:

```
(x₁ <= x₃ && x₃ <= x₂ &&
    y₃ <= y₁ && y₁ <= y₄) ||
(x₃ <= x₁ && x₁ <= x₄ &&
    y₁ <= y₃ && y₃ <= y₂)
```

Implement this. Give an example to show that the test does not work when the (sensible) lines can be sloping.

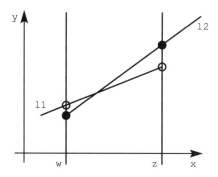

Figure 2.4 Checking line intersections.

2.64 To test for arbitrary lines intersecting, we first check that there is some overlap in their x values; in Figure 2.4 it is the range from w to z. Write a function which checks whether for two sensible lines there is such an overlap.

2.65 If there is an overlap, then we can check whether the lines intersect as illustrated in Figure 2.4. The lines intersect if over their common x values they cross. In the figure, l1 is above l2 at w, below it at z. Write a function which checks for intersection in this way. Your definition should be able to deal with the case of either of the lines being vertical.

2.66 Design test data for your function. There are a number of cases to be checked, depending upon whether one or both of the lines are vertical, whether the lines do or do not cross in their overlap and whether they indeed have an overlap. You should also examine extreme cases: where intersection is at one of the ends of the overlap, and where the lines intersect in more than one point.

    Explain the cases that your particular data are intended to test, and how you have covered all possible cases.

SUMMARY

This chapter has covered the basic types in Haskell: numbers – the integers and the fractions, represented by floating point numbers – Booleans, characters, strings and tuples. Together with each type, we gave the operators and predefined functions from the standard prelude. Information about the operators is found in Appendix E, and some functions from the standard preludes are discussed in Appendix H of this text.

We have also covered the main forms of function definition using

- pattern matching;
- guards and if .. then .. else ..;
- local definitions – where clauses and let expressions.

and have shown how the layout of definitions in Haskell is significant, and is used in particular to describe the scope of definitions.

3 Reasoning about programs

This short chapter introduces the important idea that we can write down logical arguments about functional programs. These **proofs** of program properties have the advantage that they can address the behaviour of a program over *all* its inputs, rather than testing which can only look at behaviour on a finite set of inputs, which it is hoped are representative of its behaviour as a whole.

After introducing **mathematical induction**, the most powerful method for proving properties of functions over the natural numbers, we apply it in a series of examples, and give advice about how to build proofs of program properties.

3.1 Informal proof: an introduction

In this section we look at two straightforward methods of proof used to infer properties of functional programs, before looking at the more powerful method of induction in the following section.

Direct proofs

As a first example, suppose we define the function

```
swap :: (Int,Int) -> (Int,Int)
swap (a,b) = (b,a)
```

The program takes a pair of numbers, and swaps them about. As well as being a program, we can read this as an equation which *describes* the behaviour of the function. The equation says that *for all possible values* of a and b, swap (a,b) is equal to (b,a). Using the equation, we can *prove* that the function has various properties. It is not hard to see that swapping twice should have the same effect as making no change; we could see evidence for this from testing, but we can prove it directly from the equation, working just as we do in calculation:

```
swap (swap (a,b))
  = swap (b,a)
  = (a,b)
```

for all a and b. In a similar way if we define cycl and recycl thus

```
cycl , recycl :: (Int,Int,Int) -> (Int,Int,Int)
cycl (a,b,c) = (b,c,a)
recycl (a,b,c) = (c,a,b)
```

then we can show that, for all a, b and c,

```
cycl (recycl (a,b,c)) = (a,b,c)
recycl (cycl (a,b,c)) = (a,b,c)
```

As can be seen from the examples here, the properties we prove often summarize part of the behaviour of a function. In the case of swap, we choose to show that the effect of the function is reversed by applying the function a second time, while in the latter examples we show that cycl reverses recycl, and vice versa.

Definedness

Before we discuss other methods of proof, we need to talk about an aspect of programming upon which we have only touched thus far. Evaluating an expression can have one of two outcomes:

- the evaluation can halt, or **terminate**, to give an answer; or
- the evaluation can go on forever.

Examples of the two are given by the expressions

```
totalSales 2                    totalSales (-2)
```

for the definition of `totalSales` given in Section 2.2.

In the case that evaluation goes on forever, we say that the value of the expression is **undefined**. In writing proofs we often have to look only at cases where a value is **defined**, since it is only for defined values that many familiar properties hold. One of the simplest examples is given by the expression

```
0*e
```

which we expect to be 0 irrespective of the value of e. That is certainly so if e has a defined value, but if e is `totalSales (-2)`, the value of

```
0 * totalSales (-2)
```

will itself be undefined, *not* zero.

In many of the proofs we give, we state that results hold for all defined values; in practice this is not a problem, as these are exactly the cases we are interested in evaluating.

We re-visit the topics of definedness and undefinedness when we examine evaluation in more detail in Chapter 13. Undefinedness is discussed in Section 13.9 in particular.

Proof by cases

In Chapter 1 we saw the definition

```
maxi :: Int -> Int -> Int
maxi n m
  | n>=m       = n
  | otherwise  = m
```

This is a program to give the maximum of two numbers; it is a conditional equation which says that the value of maxi n m is either n or m, whichever is larger.

We can *deduce* from this equation various important properties of maxi. For instance, for any defined numbers n and m

        maxi n m ⩾ n

How do we deduce this property? We know that m > n or n ⩾ m for all defined n and m. There are therefore two cases.

- If n ⩾ m holds then from the definition, maxi n m = n and so we get maxi n m ⩾ n;

- if, on the other hand, m > n holds, then maxi n m = m which is greater than n and so maxi n m ⩾ n.

Since maxi n m ⩾ n holds in both the possible cases, it will be the case in general.

It is interesting to see that the proof has a similar structure to the function definition: both use cases depending upon the relative size of m and n. We can also see a relation to testing: instead of picking a typical representative of the two cases, we use the *variables* n and m and look at the two cases that can apply to those variables.

We can use the properties of maxi in proving things about the functions which use maxi. We have, in a variant of the function from Section 2.2,

```
maxSales 0 = sales 0
maxSales r = maxi (maxSales (r-1)) (sales r)
```

Using maxi n m ⩾ n, which we saw above holds for all defined values n and m, we get for positive r that

```
maxSales r
  = maxi (maxSales (r-1)) (sales r)
  ⩾ maxSales (r-1)
```

The inequality follows from maxi n m ⩾ n by replacing m by sales r and n by maxSales (r-1).[1]

---

[1] Note that if sales gives defined values, then maxSales will too, since the value at r only uses maxSales at the smaller argument (r-1). After (r-1) steps evaluation reaches the base case of the definition, maxSales 0 = sales 0.

For s ⩾ t we can then deduce `maxSales s ⩾ maxSales t` from the chain of inequalities

`maxSales s ⩾ maxSales (s-1) ⩾ ... ⩾ maxSales t`

EXERCISES

3.1 Prove that `cycl (recycl (a,b,c)) = (a,b,c)` for all a, b and c.

3.2 Prove that `cycl (cycl (cycl (a,b,c))) = (a,b,c)` for all a, b, c.

3.3 Prove that `maxi n m ⩾ m` for defined n and m.

3.4 If we define

    `sumThree (a,b,c) = a+b+c`

give a proof that for integers a, b and c

    `sumThree (cycl (a,b,c)) = sumThree (a,b,c)`

3.5 Given the following definition

```
swapIf :: (Int,Int) -> (Int,Int)
swapIf (a,b)
  | a <= b     = (a,b)
  | otherwise  = (b,a)
```

prove that for all defined a and b,

    `swapIf (swapIf (a,b)) = swapIf (a,b)`

3.2 Proof by induction

In the previous section we gave two methods of proof that a property holds for all values – for all natural numbers, for instance. The first one worked directly for all values at once, using a single equation; the second made a proof by cases, for example, depending upon the cases of whether m > n or n ⩾ m. This section introduces a powerful method of proof by **induction** which we use to prove properties for all natural numbers 0, 1, 2, ..., n, ...

Assumptions in proofs

Before looking at the method of induction, we look at the idea of proofs and formulas which contain **assumptions**. Taking a particular example, it follows from elementary arithmetic that if we *assume* that petrol costs 27 pence per litre, then we can prove that four litres will cost £1.08.

What does this tell us? It does *not* tell us outright how much four litres will cost; it only tells us the cost if the assumption is valid. To be sure that the cost will be £1.08, we need to supply some evidence that the assumption is justified: this might be another proof – perhaps based on petrol costing £1.20 per gallon – or direct evidence.

We can write what we have proved as a formula,

1 litre costs 27 pence ⇒ 4 litres cost £1.08

where the arrow or implication, ⇒, suggests that the second proposition follows from the first.

As we have seen, we prove an implication like $A \Rightarrow B$ by assuming A in proving B. If we then find a proof of A, the implication tells us that B is also valid. Yet another way of looking at this is to see a proof of $A \Rightarrow B$ as a *machine* for turning a proof of A into a proof of B.

We use this idea in proof by induction, as one of the tasks in building an induction proof is the induction step, where we prove that one property holds assuming another. We turn to induction now.

Proof by mathematical induction

To prove the statement P(n) for all natural numbers n we have to do two things.

> **Base case**   Prove P(0).
> **Induction step** For n>0, prove P(n) *assuming* that P(n-1) holds.

How does this give a proof of P(n) for every n? The base case gives P(0), and the rest of the cases follow from the induction step. As we argued above, we can think of the induction step as a machine which turns proofs into proofs: see Figure 3.1. For example, if we give it a proof of P(7), say, it will give us a proof of P(8).

Starting at the proof of P(0), that is P(1-1), using the machine we get a proof of P(1). If we feed that proof into the machine again, we get a proof of P(2), and in a similar way we get proofs of P(3), P(4), ... In other words we get proofs of P(n) for all possible values of n.

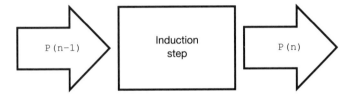

Figure 3.1   P(n-1) ⇒ P(n).

EXAMPLE: Factorial ─────────────────────────────────

Suppose we define

```
fac :: Int -> Int

fac 0 = 1
fac n = n * fac (n-1)
```

and suppose we want to prove that `fac` gives a positive result for all natural numbers. Formally, we want to prove

```
P(n):   fac n > 0
```

for all natural numbers n. To do this, we use mathematical induction, and so we have to give the two steps:

- prove P(0): fac 0 > 0;
- prove P(n) for n>0, assuming P(n-1): That is, we have to show for n>0 that fac n > 0 assuming that fac (n-1) > 0 is already proven.

Proof. As we said above, the proof has two parts.
The *base case* requires a proof of fac 0 > 0. Now, fac 0 = 1, and since 1 is greater than 0 we have fac 0 > 0 as we require.
We then have to prove the *induction step*. In this we have to show

```
P(n): fac n > 0
```

on the assumption that n>0 and P(n-1) holds. Now, we know from the definition of fac that for n>0

```
fac n = n * fac (n-1)
```

We have assumed that P(n-1) holds, so that fac (n-1) > 0. This means that fac n is a product of two positive numbers, n and fac (n-1), and is therefore positive. In other words, fac n > 0, completing the proof of the induction step, and the proof itself.

■

We use the box, ■, to signify the end of a proof.

Induction and recursion

Taking the factorial example as a guide, we can see a strong resemblance between making a proof by induction, and a definition by recursion. The function definition has two cases: the value is given outright at zero:

fac 0 = 1   (†)

and for n>0 the value, fac n, is given in terms of fac (n-1) (and n):

fac n = n * fac (n-1)   (‡)

The equation (‡) acts like the machine of the induction proof, turning a value at (n-1) into a value at n. Just as we explained how the two parts of an induction give proofs of P(n) for each n, the two equations give a value to the function fac at each n. To start, (†) gives a value at 0; using (‡) on this gives a value at 1, repeating this gives values at 2, 3 and so forth.

Seeing this link can make induction seem less alien: if we think of an induction proof building proofs P(0), P(1) and so on just as a function definition builds the results fac 0, fac 1, ... the way in which P(n-1) is assumed while we are proving P(n) is no different from the way we use the value fac (n-1) while defining fac n. In particular, it is no more 'circular' than a recursive definition of a function like factorial.

This relationship between induction and recursion is no accident, and each time we meet a way of defining functions over a data type we shall also find an induction principle which allows us to prove properties of these functions. In the following section we give further examples of proofs built by induction over the natural numbers.

3.3   Building induction proofs

Here we look at some details of how to build proofs using induction. As we said before, the structure of a proof is often very similar to the structure of the functions it involves. Induction proofs usually go with functions defined by primitive recursion, that is functions fun defined thus:

- `fun 0` is defined outright;
- `fun n` for values of n>0 is defined using `fun (n-1)`.

This mirrors the induction proof, in which `P(0)` is proved outright and `P(n)` for n>0 is proved using `P(n-1)`.

Induction proofs all follow a similar pattern, and we first give a template which can be filled in to help build a proof.

A proof template

The template in Figure 3.2 gives the overall structure of the proof, and it is evident that we have used this structure in the example above. It is sensible to write down the goal first, and especially to be clear about what are the sub-goals `P(0)` and `P(n)` (the former being obtained from `P(n)` by replacing n by 0) before trying to find the proofs themselves.

Next we look at how to get the proofs for stages 3 and 4. Before that, we say something about the equations involved.

Stage 0	Write down the goal of the proof, in English
Stage 1	Write down the goal of the proof: proving,

- `P(n)`, for all n

Stage 2	Write down the two sub-goals of the induction proof,

- `P(0)`
- `P(n)` for n>0 assuming `P(n-1)`

Stage 3	Prove `P(0)`
Stage 4	Prove `P(n)` for n>0, remembering that you can, and probably *should*, use `P(n-1)` somewhere in the proof.

Figure 3.2   Induction template.

Equations

In all proofs involving functions, the resources we have are the *definitions* of the functions involved. The equations describe the effect of the functions on any value of the variables. Consider the functions `power2` and `sumPowers`, defined by

```
power2 :: Int -> Int

power2 0 = 1                                    (1)
power2 r = 2 * power2 (r-1)                     (2)
```

```
sumPowers :: Int -> Int

sumPowers 0 = 1                                              (3)
sumPowers r = sumPowers (r-1) + power2 r                     (4)
```

We have used the variable 'r' rather than 'n' so that the variables in the definitions do not get confused with the variables in the proof.

In applying any function defined by a sequence of equations, we use the first equation which applies. In the cases of power2 and sumPowers equations (2) and (4) will apply for any non-zero r. For example, if we replace r with (n+1) in (2) we get

```
power2 (n+1) = 2 * power2 n
```

As a general piece of advice, it is best to change the names of variables in definitions so that they are different from those used in a proof.

Finding proofs

We look at the example of proving that

```
sumPowers n + 1 = power2 (n+1)
```

for all natural numbers n. The binding power of function application implies that the left-hand side means (sumPowers n) + 1, rather than sumPowers (n+1). The template for this example is given in Figure 3.3.

Here we look at how to find proofs of P(0) and P(n) for n>0. In proving the former, we have the defining equations to use; in proving P(n) for n>0 we can also use P(n-1). Indeed, we *expect* to use the induction

---

Stage 0	To prove that the sum of powers of two up to n, plus 1, is equal to the (n+1)st power of two.
Stage 1	To prove

P(n): sumPowers n + 1 = power2 (n+1)

Stage 2	We need to establish the subgoals:

- sumPowers 0 + 1 = power2 (0+1)
- sumPowers n + 1 = power2 (n+1) for n>0

in the second case assuming that

- sumPowers (n-1) + 1 = power2 n

Figure 3.3 Template for power2 example.

hypothesis `P(n-1)` in proving `P(n)`, and it is worth checking a proof which does not use it.

The main pieces of advice for constructing proofs of equalities are:

- look separately at each side;
- use the definitions, and general facts (of, for example, arithmetic) to simplify each side;
- explain each step of the proof.

This is precisely what happens in

```
sumPowers 0 + 1
   = 1 + 1                                              by (3)
   = 2                                                  arithmetic


power2 1
   = 2                                                  by (1),(2)
```

In the induction step, we start the same way, and get

```
sumPowers n + 1
   = sumPowers (n-1) + power2 n + 1                     by (4)


power2 (n+1)
   = 2 * power2 n                                       by (2)
```

Note that in the case of `power2`, we use the value of the power function at `(n+1)`; we replace `r` by `(n+1)` to do this. Now, to make any more progress we have to use the induction hypothesis, `P(n-1)`, which equates `sumPowers (n-1) + 1` and `power2 n`. Both of these are involved here, and continuing the proof on the left-hand side we get

```
sumPowers n + 1
   = sumPowers (n-1) + power2 n + 1                     as above
   = sumPowers (n-1) + 1 + power2 n                     arithmetic
   = power2 n + power2 n                                by P(n-1)
   = 2 * power2 n                                       arithmetic
```

which finally equates the two sides. This completes stage 4 of the proof, and so the proof itself.

∎

The proof we have just completed relates the two functions `power2` and `sumPowers`; instead of actually calculating the sum in `sumPowers`, we could use `power2` instead, giving the simpler definition:

```
sumPowers n = power2 (n+1) - 1
```

This process of replacing one definition by another is often called **program transformation** and it is a powerful technique for developing one (more efficient, for instance) program from another.

The general advice when proving general properties and not just equalities is similar: use the definitions and induction hypothesis to simplify the property to something which can be proved. We can see this in the following example.

EXAMPLE: Sales analysis ─────────────────────────────────

This section looks at an example from the programs we have developed so far. We reintroduced the `maxSales` function in Section 3.1 above. From the same application area we have

```
totalSales :: Int -> Int

totalSales 0 = sales 0
totalSales n = totalSales (n-1) + sales n
```

`maxSales n` is intended to give the maximum sales in the weeks 0 to n, while `totalSales n` gives the total sales for that `(n+1)`-week period. We would expect that the total sales for weeks 0 to n would be no larger than the total would have been if the sales in each week were equal to the maximum for the period. Formally, we want to prove for all n that

```
P(n):  totalSales n ≤ (n+1) * maxSales n
```

To prove this by induction we have to

- prove P(0): `totalSales 0 ≤ (0+1) * maxSales 0`;
- prove P(n): `totalSales n ≤ (n+1) * maxSales n`, for n>0

assuming that P(n-1): `totalSales (n-1) ≤ n * maxSales (n-1)` is valid.

Proof. First we have to prove the base case. We look at each side separately:

```
totalSales 0                (0+1) * maxSales 0
  = sales 0                   = 1 * sales 0
                              = sales 0
```

Since they are equal, this gives `P(0)`. We then have to prove `P(n)` for n>0. We start by looking at the left-hand side.

```
totalSales n
  = totalSales (n-1) + sales n            by def of totalSales
  ≤ n * maxSales (n-1) + sales n          by P(n-1)
```

Again, after each step of the proof we have added an explanation. The first equality comes from the definition of `totalSales`; the inequality comes from `P(n-1)`, which we assume while proving `P(n)`.

How are `maxSales (n-1)` and `sales n` related to the right-hand side, `maxSales n`? The definition of `maxSales` says that it is the maximum of the two values. As we argued earlier, this means that

```
maxSales n ⩾ maxSales (n-1)                      (†)
maxSales n ⩾ sales n                             (‡)
```

and so

```
totalSales n
  ≤ n * maxSales (n-1) + sales n          as above
  ≤ n * maxSales n + maxSales n           by (†), (‡)
  = (n+1) * maxSales n                    by arithmetic
```

which is exactly what we wanted to prove. This completes the proof of the induction step, and therefore the whole proof.

∎

EXERCISES

The first exercises here refer to the sales analysis examples introduced in Section 2.2 and further discussed in Section 3.1.

3.6 After defining the function

```
productSales :: Int -> Int
productSales 0 = sales 0
productSales n = sales n * productSales (n-1)
```

we can define

```
zeroInPeriod2 :: Int -> Bool
zeroInPeriod2 n = (productSales n == 0)
```

zeroInPeriod2 is intended to be a new way of defining 'zeroInPeriod'. Prove that it has the same behaviour by proving for all natural numbers n that

```
zeroInPeriod n = zeroInPeriod2 n
```

In the following questions, you may assume that for all n, sales n $\geqslant$ 0.

3.7   Give a proof that for all natural numbers n, totalSales n $\geqslant$ 0.

3.8   Define a function minSales which returns the minimum sales value in the weeks 0 to n. Define the function

```
zeroInPeriod3 n = (minSales n == 0)
```

and give a proof that for all natural numbers n,

```
zeroInPeriod n = zeroInPeriod3 n
```

3.9   Define a function which checks whether all sales in a period are zero. Show that this has the same behaviour as a function which checks whether the total sales for the period are zero.

3.10   Prove that for all natural numbers n,

```
fac (n+1) ⩾ power2 n
```

3.11   Prove that for all natural numbers n,

```
fib (n+1) ⩾ power2 (n div 2)
```

You need to use a slightly strengthened version of induction here, in which we infer P(n) from P(n-1) and P(n-2).

3.12   [Harder] We can say that all sales in a period 0 to n are the same explicitly, thus

```
equalSales1 :: Int -> Bool
equalSales1 0 = True
equalSales1 n = equalSales1 (n-1) && (sales (n-1) == sales n)
```

We can also define the function this way

```
equalSales2 :: Int -> Bool
equalSales2 n = (totalSales n == (n+1)*maxSales n)
```

Prove that the two functions have the same behaviour.

SUMMARY

This chapter has shown how we can prove that programs have properties. Such proofs cover all possible inputs, and so are more powerful than tests, which cover only a selection of representative cases.

The first proofs we have given use the defining equations to reason directly about function behaviour. If a function definition contains cases given by guards, it is likely that the proof will break into cases also.

Many functions are defined by recursion; we use the method of *induction* to cover proofs involving these functions. To help with induction proofs, the chapter contains suggestions for

- a template for the overall structure of the proof, making clear what are the two sub-goals of the induction proof;

- changing the names of the variables used in definitions, to avoid confusion with the variables used in the induction proof;

- how to find proofs for the sub-goals P(0) and P(n) for n>0. In finding proofs of equations, it is suggested that the definitions are used to simplify the two sides of the equations as much as possible, before applying the induction hypothesis if this is appropriate.

As with earlier chapters, a full understanding of proof can only come from practice in building proofs for yourself.

Data structures: lists

Collections of objects often occur in the situations we try to model in a program. For instance:

- A telephone directory is a collection of pairs of names and numbers.

- A book is a collection of chapters, each of which is a collection of sections. Sections, in turn, are made up of paragraphs, and so on.

- A bill from a shop is a collection of prices (numbers), or of pairs of names and prices.

- A simple picture is a collection of lines.

Lists in Haskell represent collections of objects of a particular type, and in this chapter we begin to write programs which handle lists.

4.1 Lists in Haskell

For any type `t`, there is a type of lists of items of type `t`, and this type is written `[t]`. For instance,

```
[1,2,3,4,1,4] :: [Int]
[True]        :: [Bool]
```

We read these as '`[1,2,3,4,1,4]` is a list of `Int`' and '`[True]` is a list of `Bool`'. `String` is a synonym for `[Char]` and the two lists which follow are the same.

```
['a','a','b'] :: [Char]
"aab"         :: [Char]
```

We can build lists of items of any particular type, and so we can have lists of functions and lists of lists of numbers, for instance.

```
[totalSales,totalSales]  :: [ Int -> Int ]
[ [12,2] , [2,12] , [] ] :: [ [Int] ]
```

As can be seen, the list with elements e_1, e_2 to e_n is written by enclosing the elements in square brackets, thus

```
[e₁,e₂,...,eₙ]
```

As a special case the empty list, `[]`, which contains no items, is an element of every list type.

```
[] :: [Int]
[] :: [[Bool]]
[] :: [ Int -> Int ]
...
```

Lists are collections in which the *order* of the items is significant. `[1,2]` and `[2,1]` are different lists, because although they contain the same items, their ordering is different. The first element of `[1,2]` is 1, while of `[2,1]` it is 2. The *number of occurrences* of an item also matters: `[True]` contains one item, `[True,True]` contains two, which happen to be the same.

There are some other ways of writing down lists of numbers.

●   `[n .. m]` is the list `[n,n+1,...,m]`; if n exceeds m, the list is empty.

```
[2 .. 7] = [2,3,4,5,6,7]
[3.1 .. 7.0] = [3.1,4.1,5.1,6.1]
```

- [n,p .. m] is the list of numbers from n to m in steps of p-n. For example,

  ```
  [7,6 .. 3] = [7,6,5,4,3]
  [0.0,0.3 .. 1.0] = [0.0,0.3,0.6,0.9]
  ```

- In both cases it can be seen that if the step size does not allow us to reach m exactly, the last item of the list is the largest in the sequence which is less than or equal to m.

EXERCISES

4.1 Give Haskell type definitions, using type, for the examples of the telephone directory, book and shop bill given at the start of the chapter.

4.2 How many items does the list [2,3] contain? How many does [[2,3]] contain? What is the type of [[2,3]]?

4.3 What is the result of evaluating [2 .. 2]? What about [2,7 .. 4]?

4.2 Defining functions over lists

Suppose we want to define the function

```
sumList :: [Int] -> Int
```

which sums a list of integers. Our definition will have to cover lists of length 0, 1, 2 and so on. How can the definition work for all cases? We can divide up the type of lists as follows: every list is either

- the empty list, [], or
- non-empty. In this case it will have a first element, or **head**, and a remainder, or **tail**. For instance, [2,3,4,5] has head 2 and tail [3,4,5]. A list with head a and tail x is written (a:x).

We can now look at the definition of sumList. It will divide into the two cases suggested above.

- The sum of the empty list is 0.
- The sum of a non-empty list, (a:x), is given by adding a to the sum of x.

For example, in the case of [2,3,4,5]

| 2 | 3 | 4 | 5 |

2 + ◁ .... sumList [3,4,5] .... ▷

The Haskell definition will be

```
sumList []    = 0                          (1)
sumList (a:x) = a + sumList x              (2)
```

As we did earlier, in making a calculation we use the first equation whose patterns are matched by the corresponding arguments, so that in the case of sumList,

```
sumList [2,3,4,5]
= 2 + sumList [3,4,5]                       by (2)
= 2 + (3 + sumList [4,5])                   by (2)
= 2 + (3 + (4 + sumList [5]))               by (2)
= 2 + (3 + (4 + (5 + sumList [])))          by (2)
= 2 + (3 + (4 + (5 + 0)))                   by (1)
= ... = 14                                  arithmetic
```

The list constructor

The last section introduced the operator ':', which is sometimes called 'cons'. This operator or **constructor** (hence the name 'cons') builds a list from an item and a list, and we can see every non-empty list as being built this way. For instance,

```
[5]   = 5:[]
[4,5] = 4:[5] = 4:(5:[])
[2,3,4,5] = 2:3:4:5:[]
```

In the final expression, we have used the fact that ':' associates to the right – this means that

```
a:b:c = a:(b:c)
a:b:c ≠ (a:b):c
```

All the notation for lists given so far can be defined using ':'. Lists can be of any type, so

```
(:) :: Int -> [Int] -> [Int]
(:) :: Bool -> [Bool] -> [Bool]
   ...
```

These types express the fact that the elements of a list must all be of the same type: you cannot put an integer onto the front of a Boolean list, for instance. In fact we can express the type of (:) in a single expression

```
(:) :: t -> [t] -> [t]
```

where t is a type variable, which stands for any type (such as Int or Bool). We look at the details of this in Chapter 6.

To illustrate another function on lists, suppose we want to double every element of a numerical list.

| 2 | 3 | 4 | 2 |

We can double the first element, or head, simply by multiplying it by two. The final result is built by putting this on the front of the doubled tail, using ':':

4 : | 6 | 8 | 4 |

This is the list

| 4 | 6 | 8 | 4 |

as required. The Haskell definition will be

```
double :: [Int] -> [Int]

double []    = []
double (a:x) = (2*a) : double x
```

and the calculation of an example gives

```
double [2,3]
= (2*2) : double [3]
= 4 : double [3]
= 4 : ( (2*3) : double [] )
= 4 : ( 6 : double [] )
= 4 : ( 6 : [] )
= 4 : [6]
= [4,6]
```

Standard list functions and operators

The length of a list is given by `length`, which is built into the standard prelude. It can be defined in this way

```
length []    = 0
length (a:x) = 1 + length x
```

The empty list has length zero; a non-empty list, `a:x`, is one item longer than its tail, `x`.

When we introduced strings as lists of `Char`, we saw that `++` could be used to join or append two strings. This is true for lists of any type, so that

```
[2] ++ [3,4,5] = [2,3,4,5]
[] ++ [2,3] ++ [] ++ [4,5] = [2,3,4,5]
```

Only lists of the same type can be joined, so the type of `++` will be

```
(++) :: [Int] -> [Int] -> [Int]
(++) :: [Bool] -> [Bool] -> [Bool]
  ...
```

How is `++` defined? Joining `[]` and any list `y` will give the result `y`

```
[] ++ y = y
```

but now we should look at the case of joining `a:x` to `y`. In pictures, we have

a	x		++		y	

Taking off the head, `a`, we can combine `x` and `y`

	x		++		y	

and then put `a` at the front, using ':', thus

a :

	x		++		y	

The full definition of append in Haskell is thus

```
[] ++ y    = y
(a:x) ++ y = a : (x++y)
```

The associativity and binding powers of the full collection of list operators are given in Appendix E.

Pitfalls: cons and append

++ and ':' do similar but different things!

- ++ takes two lists and returns a list, so for instance

    [2] ++ [3,4,5] = [2,3,4,5]

  but 2 ++ [3,4,5] gives the Gofer error

  ```
  ERROR: Type error in application
  *** expression    : 2 ++ [2,3]
  *** term          : 2
  *** type          : Int
  *** does not match : [Int]
  ```

  since the first argument of ++ is expected to be a list of Int rather than an Int.
- ':' takes an element and a list, giving a list

    2 : [3,4,5] = [2,3,4,5]

  while [2] : [3,4,5] gives the Gofer error:

  ```
  ERROR: Type error in application
  *** expression    : [2] : [3,4,5]
  *** term          : [2]
  *** type          : [Int]
  *** does not match : Int
  ```

  as there is an attempt to use ':' to make an integer list, [2], the first element of a list of integers. The type of the first argument to ':' here has to be an Int, rather than of type [Int].

In both cases the Hugs error is less specific, saying,

```
ERROR: Cannot construct instance Num [a] in expression
```

The simplest way to remember the behaviour is by the equations

```
item :  list = list
list ++ list = list
```

EXERCISES

4.4 Write out `[True,True,False]` and `[2]` in full using ':' and `[]`.

4.5 Give calculations of

```
sumList [34,2,0,1]
double [0]
"tea"++"cup"
```

4.6 Design test data for the functions `sumList` and `double`.

4.7 Define a function

```
productList :: [Int] -> Int
```

which returns the product of a list of integers. You should take the product of an empty list to be 1. Why is 1 a better choice than 0?

4.8 Define a function

```
and :: [Bool] -> Bool
```

which returns the conjunction of a list. Informally,

```
and [e₁,e₂,...,eᵢ] = e₁ && e₂ && ... && eᵢ
```

The conjunction of an empty list should be `True`.

4.9 Define a function

```
concat :: [[Int]] -> [Int]
```

which 'flattens' a list of lists of numbers into a single list of numbers. For example,

```
concat [[3,4],[],[31,3]] = [3,4,31,3]
```

An informal definition is given by

```
concat [e₁,e₂,...,eᵢ] = e₁ ++ e₂ ++ ... ++ eᵢ
```

4.3 Designing functions over lists

Previous sections have introduced the list types, and given some elementary definitions of functions over lists. Here we go into more detail about how more complex list manipulating functions can be designed in Haskell. We begin by looking at a sequence of examples.

EXAMPLE: Sorting ─────────────────────────────────

The task here is to write a function which will sort a list of numbers into ascending order. A list like

7	3	9	2

is sorted by taking the tail [3,9,2] and sorting it to give

2	3	9

It is then a matter of inserting the head, 7, in the right place in this list, giving

2	3	7	9

In Haskell, we have the definition of iSort – the 'i' is for *insertion* sort.

```
iSort :: [Int] -> [Int]

iSort []    = []                      (1)
iSort (a:x) = ins a (iSort x)         (2)
```

This is a typical example of top-down definition. We have defined iSort assuming we can define ins. The development of the program has been in two separate parts, since we have a definition of the function iSort using a simpler function ins, together with a definition of the function ins itself. Solving each sub-problem is simpler than solving the original problem itself.

Now we have to define the function

```
ins :: Int -> [Int] -> [Int]
```

To get some guidance about how ins should behave, we look at some examples. Inserting 7 into [2,3,9] was given above, while inserting 1 gives

1	2	3	9

Looking at these two examples we see that

- The case of 1. If the item to be inserted is smaller than (or equal to) the head of the list, we cons it to the front of the list.
- The case of 7. If the item is greater than the head, we insert it in the tail of the list, and cons the head to the result, thus:

$$2 \quad : \quad \boxed{\begin{array}{c|c|c} 3 & 7 & 9 \end{array}}$$

The function can now be defined, including the case that the list is empty.

```
ins a []     = [a]                        (3)
ins a (b:y)
  | a <= b     = a:(b:y)                   (4)
  | otherwise  = b : ins a y               (5)
```

We now show the functions in action, in the calculation of iSort [3,9,2]

```
iSort [3,9,2]
= ins 3 (iSort [9,2])                      by (2)
= ins 3 (ins 9 (iSort [2]))                by (2)
= ins 3 (ins 9 (ins 2 (iSort [])))         by (2)
= ins 3 (ins 9 (ins 2 []))                 by (1)
= ins 3 (ins 9 [2])                        by (3)
= ins 3 (2 : ins 9 [])                     by (5)
= ins 3 [2,9]                              by (3)
= 2 : ins 3 [9]                            by (5)
= 2 : [3,9] = [2,3,9]                      by (4)
```

Developing this function has shown the advantage of looking at examples while trying to define a function; the examples can give a guide about how the definition might break into cases, or the pattern of the recursion. We also saw how using top-down design can break a larger problem into smaller problems which are easier to solve.

EXERCISES

4.10 Can you use the iSort function to find the minimum and maximum elements of a list of numbers? How would you find these elements without using iSort?

4.11 Design test data for the ins function. Your data should address different possible points of insertion, and also look at any exceptional cases.

4.12   By modifying the definition of the `ins` function we can change the behaviour of the sort, `iSort`. Redefine `ins` in two different ways so that

- the list is sorted in descending order;
- duplicates are removed from the list. For example,

    ```
    iSort [2,1,4,1,2] = [1,2,4]
    ```

    under this definition.

4.13   Design test data for the duplicate-removing version of `iSort`, explaining your choices.

EXAMPLES: Membership and selection ──────────────────

Given a list, how can we decide whether a particular item belongs in it? We define the function

```
member :: [Int] -> Int -> Bool
```

whose result is a Boolean value, signalling whether the second argument appears in the first. An item `b` can appear in a list `(a:x)` in two ways:

- it can be equal to `a`, or
- it can appear in the tail `x`.

The function definition reflects this

```
member []    b = False
member (a:x) b = (a==b) || member x b
```

Often the function receives the definition

```
mem []    b = False
mem (a:x) b
   | a==b        = True
   | otherwise   = mem x b
```

this has the same effect as the definition of `member`, but it is less clear. The 'or' which appeared in the informal definition has been replaced with a guard. It is clearer in general to use the Boolean operations `not`, `||` and `&&` to combine Boolean values, rather than to use guards.

Given a string, how can we *select* or *filter* the digits from it, so that

```
digits :: String -> String
digits "the34reIs32w" = "3432"
```

There are two cases when the string is non-empty, so having the form (first:rest).

- When first is a digit, it will be the first element of the output string.
- When it is not a digit, it will not appear in the output string.

In either case, the remainder of the output is given by finding the digits in rest. As a Haskell definition, we have

```
digits [] = []
digits (first:rest)
  | isDigit first      = first : digits rest
  | otherwise          =        digits rest
```

in which we use the function isDigit :: Char -> Bool to test whether a character is a digit. An example calculation gives

```
digits "s32w"
  ??  isDigit 's' = False
= digits "32w"
  ??  isDigit '3' = True
= '3' : digits "2w"
  ??  isDigit '2' = True
= '3' : ('2' : digits "w")
  ??  isDigit 'w' = False
= '3' : ('2' : digits "")
= '3' : ('2' : [])
= "32"
```

EXERCISES

4.14 Define a function

```
memberNum :: [Int] -> Int -> Int
```

so that memberNum l s returns the *number* of times the item s appears in the list l; design test data for your function.

4.15 Give a definition of `member` which uses the function `memberNum`.

4.16 Define a function

```
unique :: [Int] -> [Int]
```

which returns the list of numbers which occur exactly once in a list. For instance

```
unique [2,4,2,1,4] = [1]
```

You will probably find that the function `memberNum` is useful in your definition.

4.17 If you are allowed to assume that the list argument of `member` is sorted into ascending order, can you modify the definition so that it is not in general necessary to examine the whole list in order to be able to conclude that an item is *not* an element of the list? You may like to consider the example

```
member [2,4,6] 3
```

for guidance.

4.18 For the original definitions of `member` and `mem` give evaluations of

```
member [2,4,6] 4
mem [2,4,6] 4
```

The evaluation using `member` can be shortened if you notice that

```
True || e = True
```

whatever the value of e. This is an example of 'lazy' evaluation; we only evaluate the argument e if we need to.

4.4 Pattern matching

Patterns in Haskell are given by:

- Constant integers, characters and Booleans: -2, '1', True.
- Variables: x, varNumber17.
- Tuples of patterns: for example $(p_1, p_2, \ldots, p_k)$, where $p_1, \ldots$ are themselves patterns.
- List patterns: [] and $(p_1:p_2)$, where p_1 and p_2 are patterns.
- Wild cards: _.
- Constructor patterns, which will be introduced in Chapter 10 below.

As can be seen from this, patterns can be *nested*: a tuple or list pattern can be built itself from patterns. Indeed, we saw this earlier with the definition of the shift function.

There is one further condition on patterns: no variable may be *repeated* in the patterns of a conditional equation.

A pattern match does two things; first it checks whether an argument is of the correct form, and second it associates values with variables within the pattern, so that those values can be used within a definition. For instance, when [2,3,4] is matched against (a:x) the match *succeeds*, since the list [2,3,4] has a head and a tail. Moreover, 2 will be associated with a and [3,4] with x. If the pattern is used in the definition

```
sumList (a:x) = a + sumList x
```

we have

```
sumList [2,3,4] = 2 + sumList [3,4]
```

When does an argument a match a pattern p?

- If p is a constant, this happens when a equals p.
- If p is a variable, x say, a will match p and will be associated with x in the definition.
- If p is a tuple of patterns, for example $(p_1, p_2, \ldots, p_k)$, a will match if a is a tuple itself, $(a_1, a_2, \ldots, a_k)$ and each a_i matches p_i.
- If p is a list pattern $(p_1:p_2)$, a will match if it is a non-empty list. Its head is matched with p_1 and its tail with p_2.
- If p is a wild card _, then a will match p, but no association is set up; the wild card simply acts as a *test*.

We next introduce a new construct which allows pattern matching to occur within an expression.

The case construction

So far we have seen how to perform a pattern match over the arguments of functions; sometimes we might want to pattern match over other values. This can be done by a case expression, which we introduce by means of an example.

Suppose we are asked to find the first digit in the string st, returning '\0' in case no digit is found. We can use the function digits of Section 4.3 to give us the list of *all* the digits in the string: digits st. If this is not empty, that is if it matches (a:x), we want to return its first element, a; if it is empty, we return '\0'.

We therefore want to pattern match over the value of (digits st) and for this we use a case expression as follows:

```
firstDigit :: String -> Char

firstDigit st
  = case (digits st) of
        []    -> '\0'
        (a:_) -> a
```

A case expression has the effect of distinguishing between various alternatives – here those of an empty and a non-empty list – and of extracting parts of a value, by associating values with the variables in a pattern. In the case of matching e with (a:_) we associate the head of e with a; as we have used a wild-card pattern in (a:_), the tail of e is not associated with any variable.

In general, a case expression has the form

```
case e of
    p₁ -> e₁
    p₂ -> e₂
    ...
    pₖ -> eₖ
```

where e is an expression to be matched in turn against the patterns p_1, $p_2, \ldots, p_k$. If p_i is the first pattern which e matches, the result is e_i in which the variables in p_i are associated with the corresponding parts of e.

EXAMPLE: Summing a list of pairs _____

In the remainder of this section we look at the example of the function to sum a list of pairs of numbers, and see that there is often more than one way to define a particular function using pattern matching. Obviously,

```
sumPairs :: [(Int,Int)] -> Int
sumPairs [] = 0
```

but there are a number of possibilities for the case of the non-empty list. We can choose to use a simple list pattern, thus

```
sumPairs (a:x) = fst a + snd a + sumPairs x              (1)
```

A non-empty list will match `(a:x)`. The components of its head, `a`, are accessed using the built-in functions `fst` and `snd`.

We also use a simple list pattern in the second definition, but use a `where` clause to define the first and second parts of the pair `a`.

```
sumPairs (a:x) = c + d + sumPairs x                    (2)
                 where
                 c = fst a
                 d = snd a
```

Alternatively again, we can use a conformal pattern match to extract the components in a `where` clause

```
sumPairs (a:x) = c + d + sumPairs x                    (3)
                 where
                 (c,d) = a
```

A conformal pattern match p = e will only succeed if e matches the pattern p. In this case, `a` will be a pair, and so the match will always succeed. On the other hand, if p were the pattern `(a:x)`, e would fail to match p if its value was the empty list.

As an alternative to definitions (1) to (3), we can give a nested pattern.

```
sumPairs ((c,d):x) = c + d + sumPairs x                (4)
```

In this case a non-empty list of pairs is matched – to succeed the list must be non-empty, as it is built using ':', and have as its first element a pair `(c,d)`. The three components c, d and x are then used on the right-hand side.

The final definition uses a different strategy, in which an auxiliary function to sum a pair of numbers is defined separately

```
sumPairs (a:x) = sumPair a + sumPairs x                (5)
sumPair  (c,d) = c+d
```

The pattern match over the pair is made in the definition of `sumPair`, while the match over the list is in the main function `sumPairs`.

Each of these forms of definition has its advantages. The first three use a simple top-level pattern, and extract the components of the pair in different ways; in the fourth, a nested pattern is used to extract the components at top level. The final definition separates the processing of the list from the processing of the items. This *separation* makes the function potentially easier to modify: we could change the function to sum a list of triples, or pairs of pairs of numbers without modifying the `sumPairs` function.

As was explained above, pattern matching in Haskell is *sequential*. Take the example of a function to *zip* together two lists into a list of pairs, so that

```
zip [2,3,4] [4,5,78] = [(2,4),(3,5),(4,78)]
zip [2,3] [1,2,3]    = [(2,1),(3,2)]
```

Note that in the second case, elements from the longer list are thrown away if there is no corresponding element in the other list. The function is defined by

```
zip (a:x) (b:y) = (a,b) : zip x y
zip _ _         = []
```

The second equation will only be used if the arguments fail to match the first, which means that at least one of the lists is empty. It could be written with all the patterns disjoint, but the definition is correspondingly longer:

```
zip (a:x) (b:y) = (a,b) : zip x y
zip (a:x) []    = []
zip []    y     = []
```

EXERCISES

4.19 Modify definitions (2) and (4) of sumPairs to sum a list of triples of numbers, (c,d,e).

4.20 Modify definitions (3) and (5) of sumPairs to sum a list of pairs of pairs of numbers, ((c,d),(e,f)).

4.21 Do a calculation of

```
sumPairs [ (2,3) , (6,-7) ]
```

for each of the definitions (1) to (5) of sumPairs.

4.22 Define a function zip3 to zip together three lists of numbers. Can you modify your definition so that there is no overlap between the equations?

4.23 Define a function

```
unZip :: [ (Int,Int) ] -> ( [Int] , [Int] )
```

which takes a list of pairs into a pair of lists. You might find it helpful first to define two functions

```
unZipLeft, unZipRight :: [ (Int,Int) ] -> [Int]
```

which give the lists of first elements and second elements, respectively,

```
unZipLeft  [(2,4),(3,5),(4,78)] = [2,3,4]
unZipRight [(2,4),(3,5),(4,78)] = [4,5,78]
```

4.5   A library database

A library uses a database to keep a record of the books on loan to borrowers.

Types

In modelling this situation, we first look at the types of the objects involved. People and books are represented by strings

```
type Person = String
type Book   = String
```

The database can be represented in a number of different ways. We choose to make it a list of (Person,Book) pairs. If the pair ("Alice" , "Spot") is in the list, it means that "Alice" has borrowed the book called "Spot". We therefore define

```
type Database = [ (Person , Book) ]
```

An example object of this type is

```
exampleBase
= [ ("Alice" , "Postman Pat") , ("Anna" , "All Alone") ,
    ("Alice" , "Spot") , ("Rory" , "Postman Pat") ]
```

After defining the types of the objects involved, we consider the functions which work over the database.

- Given a person, we want to find the book(s) they have borrowed, if any.
- Given a book, we want to find the borrower(s) of the book, if any. (It is assumed that there may be more than one copy of any book.)
- Given a book, we want to find out whether it is borrowed.
- Given a person, we may want to find out the number of books they have borrowed.

Each of these **lookup** functions will take a `Database`, and a `Person` or `Book`, and return the result of the query. Their types will be

```
books       :: Database -> Person -> [Book]
borrowers   :: Database -> Book -> [Person]
borrowed    :: Database -> Book -> Bool
numBorrowed :: Database -> Person -> Int
```

Note that `borrowers` and `books` return lists; these can contain zero, one or more items, and so in particular can signal that a book has no borrowers, or that a person has no books on loan.

Two other functions need to be defined. We need to be able to make a loan of a book to a person, and also to return a loan. These functions will take a database, plus the loan information, and return a *different* database, which is the original with the loan added or removed. These **update** functions will have type

```
makeLoan   :: Database -> Person -> Book -> Database
returnLoan :: Database -> Person -> Book -> Database
```

Defining the lookup functions

We start by looking at the function

```
books :: Database -> Person -> [Book]
```

which forms a model for the other lookup functions `borrowers`, `borrowed` and `numBorrowed`. For the `exampleBase`, we have

```
books exampleBase "Alice" = [ "Postman Pat" , "Spot" ]
books exampleBase "Rory"  = [ "Postman Pat" ]
```

How are these found? We have looked already at two functions whose design can help.

- The function `digits` of Section 4.3, shows how to *filter* certain items from a list. In the example above we need to find the pairs whose first halves are equal to "Alice" and then to return the second halves of those pairs.

- The function `sumPairs` of the same section is defined over a list of pairs, and the discussion of pattern matching there is relevant here.

To design a function it is often helpful first to think of the left-hand side. In checking through the database we will need to check each pair one-by-one, and so we will pattern match over the first argument.

The sumPairs function gives guidance about the exact form of the left-hand sides when dealing with a list of pairs. If we take our guidance from definition (4) of sumPairs we will use a nested pattern like ((c,d):x) to describe a non-empty list of pairs. The left-hand sides will be

```
books []                 borrower =
books ((pers,bk):rest) borrower =
```

No books can be borrowed by borrower in an empty database, as no books are borrowed by anybody

```
books [] borrower = []
```

Now, informally, given a list ((pers,bk):rest), the book bk will be included in the output if pers is borrower; otherwise it will not be included, much like the definition of digits. This completes the definition.

```
books :: Database -> Person -> [Book]
books [] borrower = []
books ((pers,bk):rest) borrower
  | pers == borrower   = bk : books rest borrower
  | otherwise          =      books rest borrower
```

As we said at the start, books forms a model for the other lookup functions, which we leave as an exercise.

Defining the update functions

The database is modified, or updated, by the functions

```
makeLoan   :: Database -> Person -> Book -> Database
returnLoan :: Database -> Person -> Book -> Database
```

Making a loan is done by adding a pair to the database, which can be done simply by putting it on the front of the list of pairs.

```
makeLoan dBase pers bk = (pers,bk) : dBase
```

Note that there is no pattern match over the database here – the same operation is used whether the database is empty or not. Also, the function is not recursive.

To return a loan, we need to check through the database, and to remove the first pair (pers,bk)

```
returnLoan ((p,b):rest) pers bk
  | p==pers && b==bk    = rest
  | otherwise           = (p,b) : returnLoan rest pers bk

returnLoan [] pers bk
  = error ("returnLoan failed on " ++ pers ++ " " ++ bk)
```

the function signals an error when called on a database which does not contain the pair (pers,bk). An alternative would be to return the database unchanged when a pair is not present.

There is some ambiguity in the way that the function is described: should all loans of bk to pers be cancelled by returnLoan, or just the first? To remove them all, we can modify the definition to

```
returnLoan2 ((p,b):rest) pers bk
  | p==pers && b==bk    =          returnLoan rest pers bk
  | otherwise           = (p,b) : returnLoan rest pers bk

returnLoan2 [] pers bk = []
```

This function will not signal an error when the pair to be removed is not present.

Testing

A Haskell interpreter acts like a calculator, and this is useful when we wish to test functions like those in the library database. Any function can be tested by typing expressions to the Gofer or Hugs prompt. For example,

```
makeLoan [] "Alice" "Fireman Sam"
```

To test more substantial examples, it is sensible to put test data into a script, so we might include the definition of exampleBase as well as various tests

```
test1 = borrowed exampleBase "Spot"
test2 = makeLoan exampleBase "Alice" "Fireman Sam"
```

and so on. Adding them to the script means that we can repeatedly do them without having to type them out in full each time. Another device which can help is to use $$, which is short for 'the last expression evaluated'.

The following sequence makes a loan, then another, then returns the first.

```
makeLoan exampleBase "Alice" "Fireman Sam"
makeLoan $$ "Rory" "Gorilla"
returnLoan $$ "Alice" "Fireman Sam"
```

EXERCISES

4.24 Go through the calculation of

```
books exampleBase "Alice"
books exampleBase "Rory"
```

4.25 Define the functions `borrowers`, `borrowed` and `numBorrowed`.

4.26 Criticize the following suggested definition of `books`.

```
books [] borrower = []
books ((pers,bk):rest) borrower
  | pers == borrower    = [ bk ]
  | otherwise           = books rest borrower
```

4.27 Give calculations of

```
returnLoan exampleBase "Alice" "Spot"
returnLoan exampleBase "Alice" "All Alone"
```

4.28 Modify the definition of `returnLoan` to return the database unchanged when a pair is not present.

4.29 What is wrong with the following attempted definition of `returnLoan`?

```
returnLoan ((p,b):rest) pers bk
  | p==pers && b==bk    = rest
  | otherwise           = returnLoan rest pers bk
... as above ...
```

4.30 Why has the `[]` case of `returnLoan` been changed in `returnLoan2`? You might find it helpful to run through an example calculation.

4.31 Define a function `layout`

```
layout :: [Book] -> String
```

which takes a list of books, and which returns a `String` which displays the books one per line. Your function should join the strings together, placing newline characters between the strings.

4.32 How could you combine `layout` and `books` to give a function

    booksLayout :: Database -> Person -> String

which displays the books on loan to a person one per line?

4.33 [Harder] How would you modify your database and access functions so that

- There was a maximum number of books which could be loaned to a particular person?
- There is a list of keywords associated with each book, so that books could be found by the keywords associated with them?
- Dates are associated with loans, so that overdue books could be found if necessary, and the list of books borrowed by a borrower could be sorted by order of the date due? [To achieve this, you will need to think about how dates can be represented, and how ordering of dates is implemented.]

4.6 List comprehensions

This section introduces **list comprehensions** which provide an alternative way of writing down some lists and list-manipulating functions. Specifically they are useful for writing down lists built on the basis of others.

A series of examples

For example, if the list `ex` is `[2,4,7]` then

    [2*a | a<-ex]   (1)

will be

    [4,8,14]

as it contains each of the elements a of the list ex, doubled: `2*a`. We can read (1) as saying

> Take all `2*a` where a comes from ex.

where the symbol `<-` is meant to resemble the mathematical symbol for being an element, ϵ. In a similar way,

    [isEven n | n<-ex] = [True,True,False]

if the function `isEven :: Int -> Bool` has the obvious definition.

In list comprehensions a<-ex is called a **generator** because it generates the data from which the results are built. On the left-hand side of the '<-' there is a variable, a, while on the right-hand side we put a list, in this case ex.

We can combine a generator with one or more **tests**, which are Boolean expressions, thus:

$$[\ 2*a \ | \ a \ <- \ ex \ , \ isEven \ a \ , \ a>3 \ ] \hspace{2cm} (2)$$

(2) is paraphrased as

Take all 2*a where a comes from ex, a is even and greater than 3.

The result of (2) will therefore be the list [8], as 4 is the only even element of [2,4,7] which is greater than 3.

As well as placing a variable to the left of the arrow '<-', we can put any pattern. For instance,

```
addPairs :: [(Int,Int)] -> [Int]

addPairs pairList = [ a+b | (a,b) <- pairList ]
```

Here we choose all the pairs in the list pairList, and add their components to give a single number in the result list. For example,

```
addPairs [(2,3),(2,1),(7,8)] = [5,3,15]
```

We can add tests in such a situation, too.

```
newAddPairs :: [(Int,Int)] -> [Int]

newAddPairs pairList = [ a+b | (a,b) <- pairList , a<b ]
```

and in the example,

```
newAddPairs [(2,3),(2,1),(7,8)] = [5,15]
```

since the second pair in the list, (2,1), fails the test.

It is possible to put multiple generators into a list comprehension, and to combine generators and tests. These topics, as well as rules which govern how list comprehensions are evaluated together with a sequence of larger examples, are examined when we revisit the subject in Section 13.3. Readers who are interested are encouraged to look forward to the material, which should make sense without reading the intervening chapters.

Revisiting some earlier definitions

Here we look back at some of the examples given earlier in this chapter, and see how list comprehensions can be used to give alternative definitions. To double every element of a list, we can say

```
double :: [Int] -> [Int]
double l = [ 2*a | a<-l ]
```

In comparison to the original definition in Section 4.2, there is no pattern matching in the definition; whether l is empty or not, we simply take all the elements a and double them.

To find all the digits in a string – another example from Section 4.2 – we can say

```
digits :: String -> String
digits st = [ ch | ch<-st , isDigit ch ]
```

The notation is most useful when we combine performing some transformation, as is done in double, with the selection of elements, as in digits. A perfect case of this is given by the database functions of the preceding section.

Suppose we have to find all the books borrowed in the database db by the borrower borrower. We should run through all pairs (per,bk) in the database, and return the bk part when the per part is the borrower. Precisely this is given by

```
books :: Database -> Person -> [Book]

books db borrower
    = [ bk | (per,bk) <- db , per==borrower ]          (3)
```

A number of other examples are covered in the exercises.

A pitfall

This section addresses an important pitfall to do with the behaviour of variables: the definition (3) of books above might appear to be over-complicated. We imagine that we can say

```
books db borrower
    = [ bk | (borrower,bk) <- db ]                     (4)
```

The effect of this is to return all the books borrowed by *all* borrowers, not just the particular borrower `borrower`.

The reason for this is that the `borrower` in `(borrower,bk)` is a *new* variable, and not the variable on the left-hand side of the definition, so in fact (4) has the same effect as

```
books db borrower = [ bk | (new,bk) <- db ]
```

where it is clear that there is no constraint on the value of `new` to be equal to `borrower`.

EXERCISES

4.34 For the single generator examples of list comprehensions given in this section, show that it is never necessary to have more than one test.

4.35 How can the function

```
member :: [Int] -> Int -> Bool
```

be defined using a list comprehension and an equality test?

4.36 Re-implement the database manipulating functions of the previous section using list comprehensions rather than the explicit recursive definitions given there.

4.7 Extended exercise: supermarket billing

This collection of exercises looks at supermarket billing.[1] A scanner at a checkout will produce a list of bar codes, like

```
[1234,4719,3814,1112,1113,1234]
```

which has to be converted to a bill

---

[1] I am grateful to Peter Lindsay *et al.* of the Department of Computer Science at the University of New South Wales, Australia for the inspiration for this example, which was suggested by their lecture notes.

```
          Haskell Stores

Dry Sherry, 1lt..........5.40
Fish Fingers.............1.21
Orange Jelly.............0.56
Hula Hoops (Giant).......1.33
Unknown Item.............0.00
Dry Sherry, 1lt..........5.40

Total...................13.90
```

We have to decide first how to model the objects involved. Bar codes and prices (in pence) can be modelled by integers; names of goods by strings. We say therefore that

```
type Name    = String
type Price   = Int
type BarCode = Int
```

The conversion will be based on a *database* which links bar codes, names and prices. As in the library, we use a list to model the relationship.

```
type Database = [ (BarCode,Name,Price) ]
```

The example database we use is

```
codeIndex :: Database
codeIndex = [ (4719, "Fish Fingers" , 121),
              (5643, "Nappies" , 1010),
              (3814, "Orange Jelly", 56),
              (1111, "Hula Hoops", 21),
              (1112, "Hula Hoops (Giant)", 133),
              (1234, "Dry Sherry, 1lt", 540)]
```

The object of the script will be to convert a list of bar codes into a list of (Name,Price) pairs; this then has to be converted into a string for printing as above. We make the type definitions

```
type TillType = [BarCode]
type BillType = [(Name,Price)]
```

and then we can say that the functions we wish to define are

```
makeBill   :: TillType -> BillType
formatBill :: BillType -> String
printBill  :: TillType -> String
```

The `printBill` function will combine the effects of `makeBill` and `formatBill`,

```
printBill tt = formatBill (makeBill tt)
```

The length of a line in the bill is decided to be 30. This is made a constant, thus

```
lineLength :: Int
lineLength = 30
```

Making `lineLength` a constant in this way means that to change the length of a line in the bill, only one definition needs to be altered; if 30 were used in each of the formatting functions, then each would have to be modified on changing the line length.

The rest of the script is developed through the sequences of exercises which follow.

First we develop the `formatBill` function from the bottom up: we design functions to format prices, lines, and the total, and using these we finally build the `formatBill` function itself.

EXERCISES

4.37 Given a number of pence, 1023 say, the pounds and pence parts are given by 1023 `div` 100 and 1023 `mod` 100. Using this fact, and the `show` function, define a function

```
formatPence :: Int -> String
```

so that, e.g. `formatPence 1023 = "10.23"`

4.38 Using the `formatPence` function, define a function

```
formatLine  :: (Name,Price) -> String
```

which formats a line of a bill, thus

```
formatLine ("Dry Sherry, 1lt",540)
                = "Dry Sherry, 1lt..........5.40\n"
```

Recall that `'\n'` is the newline character, that `++` can be used to join two strings together, and that `length` will give the length of a string.

You may find it helpful to define a function

```
rep :: Int -> Char -> String
```

which builds a string containing a given number of the same character. For example,

```
rep 4 'n' = "nnnn"
```

4.39 Using the `formatLine` function, define

```
formatLines :: [ (Name,Price) ] -> String
```

which applies `formatLine` to each `(Name,Price)` pair, and joins the results together.

4.40 Define a function

```
makeTotal :: BillType -> Int
```

which takes a list of `(Name,Price)` pairs, and gives the total of the prices. For instance,

```
makeTotal [(" ... ",540),(" ... ",121)] = 661
```

4.41 Define the function

```
formatTotal :: Int -> String
```

so that, for example,

```
formatTotal 661 = "\nTotal....................6.61"
```

4.42 Using the functions `formatLines`, `makeTotal` and `formatTotal`, define

```
formatBill :: BillType -> String
```

so that on the input

```
[("Dry Sherry, 1lt",540),("Fish Fingers",121),
("Orange Jelly",56),("Hula Hoops (Giant)",133),
("Unknown Item",0),("Dry Sherry, 1lt",540)]
```

the example bill at the start of the section is produced.

This completes the definition of the formatting functions; now we have to look at the database functions which accomplish the conversion of bar codes into names and prices.

EXERCISES

4.43 Define a function

```
look :: Database -> BarCode -> (Name,Price)
```

which returns the `(Name,Price)` pair corresponding to the `BarCode` in the `Database`. If the `BarCode` does not appear in the database, then the pair `("Unknown Item", 0)` should be the result. (You can assume that each bar code occurs only once in the database, so you do not have to worry about returning multiple results.)

4.44 Define a function

```
lookup :: BarCode -> (Name,Price)
```

which uses `look` to look up an item in the particular database `codeIndex`.

4.45 Define the function

```
makeBill   :: TillType -> BillType
```

which applies `lookup` to every item in the input list. For instance, when applied to `[1234,4719,3814,1112,1113,1234]` the result will be the list of (Name,Price) pairs given in Exercise 4.42. Note that 1113 does not appear in `codeIndex` and so is converted to ("Unknown Item",0).

This completes the definition of `makeBill` and together with `formatBill` gives the conversion program. We conclude with some further exercises.

EXERCISES

4.46 Modify your script so that the bill is printed with the items sorted. Why are supermarket bills not printed in this form?

4.47 You are asked in addition to add a discount for multiple buys of sherry: for every two bottles bought, there is a `1.00` discount. From the example list of bar codes `[1234,4719,3814,1112,1113,1234]` the bill should resemble:

```
    Haskell Stores

Dry Sherry, 1lt..........5.40
Dry Sherry, 1lt..........5.40
Fish Fingers.............1.21
Hula Hoops (Giant).......1.33
Orange Jelly.............0.56
Unknown Item.............0.00

Discount.................1.00

Total...................12.90
```

You will probably find it helpful to define functions

```
makeDiscount :: BillType -> Int
formatDiscount :: Int -> String
```

which you can use in a redefined

```
formatBill :: BillType -> String
```

4.48 Design functions which update the database of bar codes. You will need a function to add a `BarCode` and a `(Name, Price)` pair to the `Database`, while at the same time removing any other reference to the bar code already present in the database.

4.49 Re-design your system so that bar codes which do not appear in the database give no entry in the final bill. There are (at least) two ways of doing this:

- keep the function `makeBill` as it is, and modify the formatting functions, or
- modify the `makeBill` function to remove the 'unknown item' pairs.

4.50 [Project] Design a script of functions to analyse collections of sales. Given a list of `TillType`, produce a table showing the total sales of each item. You might also analyse the bills to see which *pairs* of items are bought together; this could assist with placing items in the supermarket.

4.8 Example: text processing

In word processing systems it is customary for lines to be filled and broken automatically, to enhance the appearance of the text. This book is no exception. Input of the form

```
The heat bloomed      in December as the
    carnival  season
            kicked into  gear.
Nearly helpless with sun and glare, I avoided Rio's
brilliant sidewalks
   and glittering beaches,
panting in dark   corners
and waiting out the inverted southern summer.
```

would be transformed by *filling* to

```
The heat bloomed in December as the
carnival season kicked into gear.
Nearly helpless with sun and glare,
I avoided Rio's brilliant sidewalks
and glittering beaches, panting in
dark corners and waiting out the
inverted southern summer.
```

To align the right-hand margin, the text is *justified* by adding extra inter-word spaces on all lines but the last.

```
The heat bloomed in December as the
carnival  season  kicked into gear.
Nearly helpless with sun and glare,
I avoided Rio's brilliant sidewalks
and glittering beaches, panting  in
dark  corners  and  waiting out the
inverted southern summer.
```

An input file in Haskell can be treated as a string of characters, so programs to handle files or to work interactively can be string-manipulating operations.

The first step in processing text will be to split an input string into *words*, discarding any white space. The words are then re-arranged into lines of the required length. These lines can then have spaces added so as to justify the text. We therefore start by looking at how text is split into words. We first ask, given a string of characters, how should we define a function to take the first word from the front of a string?

A word is any sequence which does not contain the *whitespace* characters space, tab and newline.

```
whitespace = ['\n','\t',' ']
```

In defining getWord we will use the standard function elem which tests whether an object is an element of a list. For instance, the expression elem 'a' whitespace is False.

To guide the definition, consider two examples:

• getWord " boo" should be "" as the first character is whitespace;

• getWord "cat dog" is "cat". We get this by putting 'c' on the front of "at", which is getWord "at dog".

```
getWord :: String -> String
getWord []   = []                        (1)
getWord (a:x)
  | elem a whitespace  = []              (2)
  | otherwise          = a : getWord x   (3)
```

Consider an example

```
getWord "cat dog"
= 'c' : getWord "at dog"           by (3)
= 'c' : 'a' : getWord "t dog"      by (3)
```

```
= 'c' : 'a' : 't' : getWord " dog"                    by (3)
= 'c' : 'a' : 't' : []                                by (2)
= "cat"
```

In a similar way, the first word of a string can be dropped.

```
dropWord :: String -> String
dropWord []    = []
dropWord (a:x)
  | elem a whitespace  = (a:x)
  | otherwise          = dropWord x
```

It is easy to check that dropWord "cat dog" = " dog". We aim to use the functions getWord and dropWord to split a string into its constituent words. Note that before we take a word from the string " dog", we should remove the whitespace character(s) from the front. The function dropSpace will do this.

```
dropSpace :: String -> String
dropSpace []    = []
dropSpace (a:x)
  | elem a whitespace  = dropSpace x
  | otherwise          = (a:x)
```

How is a string st to be split into words? Assuming st has no whitespace at the start:

- the first word in the output will be given by applying getWord to st;
- the remainder will be given by splitting what remains after removing the first word and the space following it: dropSpace (dropWord st).

The top-level function splitWords calls split after removing any white-space at the start of the string.

```
type Word = String

splitWords :: String -> [Word]
splitWords st = split (dropSpace st)

split :: String -> [Word]
split [] = []
split st
  = (getWord st) : split (dropSpace (dropWord st))
```

Consider a short example.

```
splitWords "  dog cat"
= split "dog cat"
= (getWord "dog cat")
            : split (dropSpace (dropWord "dog cat"))
= "dog" : split (dropSpace " cat")
= "dog" : split "cat"
= "dog" : (getWord "cat")
            : split (dropSpace (dropWord "cat"))
= "dog" : "cat" : split (dropSpace [])
= "dog" : "cat" : split []
= "dog" : "cat" : []
= [ "dog" , "cat" ]
```

Now we have to consider how to break a list of words into lines. As before, we look how we can take the first line from a list of words.

```
type Line = [Word]
getLine :: Int -> [Word] -> Line
```

getLine takes two parameters. The first is the length of the line to be formed, and the second the list from which the words are taken. The definition uses length to give the length of a list. The definition will have three cases:

- In the case that no words are available, the line formed is empty.
- If the first word available is w, then this goes on the line if there is room for it: its length, length w, has to be no greater than the length of the line, len. The remainder of the line is built from the words that remain by taking a line of length len-(length w+1).
- If the first word does not fit, the line has to be empty.

```
getLine len []      = []
getLine len (w:ws)
   | length w <= len    = w : restOfLine
   | otherwise          = []
     where
     newlen      = len - (length w + 1)
     restOfLine  = getLine newlen ws
```

Why is the rest of the line of length len-(length w+1)? Space must be allocated for the word w *and* the inter-word space needed to separate it from the word which follows. How does the function work in an example?

```
getLine 20 ["Mary","Poppins","looks","like",...
= "Mary" : getLine 15 ["Poppins","looks","like",...
= "Mary" : "Poppins" : getLine 7 ["looks","like",...
= "Mary" : "Poppins" : "looks" : getLine 1 ["like",...
= "Mary" : "Poppins" : "looks" : []
= [ "Mary" , "Poppins" , "looks" ]
```

A companion function,

```
dropLine :: Int -> [Word] -> Line
```

removes a line from the front of a list of words, just as dropWord is a companion to getWord. The function to split a list of words into lines of length at most lineLen can now be defined:

```
splitLines :: [Word] -> [Line]
splitLines [] = []
splitLines x
   = getLine lineLen x
            : splitLines (dropLine lineLen x)
```

This concludes the definition of the function splitLines which gives filled lines from a list of words. To fill a text string into lines, we write

```
fill :: String -> [Line]
fill st = splitLines (splitWords st)
```

To make the result into a single string we need to write a function

```
joinLines :: [Line] -> String
```

This is left as an exercise, as is justification of lines.

EXERCISES

4.51 Give a definition of the function

```
joinLine :: Line -> String
```

which turns a line into printable form. For example,

```
joinLine [ "dog" , "cat" ] = "dog cat"
```

4.52 Using the function `joinLine`, or otherwise, define the function

```
joinLines :: [Line] -> String
```

which joins together the lines, separated by newlines.

4.53 [Harder] Modify the function `joinLine` so that it justifies the line to length `lineLen` by adding the appropriate number of spaces between the words.

4.54 Design a function

```
wc :: String -> (Int, Int, Int)
```

which when given a text string returns the number of characters, words and lines in the string. The end of a line in the string is signalled by the newline character, `'\n'`. Define a similar function

```
wcFormat :: String -> (Int, Int, Int)
```

which returns the same statistics for the text *after* it has been filled.

4.55 Define a function

```
isPalin :: String -> Bool
```

which tests whether a string is a palindrome – that is whether it reads the same both backwards and forwards. An example is the string

```
Madam I'm Adam
```

Note that punctuation and white space are ignored in the test, and that no distinction is made between capital and small letters. You might first like to develop a test which simply tests whether the string is exactly the same backwards and forwards, and only afterwards take account of punctuation and capital letters.

4.56 [Harder] Design a function

```
subst :: String -> String -> String -> String
```

so that `subst oldSub newSub st` is the result of replacing the first occurrence in `st` of the substring `oldSub` by the substring `newSub`. For instance,

```
subst "much  " "tall " "How much  is that?"
  = "How tall is that?"
```

If the substring `oldSub` does not occur in `st`, the result should be `st`.

4.9 Definition forms

Many of the definitions of list processing functions fall into a small number of different sorts. In this section we look back over the chapter and discuss the patterns which emerge. These patterns of definition are revisited in the next part of the book.

Combining the items – folding

The first example of the chapter, sumList (Section 4.2), shows the total of a list of integers being computed. The total of the list is given by **folding** + into the list, thus:

```
sumList [2,3,71] = 2+3+71
```

In a similar way,

- ++ can be folded into a list of lists to concatenate it;
- && can be folded into a list of Booleans to take their conjunction; and
- maxi can be folded into a list of integers to give their maximum.

Applying to all – mapping

Many functions call for all the elements of a list to be transformed in some way – this we call **mapping**. The first example, given in Section 4.2, is of doubling every element of a list of integers.

```
double [2,3,71] = [4,6,142]
```

Other examples include:

- taking the second element of each pair in a list of pairs;
- converting every item in a list of bar codes to the corresponding (Name,Price) pair;
- formatting each (Name,Price) pair in a list.

Selecting elements – filtering

Selecting all the elements of a list with a given property is also common. Section 4.3 has the example of the function which selects the digits from a string

```
digits "29 February 1996" = "291996"
```

Among the other cases are

- select each pair which has a particular person as its first element;
- select each pair which is *not* equal to the loan pair being returned.

Breaking up lists

A common pattern in the text processing example is to take or drop items, such as characters, from a list while they have some property. The first example is getWord,

```
getWord "cat dog" = "cat"
```

but others include dropWord, dropSpace and getLine, where the condition depends upon the part selected so far as well as the item in question.

Combinations

These patterns of definition are often used together. In defining books for the library database, which returns all the books on loan to a given person, we filter out all pairs involving the person, and then take all second components of the results. Combinations of mapping and filtering are often most effectively given by a list comprehension, as indeed we saw for the books example in Section 4.6.

Other combinations of functions are also common.

- Definition (5) of sumPairs can be seen applying sumPair to each pair (mapping) followed by adding the results (folding +).
- Formatting the item part of a supermarket bill involves processing each item in some way, then combining the results, using ++.

Primitive recursion and folding

The form of many definitions is primitive recursive. Sorting by insertion is a classic example

```
iSort []    = []
iSort (a:x) = ins a (iSort x)
```

Haskell provides a mechanism to turn a prefix function, like ins into an infix version. The name is enclosed by back quotes, `, so

```
iSort (a:x) = a `ins` (iSort x)
```

and, in a given example, we have

```
iSort [4,2,3] = 4 'ins' 2 'ins' 3 'ins' []
```

Looked at this way, the definition looks like 'ins' folded into the list [4,2,3]. We shall look at this again in more detail in Chapter 15.

The last 10%

The different kinds of definition discussed so far have all been primitive recursive: we were able to define the result for (a:x) in terms of the result for x. It has been said that at least 90% of all definitions of list processing functions are primitive recursive. Some are not, however; in this chapter a notable example is splitLines:

```
splitLines [] = []
splitLines x
  = getLine lineLen x
          : splitLines (dropLine lineLen x)
```

For a non-empty list x, the result splitLines x is defined using splitLines not on x but on (dropLine lineLen x).

This works because (dropLine lineLen x) will always be shorter than x itself, at least in sensible cases where no word in the text is longer than the line length lineLen!

4.10 Program design

Section 2.14 contains advice about program design which is equally applicable to list processing programs. In the supermarket billing example, for instance, we worked bottom-up to build the formatting functions; and in defining sumPairs we saw the importance of thinking about the kind of pattern matching to be used.

Change is unavoidable

This section builds on the earlier advice and the experience of the last chapter. As we construct larger systems, one fact will confront us: however well we think of our designs in advance, we will be forced to make modifications as we proceed; two scenarios follow.

- On seeing the prototype output of our billing system, it may be decided to make the lines of the bill a different length. If we have made the line length a constant, all we need to do is to modify one definition; if not, we have to look for each use of the length in the script.

- A function returns a result of type t; on design it is seen that in some cases the operation can *fail*. We therefore have to modify the result type to (t, Bool), with a False value to signal failure, and change the script accordingly. In particular, a function processing lists of these items will have to be modified. We saw in definition (5) of sumPairs that processing the items separately in the function sumPair meant that only one definition had to be modified.

These two examples show how changes can be demanded during program development. To make change possible it is helpful to follow the design principles we have given, as well as those which follow.

- Each function should do one thing: if we have to, say, process some data and then format the results, these should be two separate functions. If we have to change the formatting, then we only have to modify one of them; if there was a single function doing both tasks, we would have to modify a more complex piece of program.

- Each part of the problem should be performed by an identifiable function. It is possible to write a collection of functions which perform formatting, say, and to use them to format a piece of text. For instance

```
top text = form1 (process text) ++ form2 (process text)
```

It is clearer to say

```
top text = form (process text)
form out = form1 out ++ form2 out
```

since in the second group of definitions we can see that all the formatting is done by form, and that therefore it is this function which should be modified if we want a changed format.

Designing definitions

The advice on making definitions from Section 2.14 is still most relevant. We should know the type of the function we are designing, and we should be clear about its purpose. For lists, we have just seen a classification of the different kinds of definition which commonly occur; keeping these in mind can help to focus how we want a definition to work, especially when we remember that they can be combined.

If we try to write a direct recursive definition of a function, we can meet two kinds of problem.

- We might find that another function has to be defined. Suppose we want to write a function to decide whether one string is a substring of another.

  ```
  subString :: String -> String -> Bool
  ```

  so that, for instance

  ```
  subString "cat" "scathing" = True
  subString "cat" "cart" = False
  ```

  We will have

  ```
  subString st (a:x) = subString st x || ...
  ```

  In the ... part, we have to write a function which decides whether `st` is a substring of `(a:x)` starting at the front. This itself will require a recursive definition.

- In making a definition we may need to generalize our goal, making the original goal a particular case of the new function. For instance, in text processing, we had the function

  ```
  getLine :: [Word] -> [Word]
  ```

  which gets a line from the start of a list of words. This cannot be defined directly, but only by defining the generalization,

  ```
  getLine :: Int -> [Word] -> [Word]
  ```

  where the extra parameter gives the length of line to be found. The recursion then uses `getLine` with *different* values of line length. Another example occurs when we try to find the definition of the list `[1 .. n]`. The natural definition says

  ```
  [1 .. n] = 1:[2 .. n]
  ```

  which is given by a two-argument recursion

  ```
  [m .. n] | m>n          = []
           | otherwise    = m:[m+1 .. n]
  ```

Error handling

Some functions can have cases where a result is not defined. In defining `returnLoan` for the library database, there is a case that we might try to return a loan which has not been made, for instance. Three options are possible.

- We return the database unchanged. The way the program behaves is not affected by the error case. We could check that a loan has been made before calling the `returnLoan` function if we are concerned about this case.

- We make the result

  ```
  error "problem in returnLoan"
  ```

  in this case. If this happens, evaluation stops and the error message is printed. The program is stopped by the error case.

- We change the type of the result to (Database, Bool) with the second value being `False` if the loan was not present. After calling the `returnLoan` function we can look at the second part of the result to see whether the loan was present or not. This neither ignores the error, nor halts the program; it allows the function calling `returnLoan` to acknowledge the error without stopping the program.

Different strategies will be used in different circumstances, depending upon what is needed in each case. We return to the topic in the final part of the book.

SUMMARY

This chapter has introduced the list types – for each type t there is a type [t] of lists of items of type t. After giving the syntax of list constants we have discussed a range of examples of list-based programs: sorting, adding a list, selecting elements and a number of case studies which use lists to represent data objects such as books, supermarket bills, databases, text and so forth. The chapter is concluded by discussions of the forms taken by list definitions and of program design, which build both on earlier insights and on the present chapter.

Reasoning about lists

Now we have seen the introduction of lists, it is possible to show many more proofs of properties of functions, which we prove by *structural induction*, the list analogue of induction over the natural numbers. The form of proofs is similar, and we will again give guidelines for constructing proofs.

As with numbers earlier, some proofs can work directly or by case analysis. We shall see some examples of this as we look at induction proofs by means of a series of examples and exercises. We shall also look at more complicated examples where we need to generalize the induction hypothesis before a proof can be found successfully; the latter material can be omitted on first reading the chapter.

5.1 Structural induction

Structural induction gives a method of proof for statements P(x) for all *finite* lists x, where

- [] is a finite list;
- (a:x) is a finite list if x is a finite list.

Note that the Haskell list types in fact contain more elements than this; hence the adjective 'finite'. In the final part of the book we shall see that *infinite* lists can also be defined and used to good effect in Haskell.

Proof by structural induction

To prove the property P(x) for all finite lists x we have to do two things.

> **Base case**   Prove P([]).
> **Induction step** Prove P(a:x) assuming that P(x) holds already.

Again we can picture the induction step as a machine, Figure 5.1, turning proofs into proofs – if we know that P(x) holds, then we can use the machine to tell us that P(a:x) holds.

Starting with a proof of P([]) we can get a proof of P(x) for any finite x. For instance, if x is [2,37], we have P([]), and from the induction step, we have P([37]), and from the induction step again, P([2,37]).

Again, as for the natural numbers there is a relationship between definitions by primitive recursion and proofs by structural induction over lists. The value of a function at [] is given outright, while at (a:x), the value at x is used.

An induction template

To help construct proofs by structural induction, we supply a template to follow. The template is useful in forcing us to be clear about what are the specific goals of each part of the proof by induction.

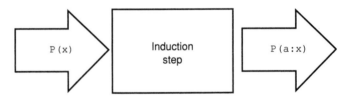

Figure 5.1 P(x) ⇒ P(a:x).

Stage 0	Write down the goal of the proof, in English
Stage 1	Write down the goal of the proof: proving,

- $P(x)$, for all finite lists x

Stage 2	Write down the two sub-goals of the induction proof,

- $P([])$
- $P(a:x)$ assuming $P(x)$

Stage 3	Prove $P([])$
Stage 4	Prove $P(a:x)$, remembering that you can, and probably *should*, use $P(x)$ somewhere in the proof.

Finding proofs

The advice is similar to that we followed in Section 3.2.

In the remainder of this chapter we will always *change the names* of the variables used in definitions, to avoid confusion with the variables used in the induction proof. Remember that the equations can be used at *any* instance whatever, provided that we use the *first* equation for which our input matches the patterns of the equation.

In finding proofs of equations, we will aim to use the definitions to simplify the two sides of the equations as much as possible, before applying the induction hypothesis in the proof of $P(a:x)$.

Next we look at a sequence of example proofs.

5.2 Proofs by structural induction

EXAMPLE: Sum and double

As we began to look at lists we wrote functions to give the total of a numerical list and to double each item in a numerical list.

```
sumList []    = 0                          (1)
sumList (b:y) = b + sumList y              (2)

double []    = []                          (3)
double (b:y) = (2*b) : double y            (4)
```

They are related – we can get the sum of a doubled list by doubling the sum of the list:

```
sumList (double x) = 2 * sumList x         (5)
```

which we aim to prove by structural induction. Following the template, our goals are

- Base case

```
sumList (double []) = 2 * sumList []              (6)
```

- Induction step

```
sumList (double (a:x)) = 2 * sumList (a:x)        (7)
```

assuming

```
sumList (double x) = 2 * sumList x                (8)
```

Proof. We begin by looking at each side of (6), and simplifying it.

```
sumList (double [])
= sumList []                                    by (3)
= 0                                             by (1)
```

The right-hand side is

```
2 * sumList []
= 2 * 0                                         by (1)
= 0                                             arithmetic
```

which shows that (6) holds. Next we have to prove (7), using the assumption (8). Simplifying the left-hand side we have

```
sumList (double (a:x))
= sumList (2*a : double x)                      by (4)
= 2*a + sumList (double x)                      by (2)
```

and, by the assumption (8), this is

```
= 2*a + 2 * sumList x                           by (8)
= 2 * (a + sumList x)                           arithmetic
```

Now, the right-hand side is

```
2 * sumList (a:x)
= 2 * (a + sumList x)                           by (2)
```

which shows the two sides are equal, and completes the proof. ∎

Associativity of append

The operation to join or *append* two lists is defined by

```
[]    ++ v = v                              (1)
(c:u) ++ v = c:(u++v)                       (2)
```

We say that it is associative because for all finite lists x, y and z,

```
x ++ (y ++ z) = (x ++ y) ++ z
```

We will show this by induction on x – this is a sensible choice because in the definition above we do recursion on the left-hand argument. In the proof y and z will be arbitrary, and so the result will hold for all choices of y and z. The result will therefore hold for all finite lists x, y and z.

Our goals in the proof will be

- Base case

```
[] ++ (y ++ z) = ([] ++ y) ++ z             (3)
```

- Induction step

```
(a:x) ++ (y ++ z) = ((a:x) ++ y) ++ z       (4)
```

assuming

```
x ++ (y ++ z) = (x ++ y) ++ z               (5)
```

At each stage we say which of the defining equations has been used to make the simplification. It can sometimes be helpful to show which part of an expression the simplification applies to – we do this by underlining in the proof which follows.

Proof. First we look at the base case, and examine the left-hand side

```
 [] ++ (y ++ z)
= (y ++ z)                                  by (1)
```

Note that here we have replaced v by (y ++ z) in (1). This is valid since we can replace v by *any* value. On the right-hand side

```
 ([] ++ y) ++ z
= (y ++ z)                                  by (1)
```

which shows that (3) holds. In the induction case we again look at each side

```
 (a:x) ++ (y ++ z)
= a:(x ++ (y ++ z))                         by (2)
```

$$\frac{((a:x) \text{ ++ } y) \text{ ++ } z}{= \underline{(a:(x \text{ ++ } y)) \text{ ++ } z}} \qquad \text{by (2)}$$
$$= \overline{a:((x \text{ ++ } y) \text{ ++ } z)} \qquad \text{by (2)}$$

In the second sequence, we use two instances of (2). In the first x replaces u and y replaces v; in the second (x ++ y) replaces u and z replaces v. The two sides are equal given the induction hypothesis.

■

EXAMPLE: Membership

The test for membership of a list is given by

```
member :: String -> Char -> Bool

member []    d = False                          (1)
member (c:z) d = (c==d) || member z d           (2)
```

which uses the 'or' operation

```
True  || w = True                               (3)
False || w = w                                  (4)
```

We claim that if we join two finite lists x and y,

```
member (x++y) b = member x b || member y b
```

We aim to prove this by induction on x. The goals will be

- Base case

```
    member ([]++y) b = member [] b || member y b        (3)
```

- Induction step

```
    member ((a:x)++y) b = member (a:x) b || member y b  (4)
```

  assuming

```
    member (x++y) b = member x b || member y b          (5)
```

Proof. Examining the base case first, we have

```
member ([]++y) b
= member y b                                    by (++ 1)

member [] b || member y b
= False || member y b                           by (1)
= member y b                                    by (4)
```

and so the base case holds. In the induction step, we first look at the left-hand side

```
member ((a:x)++y) b
= member (a:(x++y)) b                               by (++ 2)
= (a==b) || member (x++y) b                         by (2)
= (a==b) || (member x b || member y b)              by (5)
```

On the right-hand side,

```
member (a:x) b || member y b
= ((a==b) || member x b) || member y b              by (2)
```

These are equal, if we can show that '||' is associative. This we do now. ■

To prove a result for all Booleans, we need to prove it for True and False.[1] Our aim is to show associativity of 'or':

```
x || (y || z) = (x || y) || z
```

In the case that x is True, each side reduces to True; in the False case they reduce to (y || z), giving the result.

EXERCISES

5.1   Prove that for all finite lists x,

```
x ++ [] = x
```

5.2   Try to prove

```
x ++ (y ++ z) = (x ++ y) ++ z
```

by structural induction on z. What goes wrong with the proof?

---

[1] This establishes the result for all *defined* Booleans; we need to show that it also holds for an undefined value if it is to hold for all Booleans. This will be the case for the example of associativity given here.

5.3 Prove for all finite lists x and y that

```
sumList (x ++ y) = sumList x + sumList y
```

and therefore that

```
sumList (x ++ y) = sumList (y ++ x)
```

5.4 Show that for all finite lists x and y,

```
double (x ++ y) = double x ++ double y
length (x ++ y) = length x + length y
```

and that for all finite lists x,

```
length (double x) = length x
```

5.5 By induction on x prove that for all finite lists x and y,

```
sumList (x ++ (a:y)) = a + sumList (x ++ y)
```

5.6 Using the previous exercise or otherwise, prove that for all finite lists x,

```
sumList (double x) = sumList (x ++ x)
```

5.7 We can flatten a list of lists using

```
concat []    = []
concat (c:z) = c ++ concat z
```

Prove that for all w

```
concat [w] = w
```

and that for all finite lists x and y

```
concat (x ++ y) = concat x ++ concat y
```

5.8 Complete the sketch proof of the associativity of '||'.

5.3 Case studies

The examples examined so far are for small-scale definitions; the same methods apply to larger-scale examples equally well. In this section we give a sequence of exercises coming from the case studies.

EXERCISES

5.9 Show that for all finite databases db and all people per

    numBorrowed db per = length (books db per)

5.10 Show that for all finite databases db and all books bk

    borrowed db bk = (borrowers db bk /= [])

5.11 If pers is not equal to per show that for all finite databases db,

    books (makeLoan db per bk) pers = books db pers

On the other hand, show that

    books (makeLoan db per bk) per = bk : books db per

5.12 Using the function

    sorted :: [Int] -> Bool

    sorted []   = True
    sorted [a]   = True
    sorted (a:b:x) = (a<=b) && sorted (b:x)

show that iSort satisfies

    sorted (iSort x) = True

for all finite lists of defined numbers, x. You need the numbers to be defined to make sure that any comparisons a<=b will give a result.

5.13 Show that for all finite tt of tillType,

    length (makeBill tt) = length tt

5.14 Under suitable assumptions show that the length of a line in the supermarket bill is lineLength.

5.15 Show that, assuming the characters in st are defined,

    member (getWord st) ' ' = False

5.16 Formulate and prove a result which says that getLine will only give lines of the appropriate length, at most. You will probably need to define a function which gives the length of a list of words, counting one for each space between words as well as the lengths of the words themselves.

5.4 Generalizing the proof goal

It is not always easy to build a proof in a straightforward way, by induction over a goal we set ourselves. In this section we explore an example in which only after two false starts are we able to build a proof of the property we seek. The section is more technical than the rest of the chapter and can be omitted on first reading.

The shunting function

The `shunt` function moves the elements from one list onto another, thus

```
shunt :: [Int] -> [Int] -> [Int]

shunt []     y = y                              (1)
shunt (a:x)  y = shunt x (a:y)                  (2)
```

Starting with an empty second argument, we have

```
  shunt [2,3,1] []
= shunt [3,1] [2]
= shunt [1] [3,2]
= shunt [] [1,3,2]
= [1,3,2]
```

and so we can reverse lists using this function:

```
rev :: [Int] -> [Int]
rev l = shunt l []                              (3)
```

Now we turn to looking at properties of the `rev` function.

First proof attempt

Reversing a list twice should give us back the list we started with, and so we aim to prove that `rev (rev x) = x` (call this property Q) for all finite lists x. The base case is easily established, but when we look at the induction step, we meet our first problem:

```
  rev (rev (a:x))
= shunt (shunt (a:x) []) []              by (3)
= shunt (shunt x [a]) []                 by (2)
```

This has no direct relationship to `rev` and to the induction hypothesis, talking as it does of (`shunt x [a]`). A clue to the problem is that `rev` is not the function defined by recursion – it is simply a specialization of `shunt`. Can we find a *generalization* of `Q(x)` which talks explicitly about `shunt` and which is to be proved by induction?

Now, `rev` specializes `shunt` by replacing `y` with `[]`. If we replace this by `y`, we have

        shunt (shunt x y) []

and this should be equal to `shunt y x`. When `y` is replaced by `[]`, we get `Q(x)`. We therefore aim to prove this generalization.

Second proof attempt

Our aim is to show

        shunt (shunt x y) [] = shunt y x

for all finite lists `x` and `y`. In the case that `x` is `[]`, the proof is simple. Now we look at the induction step:

        shunt (shunt (a:x) y) []
        = shunt (shunt x (a:y)) []   by (2)

We would now like to claim by induction that this equals `shunt (a:y) x`, but to do this we need the induction hypothesis to give the result that

        shunt (shunt x (a:y)) [] = shunt (a:y) x

rather than

        shunt (shunt x y) [] = shunt y x

To get around this, we strengthen the induction hypothesis to become

        shunt (shunt x z) [] = shunt z x

for all finite lists `z` so that in particular it will hold when (`a:y`) replaces `z`. We now try again.

The successful proof attempt

In logical notation, our induction formula `P(x)` is

        ∀ z. shunt (shunt x z) [] = shunt z x

Now we can state what is required. The goals will be

- Base case

$$\forall z. \; \texttt{shunt (shunt [] z) [] = shunt z []} \qquad (4)$$

- Induction step

$$\forall z. \; \texttt{shunt (shunt (a:x) z) [] = shunt z (a:x)} \qquad (5)$$

assuming

$$\forall z. \; \texttt{shunt (shunt x z) [] = shunt z x} \qquad (6)$$

Proof. In the base case we prove

$$\forall z. \; \texttt{shunt (shunt [] z) [] = shunt z []} \qquad (4)$$

by proving it for an arbitrary y in place of z.
The left-hand side simplifies to the right-hand side in one step.

```
shunt (shunt [] y) []
= shunt y []                                              by (1)
```

In a similar way we prove

$$\forall z. \; \texttt{shunt (shunt (a:x) z) [] = shunt z (a:x)} \qquad (5)$$

by proving it for an arbitrary y. Simplifying the left-hand side, we have

```
shunt (shunt (a:x) y) []
= shunt (shunt x (a:y)) []                                by (2)
```

Now, by (6), at the particular value (a:y) for z,

```
= shunt (a:y) x                                           by (6)
= shunt y (a:x)                                           by (2)
```

This is the right-hand side, and so the proof is complete for an arbitrary y, giving a proof of (5), and completing the induction proof.

■

This example shows that we may have to generalize what has to be proved in order for induction proofs to work. This seems paradoxical: we are making it harder for ourselves, apparently. We are in one way, but at the same time we make the induction hypothesis *stronger*, so that we have *more* resources to use when proving the induction step.

EXERCISES

5.17   Prove for all finite lists x and y that

```
rev (x ++ y) = rev y ++ rev x
```

5.18   Given the definition

```
rev2 []    = []
rev2 (a:x) = rev2 x ++ [a]
```

prove that for all finite lists x,

```
rev x = rev2 x
```

5.19   Using the function

```
facAux :: Int -> Int -> Int
facAux 0 p = p
facAux n p = facAux (n-1) (n*p)
```

we can define

```
fac2 n = facAux n 1
```

Prove that for all natural numbers n,

```
fac n = fac2 n
```

SUMMARY

This chapter has shown that in many cases a straightforward attempt will yield a proof that a recursively defined function has certain properties, with the induction proof following the pattern of the recursive definition.

The base case, for the empty list [], is proved outright, while the case of the non-empty list (a:x) is proved from the induction hypothesis for the list x.

In cases where the straightforward approach fails, as examined in the optional Section 5.4, there might well need to be a search for the appropriate generalization of the property before it can be proved by an induction. The example given illustrated how the failed proof attempts can be used to guide the re-formulation of the problem before a proof is tried again.

Part II

Abstraction

The first part of the book introduced the basics of functional programming in Haskell. Definitions over lists, numbers, Booleans and so forth are written using pattern-matching conditional equations. These equations themselves have multiple clauses, guarded by Boolean expressions, and local definitions in `where` clauses. In this part we introduce three important new ideas.

- Functions are themselves data objects. In particular they can be the arguments to other functions or results of other functions.

- A single definition can apply to a whole collection of types, rather than to a single type.

- Names can be **overloaded**, having different definitions at different types; equality (==) is an example of this.

Putting these three ideas together gives us a very powerful way of building general functions, which can be re-used in different ways at different types.

This part is entitled **abstraction** because the usual way of forming these general functions is to abstract from a particular function – like a function to double every integer in a list of integers – to form something more general – in this case the **higher-order** function which applies a function like `times2` to every item in a list.

The concluding chapter of this part discusses how the types of Haskell expressions and definitions are checked, first using the simple types of the first part, and then using the **polymorphic** types and **type classes** introduced here.

6 Generalization

In this chapter it is shown that functions may take functions as arguments; as a result, many definitions become polymorphic: they may be used over whole collections of types rather than over a single type.

6.1 Functions as arguments

This section introduces the idea that functions (just as much as numbers, tuples and so on) can be arguments of other functions, which are called for this reason **higher-order** functions. We do this in the context of an example, and in the light of what was said about general forms of definition in Section 4.9.

EXAMPLE: Double and treble

One of the first functions we defined over lists of integers was

```
double :: [Int] -> [Int]
double []    = []
double (a:x) = (2*a) : double x
```

which returns a list containing the elements of the argument list doubled; similarly,

```
treble :: [Int] -> [Int]
treble []    = []
treble (a:x) = (3*a) : treble x
```

returns a list containing the trebles of the items in the input list. In the terminology of Section 4.9 both are mapping functions, which return a list produced by transforming each element of the input list in some way. The pattern of the definitions is the same; what differs is the way in which the elements of the lists are **transformed** in each case.

Each transformation of the elements can be written down as a function:

```
times2,times3 :: Int -> Int

times2 n = 2*n
times3 n = 3*n
```

Any function from integers to integers can be used in mapping – we could therefore make a function from integers to integers an **argument** of a general mapping function. double and treble can then be seen as two examples of a general mapping function *applied* to times2 and times3.

The general mapping function between lists of integers will have to take *two* arguments:

- the transformation to be applied to each element: a function; and
- the list input.

```
mapInt f []    = []
mapInt f (a:x) = f a : mapInt f x
```

The definition has two cases:

- when the input is empty, so is the result;
- on input `(a:x)`, the head of the result is given by `f` applied to `a`, and the tail by applying `f` to every element in the tail – by `mapInt f x` in other words.

As we said earlier, particular mapping functions are given by applying `mapInt` to the appropriate arguments, thus

```
double l = mapInt times2 l
treble l = mapInt times3 l
```

An example calculation gives

```
mapInt times2 [2,3]
= times2 2 : mapInt times2 [3]
= 4 : mapInt times2 [3]
= 4 : ( times2 3 : mapInt times2 [] )
= 4 : ( 6 : mapInt times2 [] )
= 4 : ( 6 : [] )
= 4 : [6]
= [4,6]
```

which mirrors exactly the example calculation in Chapter 4. As we saw in that chapter, a list comprehension can also be used to define the operation of applying to every member of a list, thus

```
mapInt f l = [ f a | a <-l ]
```

What is the type of `mapInt`? It has two arguments, and so its type will be

$$t_1 \rightarrow t_2 \rightarrow t$$

where t_1 is the type of the first argument, t_2 the type of the second and t the type of the result.

The first argument is a transformation or function from `Int` to `Int`, and so t_1 is (`Int -> Int`); the second argument and result are lists of integers, so t_2 and t are `[Int]`. Putting this together, we have

```
mapInt :: (Int -> Int) -> [Int] -> [Int]
```

Why higher-order functions?

What is the advantage of defining the `mapInt` function, and using it in the definition of `double` and `treble`? There are three separate reasons for using `mapInt`.

- It becomes easier to *understand* the definition, since it makes clear that it is a mapping by using the `mapInt` function. To understand the function therefore we simply have to understand the function mapped along the list.

- It becomes easier to *modify* the definition of `double` if that is necessary. If we want to change the transformation of the elements, all we need to do is to change the function which gives the transformation, `times2`; we leave the top-level definition unchanged.

- It becomes easier to *re-use* definitions – once `mapInt` is defined it can be used in a variety of circumstances, which were perhaps not originally intended. We could, for instance, use it to add value-added tax to a list of prices in pence.

If we define higher-order functions to reflect the sorts of definition we are accustomed to see, such as those in Section 4.9, then we are likely to be able to use them again and again, in differing circumstances.

EXAMPLES: Sales analysis revisited ───────────────────

Here we examine the sales analysis functions introduced in Section 2.2. These functions were all defined to analyse a *fixed* function `sales`; we can instead define functions which take a function as an argument, so that the sales analysis examples are particular *applications* of the new functions.

We first look at a function to give the sum f 0 + ... + f n, where f is of type (`Int -> Int`).

```
total :: (Int -> Int) -> Int -> Int
total f n
  | n==0      = f 0
  | otherwise = total f (n-1) + f n
```

Now `totalSales` is given by

```
totalSales n = total sales n
```

but once we have `total` it can be used to define many other functions as well. For example, we can sum the squares of integers 0 to n:

```
sumSquares :: Int -> Int
sumSquares n = total sq n

sq :: Int -> Int
sq x = x*x
```

Other functions inspired by the sales analysis study are

```
maxFun :: (Int -> Int) -> Int -> Int
maxFun f n
  | n==0        = f 0
  | otherwise   = maxi (maxFun f (n-1)) (f n)
```

which gives the maximum of the values f 0 to f n, and,

```
zeroInRange :: (Int -> Int) -> Int -> Bool

zeroInRange f 0 = (f 0 == 0)
zeroInRange f n = zeroInRange f (n-1) || (f n == 0)
```

which decides whether there is a zero value for f on inputs 0 to n. Both these functions have many uses beyond the sales analysis example.

EXAMPLE: Folding ───────────────────────────────────────

Another definition form over lists identified in Section 4.9 was folding: we give a higher-order function implementing this now.

The sum and maximum of a list are given by folding in the functions + and maxi, which have type (Int -> Int -> Int), thus

$$e_1 + e_2 + \ldots + e_n$$
$$e_1 \text{ `maxi` } e_2 \text{ `maxi` } \ldots \text{ `maxi` } e_n$$

(recall that `maxi` is the infix form of the prefix function maxi). For the one element list [e] the result is e; the result for a general list is suggested by bracketing thus:

$$e_1 \text{ `maxi` } (e_2 \text{ `maxi` } \ldots \text{ `maxi` } e_n)$$

which is

$$e_1 \text{ `maxi` } (\text{maxList } [e_2 \ldots e_n])$$

After replacing the infix function by its prefix form, we have

```
maxi e₁ (maxList [e₂ ... eₙ])
```

Guided by this, in general we should have

```
foldInt :: (Int -> Int -> Int) -> [Int] -> Int

foldInt f [a]     = a
foldInt f (a:b:x) = f a (foldInt f (b:x))
```

The type declaration for foldInt states that f is a function taking two integers and returning an integer; the second argument is a list of integers, and the result is an integer, as should be expected.

The functions to find the sum and maximum are given by

```
sumList l = foldInt (+) l
maxList l = foldInt maxi l
```

where (+) is used for the *prefix* form of the infix operator '+'.

EXAMPLE: Filtering lists ───────────────────────────────

Often programs require certain items to be selected or *filtered* from a list. For example, we might want to pick out the digits or the letters in a string of characters, so that

```
digits  "29 February 1996" = "291996"
letters "29 February 1996" = "February"
```

Each character has to be tested to see whether it has the property we want, such as being a digit. The test takes a character, and returns an answer, which will be a Boolean value. We can therefore think of a **property** of characters as a function of type

```
Char -> Bool
```

Examples of these are

```
isDigit, isLetter :: Char -> Bool

isDigit ch = ('0'<=ch && ch<='9')
isLetter ch = ('a'<=ch && ch<='z') || ('A'<=ch && ch<='Z')
```

The type of our function to filter elements from strings will be

```
filterString :: (Char -> Bool) -> [Char] -> [Char]
```

The first argument is the property for which we are testing, the second is the string to be filtered. Now we can define the function

```
filterString p [] = []
filterString p (a:x)
  | p a        = a : filterString p x
  | otherwise  =     filterString p x
```

For a non-empty string, (a:x), there are two cases. We test whether a has the property by applying p to it; this gives a Boolean.

- In case p a is True, a is the first element of the result, with the remainder coming from filtering x.
- In case p a is False, the result comes from filtering x.

The functions digits and letters are now defined from filterString:

```
digits  st = filterString isDigit st
letters st = filterString isLetter st
```

An alternative definition of filterString is provided by

```
filterString p x = [ a | a<-x , p a ]
```

Just as before, the advantages of using a higher-order function are re-usability (of the function filterString) and the ease with which we can modify one of the functions, such as letters, so that it picks out only the small letters. This can be done simply by modifying the property passed to filterString.

EXERCISES

6.1   Give definitions of functions to take a list of integers, l, and

- return the list consisting of the squares of the integers in l;
- return the sum of squares of items in l;
- check whether all items of the list are greater than zero.

6.2   Write definitions of functions to

- give the minimum value of a function on inputs 0 to n;
- test whether the values of f on inputs 0 to n are all equal;
- test if all values of f on inputs 0 to n are greater than zero; and
- check whether the values f 0, f 1 to f n are in increasing order.

6.3   State the type of and define a function `twice` which takes a function from integers to integers and an input integer, and whose output is the function applied to the input twice. For instance, with the `times2` function and 7 as input, the result is 28.

6.4   Give the type of and define a function `iter` so that

```
iter n f x = f (f (f ... (f x)...))
```

where f occurs n times on the right-hand side of the equation. For instance, we should have

```
iter 3 f x = f (f (f x))
```

and `iter 0 f x` should return x.

6.5   Using `iter` and `times2` define a function which on input n returns 2^n; remember that 2^n means one multiplied by two n times.

6.2   Polymorphism

The second concept which gives functional programming its power is explored in this section. As an illustration we examine how to find the length of a list, a topic first discussed in Section 4.2.

```
length []    = 0
length (a:x) = 1 + length x
```

The length function takes a list as argument – the patterns used on the left-hand side of the equations are [] and (a:x) – but there is no constraint on the type of elements of the list in the definition. The definition will therefore be applicable to lists of any type, returning an integer in each case.

The length function has a **polymorphic** type. Before we explain these types, we look again at the role of variables in equations. We then give a sequence of examples of polymorphic functions, and see that many functions we have seen already are in fact polymorphic.

Variables

When we write a definition like

```
square :: Int -> Int
square x = x*x
```

we use the variable x to mean that the equation holds for *all* values x (of type `Int`). Given an equation involving a variable, any **instance** of it will also be valid; an instance is given by replacing or **substituting** for the variable by an expression, so, for example

```
square 2     = 2*2
square (3+4) = (3+4)*(3+4)
square (x+1) = (x+1)*(x+1)
```

In the first instance, x was replaced by the value 2; in the second by the expression `(3+4)`; and in the third by the expression `(x+1)`, which itself contains a variable. Note that in each case, all three xs are replaced with the *same* expression.

Equations and formulas can contain more than one variable:

```
sumSq n m = n*n + m*m
```

In taking an instance, different variables can take different values,

```
sumSq 3 4 = 3*3 + 4*4
```

but, all occurrences of each variable, such as n, are replaced by the same value: 3 in this case.

Type variables

How can we express that `[]` is of type `[Int]`, `[[Bool]]` and so forth? By saying that it has type

```
[] :: [t]                                    (1)
```

where t is a **type variable**. Type variables in Haskell are written in exactly the same way as ordinary variables – they must begin with a small letter. Our convention in this book is to use single letters from near the end of the alphabet t, u, v and so on, as type variables.

How is (1) interpreted? Informally, it says that `[]` is of all list types. Just as for ordinary variables, any instance of (1) will hold, so

```
[] :: [Int]
[] :: [[Bool]]
[] :: [Int -> Int]
[] :: [[u]]
```

where in the four cases t is replaced by the types `Int`, `[Bool]`, `Int -> Int` and `[u]`.

When an function or object has a type involving one or more type variables, it has a **polymorphic** type – polymorphic means that it has 'many forms', or types. Often we call the function itself polymorphic too.

An important polymorphic function is the list constructor 'cons' or ':' which can now be given its proper type. It takes an object and a list of items *of the same type* and gives a list of that type. If we call the arbitrary type 't', then

```
(:) :: t -> [t] -> [t]
```

which has as instances the types we listed in Section 4.2.

Polymorphic definitions

When do definitions give rise to polymorphic functions? The length function

```
length []    = 0
length (a:x) = 1 + length x
```

has the type

```
length :: [t] -> Int
```

because the argument is an arbitrary list, and the result an integer. Another example is the function to join two lists, ++. It must join lists of the same type, since the result list must consist of elements of the same type, but that type is arbitrary, so

```
(++) :: [t] -> [t] -> [t]
```

To reverse a list `(a:x)`, we attach a to the end of x reversed

```
rev []    = []
rev (a:x) = rev x ++ [a]
```

in this definition there is no constraint on the type of elements, so

```
rev :: [t] -> [t]
```

A particularly simple example is the **identity** function which simply
returns its argument: the type of the output is the same as that of the
input, so

```
id :: t -> t

id x = x
```

Zipping two lists together results in a list of pairs:

```
zip (a:x) (b:y) = (a,b) : zip x y
zip _ _         = []
```

There is no constraint on the type of the two argument lists, and *no relation
between their types*. Because there is no relationship, we make the type of the
first [t], and the second [u]. The type will then be

```
zip :: [t] -> [u] -> [ (t,u) ]
```

Instances of this type include

```
[Int] -> [Bool] -> [(Int,Bool)]
[Int] -> [Int]  -> [(Int,Int)]
```

We can see from this that multiple type variables behave just like multiple
ordinary variables: different variables can be replaced by different values
(and by the same, of course, as in the second example).

The polymorphic types given in this section are most general types for
the functions. A type w for f is a **most general type** of f if all types of f are
instances of w. As we said, the type of zip given above is most general,
however the type [t]->[t]->[(t,t)], while it is a type for the function, is
not sufficiently general, since [Int] -> [Bool] -> [(Int,Bool)] is not an
instance of it, for example.

EXAMPLES DEFINED ALREADY

Many of the functions we have defined already are in fact polymorphic. In
the supermarket billing example we mentioned the function which builds a
string containing a character repeated a number of times.

```
rep :: Int -> Char -> String
rep 0 ch = []
rep n ch = ch : rep (n-1) ch
```

We can use the Gofer system to deduce the most general type of a function, such as `rep` by commenting out its type declaration in the script, thus

```
-- rep :: Int -> Char -> String
```

and then by typing

```
:type rep
```

to the prompt. The result we get in that case is

```
rep :: Int -> a -> [a]
```

which is perhaps a surprise at first, but looking at the definition we can see that it says nothing about the type of the elements of the list, except in the type declaration. We can therefore use this function to build lists of numbers, lists of lists of strings and so on.

Other examples are more obviously polymorphic; from Section 2.10 we have

```
fst :: (t,u) -> t              snd :: (t,u) -> u

fst (x,_) = x                  snd (_,y) = y

shift :: ((t,u),v) -> (t,(u,v))
shift ((a,b),c) = (a,(b,c))
```

from Section 4.3:

```
head :: [t] -> t               tail :: [t] -> [t]

head (a:_) = a                 tail (_:x) = x
```

Why polymorphism?

What are the advantages of Haskell allowing definitions to be polymorphic? The main advantage is that by making definitions more general, there is a much greater chance of their being re-used. We originally wrote the function `rep` to build strings, but in its polymorphic form we can see it as a general list-creating function, usable over arbitrary types of list.

Many list-processing functions are polymorphic: we have seen a number here and will see more when polymorphism and higher-order functions are combined. We can write a library of list-processing functions once and for all, and re-use them on each new type of list. In a non-polymorphic language, they need to be re-defined for each new type. This is both inefficient and unsafe: if we have more than one copy of a function definition in our system, we run the risk of these versions becoming different or inconsistent.

EXERCISES

6.6 Define the 'flatten' function, `concat` so that

```
concat [e₁,...,eₖ] = e₁ ++ ... ++ eₖ
```

What is the type of `concat`?

6.7 Give a function `unZip` which turns a list of pairs into a pair of lists. What is its type?

6.8 Define the function

```
last :: [t] -> t
```

which returns the last element of a non-empty list, and define

```
init :: [t] -> [t]
```

which returns all but the last element of such a list. For instance, we should have

```
last "Greggery Peccary" = 'y'
init "Greggery Peccary" = "Greggery Peccar"
```

6.9 Define the functions

```
take, drop :: Int -> [t] -> [t]
```

so that `take n l` consists of the first n elements of l, and `drop n l` consists of l with its first n elements dropped. In either case if the length of the list is less than n as many elements as possible are taken or dropped.

6.3   Putting the two together

Now we can explain some of the most commonly used and important higher-order functions: they are polymorphic *and* higher order.

Mapping, filtering and folding

At the start of the chapter we defined functions

- to map a function from numbers to numbers along a list of numbers;
- to fold a binary function along a list of numbers; and
- to filter characters with given properties from a string, or list of characters.

If we examine the definitions given, we see nothing particular to do with numbers or strings:

- any function from one type to another can be mapped along a list of items of the first type;
- a binary function over any type can be folded into a list of elements of that type; and
- a list of items of any type can be filtered according to an appropriate property.

The definitions of the general functions are exactly the same as their special cases – all that is changed are their types.

Map

To map f along the list (a:x),

- the head is given by f applied to a, and
- the tail is given by mapping f along x.

f mapped along [] gives [].

```
map :: (t -> u) -> [t] -> [u]
map f []    = []
map f (a:x) = f a : map f x
```

Alternatively,

```
map f x = [ f a | a <- x ]
```

What does the type say? map is a function of two arguments; the first is a function, from one type (call it 'thing') to another ('item'), the second argument will be a list of things, to be transformed into the result. This result is a list of items, given by mapping the function along the list of things. (Calling t and u 'thing' and 'item' may see silly, but it can help to emphasize that the type variables stand for arbitrary types.) Examples of the use of map abound

```
map times2 [2,3,4] = [4,6,8]
map isEven [2,3,4] = [True,False,True]
map small "Bongo Fury" = "bongo fury"
map length ["Clear","Spot"] = [5,4]
```

(The definitions of isEven and small are left as an exercise.) Moreover, we can redefine many of the functions of Chapter 4 using map and other polymorphic higher-order functions. For example, in making a supermarket bill, we have to format a number of lines, and to join the result together, we can write

```
formatLines :: [Line] -> String
formatLines ls = concat (map formatLine ls)
```

where concat is the built-in polymorphic function to join a list of lists together into a single list.

Fold

The definition of fold will have two cases. Folding f into the singleton list [a] gives a. Folding f into a longer list is given by

```
fold f [e₁,e₂,...,eₖ]
= e₁ `f` (e₂ `f` ( ... `f` eₖ)...)
= f e₁ (fold f [e₂,...,eₖ])
```

The Haskell definition is therefore

```
fold :: (t -> t -> t) -> [t] -> t

fold f [a]     = a
fold f (a:b:x) = f a (fold f (b:x))
```

in which the operation to be folded in must be a binary function over the type t. Examples include

```
fold (||) [False,True,False] = True
fold (++) ["Freak ", "Out" , "", "!"] = "Freak Out!"
fold min [6] = 6
fold (*) [1 .. 6] = 720
```

The function `fold`, which is known as `foldr1` in the Haskell standard prelude, gives an error when applied to an empty list argument.

We can modify the definition to give an extra argument which is the value on the empty list, and write

```
foldr f s []    = s
foldr f s (a:x) = f a (foldr f s x)
```

The 'r' in the definition is for 'fold, bracketing to the right'. Using this slightly more general function, whose type we predict is

```
(t -> t -> t) -> t -> [t] -> t
```

we can now define some of the standard functions of Haskell

```
concat :: [[t]] -> [t]
concat xs = foldr (++) [] xs

and :: [Bool] -> Bool
and bs = foldr (&&) True bs
```

We shall see in fact that the most general type of `foldr` is more general than we predicted:

```
(t -> u -> u) -> u -> [t] -> u
```

and that `foldr` can be used to define another cohort of list functions. For instance, we can reverse a list thus:

```
rev :: [t] -> [t]
rev l = foldr stick [] l

stick :: t -> [t] -> [t]
stick a x = x ++ [a]
```

We see more of the fold functions in Section 6.4 and in Chapter 15.

Filter

As we explained when we introduced `filterString`, a *property* of characters is expressed by a function of type `Char -> Bool`. For an arbitrary type t, a property of objects of type t will be given by a function of type

```
t -> Bool
```

For instance, `isEven` defined by

```
isEven :: Int -> Bool
isEven n = (n 'mod' 2 == 0)
```

is a property of integers, and

```
nonEmpty :: String -> Bool
nonEmpty st = (st /= "")
```

is a property of strings.

Filtering an empty list gives an empty list. On a non-empty list `(a:x)`, there are two cases in the definition of `filter p (a:x)`.

- If a has the property, that is the guard `p a` is `True`, then a is the head of the result; the tail is given by filtering x.
- If the guard is `False`, a is not to be included, and so the result is given by filtering x.

The definition of `filter` is therefore given by

```
filter :: (t -> Bool) -> [t] -> [t]

filter p [] = []
filter p (a:x)
  | p a        = a : filter p x
  | otherwise  =     filter p x
```

and we have

```
filter isEven [2,3,4] = [2,4]
filter nonEmpty ["Freak ", "Out" , "", "!"]
            = ["Freak ", "Out" , "!"]
```

A list comprehension serves to provide an equivalent definition

```
filter p x = [ a | a <- x , p a ]
```

EXERCISES

6.10 How would you define the sum of the squares of the natural numbers 1 to n using map and `foldr`?

6.11 Define a function to give the sum of squares of the positive integers in a list of integers.

6.12 How would you define the function `length` using map and `sumList`?

6.13 Given the function

```
addUp l = filter greaterOne (map addOne l)
```

where

```
greaterOne n = n>1
addOne n     = n+1
```

you are asked to redefine it using `filter` before map, thus

```
addUp l = map fun1 (filter fun2 l)
```

What are the functions fun1 and fun2?

6.14 What is the effect of

```
map addOne (map addOne l)
```

Can you conclude anything in general about

```
map f (map g l)
```

where f and g are arbitrary functions?

6.15 What is the effect of

```
filter greaterOne (filter lessTen l)
```

where lessTen n = n<10. Can you conclude anything in general about

```
filter p (filter q l)
```

where p and q are arbitrary properties?

6.16 How does the function

```
mystery l = foldr (++) [] (map sing l)
```

behave, where sing a = [a] for all a?

6.17 The function `formatLines` will format a list of lines using the function

```
formatLine :: Line -> String
```

to format each line in the list. Define a function

```
formatList :: (t -> String) -> [t] -> String
```

which takes as a parameter a function of type

```
t -> String
```

to format each item of the list which is passed as the second parameter. Show how `formatLines` can be defined using `formatList` and `formatLine`.

6.4 Using the higher-order functions

Here we look at the higher-order functions (HOFs) `map`, `filter` and the folds `fold` and `foldr` in some longer examples. We see in particular how they are used in combination.

EXAMPLE: Library database —————————————————————

Section 4.5 contains an example library database, in which the functions were defined directly, using recursion. Here we consider how the HOFs can be used instead.

Recall that a `Database` is a list of `Person`, `Book` pairs. The function

```
books :: Database -> Person -> [Book]
```

takes a `Database` and a person, `per`, and gives as a result the list of all books borrowed by `per`. The algorithm has two phases:

● all pairs whose first half is `per` have to be found – a filter;

● for each of these pairs, we take the second half – a map.

So we can say

```
books db per = map snd (filter isPer db)
               where
               isPer (p,b) = (p == per)
```

There are two things worth noting about this definition.

- The isPer function checks whether the first half of a pair is per. As it is defined in a where clause it can use per in its definition, since the variables on the left-hand side of an equation can be used in the where defined functions.

- There is no pattern matching in the definition, unlike the earlier definition, where we had to make cases for the database argument. Using map and filter means that the definition is itself higher level, and is substantially easier to read. (Of course, pattern matching has to happen somewhere; in fact, it takes place in the definitions of map and filter themselves.)

As a second example, consider the function

```
returnLoan :: Database -> Person -> Book -> Database
```

designed to return the loan of book b to person p. We can say

```
returnLoan db p b
  = filter notPB db
    where
    notPB pr = (pr /= (p,b))
```

if we wish to remove *all* pairs (p,b). To remove the *first* pair (p,b) we could define a version of filter which removes a first occurrence only. This could be re-used as required later.

EXAMPLE: Supermarket billing ⎯⎯⎯⎯⎯⎯⎯⎯⎯⎯⎯⎯⎯⎯⎯⎯⎯

In following this section you will need to refer to the supermarket billing exercise in Chapter 4. Many of the operations of this exercise can be written using the HOFs. For instance, we are asked to

- format each line (mapping) and then to join the results together (folding in the function (++));

- look up individual items in a database of bar codes (map and filter), and then to look up a list of such items (map again);

- find the number of bottles of sherry bought (filter and other functions), and to calculate a discount from that.

EXERCISES

6.18 Define the functions `borrowers` and `numBorrowed` of the library database making use of higher-order functions rather than recursion and pattern matching.

6.19 Define a function

```
filterFirst :: (t -> Bool) -> [t] -> [t]
```

so that `filterFirst p l` removes the first element of l which does not have the property p. Use this to give a version of `returnLoan` which only returns one copy of a book. What does your function do on a list all of whose elements have property p?

6.20 Can you define a function

```
filterLast :: (t -> Bool) -> [t] -> [t]
```

which removes the last occurrence of an element of l without property p? How could you define it using `filterFirst`?

6.21 Using the HOFs described earlier, redefine the functions `formatLines`, `lookup` and `makeBill` of the supermarket billing example.

6.22 How can you define the `makeDiscount` operation without using recursion? How would you modify `makeBill` so that unknown items are not a part of the bill?

6.5 Generalizing: splitting up lists

Many list manipulating programs involve splitting up lists in some way, as a part of their processing. One way of doing this is to select some or all the elements with a particular property – this we have seen with `filter`. Other ways of processing include taking or dropping elements of the list from the front – this we saw in the text processing example. If we know the number of elements to be dropped, we can use

```
take, drop :: Int -> [t] -> [t]
```

where `take n l` and `drop n l` are intended to take or drop n elements from the front of the list; if the list contains less than n elements, we drop as many as possible. So,

```
take _ []    = []
take 0 _     = []
take n (a:x) = a : take (n-1) x
```

and `drop` is defined similarly.

In Chapter 4 we looked at an example of text processing, in which lists were split to yield words and sentences. The functions `getWord` and `dropWord` defined there were *not* polymorphic, as they were designed to split at whitespace characters.

It is a general principle of functional programming that programs can often be rewritten to use more general polymorphic and/or higher-order functions, and we illustrate that here.

The function `getWord` was originally defined thus:

```
getWord :: String -> String
getWord []    = []
getWord (a:x)
  | elem a whitespace   = []                                    (1)
  | otherwise           = a : getWord x
```

What forces this to work over strings is the test in (1), where a is checked for membership of `whitespace`. We can generalize the function to have the test as a parameter.

How is this to be done? Recall that a property over the type `t` is represented by a function of type (`t -> Bool`). Making this test a parameter we have

```
getUntil :: (t -> Bool) -> [t] -> [t]
getUntil p []    = []
getUntil p (a:x)
  | p a        = []
  | otherwise  = a : getUntil p x
```

in which the test `elem a whitespace` has been replaced by the test `p a`, the arbitrary property p applied to a. We can of course recover `getWord` from this definition.

```
getWord l = getUntil p l
            where
            p a = elem a whitespace
```

Built into Haskell are the functions `takeWhile` and `dropWhile`, which are like `getUntil` and `dropUntil`, except that they take elements until the condition *fails* to be `True`. For instance,

```
takeWhile :: (t -> Bool) -> [t] -> [t]
takeWhile p []    = []
takeWhile p (a:x)
  | p a         = a : takeWhile p x
  | otherwise   = []
```

getUntil can be defined using takeWhile, and vice versa.

EXERCISES

6.23   Give the generalization dropUntil corresponding to the dropWord function.

6.24   How would you define the function dropSpace using dropUntil?

6.25   How would you split a string into lines using getUntil and dropUntil?

6.26   The function getLine of Chapter 4 has a polymorphic type – what is it? How could you generalize the test in this function? If you do this, does the type of the function become more general – explain your answer?

SUMMARY

This chapter has introduced two of the most fertile ideas in functional programming.

- We have seen that functions can be arguments to other functions, which are called higher-order. A function parameter can represent an operation to be mapped along a list, or a property used to filter the elements of a list, for example.

- We have also seen that definitions can be of polymorphic objects; a mapping operation can be applied to all types of list, for instance. Polymorphic definitions are found where definitions constrain the types only weakly; in defining the function to give the length of a list, all that is required of the argument is that it is a list; the type of the elements is irrelevant.

These two properties combined give us functions like map, filter and fold, all of which can be combined and used in diverse situations. Higher-order polymorphic functions are ideal candidates for libraries of re-usable functions.

We saw in the final section that in many situations where functions of a monomorphic type have been defined, it is possible to *generalize* them. This is done by supplying them with the appropriate parameters (which are often themselves functions) and makes them general polymorphic operations which are widely applicable. We looked at the particular example of generalizing the functions originally defined in the context of text processing.

Functions as values

As we saw in the previous chapter, functions can be arguments of other, *higher-order*, functions. Functions and operators can also give functions as *results*, another way of making them higher-order. After showing a number of ways that we can describe functions in Haskell, this chapter shows how functions are returned as results of other functions, and re-examines some of our examples to see how the ideas fit into programs we built earlier.

A longer example – building an index for a document – is used to show how these new ideas fit into program development; after considering this we draw some general conclusions for program design. The chapter concludes with some examples of program verification involving higher-order polymorphic objects, where it is shown that the theorems proved about them are re-usable in exactly the same way as are the functions themselves.

7.1 Function composition

One of the simplest ways of structuring a program is to do a number of things one after the other – each part can be defined separately. In a functional program this is achieved by **composing** a number of functions together: the output of one function becomes the input of another, as in Figure 7.1.

In Chapter 4 we gave the function `fill`, to take a text (that is a `String`) and to split it into filled lines. It was written thus:

```
fill :: String -> [Lines]
fill st = splitLines (splitWords st)          (1)
```

so that first the text is split into a list of words which is then split into lines. The component functions have types

```
splitWords :: String -> [Word]
splitLines :: [Word] -> [Line]
```

Because composition is so frequently used, there is a Haskell notation for it, '.', an infix dot. The definition of `fill` can be rewritten

```
fill = splitLines . splitWords
```

This definition has exactly the same effect as the definition (1), but says directly that the function `fill` is a composition of the two, without the necessity of applying either side to an argument. It is easier to read, and makes explicit the fact that `fill` is a composition.

How is composition, '.', defined? For any functions f and g, the effect of f.g is given by the equation

```
(f.g) x = f (g x)
```

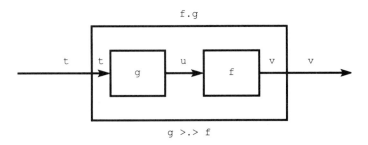

Figure 7.1 Function composition.

Not all pairs of functions can be composed. The output of g, g x, becomes the input of f, so that the output type of g must equal the input type of f. In the example, the output type of splitWords and the input type of splitLines are both [Word].

The type constraint can be expressed by giving '.' the type

```
(.) :: (u -> v) -> (t -> u) -> (t -> v)
```

which shows that, if we call the first input f and the second g,

- the input of f and the output of g are of the same type: u;
- the result f.g has the same input type, t, as g and the same output type, v, as f.

and is illustrated in Figure 7.1.

Composition is **associative**, that is f.(g.h) is equal to (f.g).h for all f, g and h. We can therefore write f.g.h unambiguously to mean 'do h, then g, then f'.[1]

Forward composition

The order in f.g is significant, and can be confusing; f.g means 'first apply g and then apply f to the result', and *not* the other way round, even though f occurs to the left of g.

The reason we write (f.g) for 'g then f' is that we write arguments to the right of functions. The argument is therefore closer to g than to f, and the order of the functions in (f.g) x is the same as in the repeated application, f (g x).

It is simple in Haskell to define an operator for composition which takes its arguments in the opposite order to '.'. This we do thus:

```
infixl 9 >.>

(>.>) :: (t -> u) -> (u -> v) -> (t -> v)

g >.> f = f . g
```

This definition has the effect that

```
(g >.> f) x = (f.g) x = f (g x)
```

---

[1] For technical reasons, the '.' is treated as right associative in the Haskell standard prelude.

showing that, as it were, the order of the f and g is swapped before the functions are applied.

Our example `fill` function can then be written

```
fill = splitWords >.> splitLines
```

which we can read as `splitWords` *then* `splitLines`, with the order that the functions are applied going from left to right.

The notation '>.>' contains a '.' to show that it is a form of composition, with the arrows showing the direction in which information is flowing.

Pitfalls of composition

There are a number of pitfalls associated with composition, which can trap the unwary.

- There is an error caused by the binding power of function application. It is a common error to write `f.g x` thinking it means `f.g` applied to x. Because function application binds more tightly than anything else, it is interpreted by the system as `f.(g x)`, which will in general lead to a type error.

  For example, if `succ` is defined by `succ x = x+1` then evaluating

  ```
  succ.succ 1
  ```

  gives the type error message

  ```
  *** expression      : succ . succ 1
  *** term            : succ 1
  *** type            : Int
  *** does not match : a -> b
  ```

  since there is an attempt to treat `succ 1` as a function to be composed with `succ`. Such a function needs to have type `a->b`, whereas it actually has type `Int`.

- Function application and composition can get confused. Function composition combines two functions, while application combines a function and an argument (which can be a function, of course).

  If, for example, f has type `Int -> Bool`, then

  - `f.a` means f composed with the *function* a; a therefore needs to be of type `s -> Int` for some type s;

  - `f a` means f applied to the object a, so a must therefore be an integer.

EXERCISES

7.1 Redefine the function `printBill` from the supermarket billing exercise in Chapter 4 so that composition is used. Repeat the exercise using forward composition, `>.>`.

7.2 If `id` is the polymorphic identity function, `id x = x`, explain the behaviour of the expressions `id.f` and `id f`. If `f` is of type `Int -> Bool`, at what type is `id` used in each case? What type does `h` have if `h id` is properly typed?

7.2 Functions as values and results

We have seen that functions can be combined together using the composition operators '`.`' and '`>.>`'; this can be done on the right-hand side of function definitions. The simplest example of this is

```
twice f = f.f                                          (1)
```

`f` is a function, and the result is `f` composed with itself. For this to work, it needs to have the same input and output type, so we have

```
twice :: (t -> t) -> (t -> t)
```

This states that `twice` takes one argument, a function of type `(t -> t)`, and returns a result of the same type. For instance, if `succ` is the function to add one to an integer, then

```
(twice succ) 12
= (succ.succ) 12                      by (1)
= succ (succ 12)                      by '.'
= 14
```

We can generalize `twice` so that we pass a parameter giving the number of times a function is to be composed with itself

```
iter :: Int -> (t -> t) -> (t -> t)

iter 0 f = id
iter n f = f >.> iter (n-1) f
```

As an example, we can define 2^n as `iter n times2 1`, if `times2` doubles its argument.

Expressions defining functions

How else can we write down expressions which describe functions? In writing a function definition we can use a `where` clause to make a definition.

Suppose, for example, that given an integer n we are to return the function (from `Int` to `Int`) which adds n to its argument, we can say

```
addNum :: Int -> (Int -> Int)
addNum n = h
          where
          h m = n+m
```

The result is a function h, and h is itself defined by an equation in the `where` clause. This method is rather indirect – we say we shall return the function named h, and then define that function.

Lambda notation

We can instead write down directly the function we want; it is

```
\m -> n+m
```

How is this expression to be interpreted?

- Before the arrow go the arguments, in this case the single argument m.
- After the arrow comes the result, here n+m.

That the expression is a function is signalled by its beginning with '\' which is the closest ASCII character to the Greek lambda, λ, which is used in a mathematical theory of functions, called the lambda calculus, for exactly this purpose. The definition of addNum now becomes

```
addNum n = (\m -> n+m)
```

Another example is given by the 'plumbing' illustrated in Figure 7.2. The object shown is a function, whose arguments are x and y. The result of the function is

```
g (f x) (f y)
```

so the overall effect is to give a function which applies f to each of its (two) arguments before applying g to the results. The definition states this quite straightforwardly:

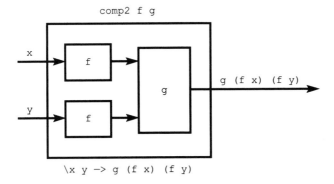

Figure 7.2 Plumbing f and g together.

```
comp2 :: (t -> u) -> (u -> u -> v) -> (t -> t -> v)

comp2 f g = (\x y -> g (f x) (f y))
```

To add together the squares of 3 and 4 we can write

```
comp2 sq add 3 4
```

where add and sq have the obvious definitions.

We shall see in the next section that partial application will make many definitions, including those of the functions here, more straight-forward. On the other hand the 'anonymous' functions given by this lambda notation are used heavily in certain sorts of program to do input/output; see Chapter 14 for more details.

EXERCISES

7.3   Give calculations of

```
iter 3 times2 1
(comp2 succ (*)) 3 4
comp2 sq add 3 4
```

7.4   Given a function f of type t -> u -> v write down an expression of the form

```
(\ ... -> ... )
```

for the function of type u -> t -> v which behaves like f but which takes its arguments in the other order.

7.5 Using the last exercise, or otherwise, give a definition of the function

```
flip :: (t -> u -> v) -> (u -> t -> v)
```

which reverses the order in which its function argument takes its arguments.

7.6 Using a lambda expression, the Boolean function `not` and the built-in function `elem` describe a function of type

```
Char -> Bool
```

which is `True` only on non-whitespace characters, that is those which are not elements of the list `" \t\n"`.

7.7 Define a function `total`

```
total :: (Int -> Int) -> (Int -> Int)
```

so that `total f` is the function which at value n gives the total

```
f 0 + f 1 + ... + f n
```

7.8 [Harder] Define a function

```
slope :: (Float -> Float) -> (Float -> Float)
```

which takes a function `f` as argument, and returns (an approximation to) its derivative `f′` as result.

7.9 [Harder] Define a function

```
integrate :: (Float -> Float) -> (Float -> Float -> Float)
```

which takes a function `f` as argument, and returns (an approximation to) the two argument function which gives the area under its graph between two end points as its result.

7.3 Partial application

The function `multiply` multiplies together two arguments.

```
multiply :: Int -> Int -> Int
multiply a b = a*b
```

so that `multiply 2 3` equals 6. What happens if `multiply` is applied to *one* argument 2? The result is a *function*, which when given an argument b will return double the value, `2*b`.

This is an example of a general phenomenon: any function taking two or more arguments can be *partially applied* to one or more arguments. This gives a powerful way of forming functions as results.

As an example, suppose that every element of a list is to be doubled. The function can be defined thus:

```
doubleList :: [Int] -> [Int]
doubleList = map (multiply 2)
```

In this definition there are two partial applications:

- `multiply 2` is a function from integers to integers, given by applying `multiply` to one rather than two arguments;
- `map (multiply 2)` is a function from `[Int]` to `[Int]` given by partially applying `map`.

How is the type of a partial application determined? There is a simple rule which explains it.

Rule of cancellation

If the type of a function `f` is

$$t_1 \rightarrow t_2 \rightarrow \ldots \rightarrow t_n \rightarrow t$$

and it is applied to arguments

$$e_1::t_1, \ e_2::t_2, \ \ldots, \ e_k::t_k$$

(where $k \leqslant n$) then the result type is given by **cancelling** the types t_1 to t_k

$$\not{t_1} \rightarrow \not{t_2} \rightarrow \ldots \rightarrow \not{t_k} \rightarrow t_{k+1} \rightarrow \ldots \rightarrow t_n \rightarrow t$$

which gives the type

$$t_{k+1} \rightarrow t_{k+2} \rightarrow \ldots \rightarrow t_n \rightarrow t$$

For example,

```
multiply 2        :: Int -> Int
multiply 2 3      :: Int
doubleList        :: [Int] -> [Int]
doubleList [2,3] :: [Int]
```

The idea of partial application is important. We have already seen that many functions can be defined as **specializations** of general operations like `map`, `filter` and so on. These specializations arise by us passing a function to the general operation – this function is often given by a partial application, as in the examples

```
map (multiply 2)
```

It is not always possible to make a partial application, since the argument to which we want to apply the function may not be its first argument. Consider the function

```
elem :: Char -> [Char] -> Bool
```

We can test whether a character `ch` is a whitespace character by writing

```
elem ch whitespace
```

where `whitespace` is the string `" \t\n"`. We would like to write the function to test this by partially applying `elem` to `whitespace`, but cannot. Instead we can write

```
\ch -> elem ch whitespace
```

In a similar vein, to filter all non-whitespace characters from a string, we can write the partial application

```
filter (\ch -> not (elem ch whitespace))
```

Syntax: associativity

Function application is **left associative** so that

```
f a b = (f a) b
f a b ≠ f (a b)
```

The function space symbol '`->`' is **right associative**, so that `t -> u -> v` means

```
t -> (u -> v)
```

and *not*

```
(t -> u) -> v
```

The arrow is not associative. If

```
f :: Int -> Int -> Int
g :: (Int -> Int) -> Int
```

then f will yield a function from `Int` to `Int` when given an `Int` – an example is `multiply`. On the other hand, when given a function of type `Int -> Int`, g yields an `Int`. An example is

```
g :: (Int -> Int) -> Int
g h = (h 0) + (h 1)
```

The function g defined here takes a function h as argument and returns the sum of h's values at 0 and 1.

How many arguments do functions have?

Partial application can appear confusing: in some contexts functions appear to take one argument, and in others two. In fact, *every function in Haskell takes exactly one argument*. If this application yields a function, then this function may be applied to a further argument, and so on. Consider the multiplication function again.

```
multiply :: Int -> Int -> Int
```

This is shorthand for

```
multiply :: Int -> (Int -> Int)
```

and so it can therefore be applied to an integer. Doing this gives (for example)

```
multiply 4 :: Int -> Int
```

This can itself be applied to give

```
(multiply 4) 5 :: Int
```

which since function application is left associative, can be written

```
multiply 4 5 :: Int
```

Our explanations earlier in the book are consistent with this full explanation of the system. We hid the fact that

```
f e₁ e₂ ... eₖ
t₁ -> t₂ -> ... tₙ -> t
```

were shorthand for

```
( ...((f e₁) e₂) ... eₖ)
t₁ -> (t₂ -> (...(tₙ -> t)...))
```

but this did no harm to our understanding of how to use the Haskell language.

Examples of partial applications will be seen throughout the material to come, and can be used to simplify and clarify many of the preceding examples. Three simple examples are the text processing functions

```
dropSpace = dropWhile (member whitespace)
dropWord  = dropWhile (not . member whitespace)
getWord   = takeWhile (not . member whitespace)
```

where

```
member st x = elem x st
```

We look at further examples in the next section, after examining partially applied operators.

Operator sections

The operators of the language can be partially applied, giving what are known as **operator sections**. Examples include

(+2)	The function which adds two to its argument.
(2+)	The function which adds two to its argument.
(>2)	The function which returns whether an integer is greater than two.
(3:)	The function which puts the integer 3 on the front of a list.
(++"\n")	The function which puts a newline at the end of a string.

The general rule here is that a section of the operator op will put its argument to the side which completes the application. That is,

```
(op a) b = b op a
(a op) b = a op b
```

When combined with higher-order functions like map, filter and composition, the notation is both powerful and elegant. For example,

```
map (+1) >.> filter (>0)
```

is the function which adds one to each member of a list, and then removes those elements which are not positive.

EXERCISES

7.10 Use partial applications to define the functions addNum, comp2 and total given in the previous section.

7.11 How would you re-define the function map (+1) >.> filter (>0) thus

```
filter sec₁ >.> map sec₂
```

where sec₁ and sec₂ are operator sections?

7.4 Examples

This section explores how partial applications and operator sections can be used to simplify and shorten definitions. Often it is possible to avoid giving an explicit function definition if we can use a partial application to return a function. Revisiting the examples of Chapter 6 we see that to double a list we can write

```
double = map (*2)
```

using an operator section (*2) to replace the times2 function, and giving the function definition directly by partially applying map.

To filter out the even elements in a numerical list, we have to check whether the remainder on dividing by two is equal to zero. As a function we can write

```
(==0).(`mod` 2)
```

this is the composition of two operator sections: first find the remainder, then check if it is equal to zero. (Why can we not write (`mod` 2 == 0)?) The filtering function can then be written

```
getEvens = filter ((==0).(`mod` 2))
```

In the library database example, when defining `books` we wrote

```
books db per = map snd (filter isPer db)
```

with the definition of `isPer` in a `where` clause. We can replace this with

```
books db per = map snd (filter ((==per).fst) db)
```

The function `(==per).fst` takes the first component of a pair, using `fst`, and then compares it with the person of interest, `per`.

Our final example comes from the list splitting study. We defined

```
getWord l = getUntil p l
            where
            p a = elem a whitespace
```

The local definition is not now needed, as we can define the function `p` by an operator section:

```
getWord l = getUntil (`elem` whitespace) l
```

Note the way that we partially apply a function to its *second* argument, by forming an operator section. This works because

```
(`elem` whitespace) a
= a `elem` whitespace
= elem a whitespace
```

as required.

Finally, the function `getWord` can itself be given a direct definition by partial application thus

```
getWord = getUntil (`elem` whitespace)
```

This definition reads like an informal explanation – to get a word, get characters until a whitespace character is found.

7.5   Currying and uncurrying

Making a function of two or more arguments accept its arguments one at a time is called **currying** after Haskell B. Curry[2] who was one of the pioneers of the λ-calculus and after whom the Haskell language is named. An

---

[2] In fact the first person to describe the idea was Schönfinkel, but 'Schönfinkeling' does not have the same elegance of expression!

uncurried version of a two argument function can be given by bundling the arguments into a pair, thus:

```
multiplyUC :: (Int,Int) -> Int
multiplyUC (a,b) = a*b
```

but it is most usual to present curried versions, as they can be partially applied.

There are two higher-order functions which convert between curried and uncurried functions.

```
curry :: ((t,u) -> v) -> (t -> u -> v)
curry g a b = g (a,b)
```

curry multiplyUC will be exactly the same function as multiply.

```
uncurry :: (t -> u -> v) -> ((t,u) -> v)
uncurry f (a,b) = f a b
```

uncurry multiply will be exactly the same function as multiplyUC. The functions curry and uncurry are inverse to each other.

Partial application of functions is done on the arguments from left to right, so a function cannot directly be applied to its second argument only. This effect can be achieved indirectly by first transforming the order in which the function takes its arguments and then partially applying it.

```
flip :: (t -> u -> v) -> (u -> t -> v)
flip f b a = f a b
```

flip map will take as its first argument the list and as its second the function to be mapped; it can be applied to its first argument, having the effect of applying map to its second only.

Another way of forming the partial application

```
('elem' whitespace)
```

is to use the flip function. We have

```
flip elem :: [t] -> t -> Bool
```

so we can form the partial application thus:

```
flip elem whitespace
```

We now turn to a more substantial example in which we use the ideas of composition, partial application and operator sections in a variety of ways.

7.6   Example: creating an index

This section explores a different aspect of text processing from those we have looked at already. How can an index for a document be produced automatically? We use the example to illustrate how higher-order functions are used in many parts of the final program. Polymorphism allows their use at different types, and their function parameters mean that they can be used to different effect in different situations.

To make the example texts shorter, a scaled-down version of the indexing problem is investigated. This is only done for ease of presentation, as all the important aspects of the system are explored here.

We should first specify what the program is to do. The input is a text string, in which lines are separated by the newline character ' \n'. The index should give every line on which the word in question occurs. Only words of length at least five are to be indexed, and an alphabetical listing of the results produced. Within each entry, a line number should not be duplicated.

We can represent the index as a list, with each entry being an item. What will a single entry be? It has to associate a collection of line numbers with a word of text; we can therefore represent each entry by a pair consisting of a list of numbers, of type [Int], and a word, of type String. The top-level function will therefore be

```
makeIndex :: Doc -> [ ([Int],Word) ]
```

where we use the type synonyms

```
type Doc  = String
type Line = String
type Word = String
```

to distinguish the different uses of the string type in the design which follows.

How can the program be designed? We focus on the **data structures** which the program will produce, and we can see the program as working by making a series of modifications to the data with which we begin. This **data-directed** design is common in Haskell functional program development.

At the top level, the solution will be a **composition** of functions. These perform the following operations, in turn.

- Split the text, a Doc, into lines, giving an object of type [Line].

- Pair each line with its line number, giving an object of type [(Int,Line)].

- Split the lines into words, associating each word with the number of the line on which it occurs. This gives a list of type [(Int,Word)].

- Sort this list according to the alphabetical ordering of words (Strings), giving a list of the same type.

- Modify the lists so that each word is paired with a list of line numbers. This gives a result of type [([Int],Word)].

- Amalgamate entries for the same word into a list of numbers, giving a list of type [([Int],Word)].

- Shorten the list by removing all entries for words of less than five letters, giving a list of type [([Int],Word)].

The definition follows; note that we have used comments to give the type of each component function in the (forward) composition.

```
makeIndex
  = splitup      >.>   --   Doc              -> [Line]
    numLines     >.>   --   [Line]           -> [(Int,Line)]
    allNumWords  >.>   --   [(Int,Line)]     -> [(Int,Word)]
    sortLs       >.>   --   [(Int,Word)]     -> [(Int,Word)]
    makeLists    >.>   --   [(Int,Word)]     -> [([Int],Word)]
    amalgamate   >.>   --   [([Int],Word)]   -> [([Int],Word)]
    shorten            --   [([Int],Word)]   -> [([Int],Word)]
```

Once the type of each of the functions is given, development of each can proceed independently. The only information necessary to use a function is its *type*, and these types are specified in the definition above. Each of the functions can now be given, in turn.

To split a string into a list of lines it must be split at each occurrence of the newline character, '\n'. How is this written as a function? One solution is to write functions analogous to getWord and dropWord, which together were used earlier in splitWords. Alternatively, we can use the functions getUntil and dropUntil from Chapter 6. The definition is left as an exercise.

```
splitup :: Doc -> [Line]
```

The next function should pair each line with its line number. If the list of lines is linels, then the list of line numbers is

```
[1 .. length linels]
```

Stepping back from the problem, it is apparent that the lists of lines and line numbers need to be combined into a *list of pairs*, by zipping the two lists together. The zip function has already been defined to do exactly this, so the required function is written thus

```
numLines :: [Line] -> [ ( Int , Line ) ]
numLines linels
  = zip [1 .. length linels] linels
```

Now the lines have to be split into words, and line numbers attached. We first consider the problem for a single line.

```
numWords :: ( Int , Line ) -> [ ( Int , Word ) ]
```

Splitting into words can be done by the function `splitWords` of Chapter 4. Each of these words is then to be paired with the (same) line number. Stepping back from the problem, we see that we have to perform an operation on every item of a list, the list of words making up the line. This is a job for `map`.

```
numWords (number , lin)
  = map addLineNo (splitWords lin)
    where
    addLineNo wd = (number,wd)
```

To apply this to the whole text, the function `numWords` has to be applied to every line. This is again done by `map`, and the individual results joined together or **concatenated**. We make a direct definition of the function, by composing its two parts. First we map the function `numWords`, then we concatenate the results, using `concat`.

```
allNumWords :: [ ( Int , Line ) ] -> [ ( Int , Word ) ]
allNumWords = concat . map numWords
```

What has been achieved so far? The text has been transformed into a list of line-number/word pairs, from which an index is to be built. For instance, the text

```
"cat dog\nbat dog\ncat"
```

will be converted to

```
[(1,"cat") , (1,"dog") , (2,"bat") , (2,"dog") , (3,"cat")]
```

The list must next be sorted by word order, and lists of lines on which a word appears be built. The ordering relation on pairs of numbers and words is given by

```
compare :: ( Int , Word ) -> ( Int , Word ) -> Bool
compare ( n1 , w1 ) ( n2 , w2 )
  = w1 < w2 || ( w1 == w2 && n1 < n2 )
```

The words are compared for dictionary order. For pairs containing the same words, ordering is by page number.

Sorting a list is most easily done by a version of the *quicksort* algorithm. The list is split into parts smaller than and larger than a given element; each of these halves can be sorted separately, and then joined together to form the result.

```
sortLs :: [ ( Int , Word ) ] -> [ ( Int , Word ) ]

sortLs []    = []
sortLs (a:x) = sortLs smaller ++ [a] ++ sortLs larger
```

The lists `smaller` and `larger` are the lists of elements of x which are smaller (or larger) than the element a. Note that it is here that duplicate copies are removed – any other occurrence of the element a in the list x does not appear in either `smaller` or `larger`.

How are the two lists defined? They are given by selecting those elements of x with given properties: a job for `filter`, or a list comprehension. Going back to the definition of `sortLs`,

```
sortLs (a:x)
  = sortLs smaller ++ [a] ++ sortLs larger
    where
    smaller = [ b | b<-x , compare b a ]
    larger  = [ b | b<-x , compare a b ]
```

After sorting the index may look something like

```
[(2,"bat") , (1,"cat") , (3,"cat") , (1,"dog") , (2,"dog")]
```

The entries for the same word need to be accumulated together. First each entry is converted to having a *list* of pages associated with it, thus

```
makeLists ::  [ (Int,Word) ] -> [ ([Int],Word) ]
makeLists
  = map mklis
    where
    mklis ( n , st ) = ( [n] , st )
```

For our example, this gives

```
[ ([2],"bat") , ([1],"cat") , ([3],"cat") ,
  ([1],"dog") , ([2],"dog") ]
```

After this, the lists associated with the same words are amalgamated.

```
amalgamate :: [ ([Int],Word) ] -> [ ([Int],Word) ]

amalgamate [] = []
amalgamate [a] = [a]
amalgamate ((l1,w1):(l2,w2):rest)
  | w1 /= w2    = (l1,w1) : amalgamate ((l2,w2):rest)    (1)
  | otherwise   = amalgamate ((l1++l2,w1):rest)          (2)
```

The first two cases are simple, with the third doing the work.

- If we have two adjacent entries with different words, case (1), then we know that there is nothing to add to the first entry – we therefore have to amalgamate entries in the *tail* only.
- If two adjacent entries have the same word associated, case (2), they are amalgamated and the function is called again on the result. This is because there may be other entries with the same word, also to be amalgamated into the leading entry.

Consider an example

```
amalgamate [ ([2],"bat") , ([1],"cat") , ([3],"cat") ]
= ([2],"bat") : amalgamate [([1],"cat"),([3],"cat")]  by (1)
= ([2],"bat") : amalgamate [ ([1,3],"cat") ]          by (2)
= ([2],"bat") : [ ([1,3],"cat") ]
= [ ([2],"bat") , ([1,3],"cat") ]
```

To meet the requirements, one other operation needs to be performed. 'Small' words of less than five letters are to be removed.

```
shorten = filter sizer
            where
            sizer (nl,wd) = length wd > 4
```

Again, the `filter` function proves useful. The index function can now be defined in full:

```
makeIndex :: Doc -> [ ([Int],Word) ]
makeIndex
  = splitup >.> numLines >.> allNumWords >.> sortLs >.>
    makeLists >.> amalgamate >.> shorten
```

As was said at the beginning of this section, function composition provides a powerful method for structuring designs: programs are written as a **pipeline** of operations, passing the appropriate data structures between them.

It is easy to see how designs like these can be modified. To take one example, the indexing program above filters out short words only as its final operation. There are a number of earlier points in the chain at which this could have been done, and it is a worthwhile exercise to consider these.

EXERCISES

7.12 Define the function `splitup` using the functions `getUntil` and `dropUntil` from Chapter 6, or the built-in functions `takeUntil` and `dropUntil`. You should be careful that your functions do not give an empty word when there are empty lines in the `Doc`; this happens in the examples `"cat\n\ndog"` and `"fish\n"`.

7.13 How would you use lambda expressions to replace the local definitions in `numWords`, `makeLists` and `shorten`?

7.14 How would you re-define `sortLs` so that duplicate copies of an item are not removed? For the index, this means that if a word occurs twice on line 123 say, then 123 occurs twice in the index entry for that word.

7.15 How could the functions `getUntil` and `dropUntil` be used in the definition of `amalgamate`?

7.16 Explain how the function `sizer` can be defined as a composition of built-in functions and operator sections; the role of `sizer` is to pick the second half of a pair, find its length, and compare the result with 4.

7.17 How is the following definition of the last conditional equation for `amalgamate` incorrect? Give an example calculation to justify your answer.

```
amalgamate ((l1,w1):(l2,w2):rest)
  | w1 /= w2    = (l1,w1) : amalgamate ((l2,w2):rest)
  | otherwise   = (l1++l2,w1) : amalgamate rest
```

7.18 Give a definition of

```
showIndex :: [ ([Int],Word) ] -> String
```

which gives a neatly laid out printable version of an index.

7.19   Modify the program so that words of less than five letters are removed as a part of the definition of `allNumWords`.

7.20   Modify the `makeIndex` function so that instead of returning the list of line numbers on which a word occurs, the function returns the total number of times which the word occurs. You will need to make sure that multiple occurrences of a word in a single line are counted. There are two ways of tackling the problem.

- Modify the program as little as is necessary – you could return the length of a list rather than the list itself, for instance.
- Take the program structure as a guide, and write a (simpler) program which calculates the number of occurrences directly.

7.21   Modify the program so that capitalized words like `"Dog"` are indexed under their uncapitalized equivalents (`"dog"`). This does not work well for proper names like `"Amelia"` – what could you do about that?

7.22   The function `sortLs` is limited to sorting lists of type `[(Int,Word)]` because it calls the `compare` function. Re-define the function so that it takes the comparison function as a *parameter*. What is its type after this re-definition?

7.7   Design revisited

We have already discussed the design of functions and scripts in Sections 2.14 and 4.10 where two fundamental points emerged.

- We can design a system before starting to write it, by thinking about it from the top down. In this way a complex task is broken into a number of smaller and simpler tasks. We can also think of the design of single functions in more than one stage: first looking at the left-hand side, then at the right, and finally at the `where` clause, if any.
- Top-down design, with separate parts of a program working independently, is important not least because nearly every practical system has to be modified during its lifetime.

We now have more facilities at our disposal. We can write functions which take functions as arguments and return functions as results; we are also able to write definitions which apply to whole collections of types, such as lists of any type whatever, at once; these definitions have polymorphic type.

This ability gives us greater freedom to separate different parts of a program. For instance, if we have to apply an operation to every element of a list we can

- write the particular operation as one function definition, op, say, and

- write a general function, map, which applies an arbitrary function to every element of a list. The particular operation becomes an *argument* of the general function.

Given this separation, we can modify the definition of op completely independently of map. The definitions we write also become easier to understand, and when they are polymorphic, they become candidates for **re-use**.

Chapter 6 showed how functions could be the results of other functions, particularly through partial application. This is useful in giving direct definitions of functions, as compositions for example, and also in allowing the parameters to HOFs (like map) to be defined directly (like multiply 2) rather than having to be defined in a where clause.

How do collections of higher-order functions arise? One way which we saw in Section 4.9 is to recognize patterns of definitions, and to build a **toolkit** of HOFs to reflect these patterns.

Once we have a toolkit of list processing functions, we can build programs up using them. This toolkit approach was used in the indexing example, where some 80% of the work was done by toolkit functions. We had to define the functions amalgamate and sortLs to complete the work. Amalgamating entries in a list is peculiar to the indexing program, and it is no surprise that we will, in any sizable program, need to define some functions from scratch rather than by re-using other definitions.

The example of sortLs is more interesting; it is monomorphic, but we can change the definition so that it becomes a polymorphic higher-order function, ready for re-use. The function used compare, which was the ordering – we now make this a *parameter*, called comp, and obtain

```
sort :: (t -> t -> Bool) -> [t] -> [t]
sort comp (a:x)
  = sort comp smaller ++ [a] ++ sort comp larger
    where
    smaller = [ b | b<-x , comp b a ]
    larger  = [ b | b<-x , comp a b ]
sort comp [] = []
```

The original sortLs is given by sort compare.

This **generalization** is not isolated; another example is that of list splitting, seen in Chapter 6. In each case we have to recognize

- the general operation – this is the higher-order function, which will often be polymorphic, and

- the particular case – this will be a function argument to the general higher-order function; this argument is monomorphic in many cases.

This split makes the definitions we make more modular, and also gives us HOFs which are candidates for re-use in a toolkit. With experience, we begin to be able to see when there are opportunities to generalize; often they can be seen during design and implementation itself, giving a modified design or implementation.

7.8 Verification

Verification can take on a different character when we look at higher-order polymorphic functions. We can start to prove equalities between functions, rather than between values of functions, and we shall also see that we are able to prove theorems which resemble their subjects in being general and re-usable, that is being applicable in many contexts.

Function-level verification

We claimed in Section 7.2 that the function `iter` is a generalization of `twice`, since

```
iter 2 f
= f >.> iter 1 f
= f >.> (f >.> iter 0 f)
= f >.> (f >.> id)
= f >.> f                                    by (1)
= f . f
```

In proving this we have used the equality between two functions

```
f >.> id = f                                               (1)
```

How is this proved? We examine how each side behaves on an arbitrary argument `a`

```
(f >.> id) a
= id (f a)
= f a
```

so that for any argument `a` the two functions have the same behaviour. As black boxes, they are therefore the same, because for no argument do they behave differently. As what interests us here is their behaviour, we say that they are equal. We call this concept of equality **extensional**, and say that

Principle of extensionality:

> Two functions f and g are equal if they have the same value at every argument.

This is called extensionality in contrast to the idea of **intensionality** in which we say two functions are the same only if they have the same definitions – we no longer think of them as black boxes, as we are allowed to look inside them to see how the mechanisms work, as it were. If we are interested in the results of our programs, all that matters are the values given by functions, not how they are arrived at. We therefore use extensionality when we are reasoning about function behaviour in Haskell. If we are interested in *efficiency* or other performance aspects of programs, then the way in which a result is found *will* be significant, however. This is discussed further in Chapter 15.

EXERCISES

7.23 Show that function composition is associative, that is, for all f, g and h,

```
f.(g.h) = (f.g).h
```

7.24 Show that for all f,

```
id >.> f = f
```

7.25 Show that the function flip defined in Section 7.5 satisfies

```
flip.flip = id
```

Hint: to show this, you might want to prove that for any f,

```
flip (flip f) = f
```

7.26 Two functions f and g are *inverses* if it can be shown that

```
f.g = id            g.f = id
```

Prove that the functions curry and uncurry of Section 7.5 are inverses. Can you think of other pairs of inverse functions?

7.27 Prove that for all natural numbers n,

```
iter n id = id
```

7.28 A function f is called **idempotent** if

```
f.f = f
```

Show that the functions abs and signum are idempotent. Can you think of any other idempotent functions?

Higher-level proofs

Our verification thus far has concentrated on first-order, monomorphic functions. Just as map, filter and fold generalized patterns of definition, we shall find that proofs about these functions generalize results we have seen already. To give some examples, we saw in Chapter 5 that

```
double (x++y) = double x ++ double y
```

for finite lists x and y. When double is defined as map (*2) it becomes clear that we have an example of a general result,

```
map f (x++y) = map f x ++ map f y
```

which is valid for *any* function f. We also claimed that

```
sumList (x++y) = sumList x + sumList y                    (sumThm)
```

for all finite lists x, y. The function sumList is given by folding in (+),

```
sumList = foldr (+) 0
```

and we have, generally

```
foldr f st (x++y)
= f (foldr f st x) (foldr f st y)                        (foldThm)
```

if f is associative, and st is an identity for f; that is,

```
f a (f b c) = f (f a b) c
f a st = a = f st a
```

for all a, b, c. Obviously (+) is associative and has 0 as an identity, and so (sumThm) is a special case of (foldThm).

Now we give two full proofs of examples in the same vein.

EXAMPLE: Map and composition ────────────────────────────

A first example concerns `map` and composition. Recall the definitions

```
map f []    = []                                    (1)
map f (a:x) = f a : map f x                         (2)
(f.g) x     = f (g x)                               (3)
```

It is not hard to see that

```
map (f.g) x = (map f . map g) x                     (4)
```

for every finite list x. Applying `(f.g)` to every member of a list should be the same as applying `g` to every member and applying `f` to every member of the result. It is proved just as easily, by structural induction. The base case requires the identity to be proved for the empty list.

```
map (f.g) [] = []                                   by (1)


(map f . map g) [] = map f (map g [])               by (3)
                   = map f []                        by (1)
                   = []                              by (1)
```

Assuming that `map (f.g) x = (map f . map g) x` is true, it is now necessary to prove that

```
map (f.g) (a:x) = (map f . map g) (a:x)
```

Again, it is enough to analyse each side of the equation.

```
map (f.g) (a:x) = (f.g) a : map (f.g) x             by (2)
                = f (g a) : map (f.g) x             by (3)


(map f . map g) (a:x)
  = map f (map g (a:x))                             by (3)
  = map f (g a : map g x)                           by (2)
  = f (g a) : map f (map g x)                       by (2)
  = f (g a) : (map f . map g) x                     by (3)
```

The induction hypothesis is exactly what is needed to prove the two sides equal, completing the proof of the induction step and the proof itself. ∎

Each Haskell list type besides containing finite lists also contains infinite and partial lists. In Chapter 13 these will be explained and it will be shown that (4) is true for *all* lists x, and therefore that the functional equation

```
map (f.g) = (map f).(map g)
```

holds in general.

Map and filter

The last proof showed how properties of functional programs could be proved from the definitions of the functions in a straightforward way. The properties can state how the program behaves – that a sorting function returns an ordered list, for instance – or can relate one program to another. This latter idea underlies **program transformation** for functional languages. This section introduces an example called **filter promotion** which is one of the most useful of the basic functional transformations.

```
filter p . map f = map f . filter (p.f)
```

The equation says that a map followed by a filter can be replaced by a filter followed by a map. The right-hand side is potentially more efficient than the left, since the map operation will there be applied to a shorter list, consisting of just those elements with the property (p.f). An example is given by the function first defined in Section 7.3.

```
filter (0<) . map (+1)
```

Instead of mapping first, the function can be replaced by

```
map (+1) . filter ((0<).(+1))
   = map (+1) . filter (0<=)
```

and it is clear that here the transformed version is more efficient, since the test (0<=) is no more costly than (0<). The proof that

```
(filter p . map f) x = (map f . filter (p.f)) x
```

for finite lists x is by structural induction and follows the reiteration of the definitions of map, filter and composition.

```
map f []    = []                                    (1)
map f (a:x) = f a : map f x                         (2)
```

```
filter p []    = []                                          (3)
filter p (a:x)
  | p a          = a : filter p x                            (4)
  | otherwise   =       filter p x                           (5)


(f.g) x      = f (g x)                                       (6)
```

The base case consists of a proof of

```
(filter p . map f) [] = (map f . filter (p.f)) []           (7)
```

This is true since

```
(filter p . map f) []
  = filter p (map f [])                          by (6)
  = filter p []                                  by (1)
  = []                                           by (3)
```

and

```
(map f . filter (p.f)) []
  = map f (filter (p.f) [])                      by (6)
  = map f []                                     by (3)
  = []                                           by (1)
```

In the induction step, a proof of

```
(filter p . map f) (a:x) = (map f . filter (p.f)) (a:x) (8)
```

is required, using the induction hypothesis

```
(filter p . map f) x = (map f . filter (p.f)) x            (9)
```

The proof begins with an analysis of the left-hand side of (8).

```
(filter p . map f) (a:x)
  = filter p (map f (a:x))                       by (6)
  = filter p (f a : map f x)                     by (2)
```

There are two[3] cases to consider: whether p (f a) is True or False. In the first case,

---

[3] We should also think about what happens when p (f a) is undefined; in this case both sides will be undefined, and so equal.

$$
\begin{array}{llr}
= \text{f a : filter p (map f x)} & \text{by (4)} \\
= \text{f a : (filter p . map f) x} & \text{by (6)} \\
= \text{f a : (map f . filter (p.f)) x} & \text{by (9)} \\
= \text{f a : map f (filter (p.f) x)} & \text{by (6)} \\
= \text{map f (a: (filter (p.f) x))} & \text{by (2)} \\
= \text{map f (filter (p.f) (a:x))} & \text{by (4)} \\
= \text{(map f . filter (p.f)) (a:x)} & \text{by (6)} \\
\end{array}
$$

A similar chain of reasoning gives the same result in case p (f a) is False. This establishes (8) assuming (9), and so together with (7) completes the proof of the filter promotion transformation in the case of finite lists; it holds, in fact, for all lists.

∎

EXERCISES

7.29 Prove that if f is associative, and st is an identity for f, the equation

```
foldr f st (x++y) = f (foldr f st x) (foldr f st y)
```

which was called (foldThm) above, holds.

7.30 Argue that the result

```
concat (x ++ y) = concat x ++ concat y
```

is a special case of (foldThm), using

```
concat = foldr (++) []
```

as the definition of concat.

7.31 Prove that for all finite lists x, and functions f,

```
concat (map (map f) x) = map f (concat x)
```

7.32 Prove that over the integers

```
(0<) . (+1) = (0<=)
```

as is used in the theorem relating map and filter.

7.33 Prove for all finite lists l that

```
filter p (filter q l) = filter (p &&& q) l
```

where the operator &&& is defined by

```
p &&& q = \b -> (p b && q b)
```

SUMMARY

The main point of this chapter has been to give the various mechanisms for expressing and combining functions. These include

- composition and forward composition which connect the output of one function to the input of another;
- lambda expressions, in which a function is described by writing down its arguments and results, without giving it a name;
- partial application, which can be used for both functions and (infix) operators.

These mechanisms allow us to return functions as results of other functions.

We then discussed how the partial application mechanism fits into Haskell as we have already explained it, and discovered the formal justification to be that *all* Haskell functions take a single argument, and may return a function as result. We also gave a rule of cancellation, which allows us to deduce the types of partial applications.

We also looked at the effects of HOFs on design, and gave the example of document indexing where a toolkit of higher order functions supported program development.

We concluded the chapter by examining the possibilities for re-using *theorems* about higher-order functions, and discovered that many results we have seen already are particular cases of theorems concerning `map`, `filter`, `fold` and so on.

Classes in Haskell

The **classes** of Haskell are the main technical innovation of the language. Using classes we are able to **overload** names to mean different things at different types; in fact we have been doing this throughout the text so far with equality, ==. We can also begin to program in an **object-oriented** style using inheritance between classes; this we examine in Chapter 12 below.

8.1 Introducing classes

Haskell contains some built-in functions which give equality, ordering, textual representations and other operations on a variety of types. At first sight they appear to have polymorphic type:

```
(==)  :: t -> t -> Bool
(<)   :: t -> t -> Bool
show  :: t -> String
```

but in fact they are different from the functions we have met so far, which fall into two kinds.

- A function like

  ```
  capitalize :: Char -> Char
  capitalize ch = chr (ord ch + offset)
                where
                  offset = ord 'A' - ord 'a'
  ```

  is *monomorphic*. Its definition allows it to be used only over characters, since the functions ord and chr are used to convert from Char to Int and vice versa.

- On the other hand, a function like

  ```
  length []    = 0                                           (1)
  length (a:x) = 1 + length x
  ```

  can be used over a whole collection of types: its type is

  ```
  length :: [t] -> Int
  ```

  where t is a type variable standing for any type whatever. We can therefore use the *same* program (1) to calculate the length of lists of type [Int], [[Bool]], [t->Char] and so on.

In contrast to these two kinds of function, the definitions of the comparison and show functions are **overloaded**. This means that

- they can be used at more than one type, unlike capitalize, *and*
- their definitions are different at different types, unlike length.

If our language is to include functions like == which are defined over some but not all types, we need some way of saying whether we have an equality function over a given type. We call the collection of types over which a function is defined a **class**; the set of types over which == is defined is the *equality class*, Eq, for instance.

Defining the equality class

How do we define a class, such as Eq? We say what is needed for a type t to be in a class. In this case we need a function == defined over t, of type t->t->Bool.

```
class Eq t where
    (==) :: t -> t -> Bool
```

Members of a class are called its **instances**. Built-in instances of Eq include the base types Int, Float, Bool, Char. Other instances are given by tuples and lists built from types which are themselves instances of Eq; examples include the types (Int,Bool) and [[Char]]. Not all types will necessarily carry an equality; we may choose not to define one, for reasons of information hiding, or there may be no natural way of defining an equality on a particular type. For example, function types like Int -> Int are not instances of Eq, since there is no algorithm which will decide whether two functions over Int have the same behaviour.

It is unfortunate that the term *instance* is used in two quite different ways in Haskell. We talked in Section 6.2 of a type t_1 being an instance of a *type* t_2, when we can substitute for a type variable in t_2 to give t_1. Here we have talked about a type being an instance of a *class*.

Functions which use equality

Many of the functions appearing in Parts I and II use equality over particular types. In Chapter 1 we saw the definition

```
allEqual :: Int -> Int -> Int -> Bool
allEqual n m p = (n==m) && (m==p)
```

which decides whether three integers are equal. If we examine the definition itself, it contains nothing which is specific to integers; the only constraint it makes is that n, m and p are compared for equality. Their type can be t for any t *in the class* Eq. This changes the type thus:

```
allEqual :: Eq t => t -> t -> t -> Bool
allEqual n m p = (n==m) && (m==p)
```

The part before the => is called the **context**. We can read the type as saying that

if t is in the class Eq then allEqual has type

t -> t -> t -> Bool

What happens if we break this constraint by trying to compare functions for equality? In Hugs if we define

```
succ :: Int -> Int
succ = (+1)
```

and try to evaluate

```
allEqual succ succ succ
```

we get the message

```
ERROR: Cannot construct instance Eq (Int -> Int) in
expression
```

This conveys that (Int -> Int) is not in the Eq class, because it is not ('we cannot construct it as') an instance of that class. Gofer gives a different message,

```
ERROR: Cannot derive instance in expression
*** Expression       : allEqual succ succ succ
*** Required instance : Eq (Int -> Int)
```

to the same effect: the instance we want, namely Eq (Int -> Int), cannot be derived.

Further equality examples

Many of the functions we have defined already use equality in an overloaded way. We can use the Hugs system to deduce the most general type of a function, such as the books function from the library database of Chapter 4, by commenting out its type declaration in the script, thus

```
-- books :: Database -> Person -> [Book]
```

and then by typing

```
:type books
```

to the prompt. The result we get in that case is

```
books :: Eq a => [ (a,b) ] -> a -> [b]
```

which is perhaps a surprise at first. This is less so if we rewrite the definition with books renamed lookupFirst, because it looks up all the pairs with a particular first part, and returns their corresponding second parts. Here it is with its variables renamed as well

```
lookupFirst :: Eq t => [ (t,u) ] -> t -> [u]

lookupFirst [] a = []
lookupFirst ((b,c):rest) a
  | b==a        = c : lookupFirst rest a
  | otherwise   =     lookupFirst rest a
```

Clearly from this definition there is nothing specific about books or people, and so it is polymorphic, if we can compare objects in the first halves of the pairs for equality. This condition gives rise to the context Eq t.

In a similar way we have from Section 4.3:

```
member :: Eq t => [t] -> t -> Bool

member []    b = False
member (a:x) b = (a==b) || member x b
```

and finally from Section 4.5, as we saw for books,

```
borrowed    :: Eq u => [ (t,u) ] -> u -> Bool
numBorrowed :: Eq t => [ (t,u) ] -> t  -> Int
```

SUMMARY

In this section we have introduced the idea of a class, which is a collection of types – its instances – with the property that certain functions are defined over them. One way we can think of a class is as an adjective: any particular type is or is not in the class, just as the weather at any particular moment might or might not be sunny.

We saw how equality could be seen as being defined over all the types in the class Eq. This allows many of the functions defined so far to be given polymorphic type, allowing them to be used over any type in the class Eq. In the following sections we explain how classes and instances are defined in general, and explore the consequences of classes for programming in Haskell.

EXERCISES

8.1 How would you extend the definition of Eq to include the 'not equal' operation, /=, as well as equality, ==?

8.2 Define the function numEqual which takes a list of items, x say, and an item, a say, and returns the number of times a occurs in x. What is the type of your function? How could you use numEqual to define member?

8.3 There are two ways that one list can be contained in another.

- One is a *sublist* of the other if all the elements of one are contained in the other, in the same order. For example [1,3] is a sublist of [1,2,3,4], but not of [4,3,2,1].
- One is a *subsequence* of the other if it is a sublist and the elements occur in a single block. For instance, [1,3] is a subsequence of [1,3,4], but not of [1,2,3,4].

Define functions to test for sublist and subsequence. Specify the test data you would use for them and explain your choice. What are the types of the functions?

8.4 Define functions

```
lookupFirst1  :: Eq t => [ (t,u) ] -> t -> u
lookupSecond1 :: Eq u => [ (t,u) ] -> u -> t
```

lookupFirst1 takes a list of pairs and an item, and returns the second part of the first pair whose first part equals the item. You should explain what your function does if there is no such pair. lookupSecond1 returns the first pair with the roles of first and second reversed.

8.2 Signatures and instances

In the last section we saw that the operation of equality, ==, is overloaded. This allows == to be used over a variety of types, and also allows for functions using == to be defined over all instances of the class of types Eq. This section explains the mechanics of how classes are introduced, and then how instances of them may be declared. This allows us to program with classes we define ourselves, rather than simply using the built-in classes of Haskell.

Declaring a class

As we saw earlier, a class is introduced by a declaration like:

```
class Visible t where
    toString :: t -> String
    size     :: t -> Int
```

The declaration introduces the name of the class, `Visible`, and then follows a **signature**, that is a list of names and their types. Any type `t` in the `Visible` class must carry the two functions in the signature:

- the `toString` function, which converts a object of the type to a `String`, and
- the `size` function, which returns a measure of the size of the argument, as an integer.

Visible things can be viewed, using the `toString` function, and we can give an estimate of their size: the size of a list might be its length, while a Boolean might have size one.

The general form of definition is:

```
class Name ty where
    ... signature involving ty ...
```

Now, how are types made instances of such a class?

Defining the instances of a class

A type is made a member or **instance** of a class by defining the signature functions for the type. For example,

```
instance Eq Bool where
    True  == True  = True
    False == False = True
    _     == _     = False
```

describes how `Bool` is an instance of the equality class. The declarations that numeric types like `Int` and `Float` are in the equality class (and indeed other built-in classes) involve the appropriate primitive equality functions supplied by the implementation.

Although we have called the class `Eq` the equality class, there is no requirement that the `==` function we define has any of the usual properties of equality apart from having the same type as equality. It is up to the user to ensure that he or she makes sensible definitions, and documents them adequately.

Taking up our other example, we might say

```
instance Visible Char where
   toString ch  = [ch]
   size _       = 1
```

shows how characters can be printed – by making them into strings of length one – and gives a measure of their size. We can also make Bool an instance, thus:

```
instance Visible Bool where
   toString True  = "True"
   toString False = "False"
   size b         = 1
```

Suppose the type t is visible: this means that we can estimate the size of a value in t, and turn a value into a string. If presented with a list of t, we can use the toString and size on t to define those functions over [t], so we can declare the following instance

```
instance Visible t => Visible [t] where ....
```

in which the *context* Visible t appears, making clear that we are only making visible lists of objects which are visible themselves. We can complete the definition by saying how we print and give the size of a list of t:

```
instance Visible t => Visible [t] where
   toString = map toString >.> concat
   size     = map size     >.> foldr (+) 1
```

To turn a list of t into a String, we turn each element of the list into a string (map toString) and then (>.>) we concatenate the results, using concat.

In a similar way we can estimate the size of a list of t: we take the size of each object (map size), and add one to the total of these sizes by foldr (+) 1. On the right-hand sides of these definitions we use toString and size over the type t; this shows that we need the context which says that t is a Visible type.

There are some limitations to what can be declared as an instance, in other words on what can appear after the => (if any) in an instance declaration. This must either be a base type like Int, or consist of a type former (or constructor) like [...] or (...,...) applied to distinct type variables.

We will *not* be able, for instance, to declare (Float,Float) as an instance; nor can we use named types (introduced by a type definition). More details of the mechanism can be found in the Haskell report (Hudak *et al.*, 1992; Peterson *et al.*, 1996). We shall explore more complex examples in the next part of the book, after introducing our own type constructors.

Default definitions

To return to our example of equality, the Haskell equality class is in fact defined by

```
class Eq t where
    (==), (/=) :: t -> t -> Bool
    a /= b = not (a==b)
```

To the equality operation is added inequality, /=. As well as this, there is a **default** definition of /= from ==. This has two purposes; it gives a definition over all equality types, but as a default it can be **over-ridden** by an instance declaration, if that is needed. If, for instance, we wanted to define a different version of /= over Bool, we could add to our instance declaration for Bool the line

```
a /= b = ... our definition ...
```

Derived classes

Functions and instances can depend upon types being in classes; this is also true of classes. The simplest example in Haskell is the class of ordered types, Ord. To be ordered, a type must carry the operations >, >= and so on, as well as the equality operations. We say

```
class Eq t => Ord t where
    (<), (<=), (>), (>=) :: t -> t -> Bool
    max, min               :: t -> t -> t
```

For a type t to be in the class Ord, we must supply over t definitions of the operations of Eq as well as the ones in the signature of Ord. Given a definition of < we can supply default definitions of the remaining operations of Ord. For instance,

```
a <= b = (a<b || a==b)
a > b  = b<a
```

From a different point of view, we can see the class Ord as **inheriting** the operations of Eq; inheritance is one of the central ideas of object-oriented programming.

A simple example of a function defined over types in the class Ord is the insertion sort function iSort of Chapter 4. Its type is

```
iSort :: Ord t => [t] -> [t]
```

Indeed, any sorting function (which sorts using the ordering given by <=) would be expected to have this type.

Multiple constraints

In the contexts we have seen so far, we have a single constraint on a type, such as Eq t. There is no reason why we should not have multiple constraints on types. This section introduces the notation we use, and some examples where it is needed.

Suppose we wish to sort a list then show the results as a string. We can write

```
vSort = iSort >.> toString
```

To sort the elements, we need the list to consist of elements from an ordered type, as we saw above. To convert the results to a String we need [t] to be Visible; this will hold if t is visible. We therefore have

```
vSort :: (Ord t,Visible t) => [t] -> String
```

showing that t must be in both the classes Ord and Visible. Such types include Bool, [Char] and so on.

In a similar way, suppose we are to use lookupFirst, and then make the results visible. We write

```
vLookupFirst db a = toString (lookupFirst db a)
```

We have twin constraints again on our list type [(t,u)]. We need to be able to compare the first halves of the pairs, so Eq t is required. We also want to turn the second halves into strings, so needing Visible u. This gives the type

```
vLookupFirst :: (Eq t,Visible u) => [(t,u)] -> t -> String
```

The types given here are valid in Haskell; the Gofer system differs from Haskell in some respects: for more details of this, see Section 8.4.

Multiple constraints can occur in an instance declaration, such as

```
instance (Eq t,Eq u) => Eq (t,u) where
  (a,b) == (c,d)  =  a==c && b==d
```

and also in the definition of a class,

```
class (Ord t,Visible t) => OrdVis t
```

In such a declaration, the class inherits the operations of both `Ord` and `Visible`.

In this particular case, the class declaration contains an empty signature. To be in `OrdVis`, the type `t` must simply be in the classes `Ord` and `Visible`. We could modify the type of `vSort` then to say

```
vSort :: OrdVis t => [t] -> String
```

The situation when a class is built on top of two or more classes is called **multiple inheritance**; this has consequences for programming style, explored in Section 10.6.

SUMMARY

This section has explained the basic details of the class mechanism in Haskell. We have seen that a class definition specifies a signature, and that in defining an instance of a class we must provide definitions of each of the signature operations. These definitions over-ride any default definitions which are given in the class declaration. Contexts were seen to contain one or more constraints on the type variables which appear in polymorphic types, instance declarations and class declarations.

EXERCISES

8.5 How would you make `Bool`, pair types, `(t,u)`, and triple types, `(t,u,v)`, into `Visible` types?

8.6 Write a function to convert an integer into a `String`, and hence show how `Int` can be an instance of `Visible`.

8.7 What is the type of the function

```
compare x y = size x <= size y
```

8.8   Complete the default definitions for the class `Ord`.

8.9   Complete the following instance declarations:

```
instance (Ord u, Ord v) => Ord (u,v) where ...
instance Ord u => Ord [u] where ...
```

where the lists should be ordered lexicographically, like the words in a dictionary.

8.3   A tour of the built-in Haskell classes

Haskell contains a number of built-in classes which we briefly introduce in this section. Many of the classes are numeric, and are built to deal with overloading of the numerical operations over integers, floating point reals, complex numbers and rationals (that is integer fractions like $\frac{22}{7}$). Rather than give complete details of the numeric types, we give an exposition of their major features.

Equality and ordering

Equality was described above; to recap, we define it by

```
class Eq t where
  (==), (/=) :: t -> t -> Bool
  x /= y   =  not (x==y)
```

Similarly, we build the ordered class on `Eq`:

```
class (Eq t) => Ord t where
  (<), (<=), (>=), (>) :: t -> t -> Bool
  max, min             :: t -> t -> t

  x <  y                 = x <= y && x /= y
  x >= y                 = y <= x
  x >  y                 = y <  x

  max x y
    | x >= y     = x
    | otherwise  = y
  min x y
    | x <= y     = x
    | otherwise  = y
```

As can be seen, given a definition of <=, all the other operations of the class can be defined by default.

Many of the Haskell types belong to these classes: among the exceptions are function types, and some of the abstract data types we meet below in Chapter 12.

Enumeration

It is useful to generate lists like [2,4,6,8] using the enumeration expression

```
[2,4 .. 8]
```

but enumerations can be built over other types as well: characters, floating point numbers, and so on. The class definition is

```
class (Ord t) => Enum t where
  enumFrom          :: t -> [t]              -- [n .. ]
  enumFromThen      :: t -> t -> [t]         -- [n,m .. ]
  enumFromTo        :: t -> t -> [t]         -- [n .. m]
  enumFromThenTo    :: t -> t -> t -> [t]    -- [n,n' .. m]
```

where enumFromTo and enumFromThenTo have default definitions, which we leave as exercises for the reader.

The textual classes

In our introduction we talked about the class Visible as an example of a user-defined class. In the standard prelude we have the classes Show, which contains types whose values can be written as strings; and Read, whose values can be read from strings. The classes have in their signatures functions supporting flexible and efficient conversion to and from strings; their details are explained in Hudak and Fasel (1992). For the purposes of this text, we will use the two functions

```
show :: (Show t) => t -> String
read :: (Read t) => String -> t
```

The operation of show is straightforward and we shall use it in the rest of this text, but read requires some explanation. The result of a read may not be properly defined: there needs to be exactly one object of the required type in the input string (which may optionally also contain whitespace or nested comments); in any other case the read will fail with an error. More details of how strings are *parsed* in this way can be found in Section 13.5 below.

It is also important to see that in many cases the type of the result of the read has to be specified, since it could potentially be of any type in the class Read. For instance, we can write

```
read "   1   " :: Int
```

which indicates that in this case we require the result of the read to be an Int.

The Haskell numeric types

One of the purposes of the Haskell[1] design was to build a functional programming language which had a strong type system – in which any type errors in definitions and expressions are found before evaluation – yet which contains a rich set of numeric types, as befits a language suitable to substantial 'real-world' tasks. Among Haskell's numeric types are:

- the fixed precision integers, Int, and the full precision integers, Integer, which represent *all* integers faithfully;
- the floating point numbers, Float, and the double-precision floating point numbers, Double;
- rational numbers, that is fractions, represented as ratios of integers; built-in is the type Rational of Integer fractions;
- complex numbers, which can be built over other types such as Float.

The design also required that the usual operations, +, /, . . . and literals 23, 57.4, . . . would be overloaded. For instance, Int and Integer will carry identical operations,[2] and have identical literals, as indeed will Float and Double; a guide to the operations over integers and floats was given in Sections 2.1 and 2.8. This overloading can lead to situations where the type of an expression is undetermined; in such a case we can give an explicit type to an expression, thus:

```
(2+3)::Int
```

The Haskell report discusses a mechanism by which a default type can be given to numeric expressions.

In this text we restrict attention to Int and Float, and so we do not go into any further details of the numeric type classes. More information can be found in the Haskell report (Hudak *et al.*, 1992; Peterson *et al.*, 1996).

---

[1] This discussion applies to Haskell, not Gofer, whose numeric types are Int and Float only.
[2] Apart from (de)coding of Char.

EXERCISES

8.10 Investigate the Haskell definition of '<' on the types `Bool` and $(t_1, t_2, \ldots t_k)$.

8.11 Define a function

```
showBoolFun :: (Bool -> Bool) -> String
```

which displays a Boolean function as a table. Generalize this to

```
showBoolFunGen :: (t -> String) -> (Bool -> t) -> String
```

whose first argument is a function to show elements of `t`. This argument is used in giving a table of the results of the function.

8.4 More advanced features

This section discusses some of the more advanced aspects of type classes in Haskell and Gofer, and can be omitted on first reading.

Default definitions

If we want to *stop* a default being over-ridden, we should remove the operation from the class, and instead give its definition at the top level and not in the signature. In the case of the operation /= in `Eq` we would give the top-level definition

```
a /= b = not (a == b)
```

which has the type

```
(/=) :: Eq t => t -> t -> Bool
```

and will be effective over all types which carry the == operation.

There are some situations when it is better to give default definitions, which can be over-ridden, rather than top-level definitions, which cannot. Over the numerical types, for instance, an implementation may well supply all the operations as hardware instructions, which will be much more efficient than the default definitions.

Haskell and Gofer classes

The systems of classes differ in substantial ways. As this is an introduction, we cannot expect to give a full account of this; details can be found in Jones (1995a) and Hudak *et al.* (1992). We should however discuss how the types of vSort and vLookupFirst given in Section 8.2 need to be modified to work in Gofer. Recall the discussion there, where we stated that in defining vSort, we required that t have equality and be visible. In fact, we need a *list* of t to be visible, and so in Gofer we write

```
vSort :: (Ord t,Visible [t]) => [t] -> String
```

and similarly

```
vLookupFirst :: (Eq t,Visible [u]) =>
    [(t,u)] -> t -> String
```

Such a declaration causes an error in Haskell: a constraint can only apply to a type variable such as t rather than a type expression, like [t]. We will use the Haskell style of classes in this book.

Types and classes

The type system of Haskell can be seen as giving monomorphic types to functions. Polymorphic types, and classes can be seen as shorthand for collections of typings, such as

```
toString :: Bool -> String
toString :: Char -> String
```

and using these we can convert strings of Bool or Char to strings also, so

```
toString :: [Bool] -> String
toString :: [Char] -> String
```

and so on.

A class is a collection of types in Haskell. Other languages such as C++ make a type and a class the same thing. Under that approach, introducing the class of visible objects would effectively give us a type[3] VisibleType

```
toString :: VisibleType -> String
```

[3] In C++ teminology this would be an abstract base class, with Bool etc. inheriting and being forced to implement the operations of that class.

with `Bool` and `Char` among its sub-classes (or sub-types). This would allow us to write

```
[True,'N',False] :: [VisibleType]
```

and to convert such a list to a `String` we could write, as before,

```
map toString >.> concat
```

At different items of the list we use *different* versions of the `toString` function; on the first we use the `Bool` function, on the second the `Char` function and so forth. This so-called **dynamic binding** is a powerful feature of many object-oriented languages, including C++, but it is not a feature of Haskell; a proposed entension which would allow dynamic binding is described in Laufer (1994).

SUMMARY

This chapter has shown how names such as `read` and `show` and operators like + can be overloaded to have different definitions at different types. The mechanism which enables this is the system of Haskell classes. A `class` definition contains a signature which contains the names and types of operations which must be supplied if a type is to be a member of the class. For a particular type, the function definitions are contained in an `instance` declaration.

In giving the type of a function, or introducing a class or instance, we can supply a context, which constrains the type variables occurring. Examples include

```
member  :: Eq t => [t] -> t -> Bool
instance  Eq t => Eq [t] where ....
class     Eq t => Ord t  where ....
```

In the examples, it can be seen that `member` can only be used over types in the class `Eq`. Lists of `t` can be given an equality, provided that `t` itself can; types in the class `Ord` must already be in the class `Eq`.

After giving examples of the various mechanisms, we looked at the classes in the standard preludes of Haskell, and concluded with an overview of some more technical issues involving classes.

In the final part of the book we shall revisit classes and see how they are used to structure larger-scale systems.

Checking types

In the first part of the book, we looked at the monomorphic part of Haskell, in which the type variables t, u and so on do not appear. We begin this chapter by reviewing the type constraints of the monomorphic language, before looking at the full language itself. Central to this are explanations of **unification**, which gives the mechanism for finding the appropriate **instance** of a polymorphic type when a polymorphic function is applied, and the mechanism by which **contexts** are handled in type checking.

9.1 Monomorphic types

Here we review the type constraints present in Haskell expressions. Expressions are written on the right-hand sides of definitions and as guards, and are given to a Haskell system prompt to be evaluated. After this we look at the constraints on the various components of definitions.

Haskell expressions

Apart from some special expression syntax for tuples and lists, Haskell expressions are formed by applying functions or operators to arguments. We said at the start of this book that every function and operator was typed, and that it is only possible to apply a function to expressions of its argument type. The rule which follows expresses exactly this.

Application rule

> **IF** f has type s->t **AND** e has type s
> **THEN** f can be applied to e, and the result, f e, has type t.

The force of the rule is to say that a function can only be applied to arguments of its argument type. The rule of cancellation is given by applying this rule k times,

Cancellation rule

> **IF** f has type t_1 -> t_2 -> $\ldots$ -> t_n -> t
> **AND** e_1 has type t_1, $\ldots$, e_k has type t_k, where $k \leqslant n$,
> **THEN** f can be applied to e_1, $\ldots$, e_k
> and the result f e_1 $\ldots$ e_k
> has type t_{k+1} -> t_{k+2} -> $\ldots$ -> t_n -> t.

As a special case of the cancellation rule, we have the rules for the operators, such as addition. For instance,

Addition rule

> **IF** e_1 and e_2 both have type Int or both have type Float
> **THEN** e_1+e_2 has type Int or Float.

A similar special case gives the rules for typing operator sections, such as (*2). Also we have the rule for conditionals.

Conditional rule

> **IF** c has type Bool
> **AND** e_1 and e_2 have type s
> **THEN** if c then e_1 else e_2 has type s.

As a converse to the rule of application, we can form functions using lambda expressions.

Function rule

> **IF** x has type s and e has type t
> **THEN** \x -> e has type s -> t.

The rule for tuples states that

Tuple rule

> **IF** e_1 has type t_1, ..., e_k has type t_k
> **THEN** $(e_1, ..., e_k)$ has type $(t_1, ..., t_k)$.

In other words, the type of a tuple of elements is the tuple of their respective types. There is no restriction here on the types of the elements, while there *is* on forming lists of elements:

List rule

> **IF** $e_1, ..., e_k$ have type t
> **THEN** $[e_1, ..., e_k]$ has type [t].

The list rule says that a collection of elements can be made into a list $[e_1, ..., e_k]$ only if the elements are all of the same type, t.

Other expression-forming operators are case and let; these are type-checked in a similar way to pattern matching and local (where-bound) definitions, which are explained in the next section.

With the exception of the rule for lists like [n .. m], these are all the rules needed to express the types of Haskell expressions, and how they are type checked in the monomorphic case. There are some more rules which come from definitions in scripts, and we look at those next.

Haskell definitions

Simple definitions in Haskell associate a name with an expression, thus

```
con :: Int
con = 32+e
```

This definition is type correct if the expression on the right-hand side has the type specified.

Definitions of functions in Haskell consist of a number of conditional equations, each of which can contain multiple clauses, and have local definitions attached. The constraints which apply are

Guard rule

Each guard must be an expression of type `Bool`.

Right-hand side rule

The expressions in each clause of a conditional equation must have the same type, t say.

If the type of the function is declared, then t is given by the cancellation rule from the declared type. For instance, if f is declared to have type `Int -> Bool -> Int`, then the values in the clauses of the conditional equation beginning

```
f x True ...
```

must have type `Int`.

Pattern rule

Each pattern must not conflict with the argument type(s) of the function. For example, we can use a variable x for an argument of type `[Int]`, but we cannot use the pattern `[a:x]` over this type.

Local definitions rule

In Haskell we can give types to locally defined functions and objects. The definitions in a `where` clause must conform to the typing restrictions above, given the additional information about the local variables used in the definitions. For instance, suppose that

```
f :: Int -> Bool -> Int
f x y
    | y           = x+2
    | otherwise   = h x + 3
          where
          h p = ...
```

the variables x and y can be used in defining h, and therefore we should type check h using the information that `x::Int` and `y::Bool`.

This completes the enumeration of the rules which govern the types of parts of definitions, in the absence of type variables.

EXERCISES

9.1 Predict the type errors you would obtain by defining the following functions

```
f n     = 37+n
f True  = 34

g 0 = 37
g n = True

h x
   | x>0         = True
   | otherwise   = 37

k x = 34
k 0 = 35
```

Check your answers by typing each definition into a Haskell script.

9.2 Express the type rules for the expressions

```
[n .. m]
[n,p .. m]
```

which form lists of numbers.

9.3 Express the type rules for the operator sections of '*'.

9.2 Polymorphic types

In Section 6.2 we saw the introduction of polymorphic types, and the intuition that a polymorphic definition arises when the variables in a definition are not constrained to be of a particular monomorphic type. To explore this idea, consider the functions

```
f (a,c) = (a , ['a' .. c])
g (m,l) = m + length l
```

In the definition of f, a is unconstrained, while c must be a character, as it appears in the enumeration ['a' .. c]. In defining g, m must be a number (since it is an argument to '+') and `l` must be a list, since we take its length, which is an `Int`. There is no constraint on the type of elements of `l`. We therefore can say that `a` will have type `t`, and `l` will have type `[u]`, giving

```
f :: (t,Char) -> (t,[Char])                    (1)
g :: (Int,[u]) -> Int
```

What happens now if we make the definition

```
h   = g.f
```

or

```
h y = g (f y)                                   (2)
```

For this to typecheck using the rules given in the monomorphic setting requires the type of (`f y`)

```
(t , [Char])
```

to be equal to the input type of `g`, which is

```
(Int , [u])
```

but these are not equal! Here is the point where we should remember that the type variables can be thought of as a shorthand for `f` and `g` having a whole collection of types,

```
f :: (Bool,Char) -> (Bool,[Char])
f :: ([v],Char) -> ([v],[Char])
    ...
```

These types are all instances of a *most general* type for `f` given in (1), and they are given by *substituting* for the type variables. In the first case we substitute `Bool` for `t`, in the second `[v]` is substituted.

What we have to do to typecheck (2) is to look for *instances* of the types of `f` and `g` so that the input type of `g` is equal to the output type of `f`:

```
f :: (Int,Char) -> (Int,[Char])               (3)
g :: (Int,[Char]) -> Int
```

and so we can give `h` the type (`Int,Char`) `-> Int`.

How do we find these instances in general? We have to *unify* the types

```
(t,[Char])                    (Int,[u])
```

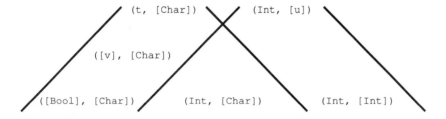

Figure 9.1 Unifying (t, [Char]) and (Int, [u]).

By this we mean that we have to find a way of substituting for the variables in the types so that we get the same result from each. In this case, we make the substitution of Int for t and Char for u to give (Int, [Char]), and this gives the types for f and g in (3). This is illustrated in Figure 9.1, where the unification is shown as finding the overlap of the two cones beneath the types.

For a function or operator application, there is an attempt to *unify* the type of the argument given (for instance Bool) with the type expected (Int, say). It will fail if two are different monomorphic types as here, and so no substitution can make them equal.

The unification in our example gives a monomorphic type, but it is possible for two types to have a polymorphic unifier, when we choose a *most general substitution* to unify the two. For instance, if we have

```
e :: (t, [t])
h :: (u, v) -> v
```

and we want to form (h e), then we have to unify (t, [t]) with (u, v). A most general unifier will replace u by t and v by [t], giving

```
e :: (t, [t])                                    (4)
h :: (t, [t]) -> [t]
```

and so (h e) :: [t]. The substitution we have given is most general because any other unification of the two can be given by substituting into (4).

Not every unification will succeed. We have seen the example of Bool and Int already, but other cases can be more subtle. First consider the example of unifying

```
[Int] -> [Int]              t -> [u]
```

We need to unify the argument and result types, simultaneously. This is achieved by substituting [Int] for the variable t, and Int for the variable u.

Now we look at

```
[Int] -> [Int]            t -> [t]
```

We can unify `[Int]` with `t`, by substituting `[Int]` for `t`; similarly, we can unify `[Int]` with `[t]`, by substituting `Int` for `t`. We *cannot* however simultaneously substitute both `Int` and `[Int]` for `t`, and so the unification will fail.

EXERCISES

9.4   Do the following pairs of types unify? If so, give a most general unifier for them; if not, explain why they fail to unify.

```
(Int -> u)        (Int,t,t)
(t -> Bool)       (t,t,[Bool])
```

9.5   Show that we can unify `(t,[t])` with `(u,v)` to give `(Bool,[Bool])`. Explain how this can be given by a substitution from (4) above.

9.6   Can the function

```
f :: (t,[t]) -> u
```

be applied to the arguments `(2,[3])`, `(2,[])` and `(2,[True])`; if so, what is the type of the result? Explain your answers.

9.7   Repeat the previous exercise for the function

```
f :: (t,[t]) -> t
```

Explain your answers.

9.8   Give the type of `f [] []` if `f` has type

```
f :: [t] -> [u] -> t -> u
```

What is the type of the function h given by the definition

```
h x = f x x ?
```

9.9   [Harder] Give an *algorithm* which decides whether two type expressions are unifiable. If they are, your algorithm should return a most general unifying substitution, if not it should give some explanation of why the unification fails.

9.10 How can you use the Haskell system to check whether two type expressions are unifiable, and if so what is their unification? Hint: you can declare to the Haskell system dummy definitions in which the defined value, `zircon` say, is equated with itself:

```
zircon = zircon
```

Values defined like this can be declared to have any type you wish.

9.3 Polymorphic type checking

While the previous section gives an informal introduction to unification, this section goes into the process of unification and type checking in a more technical way; part of it could be omitted on first reading. Here we introduce type checking in the presence of type variables; we discuss the addition of type classes in the following section.

An important example

Functions and constants can be used at different types in the same expression. A simple instance is

```
length ([]++[True,False]) + length ([]++[2,3,4])        (1)
```

The first occurrence of `[]` is at `[Bool]`, while the second is at `[Int]`. This is completely legitimate, and is one of the advantages of a polymorphic definition.

Now suppose we replace the `[]` by a variable, and define

```
funny x = length (x++[True,False]) + length (x++[2,3,4]) (2)
```

The variable x is forced to have type `[Bool]` *and* type `[Int]`; it is *forced* to be polymorphic, in other words. This is not allowed in Haskell, as there is no way of expressing the type of `funny`. It might be thought that

```
funny :: [t] -> Int
```

was the correct type, but this would mean that `funny` would have all the instance types

```
funny :: [Int] -> Int
funny :: [[Char]] -> Int
    ...
```

which it clearly does not. We conclude that constants and variables are treated differently: constants may very well appear at different incompatible types in the same expression, variables cannot.

The subsequent material, which can be omitted on first reading by skipping to the section on Haskell expressions, explains how the distinction between (1) and (2) is maintained.

Technical consequences of the example

What is the significance of disallowing definition (2) but allowing definition (1)? Taking (1) first, we have a polymorphic definition of the form

```
[] :: [t]
```

and an expression length ([]++[True,False]) + length ([]++ [2,3,4]) in which [] occurs twice; the first occurrence is at [Bool], the second at [Int]. To allow these completely independent uses to occur, we type check each occurrence of a polymorphic value with *new* type variables. In this particular instance, we type check []++[True,... with []::[u], say, and []++[2,... with []::[v].

Polymorphic use rule

> Each instance of a polymorphic definition is type checked *independently*, with a new instance of the type. That is, the variables in the type are replaced with hitherto unused type variables.

On the other hand, how is the definition of (2) disallowed? When we type check the use of a *variable* we will not treat each instance as being of an independent type. Suppose we begin with no constraint on x, so x::t, say. The first occurrence of x forces x::[Bool]. In the second, we use ++ to join lists of numbers and Booleans, which fails. In contrast, therefore, to the polymorphic use rule, we do not consider the variables to be independent, and so we implement the

Polymorphic argument rule

> The definition of a function is not permitted to *force* any of its arguments to be polymorphic. Instances of variables are therefore *not* type checked independently.

Haskell expressions

The two rules above summarize the distinction between variables and definitions. Given them, we are able to proceed with a revision of the rules of Section 9.1 for the full – polymorphic – language. The revisions involve us replacing tests for equality of types with tests for their being unifiable, which as we have seen is a more relaxed condition.

The most important rule explains what happens in application, where the type of the argument, and the argument type of the function have to be *unifiable*.

Polymorphic application rule

> **IF** f has type s->t, e has type u
> **AND** s and u can be unified, giving f :: s'->t' and e::s'
> **THEN** f can be applied to e, and the result, f e, has type t'.

The polymorphic cancellation rule is again given by applying the application rule k times. It is cumbersome to write down, but effectively each application is accompanied with a substitution to the result type, just as t is specialized to t' due to the unification of s and u in the polymorphic application rule.

The tuple rule is unchanged from Section 9.1, but the rule for lists is generalized. It is not necessary that the elements have the same type, but rather that their types are unifiable.

Polymorphic list rule

> **IF** e_1 has type t_1, . . . , e_k has type t_k
> **AND** t_1, . . . , t_k unify to type t
> **THEN** $[e_1, . . . , e_k]$ has type [t].

Haskell definitions

The type constraints from Section 9.1 carry over to the general case, except for the right-hand side rule, where an equality test is replaced by a unification.

Polymorphic right-hand side rule

> The expressions in each clause of a conditional equation must unify to some type, t say.

There is an additional rule, which explains the type of a collection of equations. First we introduce some terminology: t_1 is *at least as general as* t_2 if t_2 can be obtained by substituting for variables in t_1.

Equation-set rule

The types derived for each of a set of conditional equations should unify to a type at least as general as the type declared for the function defined by the equations. In other words, the type given to each equation must be at least as general as the type declared for the function.

Two aspects of this rule require explanation: consider the example of map. Firstly, the first equation is

```
map f [] = []
```

and from this is derived the type t -> [u] -> [v], since the only constraints are that the second argument and the result are lists. This unifies with the type given by the second equation to give the familiar type for map.

Secondly, we might have asserted

```
map :: (Int -> Bool) -> [Int] -> [Bool]
```

which is more specific than the type which unifies the equation types – hence the constraint that the unifying type is at least as general as the declared type, rather than necessarily being *equal* to the declared type.

As discussed in the monomorphic case, local definitions are checked in the same way as top-level ones. Local definitions can be polymorphic as in

```
ex1 = length (empty ++ id [True,False]) +
      length (empty ++ id [2,3,4])
      where
      empty = []
      id w  = w
```

and this makes apparent an important distinction between local definitions and variables.

EXERCISES

9.11 Explain the types of the functions defined in the where clause of

```
f x b l
 | tester l b  = appendL x ++ appendL []
 | otherwise   = appendL l
   where
   appendL x = x++l
   tester x b = b && (length l > length x)
```

9.12 Explain why the type of the standard function `foldr`

```
(t -> u -> u) -> u -> [t] -> u
```

involves two type variables rather than one. Discuss how the type of

```
foldr (&&)
```

is determined.

9.13 Give the type of

```
exam1 = ([[]],[[]])
```

and discuss how this compares with the types of

```
exam2 = (empList,empList)
        where
        empList = [[]]
```

and

```
exam3 = double [[]]
        where
        double x = (x,x)
```

9.4 Type checking and classes

Classes in Haskell restrict the use of some functions, such as `==`, to types in the class over which they are defined, in this case `Eq`. These restrictions are apparent in the *contexts* which appear in some types. For instance, if we define

```
member []     b = False
member (a:x) b = (a==b) || member x b
```

its type is

```
Eq t => [t] -> t -> Bool
```

where the context `Eq t` indicates that the type `t` must belong to the equality class `Eq`.

This section explores the way in which type checking takes place when class constraints are involved; the material is presented informally, by means of an example.

Suppose we are to apply the function `member` to an expression e, whose type is

```
Ord u => [[u]]
```

Informally, e is a list of list of objects, which belong to a type which carries an ordering. In the absence of the constraints we would unify the type expressions, giving

```
member :: [[u]] -> [u] -> Bool          e :: [[u]]
```

and so giving the application the type `[u] -> Bool`. We do the same here, but we also apply the unification to the constraints, giving

```
(Eq [u] , Ord u)                                    (1)
```

Now, we check and simplify the constraint.

- Constraints can only apply to type variables, so we need to eliminate constraints like `Eq [u]`. The only way these can be eliminated is to use the `instance` declarations. In this case the instance

  ```
  instance Eq t => Eq [t] where ....
  ```

  allows us to replace `Eq [u]` with `Eq u` in (1), giving the new context

  ```
  (Eq u , Ord u)                                    (2)
  ```

  We repeat this process until no more instances apply.
      If we fail to reduce all the type constraints to ones involving a type variable, the application fails, and an error message would be generated. This happens if we apply `member` to `[id]`; `id` is a function, and is not in a type of the class `Eq`.

- We then simplify the constraint using the `class` definitions. In our example we have both `Eq` and `Ord`, but recall that

  ```
  class Eq t => Ord t where ...
  ```

  so that any instance of `Ord` is automatically an instance of `Eq`; this means that we can simplify (2) to

  ```
  Ord u                                             (3)
  ```

  This is repeated until no further simplifications result.

For our example, we thus have the type

```
member e :: Ord u => [u] -> Bool
```

This three-stage process of unification, checking (with instances) and simplification is the general pattern for type checking with contexts in Haskell. Gofer uses a different technique which gives the context (1) for our example.

Finally, we should explain how contexts are introduced into the types of the language. They originate in types for the functions in class declarations, so that, for instance, we have

```
toString :: Visible t => t -> String
size     :: Visible t => t -> Int
```

The type checking of functions which use these overloaded functions will propagate and combine the contexts as we have seen above.

EXERCISES

9.14 Give the type of each of the individual conditional equations which follow, and discuss the type of the function which together they define.

```
merge (a:x) (b:y)
  | a<b          = a : merge x (b:y)
  | a==b         = a : merge x y
  | otherwise    = b : merge (a:x) y
merge (a:x) []     = (a:x)
merge []      (b:y) = (b:y)
merge []      []    = []
```

9.15 Define a polymorphic sorting function, and show how its type is derived from the type of the ordering relation

```
(<=) :: Ord t => t -> t -> Bool
```

SUMMARY

The chapter explains the type constraints on expressions and definitions in Haskell. Central to these is function application, where the type of an argument to a function is required to be consistent with the argument type of that function. Technically, this is expressed as the ability to *unify* the two types: we aim to find a way of specializing the two types so that they become the same. The notion of unification is explored in an intuitive way, and then some more technical details of the polymorphism of definitions and variables are examined.

After re-iterating the typing constraints for the polymorphic language, the chapter concludes with an examination of the way in which type checking is affected by the contexts generated by definitions which use functions belonging to particular classes.

Part III

Larger-scale Programming

The first part of the book introduced the main ideas of functional programming in the small. Building a bridge, the second part introduced the three abstractions of higher-order functions, polymorphism and type classes. The third part examines programming at a larger scale, and gives many examples which illustrate the ideas of Part II.

Central to this part are ideas about data representation and design – we begin by showing how user-defined concrete or **algebraic** types can model many commonly occurring forms of data. One of the ideas we have emphasized in the second part of the book is the **separation** between program parts which allows both the independent development of separate parts, and the re-use of parts of programs. A similar separation between the data implementation and use is crucial to larger-scale development, and is supported by type abstraction, given by the Haskell abstract data type mechanism.

Our account of calculation has been deliberately vague about the exact order of evaluation used: are arguments evaluated before a function is applied to them, for instance? Underpinning this approach is the fact that a change in evaluation order cannot change the results produced; all it can do is to affect whether or not a result is produced. In looking at larger-scale systems, we need to be more explicit about evaluation.

We shall see that Haskell uses **lazy evaluation** to calculate results: arguments are only evaluated if it is necessary. Indeed, evaluation of a data structure like a list will only examine the part of the list needed for the computation to continue. Lazy evaluation allows us to deal with traditional data structures in a different way: creating intermediate lists in a calculation may not be grossly inefficient, for instance. Moreover, new **infinite** data structures are possible. For example, taking the sum of the first two elements of an infinite list is quite possible, as it necessitates only that we evaluate the first two items, not the whole list. Infinite lists form a new way of structuring programs, as we can view them as **streams** or channels along which data can flow.

Most larger-scale programs interact with their environment, taking input and giving output in various forms. We show how input/output can be built on streams, and then give a **monadic** approach to I/O which allows the programmer more control of the details of the interaction. Monads provide a way of structuring many kinds of computation, and we give a brief introduction to them in concluding the discussion.

As programs become larger, the efficiency with which they can be evaluated becomes more important. We study both the time taken for programs to give results and the amount of space used during lazy evaluation of expressions.

All the ideas are backed up with examples as they are introduced and with case studies putting them and earlier ideas together to build larger systems.

10 Algebraic types

Thus far we have been able to model types of data using

- the base types, Int, Float, Bool and Char, and
- composite types: tuple types, $(t_1, t_2, \ldots, t_n)$; list types, $[t_1]$; and function types, $(t_1 \rightarrow t_2)$; where $t_1, \ldots, t_n$ are themselves types.

This gives a wide choice of types and we have seen quite complex structures, like an index for a document, represented by the appropriate combination of types: in the index example, [([Int],[Char])] was used.

However, there are other types which are difficult to model using the constructs we have seen so far. Examples include

- the type of months: January, ..., December;
- the type whose elements are either a number or a string: a house in a street will either have a number or a name, for instance;
- the type of trees, as illustrated in Figure 10.1.

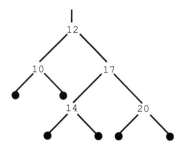

Figure 10.1 An example of a tree of integers.

All these types can be modelled by Haskell **algebraic** types, which form the subject of this chapter.

10.1 Introduction

Algebraic data type definitions begin with the keyword `data`, followed by the name of the type, an equals sign and then the **constructors** of the type being defined. The name of the type and the names of constructors begin with a capital letter.

We give a sequence of examples of increasing complexity, before discussing the general form of these type definitions.

EXAMPLE: Enumerated types ────────────────────────────

The simplest sort of algebraic type is defined by enumerating the elements of the type. For instance,

```
data Temp   = Cold | Hot
data Season = Spring | Summer | Autumn | Winter
```

introduces two types. The type `Temp` has two members, `Cold` and `Hot`, and `Season` has four members. More formally, `Cold` and `Hot` are called the **constructors** of the type `Temp`.

To define functions over these types we use pattern matching: we can match against either a constant or a variable. To describe the (British!) weather we might say

```
weather :: Season -> Temp

weather Summer = Hot
weather _      = Cold
```

Pattern matching is sequential; the first pattern to match an argument will be used. This means that the British weather is only hot in the summer, and it is cold the rest of the year. The built-in Boolean type could be defined by

```
data Bool = False | True
```

As we have seen, pattern matching is used to define functions over algebraic types. We can use it to define equality, for instance,

```
Cold == Cold  = True
Hot  == Hot   = True
_    == _     = False
```

to put Temp into the equality class Eq, but the Haskell system can be made to generate definitions of ==, ordering, enumeration and text functions automatically. We discuss the details of this at the end of this section, after looking at more examples.

EXAMPLE: Product types ──────────────────

Instead of using a tuple we can define a type with a number of components, often called a **product** type, as an algebraic type. An example might be

```
data People = Person Name Age                              (1)
```

where Name is a synonym for String, and Age for Int, written thus:

```
type Name = String
type Age  = Int
```

The definition of People should be read as saying

> To construct an element of type People, you need to supply one object, n say, of type Name, and another, a say, of type Age. The element formed from them will be Person n a.

Example values of this type include

```
Person "Electric Aunt Jemima" 77
Person "Ronnie" 14
```

As before, functions are defined using pattern matching. A general element of type `People` has the form `Person n a`, and we can use this pattern on the left-hand side of a definition,

```
showPerson :: People -> String
showPerson (Person n a) = n ++ " -- " ++ show a
```

(recall that `show` gives a printable form of an `Int`, since `Int` belongs to the `Show` class). For instance,

```
showPerson (Person "Electric Aunt Jemima" 77)
  = "Electric Aunt Jemima -- 77"
```

In this example, the type has a single constructor, `Person`, which is *binary* because it takes two elements to form a value of type `People`. For the enumerated types `Temp` and `Season` the constructors are called *nullary* (or *0-ary*) as they take no arguments.

The constructors introduced by algebraic type definitions can be used just like functions, so that `Person n a` is the result of applying the function `Person` to the arguments n and a; we can interpret (1) as giving the type of the constructor, here

```
Person :: Name -> Age -> People
```

An alternative definition of the type of people is given by the synonym

```
type People = (Name,Age)
```

The advantages of using an algebraic type are threefold.

- Each object of the type carries an explicit *label* of the purpose of the element; in this case that it represents a person.
- It is not possible accidentally to treat an arbitrary pair consisting of a string and a number as a person; a person must be constructed using the `Person` constructor.
- The type will appear in any error messages due to mis-typing; a type synonym might be expanded out and so disappear from any type error messages.

There are also advantages of using a tuple type, with a synonym declaration.

- The elements are more compact, and so definitions will be shorter.
- Using a tuple, especially a pair, allows us to re-use many polymorphic functions such as `fst`, `snd` and `zip`.

In each system that we model we will have to choose between these alternatives: our decisions will depend exactly on how we use the products, and on the complexity of the system.

The approach here works equally well with unary constructors, so we might say

```
data Age = Years Int
```

whose elements are `Years 45` and so on. It is clear from a definition like this that `45` is here being used as an age in years, rather than some unrelated numerical quantity. The disadvantage is that we cannot use functions defined over `Int` directly over `Age`.

We can use the same name, for instance `Person`, for both the type and the constructor of a type, as in

```
data Person = Person Name Age
```

We choose not to do this, as using the same name for two related but different objects can easily lead to confusion.

The examples of types given here are a special case of what we look at next.

EXAMPLE: Alternatives

A shape in a simple geometrical program is either a circle or a rectangle. These alternatives are given by the type

```
data Shape = Circle Float |
             Rectangle Float Float
```

which says that there are two ways of building an element of `Shape`. One way is to supply the radius of a `Circle`; the other alternative is to give the sides of a `Rectangle`. Example objects of this type are

```
Circle 3.0
Rectangle 45.9 87.6
```

Pattern matching allows us to define functions by cases, as in

```
isRound :: Shape -> Bool
isRound (Circle _)      = True
isRound (Rectangle _ _) = False
```

and also lets us use the components of the elements:

```
area :: Shape -> Float
area (Circle r)      = pi*r*r
area (Rectangle h w) = h*w
```

Extensions of this type, to accommodate the position of an object, are discussed in the exercises at the end of this section.

The general form

The general form of the algebraic type definitions which we have seen so far is

```
data Typename
  = Con₁ t₁₁ ... t₁ₖ₁ |
    Con₂ t₂₁ ... t₂ₖ₂ |
    ....
    Conₙ tₙ₁ ... tₙₖₙ
```

Each Con_i is a constructor, followed by k_i types, where k_i is a non-negative integer which may be zero. In the sections to come, we shall see two extensions of the definitions seen already.

- The types can be *recursive*; we can use the type we are defining, Typename, as (part of) any of the types t_{ij}. This gives us lists, trees and many other data structures.

- The Typename can be followed by one or more type variables which may be used on the right-hand side, making the definition *polymorphic*.

Recursive polymorphic types combine these two ideas, and this powerful mixture provides types which can be re-used in many different situations – the built-in type of lists is an example which we have already seen. Other examples are given in the sections which follow.

A synonym is simply a shorthand, and so a synonym type can always be expanded out (and therefore removed from the program). Synonyms cannot be recursive; and so to define new recursive types, the algebraic type mechanism has to be used.

Deriving instances of classes

As we saw earlier, Haskell has a number of built-in classes including

- Eq, a class giving equality and inequality;
- Ord, built on Eq, giving an ordering over elements of a type;
- Enum, allowing the type to be enumerated, and so giving [n .. m]-style expressions over the type;
- Show, allowing elements of the type to be turned into textual form; and
- Read, allowing items to be read from strings.

When we introduce a new algebraic type, such as Season or Shape, we might well expect to have equality, enumerations and so on. These can be supplied by the system if we ask for them, thus:

```
data Season = Spring | Summer | Autumn | Winter
                deriving (Eq,Ord,Enum,Show)

data Shape  = Circle Float |
              Rectangle Float Float
              deriving (Eq,Ord,Show)
```

We can thus compare seasons for equality and order, write expressions of the form

```
[Spring .. Autumn]
```

denoting the list

```
[Spring, Summer, Autumn]
```

and show values of the type. The same applies to Shape, except that we cannot enumerate shapes; being in Enum can only be derived for enumerated types such as Season.

We are not forced to use the derived definitions; we can give our own instances, so that, for example, all circles of negative radius are made equal. The definition of showPerson above could also form part of making People an instance of Show.

EXERCISES

10.1   Re-define the function `weather:: Season -> Temp` so that a guard is used rather than pattern matching. Which of the definitions is preferable in your opinion?

10.2   Define the type of months as a Haskell algebraic type. Give a function which takes a month to its appropriate season – in doing this you might want to use the ordering on the type, which is derived as explained above.

10.3   What would be the `weather` function for New Zealand, which is on a similar latitude to Britain, but in the Southern Hemisphere? What would be the definition for Brazil, which is crossed by the Equator?

10.4   Define a function to give the length of the perimeter of a geometrical shape, of type `Shape`.

10.5   Add an extra constructor to `Shape` for triangles, and extend the functions `isRound`, `area` and `perimeter` to include triangles.

10.6   Define a function which decides whether a shape is regular: a circle is regular, a square is a regular rectangle, and being equilateral makes a triangle regular.

10.7   Investigate the derived definitions for `Temp` and `Shape`: what form do the orderings and the `show` functions take, for example?

10.8   Define `==` over `Shape` so that all circles of negative radius are equated; how would you treat rectangles with negative sides?

10.9   The type `Shape` takes no account of the position or orientation of a shape. After deciding how to represent points, how would you modify the original definition of `Shape` to contain the centre of each object? You can assume that rectangles lie with their sides parallel to the axes, thus:

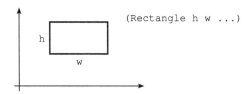

10.10 Calling the new shape type `NewShape`, define a function

```
move :: Float -> Float -> NewShape -> NewShape
```

which moves a shape by the two offsets given:

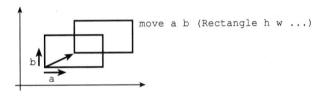

10.11 Define a function to test whether two NewShapes overlap.

10.12 Some houses have a number; others have a name. How would you implement the type of 'strings or numbers' used as a part of an address? Write a function which prints one of these objects. Give a definition of a type of names and addresses using the type you have defined.

10.13 Re-implement the library database of Section 4.5 to use an algebraic type like People rather than a pair. Compare the two approaches to this example.

10.14 [Project] The library database of Section 4.5 is to be extended in the following ways.

- CDs and videos as well as books are available for loan.
- A record is kept of the authors of books as well as their titles. Similar information is kept about CDs, but not about videos.
- Each loan has a period: books one month, CDs one week and videos three days.

Explain how you would modify the types used to implement the database, and how the function types might be changed. The system should perform the following operations. For each case, give the types and definitions of the functions involved.

- Find all items on loan to a given person.
- Find all books, CDs or videos on loan to a particular person.
- Find all items in the database due back on or before a particular day, and the same information for any given person.
- Update the database with loans; the constant today can be assumed to contain today's date, in a format of your choice.

What other functions would have to be defined to make the system usable? Give their types, but not their definitions.

10.2 Recursive types

Types are often naturally described in terms of themselves. For instance, an integer expression is either a *literal* integer, or is given by combining two expressions using an arithmetic operator such as plus or minus

```
data Expr = Lit Int |
            Add Expr Expr |
            Sub Expr Expr
```

Similarly, a tree is either nil or is given by combining a value and two sub-trees. For example, the number 12 and the trees in Figure 10.2 are assembled to give the tree in Figure 10.1. As a Haskell type we say

```
data NTree = NilT |
             Node Int NTree NTree
```

Finally, we have already used the type of lists: a list is either empty ([]) or is built from a head and a tail – another list – using the list constructor ':'. Lists will provide a good guide to using recursive (and polymorphic) definitions. In particular they suggest how polymorphic higher-order functions over other algebraic types are defined, and how programs are verified. We now look at some examples in more detail.

Expressions

The type Expr gives a model of the simple numerical expressions discussed above. These might be used in implementing a simple numerical calculator, for instance.

```
data Expr = Lit Int |
            Add Expr Expr |
            Sub Expr Expr
```

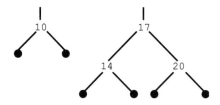

Figure 10.2 Two trees.

Some examples are

```
2              Lit 2
2+3            Add (Lit 2) (Lit 3)
(3-1)+3        Add (Sub (Lit 3) (Lit 1)) (Lit 3)
```

where the informal expressions are listed in the left-hand column, and their Expr forms in the right. Given an expression, we might want to

- evaluate it;
- print it;
- estimate its size – count the operators, say.

Each of these functions will be defined in the same way, using *primitive recursion*. As the type is itself recursive, it is not a surprise that the functions which handle the type will also be recursive. Also, the form of the recursive definitions follows the recursion in the type definition. For instance, to evaluate an operator expression we work out the values of the arguments and combine the results using the operator.

```
eval :: Expr -> Int

eval (Lit n)     = n
eval (Add e1 e2) = (eval e1) + (eval e2)
eval (Sub e1 e2) = (eval e1) - (eval e2)
```

Primitive recursive definitions have two parts:

- At the non-recursive, *base* cases – (Lit n) here – the value is given outright.
- At the recursive cases, the values of the function at the sub-expressions, eval e1 and eval e2 here, can be used in calculating the result.

The printing function has a similar form

```
showExpr :: Expr -> String

showExpr (Lit n) = show n
showExpr (Add e1 e2)
   = "(" ++ showExpr e1 ++ "+" ++ showExpr e2 ++ ")"
showExpr (Sub e1 e2)
   = "(" ++ showExpr e1 ++ "-" ++ showExpr e2 ++ ")"
```

as does the function to calculate the number of operators in an expression; we leave this as an exercise. Other exercises at the end of the section look at a different representation of expressions for which a separate type is used to represent the different possible operators. Next, we look at another recursive algebraic type, but after that we return to `Expr` and give an example of a non-primitive recursive definition of a function to re-arrange expressions in a particular way.

EXAMPLE: Trees of integers ────────────────────────────────────

Trees of integers like that in Figure 10.1 can be modelled by the type

```
data NTree = NilT |
              Node Int NTree NTree
```

The null tree is given by `NilT`, and the trees in Figure 10.2 by

```
Node 10 NilT NilT
Node 17 (Node 14 NilT NilT) (Node 20 NilT NilT)
```

Definitions of many functions are primitive recursive. For instance,

```
sumTree,depth :: NTree -> Int

sumTree NilT          = 0
sumTree (Node n t1 t2) = n + sumTree t1 + sumTree t2

depth NilT            = 0
depth (Node n t1 t2)  = 1 + max (depth t1) (depth t2)
```

with, for example,

```
sumTree (Node 3 (Node 4 NilT NilT) NilT) = 7
depth   (Node 3 (Node 4 NilT NilT) NilT) = 2
```

As another example, take the problem of finding out how many times a number, p say, occurs in a tree. The primitive recursion suggests two cases, depending upon the tree.

- For a null tree, `NilT`, the answer must be zero.
- For a non-null tree, `(Node n t1 t2)`, we can find out how many times p occurs in the sub trees `t1` and `t2` by two recursive calls; we have to make a case split depending whether p occurs at the particular node, that is depending on whether or not p==n.

The final definition is

```
occurs :: NTree -> Int -> Int

occurs NilT p = 0
occurs (Node n t1 t2) p
   | n==p        = 1 + occurs t1 p + occurs t2 p
   | otherwise   =     occurs t1 p + occurs t2 p
```

The exercises at the end of the section given a number of other examples of functions defined over trees using primitive recursion. We next look at a particular example where a different form of recursion is used.

EXAMPLE: Rearranging expressions

The next example shows a definition which uses a more general recursion than we have seen so far. After showing why the generality is necessary, we argue that the function we have defined is total: it will give a result on all well-defined expressions.

The operation of addition is associative, so that the way in which an expression is bracketed is irrelevant to its value. We can, therefore, decide to bracket expressions involving '+' in any way we choose. The aim here is to write a program to turn expressions into right-bracketed form, as shown in the following table

```
(2+3)+4                   2+(3+4)
((2+3)+4)+5               2+(3+(4+5))
((2-((6+7)+8))+4)+5       (2-(6+(7+8)))+(4+5)
```

What is the program to do? The main aim is to spot occurrences of

```
Add (Add e1 e2) e3
```
(1)

and to transform them to

```
Add e1 (Add e2 e3)
```
(2)

so a first attempt at the program might say

```
try (Add (Add e1 e2) e3)
  = Add (try e1) (Add (try e2) (try e3))
try ...
```

which is primitive recursive: on the right-hand side of their definition the function `try` is only used on sub-expressions of the argument. This function will have the effect of transforming (1) to (2), but unfortunately (3) will be sent to (4):

$$((2+3)+4)+5) \tag{3}$$
$$(2+3)+(4+5) \tag{4}$$

The problem is that in transforming (1) to (2) we may produce another pattern we are looking for at the top level: this is precisely what happens with (3) going to (4). We therefore have to call the function *again* on the result of the re-arrangement

```
assoc :: Expr -> Expr
```

```
assoc (Add (Add e1 e2) e3)
  = assoc (Add e1 (Add e2 e3))                    (5)
```

The other cases in the definition make sure that the *parts* of an expression are re-arranged as they should be.

```
assoc (Add e1 e2)
  = Add (assoc e1) (assoc e2)                      (6)
assoc (Sub e1 e2)
  = Sub (assoc e1) (assoc e2)
assoc (Lit n)
  = Lit n
```

The equation (6) will only be applied to the cases where (5) does not apply – this is when e1 is either a `Sub` or a `Lit` expression. This is always the case in pattern matching; the *first* applicable equation is used.

When we use primitive recursion we can be sure that the recursion will **terminate** to give an answer: the recursive calls are only made on smaller expressions, and so after a finite number of calls to the function, a base case will be reached.

The `assoc` function is more complicated, and we need a more subtle argument to see that the function will always give a result. The equation (5) is the tricky one, but intuitively, we can see that some progress has been made – some of the 'weight' of the tree has moved from left to right. In particular, one addition symbol has swapped sides. None of the other equations moves a plus in the other direction, so that after applying (5) a finite number of times, there will be no more exposed addition symbols at the top level of the left-hand side. This means that the recursion cannot go on indefinitely, and so the function always leads to a result.

Syntax: infix constructors

We have seen that functions can be written in infix form; this also applies to constructors. We can, for example, re-define the function `assoc` thus:

```
assoc ((e1 'Add' e2) 'Add' e3)
   = assoc (e1 'Add' (e2 'Add' e3))
   ...
```

using the infix form of the constructor, given by surrounding it with back-quotes. When an expression like this is printed, it appears in prefix form, so `(Lit 3) 'Add' (Lit 4)` appears as

```
Add (Lit 3) (Lit 4)
```

We can, however, make operators constructors. These have the same syntax as operator symbols, except that their first character must be a ':', which is reminiscent of ':', itself an infix constructor. For our type of integer expressions, we might define

```
data Expr = Lit Int |
            Expr :+: Expr |
            Expr :-: Expr
```

When an expression involving operator constructors is printed, the constructors appear in the infix position, unlike the quoted constructors above.

It is left as an exercise to complete the re-definition of functions over `Expr`.

Mutual recursion

In describing one type, it is often useful to use others; these in turn may refer back to the original type: this gives a pair of **mutually recursive** types. A description of a person might include biographical details, which in turn might refer to other people. For instance:

```
data Person = Adult Name Address Biog |
              Child Name
data Biog   = Parent String [Person] |
              NonParent String
```

In the case of a parent, the biography contains some text, as well as a list of their children, as elements of the type `Person`.

Suppose we want to define a function which prints a person's information, as a string. Printing this information will require us to print the biographical information, which itself contains information about a person. We have two mutually recursive functions:

```
showPerson (Adult nm ad bio)
  = showName nm ++ showAddress ad ++ showBiog bio
  ...
showBiog (Parent st perList)
  = st ++ concat (map showPerson perList)
  ...
```

EXERCISES

10.15 Give calculations of

```
eval (Lit 67)
eval (Add (Sub (Lit 3) (Lit 1)) (Lit 3))
showExpr (Add (Lit 67) (Lit (-34)))
```

10.16 Define the function

```
size :: Expr -> Int
```

which counts the number of operators in the expression.

10.17 Add the operations of multiplication and integer division to the type Expr, and re-define the functions eval, showExpr and size to include these new cases. What does your definition of eval do when asked to perform a division by zero?

10.18 Instead of adding extra constructors to the Expr type, as in the previous question, it is possible to factor the definition thus:

```
data Expr = Lit Int |
            Op Ops Expr Expr

data Ops  = Add | Sub | Mul | Div
```

Show how the functions eval, showExpr and size are defined for this type, and discuss the changes you have to make to your definitions if you add the extra operation Mod for remainder on integer division.

10.19 Give calculations of

```
sumTree (Node 3 (Node 4 NilT NilT) NilT)
depth    (Node 3 (Node 4 NilT NilT) NilT)
```

10.20 Complete the re-definition of functions over `Expr` after it has been defined using the infix constructors `:+:` and `:-:`.

10.21 Define functions to return the left- and right-hand sub-trees of an `NTree`.

10.22 Define a function to decide whether a number is an element of an `NTree`.

10.23 Define functions to find the maximum and minimum values held in an `NTree`.

10.24 A tree is reflected by swapping left and right sub-trees, recursively. Define a function to reflect an `NTree`.

10.25 Define functions

```
collapse, sort :: NTree -> [Int]
```

which turn a tree into a list. The function `collapse` should enumerate the left sub-tree, then the value at the node and finally the right sub-tree; `sort` should sort the elements in ascending order. For instance,

```
collapse (Node 3 (Node 4 NilT NilT) NilT) = [4,3]
sort     (Node 3 (Node 4 NilT NilT) NilT) = [3,4]
```

10.26 Complete the definitions of `showPerson` and `showBiog` which were left incomplete in the text.

10.27 It is possible to extend the type `Expr` so that it contains *conditional* expressions, `If b e1 e2`, where e1 and e2 are expressions, and b is a Boolean expression, a member of the type `BExp`.

```
data Expr = Lit Int |
            Op Ops Expr Expr |
            If BExp Expr Expr
```

The expression

```
If b e1 e2
```

has the value of e1 if b has the value `True` and otherwise it has the value of e2.

```
data BExp = BoolLit Bool |
            And BExp BExp |
            Not BExp |
            Equal Expr Expr |
            Greater Expr Expr
```

The five clauses here give

- Boolean literals, `BoolLit True` and `BoolLit False`.
- The conjunction of two expressions; it is `True` if both halves have the value `True`.
- The negation of an expression. `Not be` has value `True` if `be` has the value `False`.
- `Equal e1 e2` is `True` when the two numerical expressions have equal values.
- `Greater e1 e2` is `True` when the numerical expression `e1` has a larger value then `e2`.

Define the functions

```
eval  :: Expr -> Int
bEval :: BExpr -> Bool
```

by mutual recursion, and extend the function `showExpr` to print the redefined type of expressions.

10.3 Polymorphic algebraic types

Algebraic type definitions can contain the type variables t, u and so on, defining polymorphic types. The definitions are as before, with the type variables used in the definition appearing after the type name on the left-hand side of the definition. A simple example is

```
data Pairs t = Pair t t
```

and example elements of the type are

```
Pair 2 3    :: Pairs Int
Pair [] [3] :: Pairs [Int]
Pair [] []  :: Pairs [t]
```

A function to test the equality of the two halves of a pair is given by

```
equalPair :: Eq t => Pairs t -> Bool
equalPair (Pair x y) = (x==y)
```

The remainder of this section explores a sequence of further examples.

EXAMPLE: Lists

The built-in type of lists can be given by a definition like

```
data List t = NilList | Cons t (List t)
                deriving (Eq,Ord,Show)
```

where the syntax [t], [] and ':' is used for List t, NilList and 'Cons'. Because of this, the type of lists forms a useful paradigm for recursive polymorphic types. In particular, we can see the possibility of defining useful families of functions over such types, and the way in which program verification can proceed by induction over the structure of a type.

EXAMPLE: Binary trees

The trees of Section 10.2 carry numbers at each node; there is nothing special about numbers, and we can equally well say that they have elements of an arbitrary type at the nodes:

```
data Tree t = Nil | Node t (Tree t) (Tree t)
                deriving (Eq,Ord,Show)
```

The definitions of depth and occurs carry over unchanged:

```
depth :: Tree t -> Int
depth Nil            = 0
depth (Node n t1 t2) = 1 + max (depth t1) (depth t2)
```

as do many of the functions defined in the exercises at the end of Section 10.2. One of these is the function collapsing a tree into a list. This is done by visiting the elements of the tree 'inorder', that is visiting first the left sub-tree, then the node itself, then the right sub-tree, thus:

```
collapse :: Tree t -> [t]
collapse Nil = []
collapse (Node x t1 t2)
   = collapse t1 ++ [x] ++ collapse t2
```

For example,

```
collapse (Node 12
                (Node 34 Nil Nil)
                (Node 3 (Node 17 Nil Nil) Nil))
   = [34,12,17,3]
```

Various higher-order functions are definable, also,

```
mapTree :: (t -> u) -> Tree t -> Tree u
mapTree f Nil = Nil
mapTree f (Node x t1 t2)
  = Node (f x) (mapTree f t1) (mapTree f t2)
```

We shall return to trees in Section 12.8, where particular 'search' trees form a case study.

EXAMPLE: Union type

Type definitions can take more than one parameter. We saw earlier the example of the type whose elements were either a name or a number. In general we can form a type whose elements come either from t or from u:

```
data Union t u = One t | Two u
```

Members of the union type are either (One a), with a::t, or (Two b) with b::u. The 'name or number' type is given by Union String Int and

```
One "Duke of Prunes" :: Union String Int
Two 33312            :: Union String Int
```

We can tell whether an element is in the first half of the union by

```
isOne :: Union t u -> Bool
isOne (One _) = True
isOne (Two _) = False
```

To define a function from Union t u to Int, say, we have to deal with two cases,

```
fun :: Union t u -> Int
fun (One x) = ... x ...
fun (Two y) = ... y ...
```

In the first case, the right-hand side takes x to an Int, so is given by a function from t to Int; in the second case y is taken to an Int, thus being given by a function from u to Int.

Guided by this, we can give a higher-order function which *joins together* two functions defined on t and u to a function on Union t u. The definition follows, and is illustrated in Figure 10.3

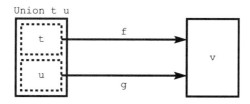

Figure 10.3 Joining together functions.

```
joinFuns :: (t -> v) -> (u -> v) -> Union t u -> v

joinFuns f g (One x) = f x
joinFuns f g (Two y) = g y
```

If we have a function f::t -> v and we wish to apply it to an element of type Union t u, there is a problem: what do we do if the element is in the second half of the union? A simple answer is to raise an error

```
applyOne :: (t -> v) -> Union t u -> v
applyOne f (One x) = f x
applyOne f (Two _) = error "applyOne applied to Two!"
```

but in the next section we shall explore other ways of handling errors in more detail.

EXERCISES

10.28 Investigate which of the functions over trees discussed in the exercises of Section 10.2 can be made polymorphic.

10.29 Define a function twist which swaps the order of a union

```
twist :: Union t u -> Union u t
```

What is the effect of (twist.twist)?

10.30 Show that any function of type t -> u can be transformed into functions of type

```
t -> Union u v
t -> Union v u
```

10.31 How could you generalize joinFuns to jFuns so that it has type

```
jFuns :: (t -> v) -> (u -> w) -> Union t u -> Union v w
```

You might find the answer to the previous exercise useful here, if you want to define jFuns using joinFuns.

The trees defined in the text are *binary*: each non-nil tree has exactly two sub-trees. We can instead define general trees with an arbitrary list of sub-trees, thus:

```
data GTree t = Leaf t | Gnode [GTree t]
```

The exercises which follow concern these trees.

10.32 Define functions

- to count the number of leaves in a GTree;
- to find the depth of a GTree;
- to sum a numeric GTree Int;
- to find whether an element appears in a GTree;
- to map a function over the elements at the leaves of a GTree; and
- to flatten a GTree to a list.

10.33 How is the completely empty tree represented as a GTree?

10.4 Case study: program errors

How should a program deal with a situation which ought not to occur? Examples of such situations include

- attempts to divide by zero, to take the square root of a negative number, and other arithmetical transgressions;
- attempts to take the head of an empty list – this is a special case of a definition over an algebraic type from which one case (here the empty list) is absent.

This section examines the problem, giving three approaches of increasing sophistication. The simplest method is to stop computation, and to report the source of the problem. This is indeed what the Haskell system does in the cases listed above, and we can do this in functions we define ourselves using the error function

```
error :: String -> t
```

An attempt to evaluate

```
error "Circle with negative radius"
```

results in the message "Circle with negative radius" being printed after computation stops.

The problem with this approach is that all the useful information in the computation is lost; instead of this, the error can be dealt with in some way *without* stopping computation completely. Two approaches suggest themselves, and we look at them in turn now.

Dummy values

The function tail is supposed to give the tail of a list, and it gives an error message on an empty list:

```
tail :: [t] -> [t]
tail (a:x) = x
tail []    = error "tail of []"
```

We could re-define it to say

```
tl :: [t] -> [t]
tl (a:x) = x
tl []    = []
```

Now, an attempt to take the tail of *any* list will succeed. In a similar way we could say

```
divide :: Int -> Int -> Int
divide n m
  | (m /= 0)   = n 'div' m
  | otherwise  = 0
```

so that division by zero gives some answer. For tl and divide there have been obvious choices about what the value in the 'error' case should be; for head there is not, and instead we can supply an extra parameter to head, which is to be used in the case of the list being empty.

```
hd :: t -> [t] -> t
hd b (a:x) = a
hd b []    = b
```

This approach is completely general; if a function f (of one argument, say) usually raises an error when cond is True, we can define a new function

```
fErr b x
  | cond       = b
  | otherwise  = f x
```

This approach works well in many cases; the only drawback is that we have no way of telling when an error has occurred, since we may get the result b from either the error or the 'normal' case. Alternatively we can use an error type to trap and process errors.

Error types

The previous approach works by returning a dummy value when an error has occurred. Why not instead return an error *value* as a result? We define the type

```
data Err t = OK t | Error
```

which is effectively the type t with an extra value Error added. We can now define a division function errDiv thus

```
errDiv :: Int -> Int -> Err Int
errDiv n m
  | (m /= 0)    = OK (n 'div' m)
  | otherwise   = Error
```

and in the general case, where f gives an error when cond holds,

```
fErr x
  | cond        = Error
  | otherwise   = OK (f x)
```

The results of these functions are now not of the original output type, t say, but of type Err t. These Err types allow us to *raise* an error, potentially. We can do two things with a potential error which has been raised

- we can *transmit* the error through a function;
- we can *trap* an error.

The function lift transmits an error value though the application of the function g; g expects an argument of type t, it can be applied to the OK elements, while Error is the result when Error is the argument.

```
lift :: (t -> u) -> Err t -> Err u
lift g Error  = Error
lift g (OK x) = OK (g x)
```

In trapping an error, we aim to return a result of type u, from an input of type Err t; we have two cases to deal with (Figure 10.4)

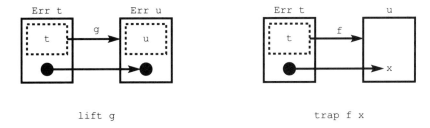

Figure 10.4   Error handling functions.

- in the OK case, we apply a function from t to u;
- in the Error case, we have to give the value of type u which is to be returned. (This is rather like the value we supplied to head earlier.)

The higher-order function which achieves this is trap, whose arguments f and x are used in the OK and Error cases, respectively.

```
trap::(t -> u) -> u -> Err t -> u

trap f x (OK a) = f a
trap f x Error  = x
```

We can see the functions lift and trap in action in the examples which follow. In the first, a division by zero leads to an Error which passes through the lifting to be trapped – 56 is therefore returned:

```
  trap (1+) 56 (lift (*3) (errDiv 9 0))
= trap (1+) 56 (lift (*3) Error)
= trap (1+) 56 Error
= 56
```

In the second, a normal division returns an OK 9. This is multiplied by three, and the trap at the outer level adds one and removes the OK:

```
  trap (1+) 56 (lift (*3) (errDiv 9 1))
= trap (1+) 56 (lift (*3) (OK 9))
= trap (1+) 56 (OK 27)
= 1 + 27
= 28
```

The advantage of the approach discussed here is that we can first define the system without error handling, and afterwards add the error handling, using the lift and trap functions together with the modified functions to *raise* the error. As we have seen numerous times already, separating a problem into two parts has made the solution of each, and therefore the whole, more accessible.

We re-visit the `Err` type in Section 14.3 where we see that it it is an example of a more general programming structure: the monad.

EXERCISES

10.34 Using the functions `lift` and `trap`, or otherwise, define a function

```
process :: [Int] -> Int -> Int -> Int
```

so that `process l n m` takes the nth and mth items of the list of numbers l, and returns their sum. Your function should return 0 if either of the numbers is not one of the indices of the list: for a list of length p, the indices are 0,...,p-1 inclusive.

10.35 Discuss the advantages and disadvantages of the three approaches to error handling discussed here.

10.36 What are the values of type `Err (Err t)`? Define a function

```
squash :: Err (Err t) -> Err t
```

which will 'squash' `OK (OK a)` to `OK a` and all other values to `Error`.

10.37 In a similar way to `lift`, define the function

```
composeErr :: (t -> Err u) ->
              (u -> Err w) ->
              (t -> Err w)
```

which composes two error-raising functions. How could you use `lift`, the function composition operator and the `squash` function to define `composeErr`?

10.38 The error type could be generalized to allow messages to be carried in the `Error` part, thus:

```
data Err t = OK t | Error String
```

How do the definitions of `lift`, `trap` and `composeErr` have to be modified to accommodate this new definition?

10.5 Design with algebraic data types

Algebraic data types provide us with a powerful mechanism for modelling types which occur both in problems themselves, and within the programs designed to solve them. In this section we suggest a three-stage method for finding the appropriate algebraic type definitions. We apply it in two examples: finding the 'edit distance' between two words and a simulation problem.

An important moral of the discussion here is that we can start to design data types *independently* of the program itself. For a system of any size, we should do this, as we will be more likely to succeed if we can think about separate parts of the system separately.

We shall have more to say about design of data types in the next chapter.

Edit distance

In discussing the stages of design, we follow the example of finding the **edit distance** between two strings. This is the shortest sequence of simple editing operations which can take us from one string to the other.

The example is a version of a practical problem: in keeping a display (of windows or simple text) up-to-date, the speed with which updates can be done is crucial. It is therefore desirable to be able to make the updates from as few elementary operations as possible; this is what the edit distance program achieves.

We suppose that there are five basic editing operations on a string. We can change one character into another, copy a character without modifying it, delete or insert a character and delete (kill) to the end of the string. We also assume that each operation has the same cost, except a copy which is free.

To turn the string "fish" into "chips", we could kill the whole string, then insert the characters one-by-one, at a total cost of six. An optimal solution will copy as much of the string as possible, and is given by

- inserting the character 'c',
- changing 'f' to 'h',
- copying 'i',
- inserting 'p',
- copying 's', and finally
- deleting the remainder of the string, "h".

In the remainder of this section we design a type to represent the editing steps, and after looking at another example of data type design, define a function to give an optimal sequence of editing steps from one string to another.

The analysis here can also be used to describe the difference between two lists of arbitrary type. If each item is a line of a file, the behaviour of the function is similar to the Unix `diff` utility.

Design stages

Now we look at the three stages of algebraic type definition in detail.

- First we have to identify the *types* of data involved. In the example, we have to define

  ```
  data Edit = ...
  ```

  which represents the editing operations.

- Next, we have to identify the different sorts of data in each of the types. Each sort of data is given by a *constructor*. In the example, we can change, copy, delete or insert a character and delete (kill) to the end of the string. Our type definition is therefore

  ```
  data Edit = Change ... |
              Copy ... |
              Delete ... |
              Insert ... |
              Kill ...
  ```

  The '...' show that we have not yet said anything about the types of the constructors.

- Finally, for each of the constructors, we need to decide what its *components* or arguments are. Some of the constructors – `Copy`, `Delete` and `Kill` – require no information; the others need to indicate the new character to be inserted, so

  ```
  data Edit = Change Char |
              Copy |
              Delete |
              Insert Char |
              Kill
              deriving (Eq, Show)
  ```

  This completes the definition.

We now illustrate how other type definitions work in a similar way.

EXAMPLE: Simulation ──────────────────────────────────

Suppose we want to model, or *simulate*, how the queues in a bank or post office behave; perhaps we want to decide how many bank clerks need to be working at particular times of the day. Our system will take as input the arrivals of customers, and give as output their departures. Each of these can be modelled using a type.

- Inmess is the type of input messages. At a given time, there are two possibilities:

  - No-one arrives, represented by the 0-ary constructor No.
  - Someone arrives, represented by the constructor Yes. This will have components giving the arrival time of the customer, and the amount of time that will be needed to serve them.

  Hence we have

  ```
  data Inmess = No | Yes Arrival Service

  type Arrival = Int
  type Service = Int
  ```

- Similarly, we have Outmess, the type of output messages. Either no-one leaves (None), or a person is discharged (Discharge). The relevant information they carry is the time they have waited, together with when they arrived and their service time. We therefore define

  ```
  data Outmess = None | Discharge Arrival Wait Service

  type Wait = Int
  ```

We return to the simulation example in Chapter 12.

Edit distance

The problem is to find the lowest-cost sequence of edits to take us from one string to another. We can begin the definition thus:

```
transform :: String -> String -> [Edit]

transform [] [] = []
```

To transform the non-empty string st to [], we simply have to Kill it, while to transform [] to st, we have to Insert each of the characters in turn:

```
transform st [] = [Kill]
transform [] st = map Insert st
```

In the general case, we have a choice: should we first use Copy, Delete, Insert or Change? If the first characters of the strings are equal we should copy; but if not, there is no obvious choice. We therefore try *all* possibilities and choose the best of them:

```
transform (a:x) (b:y)
  | a==b        = Copy : transform x y
  | otherwise   = best [ Delete    : transform x (b:y) ,
                         Insert b : transform (a:x) y ,
                         Change b : transform x y ]
```

How do we choose the best sequence? We choose the one with the lowest cost.

```
best :: [[Edit]] -> [Edit]
best [a]    = a
best (a:x)
  | cost a <= cost b    = a
  | otherwise           = b
    where
    b = best x
```

The cost is given by charging one for every operation except copy, which is equivalent to 'leave unchanged'.

```
cost :: [Edit] -> Int
cost = length . filter (/=Copy)
```

EXERCISES

The first four questions are designed to make you think about how data types are designed. *There are no right answers for them*, rather you should satisfy yourself that you have represented adequately the types you have in your informal picture of the problem.

10.39 It is decided to keep a record of vehicles which will use a particular car park. Design an algebraic data type to represent them.

10.40 If you knew that the records of vehicles were to be used for comparative tests of fuel efficiency, how would you modify your answer to the last exercise?

10.41 Discuss the data types you might use in a database of students' marks for classes and the like. Explain the design of any algebraic data types that you use.

10.42 What data types might be used to represent the objects which can be drawn using an interactive drawing program? To give yourself more of a challenge, you might like to think about grouping of objects, multiple copies of objects, and scaling.

10.43 How would you modify the edit distance program to accommodate a `Swap` operation, which can be used to transform `"abxyz"` to `"baxyz"` in a single step?

10.44 Write a definition which when given a list of edits and a string `st`, returns the sequence of strings given by applying the edits to `st` in sequence.

10.45 Give a calculation of `transform "cat" "am"`. What do you conclude about the efficiency of the `transform` function?

10.6 Algebraic types and type classes

We have reached a point where it is possible to explore rather more substantial examples of type classes.

Movable objects

We start by building a class of types whose members are geometrical objects in two dimensions. The operations of the class are those to move the objects in various different ways.

We now work through the definitions, which are illustrated in Figure 10.5. Some moves will be dictated by vectors, so we first define

```
data Vector = Vec Float Float
```

The class definition itself is

```
class Movable t where
  move     :: Vector -> t -> t
  reflectX :: t -> t
  reflectY :: t -> t
  rotate180 :: t -> t
  rotate180 = reflectX . reflectY
```

```
data Vector = Vec Float Float

class Movable t where
  move     :: Vector -> t -> t
  reflectX :: t -> t
  reflectY :: t -> t
  rotate180 :: t -> t
  rotate180 = reflectX . reflectY

data Point = Pt Float Float
            deriving Show

instance Movable Point where
  move (Vec v1 v2) (Pt c1 c2) = Pt (c1+v1) (c2+v2)
  reflectX (Pt c1 c2)  = Pt c1 (-c2)
  reflectY (Pt c1 c2)  = Pt (-c1) c2
  rotate180 (Pt c1 c2) = Pt (-c1) (-c2)

data Figure = Line Point Point |
              Circle Point Float
              deriving Show

instance Movable Figure where
  move v (Line p1 p2) = Line (move v p1) (move v p2)
  move v (Circle p r) = Circle (move v p) r

  reflectX (Line p1 p2) = Line (reflectX p1) (reflectX p2)
  reflectX (Circle p r) = Circle (reflectX p) r

  reflectY (Line p1 p2) = Line (reflectY p1) (reflectY p2)
  reflectY (Circle p r) = Circle (reflectY p) r

instance Movable t => Movable [t] where
  move v   = map (move v)
  reflectX = map reflectX
  reflectY = map reflectY
```

Figure 10.5 Movable objects.

and it shows the ways in which an object can be moved. First it can be moved
by a vector, as in

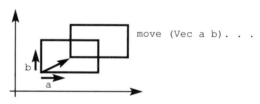

We can also reflect an object in the X-axis (the horizontal axis) or the Y-axis (the vertical), or rotate a figure through 180° around the origin (the point where the axes meet). The default definition of `rotate180` works by reflecting first in the Y-axis and then the X.

We can now define a hierarchy of movable objects; first we have the `Point`,

```
data Point = Pt Float Float
                deriving Show
```

which is moved thus:

```
move (Vec v1 v2) (Pt c1 c2) = Pt (c1+v1) (c2+v2)
```

Here we can see that the move is achieved by adding the components `v1` and `v2` to the coordinates of the point. Reflection is given by changing the sign of one of the coordinates

```
reflectX (Pt c1 c2) = Pt c1 (-c2)
reflectY (Pt c1 c2) = Pt (-c1) c2
```

For this instance we override the default definition of `rotate180` by changing the sign of both coordinates. This is a more efficient way of achieving the same transformation as the default.

```
rotate180 (Pt c1 c2) = Pt (-c1) (-c2)
```

Using the type of points we can build figures:

```
data Figure = Line Point Point |
                Circle Point Float
```

and in the instance declaration for `Figure` we use the corresponding operations on `Point`; for example,

```
move v (Line p1 p2) = Line (move v p1) (move v p2)
move v (Circle p r) = Circle (move v p) r
```

This same approach works again when we consider a list of movable objects:

```
instance Movable t => Movable [t] where
  move v   = map (move v)
  reflectX = map reflectX
```

and so on. Using overloading in this way has a number of advantages.

- The code is much easier to read: at each point we write move, rather than movePoint, and so on.

- We can re-use definitions; the instance declaration for Movable [t] makes lists of any sort of movable object movable themselves. This includes lists of points and lists of figures. Without overloading we would not be able to achieve this.

Named objects

Many forms of data contain some sort of name, a String which identifies the object in question. What do we expect to be able to do with a value of such a type?

- We should be able to identify the name of a value, and
- we ought to be able to give a new name to a value.

These operations are embodied in the Named class:

```
class Named t where
  lookName :: t -> String
  giveName :: String -> t -> t
```

and an example of Named types is given by

```
data Name t = Pair t String
```

the one-constructor type whose two components are of type t and String. The instance declaration for this type is

```
instance Named (Name t) where                           (1)
  lookName (Pair obj nm) = nm
  giveName nm (Pair obj _) = (Pair obj nm)
```

Putting together classes

An important aspect of object-oriented software development is the way in which one class can be built upon another, re-using the operations of the original class on the subclass. In this section we explore how to combine the Movable and Named classes, to give objects which are both movable and named. The section is rather more advanced, and can be omitted on first reading.

Suppose we are to add names to our movable objects – how might this be done? We examine one approach in the text, and another in the exercises.

Our approach is to build the types `Name t` where `Movable t`; we then want to establish that the type `Name t` is in both the classes `Movable` and `Named`. We have shown the latter for *any* type `t` already; so we concentrate on the former.

The crucial insight is that the naming is independent of the named type; any operation on the type can be **lifted** to work over named types thus:

```
mapName :: (t -> u) -> Name t -> Name u
```

```
mapName f (Pair obj nm) = Pair (f obj) nm
```

We can then argue that all the operations of the `Movable` class can be lifted.

```
instance Movable t => Movable (Name t) where          (2)
    move v   = mapName (move v)
    reflectX = mapName reflectX
    reflectY = mapName reflectY
```

Now we already know that `Named (Name t)` by (1) above, so if we define a class combining these attributes

```
class (Movable u, Named u) => NamedMovable u          (3)
```

we can declare the instance

```
instance Movable t => NamedMovable (Name t)
```

This last instance is established by showing that the two constraints of (3) hold when u is replaced by `Name t`, but this is exactly what (1) and (2) say given the constraint `Movable t`.

This completes the demonstration that `NamedMovable (Name t)` holds when `Movable t`. It is worth realizing that this demonstration is produced automatically by the Haskell system – we only need to type what is seen in Figure 10.6.

This section has begun to illustrate how classes can be used in the software development process. In particular we have shown how our movable objects can be named in a way which allows re-use of all the code to move the objects.

```
data Name t = Pair t String

exam1 = Pair (Pt 0.0 0.0) "Dweezil"

instance Named (Name t) where                           (1)
    lookName (Pair obj nm) = nm
    giveName nm (Pair obj _) = (Pair obj nm)

mapName :: (t -> u) -> Name t -> Name u

mapName f (Pair obj nm) = Pair (f obj) nm

instance Movable t => Movable (Name t) where            (2)
    move v    = mapName (move v)
    reflectX = mapName reflectX
    reflectY = mapName reflectY

class (Movable u, Named u) => NamedMovable u            (3)

instance Movable t => NamedMovable (Name t)
```

Figure 10.6 Named movable objects.

EXERCISES

10.46 A different way of combining the classes Named and Movable is to establish the instance

```
instance (Movable u, Named v) => NamedMovable (u, v)
```

This is done by giving the instances

```
instance Movable u => Movable (u, v) where ....
instance Named v   => Named (u, v) where ....
```

Complete these instance declarations.

10.47 Show that the method of the previous question can be used to combine instances of *any* two classes.

10.48 The example in the final part of this section shows how we can combine an arbitrary instance of the Movable class, t, with a *particular* instance of the Named class, String. Show how it can be used to combine an arbitrary instance of one class with a particular instance of another for *any* two classes whatever.

10.49 Extend the collection of operations for moving objects to include scaling and rotation by an arbitrary angle. This can be done by re-defining `Movable` or by defining a class `MovablePlus` over the class `Movable`. Which approach is preferable? Explain your answer.

10.50 Design a collection of classes to model bank accounts. These have different forms: current, deposit and so on, as well as different levels of functionality. Can you re-use the `Named` class here?

10.7 Reasoning about algebraic types

Verification for algebraic types follows the example of lists, as first discussed in Chapter 5. The general pattern of structural induction over an algebraic type states that the result has to be proved for each constructor; when a constructor is recursive, we are allowed to use the corresponding induction hypotheses in making the proof. We first give some representative examples in this section, and conclude with a rather more sophisticated proof.

EXAMPLE: Trees ───────────────────────────────────

Structural induction over the type `Tree` of trees is stated as follows:

Structural induction over trees

To prove the property `P(tr)` for all finite `tr` of type `Tree t` we have to do two things.

> `Nil` **case**   Prove `P(Nil)`.
>
> `Node` **case**   Prove `P(Node x tr1 tr2)` for all x assuming that `P(tr1)` and `P(tr2)` hold already.

We can, if we wish, follow the advice of Chapter 5 in specifying a template and in finding proofs.

Now we give a representative example of a proof. We aim to prove for all finite trees `tr` that

```
map f (collapse tr) = collapse (mapTree f tr)
```

which states that if we map a function over a tree, and then collapse the result we get the same result as collapsing before mapping over the list. The functions we use are defined as follows

```
map f []    = []                                              (1)
map f (a:x) = f a : map f x                                   (2)

mapTree f Nil = Nil                                           (3)
mapTree f (Node x t1 t2)
    = Node (f x) (mapTree f t1) (mapTree f t2)                (4)

collapse Nil = []                                             (5)
collapse (Node x t1 t2)
    = collapse t1 ++ [x] ++ collapse t2                       (6)
```

Proof. In the `Nil` case, we simplify each side, giving

```
map f (collapse Nil)
= map f []                                          by (5)
= []                                                by (1)

collapse (mapTree f Nil)
= collapse Nil                                      by (3)
= []                                                by (5)
```

This shows that the base case holds. In the `Node` case, we have to prove

```
map f (collapse (Node x tr1 tr2))
    = collapse (mapTree f (Node x tr1 tr2))
```

assuming that

```
map f (collapse tr1) = collapse (mapTree f tr1)          (7)
map f (collapse tr2) = collapse (mapTree f tr2)          (8)
```

hold. Looking at the goal, we can simplify the left-hand side thus

```
map f (collapse (Node x tr1 tr2))
= map f (collapse tr1 ++ [x] ++ collapse tr2)          by (6)
= map f (collapse tr1) ++ [f x] ++ map f (collapse tr2)
                                                       by (9)
= collapse (mapTree f tr1) ++ [f x] ++
    collapse (mapTree f tr2)                          by (7,8)
```

The final step is given by the two induction hypotheses, that the result holds for the two subtrees `tr1` and `tr2`. The result (9) is the equation

```
map g (y++z) = map g y ++ map g z                         (9)
```

discussed earlier. Examining the right-hand side now, we have

```
collapse (mapTree f (Node x tr1 tr2))
= collapse (Node (f x) (mapTree f tr1)
                       (mapTree f tr2))              by (4)
= collapse (mapTree f tr1) ++ [f x] ++
    collapse (mapTree f tr2)                         by (6)
```

and this finishes the proof in the Node case. As this is the final case of the two for trees, the proof is complete.

∎

EXAMPLE: Errors

Structural induction for the type Err t becomes proof by cases – because the type is not recursive, in none of the cases is there an appeal to an induction hypothesis. The rule is

Structural induction over the error type

To prove the property P(x) for all defined[1] x of type Err t we have to do two things.

Error **case**   Prove P(Error).
OK **case**   Prove P(OK y) for all defined y.

Our example proof is that, for all defined values x of type Err Int,

```
trap abs 2 x ⩾ 0
```

Proof. The proof has two cases. In the first x is replaced by Error:

```
trap abs 2 Error
= 2 ⩾ 0
```

In the second, x is replaced by OK y for a defined y.

```
trap abs 2 (OK y)
= abs y ⩾ 0
```

In both cases the result holds, and so the result is valid in general.

∎

---

[1] When the type is not recursive, the induction principle gives a proof for all defined objects. An object of this type is defined if it is Error, or OK y for a defined y.

Other forms of proof

We have seen that not all functions are defined by primitive recursion. The example we saw in Section 10.2 was of the function `assoc` which is used to re-arrange arithmetic expressions. Recall that

```
assoc (Add (Add e1 e2) e3)
   = assoc (Add e1 (Add e2 e3))                        (1)
assoc (Add e1 e2) = Add (assoc e1) (assoc e2)          (2)
assoc (Sub e1 e2) = Sub (assoc e1) (assoc e2)          (3)
assoc (Lit n)     = Lit n                              (4)
```

with (1) being the non-primitive recursive case. We would like to prove that the re-arrangement does not affect the value of the expression:

```
eval (assoc ex) = eval ex                              (5)
```

for all finite expressions ex. The induction principle for `expr` has three cases.

Lit **case**   Prove P(Lit n).
Add **case**   Prove P(Add e1 e2), assuming P(e1) and P(e2).
Sub **case**   Prove P(Sub e1 e2), assuming P(e1) and P(e2).

To prove (5) for all finite expressions, we have the three cases given above. The Lit and Sub cases are given, respectively, by (4) and (3), but the Add case is more subtle. For this we will prove

```
eval (assoc (Add e1 e2)) = eval (Add e1 e2)            (6)
```

by induction on the number of Adds which are left-nested at the top level of the expression e1 – recall that it was by counting these and noting that `assoc` preserves the total number of Adds overall that we proved the function would always terminate. Now, if there are no Adds at the top-level of e1, the equation (2) gives (6). Otherwise we re-arrange thus:

```
  eval (assoc (Add (Add f1 f2) e2)))
= eval (assoc (Add f1 (Add f2 e2)))
```

and since f1 contains fewer Adds at top level,

```
= eval (Add f1 (Add f2 e2))
= eval (Add (Add f1 f2) e2)          by associativity of +
```

which gives the induction step, and therefore completes the proof.

This result shows that verification is possible for functions defined in a more general way than primitive recursion.

EXERCISES

10.51 Prove that the function `weather` from Section 10.1 has the same behaviour as

```
newWeather = makeHot . isSummer
```

when

```
makeHot True  = Hot
makeHot False = Cold
isSummer = (==Summer)
```

where recall that `(==Summer)` is an operator section whose effect is to test its argument for equality with `Summer`.

10.52 Is it the case that the `area` of each `Shape` from Section 10.1 is non-negative? If so, give a proof; if not, give an example which shows that it is not the case.

10.53 If we define the `size` of an `NTree` thus

```
size NilT          = 0
size (Node x t1 t2) = 1 + size t1 + size t2
```

then prove that for all finite `NTrees`, `tr`,

```
size tr < 2 (depth tr)
```

10.54 Show for all finite `NTrees` `tr` that

```
occurs tr a = length (filter (==a) (collapse tr))
```

The next two exercises refer back to the exercises of Section 10.3.

10.55 Prove that the function `twist` has the property that

```
twist.twist = id
```

10.56 Explain the principle of structural induction for the type `GTree`. Formulate and prove the equivalent of the theorem relating `map`, `mapTree` and `collapse` for this type of tree.

SUMMARY

Algebraic types sharpen our ability to model types in our programs: we have seen in this chapter how simple, finite types like Temp can be defined, as well as the more complex Union and recursive types. Many of these recursive types are varieties of tree: we looked at numerical trees; elements of the type Expr can also be thought of as trees representing the underlying structure of arithmetical expressions.

The type of lists gives a guiding example for various aspects of algebraic types.

- The definition of the type is recursive and polymorphic, and many polymorphic higher-order functions can be defined over lists – this carries over to the various types of tree and the error type, Err, for example.
- There is a simple principle for reasoning over lists – structural induction – which is the model for structural induction over algebraic types.

The chapter also gives guidelines for defining algebraic types: the definition can be given in three parts: first the type name is identified, then the constructors are named, and finally their component types are specified. As in other aspects of program development, this separation of concerns assists the system developer to produce simple and correct solutions.

Having introduced algebraic data types we are able to give more substantial examples of classes and their instances. We can see that the overloading that classes bring both make code easier to read and more powerful; we can see in particular how software can be added to in a way that requires little modification to the code.

In the chapters to come, algebraic types will be an integral part of the systems we develop, and indeed in the next case study we exhibit various aspects of these types. We shall also explore a different approach to types: abstract data types, and see how this approach complements and contrasts with the use of algebraic data types.

11 Case study: Huffman codes

We use the case study in this chapter as a vehicle to illustrate many of the features of the previous chapters – polymorphism, algebraic types and program design – and to illustrate the **module system** of Haskell, which is introduced first.

11.1 Modules in Haskell

So far, each of the Haskell programs that we have seen is housed in a single script. If a program is of any size, we should **structure** the script, so that it is split between a number of **modules**.

A module consists of a number of definitions (of types, functions and so on), with a clearly defined **interface** stating what the module **exports** to other modules which use or **import** it.

Using modules to structure a large program has a number of advantages.

- Parts of the system can be built separately from each other. Suppose we want to monitor traffic on a network: one module might produce the statistics, while another displays them in a suitable form. If we agree which statistics are to be presented (their type etc.), that is we agree the interface, then development of the two parts of the system can go on independently.

- Parts of a system can be compiled separately; this is a great advantage for a system of any complexity.

- Libraries of components can be re-used, by importing the appropriate modules containing them.

In the definition of Haskell, there is no identification between modules and files. Nonetheless, we choose here to write one module per file. This fits well with Hugs and Gofer, which do not support the module system; their project mechanism is explained at the end of the section.

Now we look at the details of Haskell modules, before giving our example which exhibits the system in action.

Module headers

Each module is named, so an example named `Ant` might be

```
module Ant where

data Ants  = ...
anteater x = ...
```

Note that the definitions all begin in the column under the keyword `module`; it is safest to make this the leftmost column of the file.

Our convention for file names is that a module `Ant` resides in the Haskell file `Ant.hs`.

Importing a module

The basic operation on modules is to `import` one into another, so in defining
Bee we might say

```
module Bee where

import Ant

beeKeeper = ... anteater ...
```

This means that the **visible** definitions from Ant can be used in Bee. By
default the visible definitions in a module are those which appear in the
module itself. If we define

```
module Cow where

import Bee
```

the definitions of Ants and anteater will not be visible in Cow. They can be
made visible either by importing Ant explicitly, or by using the export
controls which we discuss below to modify exactly what is exported from
Bee.

The main module

Each system of modules should contain a top-level module called Main,
which gives a definition to the name main. In a compiled system, this is the
expression which is evaluated when the compiled code is executed; in an
interpreter like Gofer or Hugs, it is of less significance.

Export controls

As we explained when `import` was introduced, the default is that all top-
level definitions of a module are exported.

- This may be too much: we might wish not to export some auxiliary
  functions, such as the shunt function below

  ```
  reverse :: [t] -> [t]
  reverse = shunt []

  shunt :: [t] -> [t] -> [t]
  shunt y []    = y
  shunt y (a:x) = shunt (a:y) x
  ```

  since its only role is in defining the reverse function.

- On the other hand, it might be too little: we perhaps want to export some of the definitions we imported from other modules. The modules `Ant`, `Bee` and `Cow` above provide an example of this.

We can control what is exported by following the name of the module with a list of what is to be exported. For instance, we say in the case of `Bee`

```
module Bee ( beeKeeper, Ants(..), anteater ) where ...
```

The list contains names of defined objects, such as `beeKeeper` and also types like `Ants`; in the latter case we follow the type name with `(..)` to indicate that the constructors of the type are exported with the type itself.[1]

Such a list works on a definition-by-definition basis; we can also state that all the definitions in a module are to be exported, as in

```
module Bee ( beeKeeper, module Ant ) where ...
```

or equivalently

```
module Bee ( module Bee , module Ant ) where ...
```

where the keyword `module` followed by a module name such as `Ant` is shorthand for all the names defined in a module.

Import controls

We can control how objects are to be imported, just as we can control their export. We do this by following the `import` statement with a list of objects, types or classes. For instance, if we choose not to import `anteater` from `Ant` we can write

```
import Ant ( Ants(..) )
```

stating that we want just the type `Ants`; we can alternatively say which names we wish to *hide*:

```
import Ant hiding ( anteater )
```

Suppose that in our module we have a definition of `bear`, and also there is an object named `bear` in the module `Ant`. How can we gain access to *both* definitions? The answer is that we use the **qualified** name `Ant.bear` for the imported object, reserving `bear` for the locally defined one. A qualified name is built from the name of a module and the name of an object in that module,

---

[1] This is not necessary with types defined using `type`.

separated by a full stop. Note that there should be *no* white space between the '.' and the two names. To use qualified names we should make the import thus:

```
import qualified Ant ...
```

In the qualified case we can also state which particular items are to be imported or hidden, just as in the unqualified case above.

Interface files

Some programming languages give files which separately list the interfaces of modules; these are useful when we wish to compile modules separately, but in such a case it is likely that a compiler will generate these files automatically. This is what happens in some Haskell implementations. The interface details the names imported and exported from a module, but this information is usually clear from the `module` and `import` statements in the module itself.

Further details

Further information about the Haskell module system can be found in the language report (Hudak *et al.*, 1992; Peterson *et al.*, 1996); note that some of the details will be different in particular implementations.

Projects in Gofer and Hugs

Neither Gofer nor Hugs supports the full Haskell module system, however they do provide a useful alternative. The `module`, `import` and `export` statements are ignored by Gofer and Hugs, which means that we can use them as a form of *documentation* of files.

Gofer and Hugs allow the definition of **projects**, which are collections of files, listed in order. If we wanted to make the Ant, Bee and Cow modules into a project, we would put the list

```
Ant.hs
Bee.hs
Cow.hs
```

in a file, Animals, say. On loading the project using the command

```
:project Animals
```

the files are loaded in order. The order matters, of course; if `Bee` imports `Ant`, that is because it uses definitions in the file `Ant.hs`. We should therefore load `Ant.hs` first.

There are limitations in using projects. There is no mechanism for hiding or renaming: *all* the names defined in `Ant.hs` can be used in subsequent files, and so cannot also be defined in `Bee` or `Cow`.

EXERCISES

11.1 Can you get the effect of export controls using `import`? Can you get the effect of the qualifications of `import` using export controls? Discuss why both directives are included in the language.

11.2 Explain why you think it is the default that `imported` definitions are not themselves exported.

11.3 It is proposed to add the following option to the `module` export control and the `import` statement. If the item `-module Dog` appears, then none of the definitions in the module `Dog` is exported or imported. Discuss the advantages and disadvantages of this proposal. How would you achieve the effect of this feature in the existing Haskell module system?

11.2 Modular design

Any computer system which is used seriously will be modified during its lifetime, either by the person or team who wrote it, or more likely by others. For this reason, all systems should be designed with *change* in mind.

We mentioned this earlier when we said that systems should be documented, with types given to all top-level definitions, and comments accompanying each script and substantial definition. Another useful form of description is to link each definition with proofs which concern it; if we know some of the logical properties of a function, we have a more solid conception of its purpose.

Documentation makes a script easier to understand, and therefore change, but we can give *structure* to a collection of definitions if they are split among modules or scripts, each script concerning a separate *part* of the overall system. The directives which link the files tell us how the parts of the system fit together. If we want to modify a particular part of a system, we should therefore be able to modify a single module (at least initially), rather than starting by modifying the whole of the system as a single unit.

How should we begin to design a system as a collection of modules? The pieces of advice which follow are aimed to make modification as straightforward as possible.

- Each module should have a clearly identified role.

- Each module should do one thing *only*. If a module has two separate purposes, these should be split between two separate modules. The chance of a change to one affecting the other is thereby reduced.

- Each part of the system should be performed by one module: each module should do one thing *completely*; it should be self-contained, in other words. If performing one part of the whole is split between two modules, then either their code should be merged, or there should be a module defined with the single purpose of bringing the two components together.

- Each module should export only what is necessary. It is then clearer what the effect of an `import` is: precisely the functions which are needed are imported. This process is often called *information hiding* in software engineering, which is itself the general study of principles for programming in the large.

- Modules should be *small*. As a rule of thumb, no module should be larger than can be printed on one side of a sheet of paper.

We have also mentioned design for re-use, particularly in the context of polymorphic types and higher-order functions. The module will be the unit of re-use, and a library will be accessed by means of an `import` statement. Similar principles apply to the design of libraries. Each library should have a clearly defined purpose, like implementing a type together with basic operations over the type. In addition, we can say that

- on including a general-purpose module, it is possible to suppress the definitions which are not used;

- a qualified `import` can be used to avoid the name-clashes which can often occur: despite the (infinite) choice of names for functions, in practice we tend to choose from a very small subset!

The advice here might seem dry (or obvious) – we hope to illuminate what has been said in the case study which follows. In the next chapter we will return to the idea of information hiding when we meet abstract data types. In the remainder of this chapter we examine the case study of Huffman coding, whose foundations we explore now.

11.3 Coding and decoding

Electronic messages of various kinds are sent between machines and people by the billions each day. Such messages are usually sent as sequences of binary '*bits*'. For the transmission to be swift, the messages need to be coded as efficiently as possible. The area we explore here is how to build codes – translations of characters into sequences of bits – which produce as compact messages as possible.

Trees can be used to code and decode messages. Consider as an example the tree

We can see this as giving codes for the letters a, b and t by looking at the **routes** taken to reach the letters. For example, to get to b, we go *right* at the top node, and *left* at the next:

which gives b the code RL. Similarly, L codes a, and RR the letter t.

The codes given by trees are **prefix codes**; in these codes no code for a letter is the start (or prefix) of the code for another. This is because no route to a leaf of the tree can be the start of the route to another leaf.[2]

A message is **decoded** using the tree also. Consider the message RLLRRRLRR. To decode we follow the route through the tree given, moving right then left, to give the letter b,

where we have shown under each tree the sequence of bits remaining to be decoded. Continuing again from the top, we have the codes for a then t,

---

[2] For more information about these Huffman codes, and a wealth of material on algorithms in general, see Cormen *et al.* (1990).

so the decoded message begins with the letters `bat`.

In full, the message is `battat`, and the coded message is ten 'bits' long. The codes for individual characters are of different lengths; `a` is coded in one bit, and the other characters in two. Is this a wise choice of code in view of a message in which the letter `t` predominates? Using the tree

the coded message becomes RRRLLLRLL, a nine bit coding. A Huffman code is built so that the most frequent letters have the shortest sequences of code bits, and the less frequent have more 'expensive' code sequences, justified by the rarity of their occurrence; Morse code is an example of a Huffman code in common use.

The remainder of the chapter explores the implementation of Huffman coding, illustrating the module system of Haskell.

EXERCISES

11.4 What is the coding of the message `battat` using the tree

Compare the length of the coding with the others given earlier.

11.5 Using the first coding tree, decode the coded message RLLRLRLLRR. Which tree would you expect to give the best coding of the message? Check your answer by trying the three possibilities.

11.4 Implementation – I

We now begin to implement the Huffman coding and decoding, in a series of Haskell modules. The overall structure of the system we develop is illustrated at the end of the chapter, Figure 11.4.

As earlier, we first develop the types used in the system.

The types – Types.hs

The codes are sequences of bits, so we define

```
data Bit  =  L | R
type HCode = [Bit]
```

and in the translation we will convert the Huffman tree to a table for ease of coding.

```
type Table = [ (Char,HCode) ]
```

The Huffman trees themselves carry characters at the leaves. We shall see presently that during their formation we also use information about the frequency with which each character appears; hence the inclusion of integers both at the leaves and at the internal nodes.

```
data Tree = Leaf Char Int |
            Node Int Tree Tree
```

The file containing the module is illustrated in Figure 11.1. The name of the file, with an indication of its purpose, are listed in the first comment; the definitions themselves are also commented.

Note that we have given a full description of what is exported by the module, by listing the items after the module name. As types are being exported, we also export their constructors: explicitly in the case of `Tree` and `Bit`, implicitly for the other types.

This information could have been omitted, but we include it here as useful documentation of the interface to the file.

Coding and decoding – Coding.hs

This module uses the types in `Types.hs`, and so imports them with

```
import Types ( Tree(Leaf,Node), Bit(L,R), HCode, Table )
```

```
-------------------------------------------------------------
--                                                         --
--   Types.hs                                              --
--                                                         --
--   The types used in the Huffman coding example.         --
--                                                         --
-------------------------------------------------------------


-------------------------------------------------------------
--   The interface to the module Types is written out      --
--   explicitly here, after the module name.               --
-------------------------------------------------------------

module Types ( Tree(Leaf,Node), Bit(L,R), HCode, Table )
   where

-------------------------------------------------------------
--   Trees to represent the relative frequencies and       --
--   therefore the Huffman codes.                          --
-------------------------------------------------------------

data Tree = Leaf Char Int | Node Int Tree Tree

-------------------------------------------------------------
--   The types of bits, Huffman codes and                  --
--   tables of Huffman codes.                               --
-------------------------------------------------------------

data Bit = L | R

type HCode = [Bit]

type Table = [ (Char,HCode) ]
```

Figure 11.1 The file Types.hs.

We have chosen to list the names imported here; the statement import Types would have the same effect, but lose the extra documentation.

The purpose of the module is to define functions to code and decode messages: we only export these, and not the auxiliary function(s) which may be used in their definition. Our module therefore begins

```
module Coding ( codeMessage , decodeMessage )
```

To code a message according to a table of codes, we look up each character in the table, and concatenate the results.

```
codeMessage :: Table -> [Char] -> HCode

codeMessage tbl = concat . map (lookupTable tbl)
```

It is interesting to see that the function level definition here gives an exact implementation of the description which precedes it; using partial application and function composition has made the definition clearer.

We now define `lookupTable`, which is a standard function to look up the value corresponding to a 'key' in a table.

```
lookupTable :: Table -> Char -> HCode

lookupTable [] c = error "lookupTable"
lookupTable ((ch,n):tb) c
  | ch==c      = n
  | otherwise  = lookupTable tb c
```

Because of the `module` statement, this definition is not exported.

To decode a message, which is a sequence of bits, i.e. an element of HCode, we use a `Tree`.

```
decodeMessage :: Tree -> HCode -> [Char]
```

We saw in Section 11.3 that decoding according to the tree t has two main cases.

- If we are at an internal `Node`, we choose the sub-tree dictated by the first bit of the code.
- If at a leaf, we read off the character found, and then begin to decode the remainder of the code at the top of the tree t.

When the code is exhausted, so is the decoded message.

```
decodeMessage tr
  = decodeByt tr
    where
    decodeByt (Node n t1 t2) (L:rest)
      = decodeByt t1 rest
    decodeByt (Node n t1 t2) (R:rest)
      = decodeByt t2 rest
    decodeByt (Leaf c n) l
      = c : decodeByt tr l
    decodeByt t1 [] = []
```

The locally defined function is called `decodeByt` because it decodes 'by t'.

The first coding tree and example message of Section 11.3 can be given by

```
exam1 = Node 0 (Leaf 'a' 0)
             (Node 0 (Leaf 'b' 0) (Leaf 't' 0))
mess1 = [R,L,L,R,R,R,R,L,R,R]
```

and decoding of this message proceeds thus

```
decodeMessage exam1 mess1
  = decodeByt exam1 mess1
  = decodeByt exam1 [R,L,L,R,R,R,R,L,R,R]
  = decodeByt (Node 0 (Leaf 'b' 0) (Leaf 't' 0))
                            [L,L,R,R,R,R,L,R,R]
  = decodeByt (Leaf 'b' 0) [L,R,R,R,R,L,R,R]
  = 'b' : decodeByt exam1 [L,R,R,R,R,L,R,R]
  = 'b' : decodeByt (Leaf 'a' 0) [R,R,R,R,L,R,R]
  = 'b' : 'a' : decodeByt exam1 [R,R,R,R,L,R,R]
```

Before looking at the implementation any further, we look at how to construct the Huffman coding tree, given a text.

EXERCISES

11.6 Complete the calculation of `decodeMessage exam1 mess1` begun above.

11.7 With the table

```
table1 = [ ('a',[L]) , ('b',[R,L]) , ('t',[R,R]) ]
```

give a calculation of

```
codeMessage table1 "battab"
```

11.5 Building Huffman trees

Given a text, such as "battat", how do we find the tree giving the optimal code for the text? We can explain it in a number of stages.[3]

---

[3] The account here is based on that given in Section 17.3 of Cormen *et al.* (1990).

- We first find the frequencies of the individual letters, in this case giving

  ```
  [('b',1),('a',2),('t',3)]
  ```

- The main idea of the translation is to build the tree by taking the two characters occurring least frequently, and making a *single* character (or *tree*) of them. This process is repeated until a single tree results; the steps which follow give this process in more detail.

- Each of `('b',1)`, ... is turned into a tree, giving the list of trees

  ```
  [ Leaf 'b' 1 , Leaf 'a' 2 , Leaf 't' 3 ]
  ```

  which is sorted into frequency order.

- We then begin to *amalgamate* trees: we take the two trees of lowest frequency, put them together, and insert the result in the appropriate place.

  ```
  [ Node 3 (Leaf 'b' 1) (Leaf 'a' 2) , Leaf 't' 3 ]
  ```

- This process is repeated, until a single tree results

  ```
  Node 6 (Node 3 (Leaf 'b' 1) (Leaf 'a' 2)) (Leaf 't' 3)
  ```

  which is pictured thus

- This tree can then be turned into a `Table`

  ```
  [ ('b',[L,L]) , ('a',[L,R]) , ('t',[R]) ]
  ```

We now look at how the system is implemented in Haskell.

11.6 Design

Implementing the system will involve us in designing various modules to perform the stages given above. We start by deciding what the modules will be, and the functions they will implement. This is the equivalent at the larger scale of *divide and conquer*; we separate the problem into manageable portions, which can be solved separately, and which are put together using the `import` and `module` statements. We design these *interfaces* before implementing the functions.

The three stages of conversion are summarized in Figure 11.2, which shows the module directives of the three component files. We have added the types of objects to be exported as comments, so that these directives contain

```
Frequency.hs:
  module Frequency ( frequency )   -- [Char] -> [(Char,Int)]

MakeTree.hs:
  module MakeTree ( makeTree )     -- [(Char,Int)] -> Tree
  import Types

CodeTable.hs:
  module CodeTable ( codeTable )   -- Tree -> Table
  import Types
```

Figure 11.2   Modules for Huffman tree formation.

enough information for the exported functions in the files to be used without knowing *how* they are defined.

In fact the component functions frequency and makeTree will never be used separately, and so we compose them in the module MakeCode.hs when bringing the three files together. This is given in Figure 11.3.

Our next task is to implement each module, and we turn to that now.

```
-----------------------------------------------------------
--                                                       --
--        MakeCode.hs                                    --
--                                                       --
--        Huffman coding in Haskell.                     --
--                                                       --
-----------------------------------------------------------

module MakeCode ( codes, codeTable ) where

import Types
import Frequency ( frequency )
import MakeTree  ( makeTree )
import CodeTable ( codeTable )   --   Tree -> Table

-----------------------------------------------------------
-- Putting together frequency calculation and            --
-- tree conversion                                       --
-----------------------------------------------------------

codes :: [Char] -> Tree

codes = makeTree . frequency
```

Figure 11.3   The module MakeCode.hs.

11.7 Implementation – II

In this section we discuss in turn the three implementation modules.

Counting characters – `Frequency.hs`

The aim of the function `frequency` is to take a text, such as `"battat"` to a list of characters, in increasing frequency of occurrence, `[('b',1),
('a',2),('t',3)]`. We do this in three stages.

- First we pair each character with the count of 1, giving

  `[('b',1),('a',1),('t',1),('t',1),('a',1),('t',1)]`

- Next, we sort the list on the characters, bringing together the counts of equal characters.

  `[('a',2),('b',1),('t',3)]`

- Finally, we sort the list into increasing frequency order, to give the list above.

The function uses two different sorts – one on character, one on frequency – to achieve its result. Is there any way we can define a single sorting function to perform both sorts?

We can give a general merge sort function, which works by **merging**, in order, the results of sorting the front and rear halves of the list.

```
mergeSort :: ([t]->[t]->[t]) -> [t] -> [t]

mergeSort merge x
  | length x < 2     = x
  | otherwise        = merge (mergeSort merge first)
                             (mergeSort merge second)

    where
    first  = take half x
    second = drop half x
    half   = (length x) `div` 2
```

The first argument to `mergeSort` is the merging function, which takes two sorted lists and merges their contents in order. It is by making this operation a *parameter* that the `mergeSort` function becomes re-usable.

In sorting the characters, we amalgamate entries for the same character

```
alphaMerge x [] = x
alphaMerge [] y = y
alphaMerge ((a,n):x) ((b,m):y)
  | a==b        = (a,n+m) : alphaMerge x y
  | a<b         = (a,n) : alphaMerge x ((b,m):y)
  | otherwise   = (b,m) : alphaMerge ((a,n):x) y
```

while when sorting on frequency we compare frequencies; when two pairs have the same frequency, we order according to the character ordering.

```
freqMerge x [] = x
freqMerge [] y = y
freqMerge ((a,n):x) ((b,m):y)
  | n<m || (n==m && a<b)  = (a,n) : freqMerge x ((b,m):y)
  | otherwise             = (b,m) : freqMerge ((a,n):x) y
```

We can now give the top-level definition of frequency

```
frequency :: [Char] -> [ (Char,Int) ]
```

```
frequency
  = mergeSort freqMerge . mergeSort alphaMerge . map start
    where
    start ch = (ch,1)
```

which we can see is a direct combination of the three stages listed in the informal description of the algorithm.

Note that of all the functions defined in this module, only frequency is exported.

Making the Huffman tree – MakeTree.hs

We have two stages in making a Huffman tree from a list of characters with their frequencies.

```
makeTree :: [ (Char,Int) ] -> Tree
makeTree = makeCodes . toTreeList
```

where

```
toTreeList :: [ (Char,Int) ] -> [Tree]
makeCodes  :: [Tree] -> Tree
```

The function `toTreeList` converts each character–number pair into a tree, thus

```
toTreeList = map toLeaf
             where
             toLeaf (c,n) = Leaf c n
```

and the function `makeCodes` amalgamates trees successively into a single tree

```
makeCodes [t] = t
makeCodes ts  = makeCodes (amalgamate ts)
```

How are trees amalgamated? We have to pair together the first two trees in the list (since the list is kept in ascending order of frequency) and then insert the result in the correct place in the list. Working top-down, we have

```
amalgamate :: [ Tree ] -> [ Tree ]
```

```
amalgamate (t1:t2:ts) = insert (pair t1 t2) ts
```

When we pair two trees, we need to combine their frequency counts, so

```
pair :: Tree -> Tree -> Tree
```

```
pair t1 t2 = Node (v1+v2) t1 t2
             where
             v1 = value t1
             v2 = value t2
```

where the value of a tree is given by

```
value :: Tree -> Int
```

```
value (Leaf _ n)   = n
value (Node n _ _) = n
```

The definition of `insert`, which is similar to that used in an insertion sort, is left as an exercise. Again, the definition of the exported function uses various others whose definitions are not visible to the 'outside world'.

The code table – `CodeTable.hs`

Here we give the function `codeTable` which takes a Huffman tree into a code table. In converting the tree `Node n t1 t2` we have to convert `t1`, adding `L` at the front of the code, and `t2` with `R` at the head. We therefore write the more general conversion function

```
convert :: HCode -> Tree -> Table
```

whose first argument is the 'path so far' into the tree. The definition is

```
convert cd (Leaf c n)
     =  [(c,cd)]
convert cd (Node n t1 t2)
        = (convert (cd++[L]) t1) ++ (convert (cd++[R]) t2)
```

The `codeTable` function is given by starting the conversion with an empty code string

```
codeTable :: Tree -> Table
codeTable = convert []
```

Consider the calculation of

```
codeTable (Node 6 (Node 3 (Leaf 'b' 1) (Leaf 'a' 2))
                   (Leaf 't' 3))
= convert [] (Node 6 (Node 3 (Leaf 'b' 1) (Leaf 'a' 2))
                      (Leaf 't' 3))
= convert [L] (Node 3 (Leaf 'b' 1) (Leaf 'a' 2)) ++
  convert [R] (Leaf 't' 3)
= convert [L,L] (Leaf 'b' 1) ++
  convert [L,R] (Leaf 'a' 2) ++
  [ ('t',[R]) ]
= [ ('b',[L,L]) , ('a',[L,R]) , ('t',[R]) ]
```

The top-level file – `Main.hs`

We can now pull all the parts of the system together into a top-level file.

```
module Main (main) where

import Types
import Coding    ( codeMessage , decodeMessage )
import MakeCode ( codes, codeTable )
```

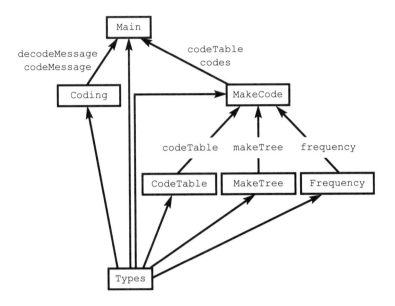

Figure 11.4   The modules of the Huffman coding system.

In this file we can include representative examples, using the major functions listed in the `import` statements.

The structure of the system is given in Figure 11.4. Modules are represented by boxes, and an arrow from A to B indicates that A.hs is imported into B.hs. An arrow is marked to indicate the functions exported by the included module, so that, for example, `codes` and `codeTable` are exported from `MakeCode.hs` to `Main.hs`.

If this coding system were to be used as a component of a larger system, a `module` directive could be used to control which of the four functions and the types are exported, after the module had been renamed. It is important to realize that the types will need to be exported (or be included in the file including `Main.hs`) if the functions are to be used.

EXERCISES

11.8   Give a definition of merge sort which uses the built-in ordering '<='. What is its type?

11.9   Modifying your previous answer if necessary, give a version of merge sort which removes duplicate entries.

11.10 Give a version of merge sort which takes an ordering function as a parameter:

```
ordering :: t -> t -> Bool
```

Explain how to implement `mergeSort freqMerge` using this version of merge sort, and discuss why you *cannot* implement `mergeSort alphaMerge` this way.

11.11 Define the `insert` function, used in the definition of `makeTree`.

11.12 Give a calculation of

```
makeTree  [('b',2),('a',2),('t',3),('e',4)]
```

11.13 Define functions

```
showTree  :: Tree  -> String
showTable :: Table -> String
```

which give printable versions of Huffman trees and code tables. One general way of printing trees is to use indentation to indicate the structure. Schematically, this looks like

```
    left sub tree, indented by 4 characters
value(s) at Node
    right sub tree, indented by 4 characters
```

SUMMARY

When writing a program of any size, we need to divide up the work in a sensible way. The Haskell module system allows one script to be included in another. At the boundary, it is possible to control exactly which definitions are exported or imported.

We gave a number of guidelines for the design of a program into its constituent modules. The most important advice is to make each module perform one clearly defined task, and for only as much information as is needed to be exported – the principle of *information hiding*. This principle is extended in the following chapter when we examine abstract data types.

The design principles were put into practice in the Huffman coding example. In particular, it was shown for the file `MakeCode.hs` and its three sub-modules that design can begin with the design of modules and their *interfaces* – that is the definitions (and their types) which are exported. Thus the design process starts *before* any implementation takes place.

12 Abstract data types

The Haskell module system allows definitions of functions and other objects to be *hidden* when one file is included in another. Those definitions hidden are only of use in defining the exported functions, and hiding them makes clearer the exact interface between the two files: only those features of the script which are needed will be visible.

This chapter shows that information hiding is equally applicable for types, giving what are known as **abstract data types**, or ADTs. In Haskell itself the module mechanism supports ADTs; in Gofer and Hugs there is a mechanism of **restricted type synonyms**. We explain both mechanisms in this chapter.

12.1 Type representations

We begin our discussion with a scenario, which is intended to show both the purpose and the operation of the abstract data type mechanism.

Suppose we are to build a calculator for numerical expressions, like those given by the `Expr` type of Section 10.2, but with variables included. The calculator is to provide the facility to set the values of variables, as well as for variables to form parts of expressions.

As a part of our system, we need to be able to model the current values of the variables, which we might call the **store** of the calculator. How can this be done? A number of models present themselves, including:

- a list of integer/variable pairs: `[(Int,Var)]`; and
- a function from variables to integers: `(Var -> Int)`.

Both models allow us to lookup and update the values of variables, as well as set a starting value for the store. These operations have types as follows.

```
initial :: Store
lookup  :: Store -> Var -> Int                    (†)
update  :: Store -> Var -> Int -> Store
```

but each model allows *more* than that: we can reverse a list, and we can compose a function with others, for instance. In using the type `Store` we intend only to use the three operations given, but it is always possible to use the model in unintended ways.

How can we give a better model of a store? The answer is to define a type which *only* has the operations `initial`, `lookup` and `update`, so that we cannot abuse the representation. We therefore hide the information about how the type is actually implemented, and only allow the operations (†) to manipulate objects of the type.

When we provide a limited interface to a type by means of a specified set of operations we call the type an **abstract data type** (or ADT). Since the 'concrete' type itself is no longer accessible and we may only access the type by means of the operations provided, these operations give a more 'abstract' view of the type.

Figure 12.1 illustrates the situation, and suggests that as well as giving a natural representation of the type of stores, there are two other benefits of type abstraction.

- The type declarations in (†) form a clearly defined **interface**, which is called the **signature** of the ADT, between the user of the type and its implementor. The only information that they have to agree on is the signature; once this is agreed, they can work independently. This is therefore another way of breaking a complex problem into simpler parts; another aspect of the *divide and conquer* method.

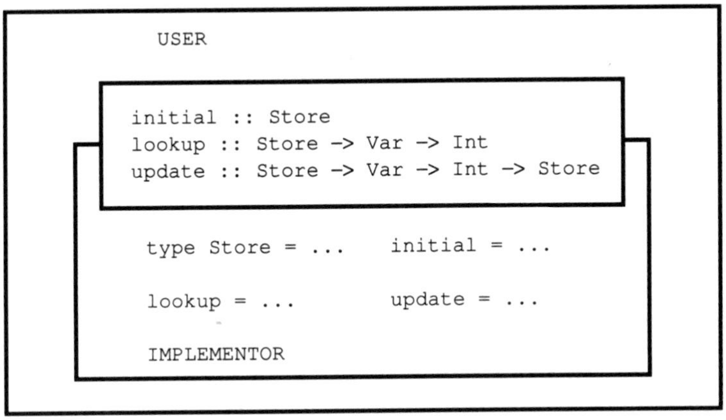

Figure 12.1 The Store abstract data type.

- We can *modify* the implementation of the Store without having any effect on the user. Contrast this with the situation where the implementation is visible to the user: we might have used pattern matching over lists, for example, and this means that potentially we may have to re-define *every* function using the type.

We shall see both aspects illustrated in the sections to come; first we look at the details of Gofer and Hugs abstract data type mechanism.

12.2 The Gofer and Hugs ADT mechanism

Continuing the Store example, we make the type abstract in Gofer or Hugs by typing

```
type
  Store = ....
  in
  initial :: Store,
  lookup  :: Store -> Var -> Int,
  update  :: Store -> Var -> Int -> Store
```

The signature is given in the section following the in. This is an offside block, and so is terminated by the first character offside of 'initial'.

The script must also contain an **implementation** of the abstract data type. The type used to implement Store replaces the ....; the definitions of the functions in the signature may appear anywhere in the script, but it is strongly recommended that they follow the type declaration.

The implementation of the Store as a list of pairs is given now

```
type
  Store = [ (Int,Var) ]
  in
  initial :: Store,
  lookup  :: Store -> Var -> Int,
  update  :: Store -> Var -> Int -> Store

initial = []

lookup [] v     = 0
lookup ((n,w):st) v
  | v==w         = n
  | otherwise    = lookup st v

update st v n    = (n,v):st
```

Only in defining the items in the signature can we use the fact that a Store is of type [(Int,Var)]. Elsewhere in the script, we can only access stores through the signature operations.

What happens if we try to break the barrier and deal with stores as lists? Trying to find the length of a store by typing length initial, for instance, provokes the type error message

```
ERROR: Type error in application
*** expression      : length initial
*** term            : initial
*** type            : Store
*** does not match : [a]
```

despite the fact that Store is implemented as [(Int,Var)].

Printing and equality

The implementation is not completely hidden, as we are able to print the objects as they are represented. For instance, evaluating initial gives the result []. In fact, this is a useful aid in testing or debugging scripts, since we get a visible form of objects which would otherwise be opaque. It is possible to tune precisely how the objects are printed by declaring Store as an instance of the Show class.

Equality is not automatically defined over `Store`. If we require it, we need to declare `Store` as an instance of `Eq`. For example, we might say

```
instance Eq Store where
  (==) = eqStore
```

where the function

```
eqStore :: Store -> Store -> Bool
```

needs to be included in the signature. If we wish to use the equality from the implementation, we simply add the definition

```
eqStore = (==)
```

otherwise we can give our own definition of equality. In the `Store` example, we might well want to equate two stores if they give the same values to each variable – the definition of this function is left as an exercise.

A different implementation of `Store` is given by the type of functions from variables to integers.

```
type
  Store = (Var -> Int)
  in
  ....

initial v   = 0

lookup st v = st v

update st v n w
  | v==w          = n
  | otherwise     = st w
```

(We have used .... here to indicate the signature for `Store` which we have seen already.) The two implementations are indistinguishable, as far as the operations of the signature are concerned. The store holds the most recent value given to a variable, and zero if the variable has not been given a value.

EXERCISES

12.1   Give an implementation of `Store` using lists whose entries are ordered according to the variable names. Discuss why this might be preferable to the original list implementation, and also its disadvantages, if any.

12.2   For the implementation of `Store` as a list type `[(Int,Var)]`, give a definition of equality which equates any two stores which give the same values to each variable. Can this operation be defined for the second implementation? If not, give a modification of the implementation which allows it to be defined.

12.3   In this question you should use the polymorphic error type, `Err t`. Suppose it is to be an error to `lookup` the value of a variable which does not have a value in the given store. Explain how you would modify the signature of `Store` and the two implementations given so that the appropriate errors are raised.

12.4   Rather than giving an error when looking up a variable which does not have a value in the particular store, extend the signature to provide a test of whether a variable has a value in a given store, and explain how you would modify the two implementations to define the test.

12.5   Suppose you are to implement a fourth operation over `Store`

```
setAll :: Int -> Store
```

so that `setAll n` is the store where every variable has the value n. Can you do this for both the example implementations? Show how if you can, and explain why, if not.

12.6   Design an ADT for the library database, first examined in Chapter 4.

12.3 Example: queues

A queue is a 'first in, first out' structure. If first `Flo` and then `Eddie` joins an initially empty queue, the first person to leave will be `Flo`. As an abstract data type, we expect to be able to add items and remove items as well as there being an empty queue.

The function `remQ` below returns a pair – the item removed together with the part of the queue that remains – if there are any items in the queue. If not, the standard function `error` is called.

```
type
  Queue t = ....
  in
  emptyQ   :: Queue t,
  isEmptyQ :: Queue t -> Bool,
  addQ     :: t -> Queue t -> Queue t,
  remQ     :: Queue t -> ( t , Queue t )
```

A list can be used to model a queue: we can add to the end of the list, and remove from the front, giving

```
type
  Queue t = [t]
  in
  ....

emptyQ   = []

isEmptyQ [] = True
isEmptyQ _  = False

addQ a x = x++[a]

remQ x
  | not (isEmptyQ x)   = (head x , tail x)
  | otherwise          = error "remQ"
```

or we can do the converse, which leaves emptyQ and isEmptyQ unchanged, and gives

```
addQ a x = (a:x)

remQ x
  | not (isEmptyQ x)   = (last x , init x)
  | otherwise          = error "remQ"
```

where the built-in functions last and init take the last element and the remainder of a list.

Although we have not said exactly how to calculate the cost of evaluation (a topic we take up in Chapter 15), we can see that in each implementation one of the operations is 'cheap' and the other is 'expensive'. The 'cheap' functions – remQ in the first implementation and addQ in the second – can be evaluated in one step, while in both cases the 'expensive' function will have to run along a list x one step per element, and so will be costly if the list is long.

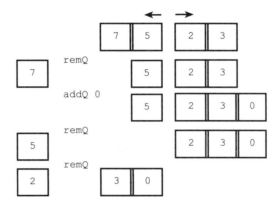

Figure 12.2 A two-list queue in action.

Is there any way of making both operations 'cheap'? The idea is to make the queue out of *two* lists, so that both adding and removing an element can take place at the head of a list. The process is illustrated in Figure 12.2, which represents a number of queues. Initially the queue containing the elements 7, 5, 2 and 3 is shown. Subsequently we see the effect of removing an element, adding the element 0, and removing two further elements. In each case the queue is represented by two lists, where the left-hand list grows to the left, and the right-hand to the right.

The function remQ removes elements from the head of the left-hand list, and addQ adds elements to the head of the right. This works until the left-hand list is empty, when the elements of the right-hand queue have to be transferred to the left (the picture might be misleading here: remember that the two lists grow in opposite directions).

This case in which we have to transfer elements is expensive, as we have to run along a list to reverse it, but we would not in general expect to perform this every time we remove an element from the queue. The implementation follows now.

```
type
  Queue t = ([t],[t])
  in
  ....

emptyQ        = ([],[])

isEmptyQ ([],[]) = True
isEmptyQ _        = False

addQ a (l,r) = (l,a:r)
```

```
remQ (a:l,r) = (a,(l,r))
remQ ([],[]) = error "remQ"
remQ ([], r) = remQ (reverse r,[])
```

As we commented for the Store types, the behaviour of this implementation will be indistinguishable from the first two, as far as the operations of the abstract data type are concerned. On the other hand, the implementation will be substantially more efficient than the single list implementations, as we explained above.[1]

EXERCISES

12.7   Give calculations of

```
"abcde" ++ "f"
init "abcdef"
last "abcdef"
```

where

```
init x = take (length x-1) x
last x = x !! (length x-1)
```

12.8   Explain the behaviour of the three queue models if you are asked to perform the following sequence of queue operations: add 2, add 1, remove item, add 3, remove item, add 1, add 4, remove item, remove item.

12.9   A double-ended queue, or deque, allows elements to be added or removed from either end of the structure. Give a signature for the ADT Deque t, and give two different implementations of the deque type.

12.10   A unique queue can only contain one occurrence of each entry (the one to arrive earliest). Give a signature for the ADT of these queues, and an implementation of the ADT.

12.11   Each element of a priority queue has a numerical priority. When an element is removed, it will be of the highest priority in the queue. If there is more than one of these, the earliest to arrive is chosen. Give a signature and implementation of the ADT of priority queues.

12.12   [Harder] Examine how priority queues could be used to implement the Huffman coding system in Chapter 11.

---

[1]   Further recent work on efficient implementation of queues can be found in Okasaki (1994).

12.4 The Haskell ADT mechanism

In the Haskell language itself, abstract data types are defined by means of the module system. In introducing modules we saw how the export part of a module statement allowed us to choose which definitions and types were to be exported. Moreover, we can control whether the constructors of a data type are exported or not. For the data type `Jerry`, if we write

```
Jerry
```

in the export list, `Jerry` is exported *without* its constructors, which has the effect of making its implementation private to the module (to make the implementation visible, recall that we write `Jerry(..)`). This means that only the functions exported by the module have access to that implementation.

This mechanism is fine for abstract data types whose implementation is indeed a data type; in the case of the examples we have seen so far, we need to wrap the implementation type in a constructor, as in

```
data StoreT = StoreC [ (Int,Var) ]
```

and then include an export statement of the form

```
module Store ( StoreT , initial , lookup , update , eqStore )
```

in which the constructor `StoreC` for the `StoreT` type is not exported.

The implementation itself needs to be modified, wrapping each list in the `StoreC` constructor; the result can be seen in Figure 12.3.

There is an advantage to making the ADT mechanism part of the module system. Suppose we want to define an auxiliary function over the implementation type, which we use in defining the functions in the signature. An example of this is the function `isEmptyQ`, in the interface to `Queue`. This is used in defining `remQ`, but might not need to be exported. We can choose *not* to export this function; in the Gofer/Hugs mechanism, if the function is to have access to the implementation, it must appear in the signature, and therefore be visible.

In the remainder of the text we shall generally use the Gofer/Hugs ADT mechanism; translation from this to the official Haskell syntax is mechanical.

```
module Store ( StoreT , initial , lookup , update , eqStore )
where

type Var = Char

data StoreT = StoreC [ (Int,Var) ]

instance Eq StoreT where
  (==) = eqStore

initial :: StoreT
initial = StoreC []

lookup  :: StoreT -> Var -> Int

lookup (StoreC []) v = 0
lookup (StoreC ((n,w):st)) v
  | (v==w)    = n
  | otherwise = lookup (StoreC st) v

update  :: StoreT -> Var -> Int -> StoreT
update (StoreC st) v n = StoreC ((n,v):st)

eqStore :: StoreT -> StoreT -> Bool
eqStore = (==)
```

Figure 12.3   Stores as a Haskell ADT.

EXERCISES

12.13 Show how the implementations of the queue and store ADTs can be given in the Haskell syntax.

12.14 Repeat the exercises earlier in the chapter using the Haskell form of ADT.

12.5 Design

This section examines the design of Haskell abstract data types, and how the presence of this mechanism affects design in general.

General principles

In building a system, the choice of types is fundamental, and affects the subsequent design and implementation profoundly. If we use abstract data types at an early stage we hope to find 'natural' representations of the types occurring in the problem. Designing the abstract data types is a three-stage process.

- First we need to identify and *name* the types in the system.
- Next, we should give an *informal description* of what is expected from each type.
- Using this description we can then move to writing the *signature* of each abstract data type.

How do we decide what should go in the signature? This is the $64,000 question, of course, but there are some general questions we can ask of any abstract data type signature.

- Can we create objects of the type? For instance, in the Queue t type, we have the object emptyQ, and in a type of sets, we might give a function taking an element to the 'singleton' set containing that element alone. If there are no such objects or functions, something is wrong!
- Can we check what sort of object we have? In a tree ADT we might want to check whether we have a leaf or a node, for instance.
- Can we extract the components of objects, if we so require? Can we take the head of a Queue t, say?
- Can we transform objects: can we reverse a list, perhaps, or add an item to a queue?
- Can we combine objects? We might want to be able to join together two trees, for example.
- Can we collapse objects? Can we take the sum of a numerical list, or find the size of an object, say?

Not all these questions are appropriate in every case, but the majority of operations we perform on types fall into one of these categories. All the operations in the following signature for binary trees can be so classified, for instance.

```
type
  Tree t = ....
  in
  nil      :: Tree t,
  isNil    :: Tree t -> Bool,
  isNode   :: Tree t -> Bool,
  leftSub  :: Tree t -> Tree t,
  rightSub :: Tree t -> Tree t,
  treeVal  :: Tree t -> t,
  insTree  :: t -> Tree t -> Tree t,
  delete   :: t -> Tree t -> Tree t,
  join     :: Tree t -> Tree t -> Tree t
```

Other functions might be included in the signature; in the case of Tree t we might want to include the size function. This function can be defined using the other operations.

```
size :: Tree t -> Int
size t
  | isNil t     = 0
  | otherwise   = 1 + size (leftSub t) + size (rightSub t)
```

This definition of size is *independent* of the implementation, and so would not have to be re-implemented if the implementation type for Tree t changed. This is a good reason for leaving size out of the signature, and this is a check we can make for any signature: are all the functions in the signature needed? We come back to this point, and the tree type, later in the chapter. Now we look at a larger-scale example.

EXERCISES

12.15 Are all the operations in the Tree t signature necessary? Identify those which can be implemented using the other operations of the signature.

12.16 Design a signature for an abstract type of library databases, as first introduced in Chapter 4.

12.17 Design a signature for an abstract type of indexes, as examined in Section 7.6.

12.6 Example: simulation

We first introduced the simulation example in Section 10.5, where we designed the algebraic types Inmess and Outmess. Let us suppose, for ease of exposition, that the system time is measured in minutes.

The Inmess No signals no arrival, while Yes 34 12 signals the arrival of a customer at the 34th minute, who will need 12 minutes to be served.

The Outmess Discharge 34 27 12 signals that the person arriving at time 34 waited 27 minutes before receiving their 12 minutes of service.

Our aim in this section is to design the ADTs for a simple simulation of queueing. We start by looking at a single queue. Working through the stages, we will call the type QueueState, and it can be described thus.

> There are two main operations on a queue. The first is to add a new item, an Inmess, to the queue. The second is to process the queue by a one minute step; the effect of this is to give one minute's further processing to the item at the head of the queue (if there is such a thing). Two outcomes are possible: the item might have its processing completed, in which case an Outmess is generated, or further processing may be needed.
>
> Other items we need are an empty queue, an indication of the length of a queue and a test of whether a queue is empty.

This description leads directly to a signature declaration

```
type
  QueueState = ....
  in
  addMessage  :: Inmess -> QueueState -> QueueState,
  queueStep   :: QueueState -> ( QueueState , [Outmess] ),
  queueStart  :: QueueState,
  queueLength :: QueueState -> Int,
  queueEmpty  :: QueueState -> Bool
```

The queueStep function returns a pair: the QueueState after a step of processing, and a *list* of Outmess. A list is used, rather than a single Outmess, so that in the case of no output an empty list can be returned.

The QueueState type allows us to model a situation in which all customers are served by a single processor (or bank clerk). How can we model the case where there is more than one queue? We call this a *server* and it is to be modelled by the ServerState ADT.

> A server consists of a collection of queues, which can be identified by the integers 0, 1 and so on. It is assumed that the system receives

one `Inmess` each minute: at most one person arrives every minute, in other words.

There are three principal operations on a server. First, we should be able to add an `Inmess` to one of the queues. Second, a processing step of the server is given by processing each of the constituent queues by one step: this can generate a list of `Outmess`, as each queue can generate such a message. Finally, a step of the simulation combines a server step with allocation of the `Inmess` to the shortest queue in the server.

Three other operations are necessary. We have a starting server, consisting of the appropriate number of empty queues, and we should be able to identify the number of queues in a server, as well as the shortest queue it contains.

As a signature, we have

```
type
  ServerState = ....
  in
  addToQueue
     :: Int -> Inmess -> ServerState -> ServerState,
  serverStep
     :: ServerState -> ( ServerState , [Outmess] ),
  simulationStep
     :: ServerState -> Inmess -> ( ServerState , [Outmess] ),
  serverStart   :: ServerState,
  serverSize    :: ServerState -> Int,
  shortestQueue :: ServerState -> Int
```

In the next section we explore how to implement these two abstract data types. It is important to realize that users of the ADTs can begin to do their programming now: all the information that they need to know is contained in the signature of the abstract data type.

EXERCISES

12.18 Are there redundant operations in the signatures of the ADTs `QueueState` and `ServerState`?

12.19 Design a signature for *round-robin* simulation, in which allocation of the first item is to queue 0, the second to queue 1, and so on, starting again at 0 after the final queue has had an element assigned to it.

12.7 Implementing the simulation

This section gives an implementation of the ADTs for a queue and a server. The `QueueState` is implemented from scratch, while the `ServerState` implementation builds on the `QueueState` ADT. This means that the two implementations are independent; modifying the implementation of `QueueState` has no effect on the implementation of `ServerState`.

The queue

In the previous section, we designed the interfaces for the ADT; how do we proceed with implementation? First we ought to look again at the description of the `QueueState` type. What information does this imply the type should contain?

- There has to be a *queue* of `Inmess` to be processed. This can be represented by a list, and we can take the item at the head of the list as the item currently being processed.

- We need to keep a record of the processing time given to the head item, up to the particular time represented by the state.

- In an `Outmess`, we need to give the waiting time for the particular item being processed. We know the time of arrival and the time needed for processing – if we also know the current time, we can calculate the waiting time from these three numbers.

It therefore seems sensible to define

```
type QueueState = (Time,Service,[Inmess])
```

where the first field gives the current time, the second the service time so far for the item currently being processed, and the third the queue itself. Now we look at the operations one by one. To add a message, it is put at the end of the list of messages.

```
addMessage  :: Inmess -> QueueState -> QueueState

addMessage im (time,serv,ml) = (time,serv,ml++[im])
```

The most complicated definition is of `queueStep`. As was explained informally, there are two principal cases, when there is an item being processed.

```
queueStep    :: QueueState -> ( QueueState , [Outmess] )

queueStep (time , servSoFar , Yes a serv : inRest)
  | servSoFar < serv
     = ((time+1, servSoFar+1 , Yes a serv : inRest) , [])
  | otherwise
     = ((time+1, 0 , inRest)
               , [Discharge a (time-serv-a) serv])
```

In the first case, when the service time so far (servSoFar) is smaller than is required (serv), processing is not complete. We therefore add one to the time, and the service so far, and produce no output message.

If processing is complete, the otherwise case, the new state of the queue is (time+1, 0 , inRest) − time is advanced by one, processing time is set to zero and the head item in the list is removed. An output message is also produced in which the waiting time is given by subtracting the service and arrival times from the current time.

If there is nothing to process, then we simply have to advance the current time by one, and produce no output.

```
queueStep (time,serv,[]) = ((time+1,serv,[]) , [])
```

Note that the case of an input message No is not handled here since these messages are filtered out by the server; this is discussed below.

The three other functions are given by

```
queueStart   :: QueueState
queueStart = (0,0,[])

queueLength :: QueueState -> Int
queueLength (time,serv,l) = length l

queueEmpty   :: QueueState -> Bool
queueEmpty (t,s,q) = (q==[])
```

and this completes the implementation.

Obviously there are different possible implementations. We might choose to take the item being processed and hold it separately from the queue, or to use an ADT for the queue part, rather than a 'concrete' list.

The server

The server consists of a collection of queues, accessed by integers from 0; we choose to use a *list* of queues.

```
type ServerState = [QueueState]
```

Note that the implementation of this ADT builds on another ADT; this is not unusual. Now we take the functions in turn.

Adding an element to a queue uses the function `addMessage` from the `QueueState` abstract type.

```
addToQueue :: Int -> Inmess -> ServerState -> ServerState

addToQueue n im st
  = take n st ++ [newQueueState] ++ drop (n+1) st
    where
    newQueueState = addMessage im (st!!n)
```

A step of the server is given by making a step in each of the constituent queues, and concatenating together the output messages they produce.

```
serverStep :: ServerState -> ( ServerState , [Outmess] )

serverStep [] = ([],[])
serverStep (q:qs)
  = (q':qs' , mess++messes)
    where
    (q' , mess)   = queueStep q
    (qs' , messes) = serverStep qs
```

In making a simulation step, we perform a server step, and then add the incoming message, if it indicates an arrival, to the shortest queue.

```
simulationStep
  :: ServerState -> Inmess -> ( ServerState , [Outmess] )

simulationStep servSt im
  = (addNewObject im servSt1 , outmess)
    where
    (servSt1 , outmess) = serverStep servSt
```

Adding the message to the shortest queue is done by `addNewObject`, which is not in the signature. The reason for this is that it can be defined using the operations `addToQueue` and `shortestQueue`.

```
addNewObject :: Inmess -> ServerState -> ServerState

addNewObject No servSt = servSt

addNewObject (Yes arr wait) servSt
  = addToQueue (shortestQueue servSt) (Yes arr wait) servSt
```

It is in this function that the input messages No are not passed to the queues, as was mentioned above.

The other three functions of the signature are standard.

```
serverStart :: ServerState
serverStart = copy numQueues queueStart
```

where numQueues is a constant to be defined, and the standard function copy returns a list of n copies of x when applied thus: copy n x.

```
serverSize :: ServerState -> Int
serverSize = length
```

In finding the shortest queue, we use the queueLength function from the QueueState type.

```
shortestQueue :: ServerState -> Int
shortestQueue [q] = 0
shortestQueue (q:qs)
  | queueLength (qs!!short) <= queueLength q   = short+1
  | otherwise                                  = 0
    where
    short = shortestQueue qs
```

This concludes the implementation of the two simulation ADTs. The example is intended to show the merit of designing in stages. First we gave an informal description of the operations on the types, then a description of their signature, and finally an implementation. Dividing the problem up in this way makes each stage easier to solve.

The example also shows that types can be implemented *independently*: since ServerState uses only the abstract data type operations over QueueState, we can re-implement QueueState without affecting the server state at all.

EXERCISES

12.20 Give calculations of the expressions

```
queueStep (12,3,[Yes 8 4])
queueStep (13,4,[Yes 8 4])
queueStep (14,0,[])
```

12.21 If we let

    serverSt1 = [(13,4,[Yes 8 4]) , (13,3,[Yes 8 4])]

then give calculations of

    serverStep serverSt1
    simulationStep (Yes 13 10) serverSt1

12.22 Explain why we cannot use the function type (Int -> QueueState) as the representation type of ServerState. Design an extension of this type which will represent the server state, and implement the functions of the signature over this type.

12.23 Given the implementations of the ADTs from this section, is your answer to the question of whether there are redundant operations in the signatures of queues and servers any different?

12.24 If you have not done so already, design a signature for round-robin simulation, in which allocation of the first item is to queue 0, the second to queue 1, and so on.

12.25 Give an implementation of the round-robin simulation which *uses* the ServerState ADT.

12.26 Give a different implementation the round-robin simulation which *modifies* the implementation of the type ServerState itself.

12.8 Example: search trees

A binary search tree is an object of type Itree t, whose elements are *ordered*.

        data Itree t = Nil | Node t (Itree t) (Itree t)

The type is called Itree because its elements will give the *implementation* of an abstract data type of trees presently.

When is a tree ordered? The tree (Node val t_1 t_2) is ordered if

- all values in t_1 are smaller than val,
- all values in t_2 are larger than val, and
- the trees t_1 and t_2 are themselves ordered;

and the tree Nil is ordered.

Search trees are used to represent sets of elements, for example. How can we create a type of search trees? The type Itree t will not serve, as it contains elements like Node 2 (Node 3 Nil Nil) Nil, which are not ordered.

The answer is to build elements of the type using only operations which create or preserve order. We ensure that only these 'approved' operations are used by making the type an abstract data type.

The abstract data type

We gave the signature of the abstract data type earlier, in Section 12.5. The implementation type[2] is

```
type
  Tree t = Itree t
  in ....
```

and the standard operations to discriminate between different sorts of tree and to extract components are defined by

```
nil :: Tree t
nil = Nil

isNil :: Tree t -> Bool
isNil Nil = True
isNil _    = False

isNode :: Tree t -> Bool
isNode Nil = False
isNode _    = True

leftSub , rightSub :: Tree t -> Tree t
leftSub Nil           = error "leftSub"
leftSub (Node _ t1 _) = t1

treeVal   :: Tree t -> t
treeVal Nil           = error "treeVal"
treeVal (Node v _ _) = v
```

Figure 12.4 contains the definitions of the insertion, deletion and join functions.

---

[2] In Haskell, we can directly define the data type

```
data Tree t = Nil | Node t (Tree t) (Tree t)
```

and then hide its constructors on export, as explained in Section 12.4.

```
insTree :: Ord t => t -> Tree t -> Tree t

insTree val Nil = (Node val Nil Nil)

insTree val (Node v t1 t2)
  | v==val        = Node v t1 t2
  | val > v       = Node v t1 (insTree val t2)
  | val < v       = Node v (insTree val t1) t2

delete :: Ord t => t -> Tree t -> Tree t

delete val (Node v t1 t2)
  | val < v       = Node v (delete val t1) t2
  | val > v       = Node v t1 (delete val t2)
  | isNil t2      = t1
  | isNil t1      = t2
  | otherwise     = join t1 t2

join :: Ord t => Tree t -> Tree t -> Tree t

join t1 t2
  = Node mini t1 newT
    where
    (OK mini) = minTree t2
    newT      = delete mini t2

minTree :: Ord t => Tree t -> Err t

minTree t
  | isNil t       = Error
  | isNil t1      = OK v
  | otherwise     = minTree t1
    where
    t1 = leftSub t
    v  = treeVal t
```

Figure 12.4   Operations over search trees.

The types of insTree, delete, join and minTree are modified from their introduction above, containing as they do the context Ord t. Recall from Chapter 8 that this constraint means that these functions can only be used over types which carry an ordering operation, <=. It is easy to see from the definitions of these functions that they do indeed use the ordering.

Inserting an element which is already present has no effect, while inserting an element smaller (larger) than the value at the root causes it to be inserted in the left (right) sub-tree. The diagram shows 3 being inserted in the tree

(Node 7 (Node 2 Nil Nil) (Node 9 Nil Nil))

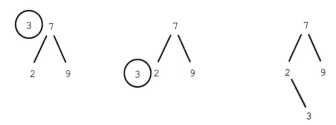

Deletion is straightforward when the value is smaller (larger) than the value at the root node: the deletion is made in the left (right) sub-tree. If the value to be deleted lies at the root, deletion is again simple if either sub-tree is Nil: the other sub-tree is returned. The problem comes when both sub-trees are non-Nil. In this case, the two sub-trees have to be joined together, keeping the ordering intact.

To join two non-Nil trees t1 and t2, where it is assumed that t1 is smaller than t2, we pick the minimum element, mini, of t2 to be the value at the root. The left sub-tree is t1, and the right is given by deleting mini from t2. The picture shows the deletion of 7 from

(Node 7 (Node 2 Nil Nil) (Node 9 (Node 8 Nil Nil) Nil))

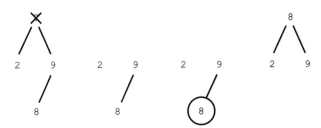

The minTree function returns a value of type Err t, since a Nil tree has no minimum. The OK constructor therefore has to be removed in the where clause of join.

Modifying the implementation

Given a search tree, we might be asked for its nth element,

```
indexT :: Int -> Tree t -> t
```

```
indexT n t                                              (†)
    | isNil t     = error "indexT"
    | n < st1     = indexT n t1
    | n == st1    = v
    | otherwise   = indexT (n-st1-1) t2
    where
      v   = treeVal t
      t1  = leftSub t
      t2  = rightSub t
      st1 = size t1
```

where the `size` is given by

```
size :: Tree t -> Int
size t
    | isNil t     = 0
    | otherwise   = 1 + size (leftSub t) + size (rightSub t)
```

If we are often asked to index elements of a tree, we will repeatedly have to find the `size` of search trees, and this will require computation.

We can think of making the size operation more efficient by *changing the implementation* of `Tree t`, so that an extra field is given in an `Stree` to hold the size of the tree:

```
data Stree t = Nil | Node t Int (Stree t) (Stree t)
```

What will have to be changed?

Incorrect

- We will have to redefine all the operations in the signature, since they access the implementation type, and this has changed. For example, the insertion function has the new definition

```
insTree val Nil = (Node val 1 Nil Nil)

insTree val (Node v n t1 t2)
    | v==val      = Node v n t1 t2
    | val > v     = Node v (n+1) t1 (insTree val t2)
    | val < v     = Node v (n+1) (insTree val t1) t2
```

wrong.

- We will have to add `size` to the signature, and redefine it thus

```
size Nil             = 0
size (Node v n t1 t2) = n
```

to use the value held in the tree.

Nothing else need be changed, however. In particular, the definition of `indexT` given in (†) is unchanged. This is a powerful argument in favour of using abstract data type definitions, and *against* using pattern matching. If (†) had used a pattern match over its argument, then it would have to be re-written if the underlying type changed. This shows that ADTs make programs more easily modifiable, as we argued at the start of the chapter.

In conclusion, it should be said that these search trees form a model for a collection of types, as they can be modified to carry different sorts of information. For, example, we could carry a count of the number of times an element occurs. This would be increased when an element is inserted, and reduced by one on deletion. Indeed *any* type of additional information can be held at the nodes – the insertion, deletion and other operations use the ordering on the elements to structure the tree irrespective of whatever else is held there. An example might be to store indexing information together with a word, for instance. This would form the basis for a re-implementation of the indexing system of Section 7.6.

EXERCISES

12.27 Explain how you would *test* the implementations of the functions over search trees. You might need to augment the signature of the type with a function to print a tree.

12.28 Using the `Itree` implementation, define the functions

```
successor :: Ord t => t -> Tree t -> Err t
closest   :: Int -> Tree Int -> Int
```

The successor of v in t is the smallest value in t larger than v, while the closest value to v in a numerical tree t is a value in t which has the smallest difference from v.

You can assume that `closest` is always called on a non-`Nil` tree, so always returns an answer.

12.29 Re-define the functions of the `Tree t` signature over the `Stree` implementation type.

12.30 To speed up the calculation of `maxTree` and other functions, you could imagine storing the maximum and minimum of the sub-tree at each node. Re-define the functions of the signature to manipulate these maxima and minima, and redefine the functions `maxTree`, `minTree` and `successor` to make use of this extra information stored in the trees.

12.31 You are asked to implement search trees with a count of the number of times an element occurs. How would this affect the signature of the type? How would you implement the operations? How much of the previously written implementation could be re-used?

12.32 Using a modified version of search trees instead of lists, re-implement the indexing software of Section 7.6.

12.33 Design a polymorphic abstract data type

```
Tree t u v
```

so that entries at each node contain an item of type `t`, on which the tree is ordered, and an item of type `u`, which might be something like the count, or a list of index entries.

On inserting an element, information of type `v` is given (a single index entry in that example); this information has to be combined with the information already present. The method of combination can be a functional parameter. There also needs to be a function to describe the way in which information is transformed at deletion.

As a test of your type, you should be able to implement the count trees and the index trees as instances.

12.9 Case study: sets

A finite set is a collection of elements of a particular type, which is both like and unlike a list. Lists are, of course, familiar, and examples include

```
[Joe,Sue,Ben]       [Ben,Sue,Joe]
[Joe,Sue,Sue,Ben]   [Joe,Sue,Ben,Sue]
```

Each of these lists is different – not only do the elements of a list matter, but also the *order* in which they occur, and their *multiplicity* (the number of times each element occurs).

In many situations, order and multiplicity are irrelevant. If we want to talk about the collection of people coming to our birthday party, we just want the names; a person is either there or not and so multiplicity is not important and the order we might list them in is also of no interest. In other words, all we want to know is the *set* of people coming. In the example above, this is the set consisting of Joe, Sue and Ben.

Like lists, queues, trees and so on, sets can be combined in many different ways: the operations which combine sets form the signature of the abstract data type. The search trees we saw earlier provide operations which concentrate on elements of a single ordered set: 'what is the successor of element e in set s?' for instance.

In this section we focus on the combining operations for sets. The signature for sets is as follows. We explain the purpose of the operations at the same time as giving their implementation.

```
type
  Set t = ....
  in
  empty        :: Set t,
  sing         :: t -> Set t,
  memSet       :: Ord t => Set t -> t -> Bool,
  union,inter,diff  :: Ord t => Set t -> Set t -> Set t,
  eqSet        :: Eq  t => Set t -> Set t -> Bool,
  subSet       :: Ord t => Set t -> Set t -> Bool,
  leqSet       :: Ord t => Set t -> Set t -> Bool,
  makeSet      :: Ord t => [t] -> Set t,
  mapSet       :: Ord u => (t -> u) -> Set t -> Set u,
  filterSet    :: (t->Bool) -> Set t -> Set t,
  foldSet      :: (t -> t -> t) -> t -> Set t -> t,
  showSet      :: (t->String) -> Set t -> String,
  card         :: Set t -> Int,
  setLimit     :: Ord t => (Set t -> Set t) -> Set t -> Set t
```

There are numerous possible signatures for sets, some of which assume certain properties of the element type. To test for elementhood, we need the elements to belong to a type in the Eq class; here we assume that the elements are in fact from an ordered type, which enlarges the class of operations over Set t. This gives the contexts Ord t, Ord u which are seen in some of the types in the signature above.

We choose to represent a set as an *ordered list of elements without repetitions*:

```
type
  Set t = [t]
```

The individual functions are described and implemented as follows. We use curly brackets '{', '}', to represent sets in examples – this is *not* part of Haskell notation.

The empty set, {}, is represented by an empty list, and the singleton set {a} consisting of the single element a by a one-element list.

```
empty  = []
sing a = [a]
```

The principal definitions over Set t are given in Figure 12.5. To test for membership of a set, we define memSet. It is important to see that we exploit the ordering in giving this definition.

Consider the three cases where the list is non-empty. In (1), the head element of the set, a, is smaller than the element we seek, and so we should check recursively in the tail x. In case (2) we have found the element, while in case (3) the head element is *larger* than b; since the list is ordered, *all* elements will be larger than b, so it cannot be a member of the list. This definition would *not* work if we chose to use arbitrary lists to represent sets.

union, inter, diff give the union, intersection and difference of two sets. The union consists of the elements occurring in either set (or both), the intersection of those elements in both sets and the difference of those elements in the first but not the second set. For example,

```
union {Joe,Sue} {Sue,Ben} =  {Joe,Sue,Ben}
inter {Joe,Sue} {Sue,Ben} =  {Sue}
diff  {Joe,Sue} {Sue,Ben} =  {Joe}
```

In making these definitions we again exploit the fact that the two arguments are ordered.

Recall that the brackets '{', '}' are not a part of Haskell; we can see them as shorthand for Haskell expressions as follows.

```
{e₁,  ...,  eₙ}
   = makeSet [e₁,  ...,  eₙ]
```

To test whether the first argument is a subset of the second, we use subSet; x is a subset of y if every element of x is an element of y.

Two sets are going to be equal if their representations as ordered lists are the same – hence the definition of eqSet as list equality; note that we require equality on t to define equality on Set t.

The ADT equality will *not* be the equality on the underlying type in every case: if we were to choose arbitrary lists to model sets, the equality test would be more complex, since [1,2] and [2,1,2,2] would represent the same set.

```
memSet [] b     = False
memSet (a:x) b
   | a<b          = memSet x b                      (1)
   | a==b          = True                           (2)
   | otherwise     = False                          (3)

union [] y          = y
union x []          = x
union (a:x) (b:y)
   | a<b           = a : union x (b:y)
   | a==b           = a : union x y
   | otherwise      = b : union (a:x) y

inter [] y = []
inter x [] = []
inter (a:x) (b:y)
   | a<b           = inter x (b:y)
   | a==b           = a : inter x y
   | otherwise      = inter (a:x) y

diff [] y = []
diff x [] = x
diff (a:x) (b:y)
   | a<b           = a : diff x (b:y)
   | a==b           = diff x y
   | otherwise      = diff (a:x) y

eqSet = (==)

subSet [] y = True
subSet x [] = False
subSet (a:x) (b:y)
   | a<b           = False
   | a==b           = subSet x y
   | a>b            = subSet (a:x) y

leqSet = (<=)

makeSet   = remDups . sort
mapSet f  = makeSet . (map f)
filterSet = filter
foldSet   = foldr
card      = length
```

Figure 12.5   Operations over the set abstract data type.

Using the function eqSet we can declare sets to be in the equality class if their elements can be compared for equality:

```
instance Eq t => Eq (Set t) where
    (==) = eqSet
```

In a similar way we can put an ordering on sets using the underlying ordering on their list representations; this is done by leqSet and allows us to declare

```
instance Ord t => Ord (Set t)
    where (<=) = leqSet
```

To form a set from an arbitrary list, makeSet, the list is sorted, and then duplicate elements are removed; definitions of sort and remDups are left as an exercise.

mapSet, filterSet and foldSet behave like map, filter and foldr except that they operate over sets. The latter two are given by filter and foldr; for mapSet we have to remove duplicates after mapping. The cardinality of a set is the number of its members. The function card gives this, as it returns the length of the list.

showSet f x gives a printable version of a set x, one item per line, using the function f to give a printable version of each element.

```
showSet f = concat . (map ((++"\n") . f))
```

The final function in the signature is a polymorphic higher order function of general use. setLimit f x gives the *limit* of the sequence

```
x , f x , f (f x) , f (f (f x)) , ...
```

The limit is the value to which the sequence settles down if it exists. It is found by taking the first element in the sequence whose successor is equal, as a set, to the element itself.

```
setLimit f x
    | eqSet x next      = x
    | otherwise         = setLimit f next
      where
      next = f x
```

As an example, take Ben to be Sue's father, Sue to be Joe's mother, who himself has no children. Now define

```
addChildren :: Set Person -> Set Person
```

to add to a set the children of all members of the set, so that for instance

```
addChildren {Joe,Ben} = {Joe,Sue,Ben}
```

Now we can give an example calculation of a set limit.

```
  setLimit addChildren {Ben}
    ??  eqSet {Ben} {Ben,Sue} = False
= setLimit addChildren {Ben,Sue}
    ??  eqSet {Ben,Sue} {Ben,Joe,Sue} = False
= setLimit addChildren {Ben,Joe,Sue}
    ??  eqSet {Ben,Joe,Sue} {Ben,Joe,Sue} = True
= {Ben,Joe,Sue}
```

The `setLimit` function is a special case of a general limit function, `generalLimit` defined in Section 12.10, in which subsequent steps are checked for equality using ==. If we declare Set t to be an instance of Eq t, this function may be used.

In the next section we build a library of functions to work with relations and graphs; this uses the Set library as its basis.

EXERCISES

12.34 Define the functions `sort` and `remDups` used in the definition of `makeSet`.

12.35 Define the function

```
symmDiff :: Ord t => Set t -> Set t -> Set t
```

which gives the *symmetric difference* of two sets. This consists of the elements which lie in one of the sets but not the other, so that

```
symmDiff {Joe,Sue} {Sue,Ben} = {Joe,Ben}
```

12.36 Complete the declaration of Ord (Set t) as discussed above. [Hint: you will need to extend the signature of the ADT to do this.]

12.37 How can you define the function

```
powerSet :: Set t -> Set (Set t)
```

which returns the set of all subsets of a set defined? Can you give a definition which uses only the operations of the abstract data type?

12.38 How are the functions

```
setUnion :: Ord t => Set (Set t) -> Set t
setInter :: Ord t => Set (Set t) -> Set t
```

which return the union and intersection of a set of sets defined using the operations of the abstract data type?

12.39 Can infinite sets (of numbers, for instance) be adequately represented by ordered lists? Can you tell if two infinite lists are equal, for instance?

12.40 The abstract data type `Set t` can be represented in a number of different ways. Alternatives include: arbitrary lists (rather than ordered lists without repetitions), and Boolean valued functions, that is elements of the type `t -> Bool`. Give implementations of the type using these two representations.

12.41 Give an implementation of the `Set` abstract data type using search trees.

12.42 Give an implementation of the `Tree` abstract data type using ordered lists. Compare the behaviour of the two implementations.

12.10 Relations and graphs

We now use the `Set` abstract data type as a means of implementing relations and, taking an alternative view of the same objects, graphs.

A binary relation relates together certain elements of a set. A family relationship can be summarized by saying that the `isParent` relation holds between Ben and Sue, between Ben and Leo and between Sue and Joe. In other words, it relates the *pairs* `(Ben,Sue)`, `(Ben,Leo)` and `(Sue,Joe)`, and so we can think of this particular relation as the set

```
isParent = {(Ben,Sue) , (Ben,Leo) , (Sue,Joe)}
```

In general we say

```
type Relation t = Set (t,t)
```

This definition means that all the set operations are available on relations. We can test whether a relation holds of two elements using `memSet`; the union of two relations like `isParent` and `isSibling` gives the relationship of being either a parent *or* a sibling, and so on.

Are there any other particular operations over relations? We first set ourselves the task of defining the function addChildren, and then the related problem of finding the isAncestor relation. The functions we define are in Figure 12.6.

```
image :: Ord t => Relation t -> t -> Set t
image rel val = mapSet snd (filterSet ((==val).fst) rel)

setImage :: Ord t => Relation t -> Set t -> Set t
setImage rel = unionSet . mapSet (image rel)

unionSet :: Ord t => Set (Set t) -> Set t
unionSet = foldSet union empty

addImage :: Ord t => Relation t -> Set t -> Set t
addImage rel st = st 'union' setImage rel st

addChildren :: Set People -> Set People
addChildren = addImage isParent
```

```
compose :: Ord t => Relation t -> Relation t -> Relation t

compose rel1 rel2
  = mapSet outer (filterSet equals (setProduct rel1 rel2))
    where
    equals ((a,b),(c,d)) = (b==c)
    outer  ((a,b),(c,d)) = (a,d)

setProduct :: (Ord t,Ord u) => Set t -> Set u -> Set (t,u)
setProduct st1 st2 = unionSet (mapSet (adjoin st1) st2)

adjoin :: (Ord t,Ord u) => Set t -> u -> Set (t,u)

adjoin st el = mapSet (addEl el) st
                 where
                 addEl el el' = (el',el)

tClosure :: Ord t => Relation t -> Relation t

tClosure rel = setLimit addGen rel
                 where
                 addGen rel' = rel' 'union' compose rel' rel
```

Figure 12.6 Functions over the type of relations, Relation t.

Working bottom-up, we first ask how we find all elements related to a given element: who are all Ben's children, for instance? We need to find all pairs beginning with Ben, and then to return their second halves. The function to perform this is image and the set of Ben's children will be

```
image isParent Ben = {Sue,Leo}
```

Now, how can we find all the elements related to a *set* of elements? We find the image of each element separately, and then take the union of these sets. The union of a set of sets is given by folding the binary union operation into the set.

```
unionSet {s₁, ..., sₙ}
  = s₁ U ... U sₙ
  = s₁ 'union' ... 'union' sₙ
```

Now, how do we add all the children to a set of people? We find the image of the set under isParent, and combine it with the set itself. This is given by the function addChildren.

The second task we set ourselves was to find the isAncestor relation – the general problem is to find the *transitive closure* of a relation, the function tClosure of Figure 12.6. We do this by closing up the relation, so we add grandparenthood, great-grandparenthood and so forth to the relation until nothing further is added.

How do we get the isGrandparent relation? We match together pairs like

```
(Ben,Sue)     (Sue,Joe)
```

and see that this gives that Ben is a grandparent of Joe. We call this the **relational composition** of isParent with itself. In general,

```
isGrandparent
  = compose isParent isParent
  = {(Ben,Joe)}
```

In defining compose we have used the setProduct function to give the *product* of two sets. This is formed by pairing every element of the first set with every element of the second. For instance,

```
setProduct {Ben,Suzie} {Sue,Joe}
  = { (Ben,Sue) , (Ben,Joe) , (Suzie,Sue) , (Suzie,Joe) }
```

setProduct uses the function adjoin to pair each element of a set with a given element. For instance,

```
adjoin Joe {Ben,Sue} = { (Ben,Joe) , (Sue,Joe) }
```

A relation rel is *transitive* if for all (a,b) and (b,c) in rel, (a,c) is in rel. The transitive closure of a relation rel is the smallest relation extending rel which is transitive. We compute the transitive closure of rel, tClosure rel, by repeatedly adding one more 'generation' of rel, using compose, until nothing more is added. To do this, we make use of the setLimit function, defined in Section 12.9 above.

Type classes

The functions of Figure 12.6 give an interesting example of type classes in action. The adjoin function requires that the types t and u carry an ordering. Haskell contains the instance declaration

```
instance (Ord t, Ord u) => Ord (t,u) ....          (†)
```

and so this is sufficient to ensure Ord (t,u), which is required for the application of mapSet within adjoin.

Similarly, in defining compose we require an ordering on the type ((t,t),(t,t)); again, knowing Ord t is sufficient to give this, since (†) can be used to derive the ordering on ((t,t),(t,t)).

Remember that the Gofer class system is different from the Haskell system we use in this book. The types of the functions here are much more complicated under the Gofer system as they explicitly contain items like Ord ((t,t),(t,t)) in the contexts. It is possible to give all the functions here Gofer types; we leave it as an exercise for the masochistic reader!

Graphs

Another way of seeing a relation is as a directed *graph*. For example, the relation

```
graph1 = { (1,2) , (1,3) , (3,2) , (3,4) , (4,2) , (2,4) }
```

can be pictured thus

where we draw an arrow joining a to b if the pair (a,b) is in the relation. What then does the transitive closure represent? Two points a and b are related by tClosure graph1 if there is a *path* from a to b through the graph. For example, the pair (1,4) is in the closure, since a path leads from 1 to 3 then to 2 and finally to 4, while the pair (2,1) is not in the closure, since no path leads from 2 to 1 through graph1.

A problem occurring in many different application areas, including networks and compilers, is to find the (strongly connected) components of a graph. Every graph can have its nodes split into sets or components with the property that every node in a component is connected by a path to all other nodes in the same component. The components of graph1 are {1}, {3} and {2,4}. We solve the problem in two stages:

- we first form the relation which links points in the same component; then

- we form the components (or equivalence classes) generated by this relation.

There is a path from a to b and vice versa if both (a,b) and (b,a) are in the closure, so we define

```
connect :: Ord t => Relation t -> Relation t
connect rel = clos 'inter' solc
            where
                clos = tClosure rel
                solc = inverse clos

inverse :: Ord t => Relation t -> Relation t
inverse = mapSet swap
            where
                swap (a,b) = (b,a)
```

Now, how do we form the components given by the relation graph1? We start with the set

```
{{1},{2},{3},{4}}
```

and repeatedly add the images under the relation to each of the classes, until a fixed point is reached. In general this gives

```
classes :: Ord t => Relation t -> Set (Set t)

classes rel
    = setLimit (addImages rel) start
        where
        start = mapSet sing (eles rel)
```

where the auxiliary functions used are

```
eles :: Ord t => Relation t -> Set t
eles rel = mapSet fst rel 'union' mapSet snd rel

addImages
      :: Ord t => Relation t -> Set (Set t) -> Set (Set t)
addImages rel = mapSet (addImage rel)
```

Searching in graphs

Many algorithms require us to *search* through the nodes of a graph: we might want to find a shortest path from one point to another, or to count the number of paths between two points.

Two general patterns of search are depth-first and breadth-first. In a depth-first search, we explore all elements below a given child before moving to the next child; a breadth-first search examines all the children before examining the grandchildren, and so on. In the case of searching below node 1 in graph1, the sequence [1,2,4,3] is depth-first (4 is visited before 3), while [1,2,3,4] is breadth-first. These examples show that we can characterize the searches as transformations

```
breadthFirst :: Ord t => Relation t -> t -> [t]
depthFirst   :: Ord t => Relation t -> t -> [t]
```

with breadthFirst graph1 1 = [1,2,3,4], for instance. The use of a list in these functions is crucial – we are not simply interested in finding the nodes below a node (tClosure does this), we are interested in the *order* that they occur.

A crucial step in both searches is to find all the descendants of a node which have not been visited so far. We can write

```
newDescs :: Ord t => Relation t -> Set t -> t -> Set t
newDescs rel st v = image rel v 'diff' st
```

which returns the *set* of descendants of v in rel which are not in the set st. Here we have a problem; the result of this function is a set and not a list, but we require the elements in some order. One solution is to add to the Set abstract data type a function

```
flatten :: Set t -> [t]                                    (†)
flatten = id
```

which breaks the abstraction barrier in the case of the ordered list implementation. An alternative is to supply as a parameter a function

```
minSet :: Set t -> Err t
```

which returns the minimum of a non-empty set and which can be used in flattening a set to a list without breaking the abstraction barrier. Unconcerned about its particular definition, we assume the existence of a flatten function of type (†). Then we can say

```
findDescs :: Ord t => Relation t -> [t] -> t -> [t]
findDescs rel l v = flatten (newDescs rel (makeSet l) v)
```

Breadth-first search

A breadth-first search involves repeatedly applying findDescs until a limit is reached. The generalLimit function finds this

```
generalLimit :: Eq t => (t -> t) -> t -> t
generalLimit f x
   | x == next    = x
   | otherwise    = generalLimit f next
     where
     next = f x
```

which works just as setLimit, with == replacing eqSet.

```
breadthFirst rel val
   = generalLimit step start
     where
     start = [val]
     step l = l ++ nub (concat (map (findDescs rel l) l))
```

A step performs a number of operations.

- First, all the descendants of elements in l which are not already in l are found. This is given by mapping (findDescs rel l) along the list l.

- This list of lists is then concatenated into a single list.

- Duplicates can occur in this list, as a node may be a descendant of more than one node, and so any duplicated elements must be removed. This is the effect of the library function

```
nub :: Eq t => [t] -> [t]
```

which removes all but the first occurrence of each element in a list.

Depth-first search

How does depth-first search proceed? We first generalize the problem to

```
depthSearch :: Ord t => Relation t -> t -> [t] -> [t]
depthFirst rel v = depthSearch rel v []
```

where the third argument is used to carry the list of nodes already visited, and so which are not to appear in the result of the function call.

```
depthSearch rel v used
   = v : depthList rel (findDescs rel used' v) used'
         where
         used' = v:used
```

Here we call the auxiliary function `depthList` which finds all the descendants of a *list* of nodes.

```
depthList rel [] used = []

depthList rel (val:rest) used
   = next ++ depthList rel rest (used++next)
     where
     next = if   elem val used
               then []
               else depthSearch rel val used
```

The definition has two equations, the first giving the trivial case where no nodes are to be explored. In the second there are two parts to the solution.

- `next` gives the part of the graph accessible below `val`. This may be `[]`, if `val` is a member of the list `used`, otherwise `depthSearch` is called.

- `depthList` is then called on the tail of the list, but with `next` appended to the list of nodes already visited.

This pair of definitions is a good example of definition by *mutual recursion*, since each calls the other. It is possible to define a single function to perform the effect of the two, but this pair of functions seems to express the algorithm in the most natural way.

12.43 Calculate

```
classes (connect graph1)
classes (connect graph2)
```

where graph2 = graph1 ∪ { (4,3) }.

12.44 Give calculations of

```
breadthFirst graph2 1
depthFirst graph2 1
```

where graph2 is defined in the previous exercise.

12.45 Using the searches as a model, give a function

```
distance :: Eq t => Relation t -> t -> t -> Int
```

which gives the length of a shortest path from one node to another in a graph. For instance,

```
distance graph1 1 4 = 2
distance graph1 4 1 = 0
```

0 is the result when no such path exists, or when the two nodes are equal.

12.46 A weighted graph carries a *weight* with each edge. Design a type to model this. Give functions for breadth-first and depth-first search which return lists of *pairs*. Each pair consists of a node, together with the length of a shortest path to that node from the node at the start of the search.

12.47 A *heterogeneous* relation relates objects of different type. An example might be the relation relating a person to their age. Design a type to model these relations; how do you have to modify the functions defined over Relation t to work over this type, if it is possible?

12.11 Commentary

This section explores a number of issues raised by the introduction of ADTs into our discussion.

First, we have not yet said anything about verification of functions over abstract data types. This is because there is nothing new to say about the *proof* of theorems: these are proved for the implementation types exactly as we have seen earlier. The theorems valid for an abstract data type are precisely those which obey the type constraints on the functions in the signature. For a queue type, for instance, we will be able to prove that

```
remQ (addQ a emptyQ) = (a , emptyQ)
```

by proving the appropriate result about the implementation. What would not be valid would be an equation like

```
emptyQ = []
```

since this breaks the information-hiding barrier and reveals something of the implementation itself.

Next we note that our *implementation* of sets gives rise to some properties which we ought to prove, often called **proof obligations**. We have assumed that our sets are implemented as ordered lists without repetitions; we ought to prove that each operation over our implementation preserves this property.

Finally, observe that both classes and abstract data types use signatures, so it is worth surveying their similarities and differences.

- Their purposes are different: ADTs are used to provide information hiding, and to structure programs; classes are used to overload names, to allow the same name to be used over a class of different types.

- The signature in an ADT is associated with a single implementation type, which may be monomorphic or polymorphic. On the other hand, the signature in a class will be associated with multiple instances; this is the whole point of including classes, in fact.

- The functions in the signature of an ADT provide the *only* access to the underlying type; there is no such information hiding over classes: to be a member of a class, a type must provide *at least* the types in the signature.

- ADTs can be polymorphic, so we can have a polymorphic type of search trees, for instance. Classes classify single types rather than polymorphic families of types; constructor classes (Peterson *et al.*, 1996; Jones, 1995b) extend classes to do exactly that.

SUMMARY

The abstract data types of this chapter have three important and related properties.

- They provide a *natural* representation of a type, which avoids being over-specific. An abstract data type carries precisely the operations which are naturally associated with the type, and nothing more.
- The signature of an abstract data type is a firm interface between the user and the implementor: development of a system can proceed completely independently on the two sides of the interface.
- If the implementation of a type is to be *modified*, then only the operations in the signature need to be changed; any operation using the signature functions can be used unchanged. We saw an example of this with search trees, when the implementation was modified to include size information.

We saw various examples of ADT development. Most importantly we saw the practical example of the simulation types being designed in the three stages suggested. First the types are named, then they are described informally, and finally a signature was written down. After that we were able to implement the operations of the signature as a separate task.

One of the difficulties in writing a signature is being sure that all the relevant operations have been included: we gave a check-list of the kinds of operations which should be present, and against which it is sensible to evaluate any of our signature definitions.

13 Lazy programming

In our calculations so far we have said that the order in which we make evaluation steps will not affect the results produced – it may only affect whether the sequence leads to a result. This chapter describes precisely the **lazy evaluation** strategy which underlies Haskell. Lazy evaluation is well named: a lazy evaluator will only evaluate an argument to a function if that argument's value is *needed* to compute the overall result. Moreover, if an argument is structured (a list or a tuple, for instance), only those parts of the argument which are needed will be examined.

Lazy evaluation has consequences for the style of programs we can write. Since an intermediate list will only be generated *on demand*, using an intermediate list will not necessarily be expensive computationally. We examine this in the context of a series of examples, culminating in a case study of parsing.

We also take the opportunity to extend the list comprehension notation. This does not allow us to write any new programs, but does make a lot of list processing programs – especially those which work by generating and then testing possible solutions – easier to express and understand.

Another consequence of lazy evaluation is that it is possible for the language to describe **infinite** structures. These would require an infinite amount of time to evaluate fully, but under lazy evaluation, only parts of a data structure need to be examined. Any recursive type will contain infinite objects; we concentrate on lists here, as infinite lists are by far the most widely used infinite structures.

After introducing a variety of examples, such as infinite lists of prime and random numbers, we discuss the importance of infinite lists for program design, and see that programs manipulating infinite lists can be thought of as processes consuming and creating 'streams' of data. Based on this idea, we explore how to complete the simulation case study.

The chapter concludes with an update on program verification in the light of lazy evaluation and the existence of infinite lists; this section can give only a flavour of the area, but contains references to more detailed presentations.

13.1 Lazy evaluation

Central to evaluation in Haskell is function application. The basic idea behind this is simple; to evaluate the function f applied to arguments a_1, a_2, $\ldots$, a_k, we simply *substitute* the expressions a_i for the corresponding variables in the function's definition. For instance, if

```
egFun1 a b = a+b
```

then

```
egFun1 (9-3) (egFun1 34 3)
= (9-3)+(egFun1 34 3)
```

since we replace a by (9-3) and b by (egFun1 34 3). The expressions (9-3) and (egFun1 34 3) are not evaluated before they are passed to the function.

In this case, for evaluation to continue, we need to evaluate the arguments to '+', giving

```
= 6+(34+3)
= 6+37
= 43
```

In this example both of the arguments are evaluated eventually, but this is not always the case. If we define

```
egFun2 a b = a+12
```

then

```
egFun2 (9-3) (egFun2 34 3)
= (9-3)+12
= 6+12
= 18
```

Here (9-3) is substituted for a, but as b does not appear on the right-hand side of the equation, the argument (egFun2 34 3) will not appear in the result, and so *is not evaluated*. Here we see the first advantage of lazy evaluation – an argument which is not needed will not be evaluated. This example is rather too simple: why would we write the second argument if its value is never needed? A rather more realistic example is

```
switch :: Int -> t -> t -> t
switch n x y
  | n>0          = x
  | otherwise    = y
```

If the integer n is positive, the result is the value of x; otherwise it is the value of y. Either of the arguments x and y might be used, but in the first case y is not evaluated and in the second x is not evaluated. A third example is

```
egFun3 a b = a+a
```

so that

```
egFun3 (9-3) (egFun1 34 3)                              (†)
= (9-3)+(9-3)
```

It appears here that we will have to evaluate the argument (9-3) *twice* since it is duplicated on substitution. Lazy evaluation ensures that *a duplicated argument is never evaluated more than once*. This can be modelled in a calculation by doing the corresponding steps simultaneously, thus

```
egFun3 (9-3) 17
= (9-3)+(9-3)
= 6+6
= 12
```

In the implementation, there is no duplicated evaluation because calculations are made over *graphs* rather than trees to represent the expressions being evaluated. For instance, instead of duplicating the argument, as in (i) below, the evaluation of (†) will give a graph in which on both sides of the plus there is the *same* expression. This is shown in (ii).

A final example is given by the pattern matching function,

```
egFun4 (a,b) = a+1
```

applied to the pair (3+2,4-17).

```
egFun4 (3+2,4-17)
= (3+2)+1
= 6
```

The argument is examined, and *part* of it is evaluated. The second half of the pair remains unevaluated, as it is not needed in the calculation. This completes the informal introduction to lazy evaluation, which can be summarized in the three points:

- arguments to functions are only evaluated when this is necessary for evaluation to continue;
- an argument is not necessarily evaluated fully: only the parts that are needed are examined;
- an argument is only evaluated once, if at all. This is done in the implementation by replacing expressions by *graphs* and calculating over them.

We now give a more formal account of the calculation rules which embody lazy evaluation.

13.2 Calculation rules

As we first saw in Section 2.11, the definition of a function consists of a number of conditional equations. Each conditional equation can contain multiple clauses and may have a number of local definitions given in a where clause. Each equation will have on its left-hand side the function under definition applied to a number of patterns.

```
f p₁ p₂ ... pₖ
    | g₁          = e₁
    | g₂          = e₂
    ...
    | otherwise   = eᵣ
      where
         v₁  a₁,₁ ... = r₁
      ....
f q₁ q₂ ... qₖ
    = ...
```

In calculating f a₁ ... aₖ there are three aspects.

Calculation – pattern matching

In order to determine which of the equations is used, the arguments are evaluated. The arguments are not evaluated *fully*, rather they are evaluated sufficiently to see whether they match the corresponding patterns. If they match the patterns p₁ to pₖ, then evaluation proceeds using the first equation; if not, they are checked against the second equation, which may require further evaluation. This is repeated until a match is given, or there are no more equations (which would generate a Program error). For instance, given the definition

```
f :: [Int] -> [Int] -> Int
f [] y        = 0                    (1)
f (a:x) []    = 0                    (2)
f (a:x) (b:y) = a+b                  (3)
```

the evaluation of f [1 .. 3] [1 .. 3] proceeds thus

```
  f [1 .. 3] [1 .. 3]                (4)
= f (1:[2 .. 3]) [1 .. 3]           (5)
= f (1:[2 .. 3]) (1:[2 .. 3])       (6)
= 1+1                                (7)
```

At stage (4), there is not enough information about the arguments to determine whether there is a match with (1). One step of evaluation gives (5), and shows there is not a match with (1).

The first argument of (5) matches the first pattern of (2), so we need to check the second. One step of calculation in (6) shows that there is no match with (2), but that there is with (3); hence we have (7).

Calculation – guards

Suppose that the first conditional equation matches (simply for the sake of explanation). The expressions a_1 to a_k are substituted for the patterns p_1 to p_k throughout the conditional equation. We must next determine which of the clauses on the right-hand side applies. The guards are evaluated in turn, until one is found which gives the value `True`; the corresponding clause is then used. If we have

```
f :: Int -> Int -> Int -> Int
f a b c
   | a>=b && a>=c      = a
   | b>=a && b>=c      = b
   | otherwise         = c
```

then

```
f (2+3) (4-1) (3+9)
   ??   (2+3)>=(4-1) && (2+3)>=(3+9)
   ??     = 5>=3 && 5>=(3+9)
   ??     = True && 5>=(3+9)
   ??     = 5>=(3+9)
   ??     = 5>=12
   ??     = False
   ??   3>=5 && 3>=12
   ??     = False && 3>=12
   ??     = False
   ??   otherwise = True
 = 12
```

We leave it as an exercise for the reader to work out which parts of the calculation above are shared.

Calculation – local definitions

Values in `where` clauses are calculated on demand: only when a value is needed does calculation begin. Given the definitions

```
f :: Int -> Int -> Int

f a b
  | notNil l    = front l
  | otherwise   = b
    where
    l = [a .. b]

front (c:d:y) = c+d
front [c]      = c

notNil []     = False
notNil (a:x) = True
```

the calculation of f 3 5 will be

```
f 3 5
   ?? notNil l
   ?? | where
   ?? | l = [3 .. 5]
   ?? |   = 3:[4 .. 5]                              (1)
   ?? = notNil (3:[4 .. 5])
   ?? = True
 = front l
        where
        l = 3:[4 .. 5]
          = 3:4:[5]                                 (2)
 = 3+4                                              (3)
 = 7
```

To evaluate the guard notNil l, evaluation of l begins, and after one step, (1) shows that the guard is True. Evaluating front l requires more information about l, and so we evaluate by one more step to give (2). A successful pattern match in the definition of front then gives (3), and so the result.

Operators and other expression formers

The three aspects of evaluating a function application are now complete; we should now say something about the built-in operators. If they can be given Haskell definitions, such as

```
True  && x = x
False && x = False
```

then they will follow the rules for Haskell definitions. The left-to-right order means that '&&' will not evaluate its second argument in case its first is `False`, for instance. This is unlike many programming languages, where the 'and' function will evaluate both its arguments.

The other operations, such as the arithmetic operators, vary. Plus needs both its arguments to return a result, but the equality on lists can return `False` on comparing `[]` and `(a:x)` without evaluating `a` or `x`. In general the language is implemented so that no manifestly unnecessary evaluation takes place.

Recall that `if ... then ... else ...`; `cases`; `let` and lambda expressions can be used in forming expressions. Their evaluation follows the form we have seen for function applications. Specifically, `if ... then ... else ...` is evaluated like a guard, `cases` like a pattern match, `let` like a `where` clause and a lambda expression like the application of a named function such as `f` above.

Finally, we turn to the way in which a choice is made between applications.

Evaluation order

What characterizes evaluation in Haskell, apart from the fact that no argument is evaluated twice, is the **order** in which applications are evaluated when there is a choice.

- Evaluation is '*from the outside in*'. In a situation like

    f e₁ (f e₂ 17)

  where one application encloses another, as seen in the expression, the outer one, `f e₁ (f e₂ 17)` is chosen for evaluation.

- Otherwise, evaluation is '*from left to right*'. In the expression

    f e₁ + f e₂

  The underlined expressions are both to be evaluated. The left-hand one, `f e₁` will be examined first.

These rules are enough to describe the way in which lazy evaluation works. In the sections to come we look at the consequences of a lazy approach for functional programming.

13.3 List comprehensions revisited

The list comprehension notation does not add any new programs to the Haskell language, but it does allow us to (re-)write programs in a new and clearer way. Building on the introduction in Section 4.6, the notation lets us combine multiple maps and filters together in a single expression. Combinations of these functions allow us to write algorithms which *generate and test*: all the elements of a particular form are generated, combinations of them are tested, before results depending upon them are returned. We begin the section with a re-examination of the syntax of the list comprehension, before giving some simple illustrative examples. After that we give the rules for calculating with list comprehensions, and we finish the section with a series of longer examples.

Syntax

A list comprehension has the form

```
[ e | q₁ , ... , qₖ ]
```

where each *qualifier* q_i has one of two forms.

- It can be a generator, p <- lExp, where p is a *pattern* and lExp is an expression of list type.
- It can be a test, bExp, which is a Boolean expression.

An expression lExp or bExp appearing in qualifier q_i can refer to the variables used in the patterns of qualifiers q_1 to q_{i-1}.

Simpler examples

Multiple generators allow us to combine elements from two or more lists

```
pairs :: [t] -> [u] -> [(t,u)]
pairs l m = [ (a,b) | a<-l , b<-m ]
```

This example is important as it shows the way in which the values a and b are chosen.

```
pairs [1,2,3] [4,5]
= [(1,4),(1,5),(2,4),(2,5),(3,4),(3,5)]
```

The first element of 1, 1, is given to a, and then *for this fixed value* all possible values of b in m are chosen. This process is repeated for the remaining values a in 1, namely 2 and 3.

This choice is not accidental, since if we have

```
triangle :: Int -> [(Int,Int)]
triangle n = [ (a,b) | a <- [1 .. n] , b <- [1 .. a] ]
```

the second generator, b <- [1 .. a] depends on the value of a given by the first generator.

```
triangle 3 = [(1,1),(2,1),(2,2),(3,1),(3,2),(3,3)]
```

For the first choice of a, 1, the value of b is chosen from [1 .. 1], for the second choice of a, the value of b is chosen from [1 .. 2], and so on.

Three numbers form a *Pythagorean triple* if the sum of squares of the first two is equal to the square of the third. The list of all triples with all sides below a particular bound, n, is given by

```
pyTriple n
  = [ (a,b,c) | a <- [2 .. n] , b <- [a+1 .. n] ,
                c <- [b+1 .. n] , a*a + b*b == c*c ]
```

```
pyTriple 100 = [(3,4,5),(5,12,13),(6,8,10),...,(65,72,97)]
```

Here the test combines values from the three generators.

Calculating with list comprehensions

How can we describe the way in which the results of list comprehensions are obtained? One way is to give a translation of the comprehensions into applications of map, filter and concat. We give a different approach here, of calculating *directly* with the expressions.

Before we do this, we introduce one piece of very helpful notation. We write e{f/x} for the expression e in which every occurrence of the variable x has been replaced by the expression f. This is the **substitution** of f for x in e. If p is a pattern, we use e{f/p} for the substitution of the appropriate parts of f for the variables in p. For instance,

```
[ (a,b) | a<-1 ]{[2,3]/1}    = [ (a,b) | a<-[2,3] ]
(a + sum x){(2,[3,4])/(a,x)} = 2 + sum [3,4]
```

since 2 matches a, and [3,4] matches x when (2,[3,4]) is matched against (a,x).

We now explain list comprehensions. The notation looks a bit daunting, but the effect should be clear. The generator v <- [a₁, ..., aₙ] has the effect of setting v to the values a₁ to aₙ in turn. Setting the value appears in the calculation as *substitution* of a value for a variable.

```
[ e | v <- [a₁,...,aₙ] , q₂ , ... , qₖ ]
= [ e{a₁/v} | q₂{a₁/v} , ... , qₖ{a₁/v} ]
++ ... ++
  [ e{aₙ/v} | q₂{aₙ/v} , ... , qₖ{aₙ/v} ]
```

As a running example for this section we take

```
[ a+b | a <- [1,2] , isEven a , b <- [a .. 2*a] ]
= [ 1+b | isEven 1 , b <- [1 .. 2*1] ] ++
  [ 2+b | isEven 2 , b <- [2 .. 2*2] ]
```

where the values 1 and 2 are substituted for a. The rules for tests are simple,

```
[ e | True  , q₂ , ... , qₖ ] = [ e | q₂ , ... , qₖ ]
[ e | False , q₂ , ... , qₖ ] = []
```

so that our example is

```
= [ 1+b | False , b <- [1 .. 2*1] ] ++
  [ 2+b | True , b <- [2 .. 2*2] ]
= [ 2+b | b <- [2,3,4] ]
= [ 2+2 | ] ++ [ 2+3 | ] ++ [ 2+4 | ]
```

and when there are no qualifiers,

```
[ e | ] = [ e ]
```

Completing the example, we have

```
[ a+b | a <- [1,2] , isEven a , b <- [a .. 2*a] ] = [4,5,6]
```

Now we consider some more examples.

```
[ (a,b) | a <- [1 .. 3] , b <- [1 .. a] ]
= [ (1,b) | b <- [1 .. 1] ] ++
  [ (2,b) | b <- [1 .. 2] ] ++
  [ (3,b) | b <- [1 .. 3] ]
= [ (1,1) | ] ++
  [ (2,1) | ] ++ [ (2,2) | ] ++
  [ (3,1) | ] ++ [ (3,2) | ] ++ [ (3,3) | ]
= [(1,1),(2,1),(2,2),(3,1),(3,2),(3,3)]
```

as we argued above. Another example contains a test:

```
[ m*m | m <- [1 .. 10] , m*m<50 ]
= [ 1*1 | 1*1<50 ] ++ [ 2*2 | 2*2<50 ] ++ ...
  [ 7*7 | 7*7<50 ] ++ [ 8*8 | 8*8<50 ] ++ ...
= [ 1  | True ] ++ [ 4  | True ] ++ ...
  [ 49 | True ] ++ [ 64 | False ] ++ ...
= [1,4,...49]
```

We now look at two longer examples, whose solutions are aided by the list comprehension style.

EXAMPLE: List permutations

A permutation of a list is a list with the same elements in a different order. The perms function returns a list of all permutations of a list.

```
perms :: Eq t => [t] -> [[t]]
```

The empty list has one permutation, itself. If x is not empty, a permutation is given by picking an element a from x and putting a at the front of a permutation of the remainder x\\[a]. (The operation '\\' returns the difference of two lists: x\\y is the list x with each element of y removed, if it is present.) The definition is therefore

```
perms [] = [[]]
perms x  = [ a:p | a <- x , p <- perms (x\\[a]) ]
```

Example evaluations give, for a one-element list,

```
perms [2]
= [a:p| a <- [2] , p <- perms [] ]
= [a:p| a <- [2] , p <- [[]] ]
= [2:p| p <- [[]] ]
= [2:[] | ]
= [[2]]
```

for a two-element list,

```
perms [2,3]
= [ a:p | a <- [2,3] , p <- perms([2,3]\\[a]) ]
= [ 2:p | p <- perms [3] ] ++ [ 3:p | p <- perms [2] ]
= [ 2:[3] ] ++ [ 3:[2] ]
= [ [2,3] , [3,2] ]
```

and finally for a three-element list,

```
perms [1,2,3]
= [ a:p | a <- [1,2,3] , p <- perms([1,2,3]\\[a]) ]
= [ 1:p | p <- perms [2,3]] ++...++
        [ 3:p | p <- perms [1,2]]
= [ 1:p | p<-[[2,3],[3,2]]] ++...++
        [ 3:p | p<-[[1,2],[2,1]]]
= [[1,2,3],[1,3,2],[2,1,3],[2,3,1],[3,1,2],[3,2,1]]
```

There is another algorithm for permutations: in this, a permutation of a list (a:x) is given by forming a permutation of x, and by inserting a into this somewhere. The possible insertion points are given by finding all the possible *splits* of the list into two halves.

```
perm :: [t] -> [[t]]

perm []    = [[]]
perm (a:x) = [ p++[a]++q | r <- perm x ,
                          (p,q) <- splits r ]
```

We get the list of all possible `splits` of a list x after seeing that on splitting (a:x), we either split at the front of (a:x), or somewhere inside x, as given by a split of x.

```
splits :: [t]->[([t],[t])]

splits []    = [ ([],[]) ]
splits (a:x) = ([],a:x) : [ (a:p,q) | (p,q) <- splits x]
```

Before moving on, observe that the type of `perms` requires that t must be in the class Eq. This is needed for the list difference operator \\ to be defined over the type [t]. There is no such restriction on the type of `perm`, which uses a different method for calculating the permutations.

Vectors and matrices

In this section we give one model for vectors and matrices of real numbers; others exist, and are suitable for different purposes.

A vector is a sequence of real numbers, [2.1,3.0,4.0], say.

```
type Vector = [Float]
```

The scalar product of two vectors (assumed to be the same length) is given by multiplying together corresponding elements and taking the total of the results.

```
scalarProduct [2.0,3.1] [4.1,5.0]
  = 2.0*4.1 + 3.1*5.0 = 23.7
```

As a first attempt we might write

```
mul l m = sum [ a*b | a<-l , b<-m ]
```

but this gives

```
mul [2.0,3.1] [4.1,5.0]
  = sum [8.2,10.0,12.71,15.5] = 46.41
```

since *all* combinations of pairs from the lists are taken. In order to multiply together corresponding pairs, we first zip the lists together.

```
scalarProduct :: Vector -> Vector -> Float
scalarProduct l m = sum [ a*b | (a,b) <- zip l m ]
```

and a calculation shows that this gives the required result. A matrix like

$$\begin{pmatrix} 2.0 & 3.0 & 4.0 \\ 5.0 & 6.0 & -1.0 \end{pmatrix}$$

can be thought of as a list of rows or a list of columns; we choose a list of rows here.

```
type Matrix = [Vector]
```

The example matrix is

```
[[2.0,3.0,4.0],[5.0,6.0,-1.0]]
```

Two matrices M and P are multiplied by taking the scalar products of rows of M with columns of P.

$$\begin{pmatrix} 2.0 & 3.0 & 4.0 \\ 5.0 & 6.0 & -1.0 \end{pmatrix} \times \begin{pmatrix} 1.0 & 0.0 \\ 1.0 & 1.0 \\ 0.0 & -1.0 \end{pmatrix} = \begin{pmatrix} 5.0 & -1.0 \\ 11.0 & 7.0 \end{pmatrix}$$

We therefore define

```
matrixProduct :: Matrix -> Matrix -> Matrix
matrixProduct m p
  = [ [scalarProduct r c | c <- columns p] | r <- m ]
```

where the function `columns` gives the representation of a matrix as a list of columns.

```
columns :: Matrix -> Matrix
columns y = [ [ z!!j | z <- y ] | j<- [0 .. s] ]
            where
            s = length (head y)-1
```

The expression `[ z!!j | z <- y ]` picks the jth element from each row z in y; this is exactly the jth column of y. `length (head y)` is the length of a row in y, and so the indices j will be in the range 0 to s = `length (head y)-1`.

Refutable patterns in generators

Some patterns are *refutable*, meaning that an attempt to pattern match against them may fail. If a refutable pattern is used on the left-hand side of an '<-', its effect is to filter from the list only the elements matching the pattern. For example,

```
[ a | (a:x) <- [[],[2],[],[4,5]] ] = [2,4]
```

The rules for calculation with generators containing a refutable pattern on their left-hand side are similar to those given above, except that before performing the substitution for the pattern, the list is filtered for the elements which match the pattern. The details are left as an exercise.

EXERCISES

13.1 Give a calculation of the expression

```
[ a+b | a <- [1 .. 4] , b <- [2 .. 4] , a>b ]
```

13.2 Using the list comprehension notation, define the functions

```
subLists,subSequences :: [t] -> [[t]]
```

which return all the sublists and subsequences of a list. A sublist is obtained by omitting some of the elements of a list; a subsequence is a continuous block from a list. For instance, both [2,4] and [3,4] are sublists of [2,3,4], but only [3,4] is a subsequence.

13.3 Give calculations of the expressions

```
perm [2]
perm [2,3]
perm [1,2,3]
```

and of the matrix multiplication

```
matrixProduct [[2.0,3.0,4.0],[5.0,6.0,-1.0]]
              [[1.0,0.0],[1.0,1.0],[0.0,-1.0]]
```

13.4 Define functions to calculate the determinant of a square matrix, and if this is non-zero, to invert the matrix.

13.5 The calculation rules for list comprehensions can be re-stated for the two cases [] and (a:x), instead of for the arbitrary list $[a_1, \ldots, a_n]$. Give these rules by completing the equations

```
[ e | v <- []    , q₂ , ... , qₖ ] = ...
[ e | v <- (a:x) , q₂ , ... , qₖ ] = ...
```

13.6 Give the precise rules for calculating with a generator containing a refutable pattern, like (a:x) <- lExp. You might need to define auxiliary functions to do this.

13.7 List comprehensions can be translated into expressions involving map, filter and concat by the following equations.

```
[ x | x<-l ]               = l
[ f x | x<-l ]             = map f l
[ e | x<-l , p x , ... ] = [ e | x <- filter p l , ... ]
[ e | x<-l , y<-m , .. ] = concat [ [e|y<-m, ..] | x<-l]
```

Translate the expressions

```
[ m*m | m <- [1 .. 10] ]
[ m*m | m <- [1 .. 10] , m*m<50 ]
[ a+b | a <- [1 .. 4] , b <- [2 .. 4] , a>b ]
[ a:p | a <- x , p <- perms (x\\[a]) ]
```

using these equations; you will need to define some auxiliary functions as a part of your translation.

13.4 Data on demand

The data structures manipulated by a program will be generated on demand, and indeed may never appear explicitly. This makes possible a style of programming, **data-directed programming**, in which complex data structures are constructed and manipulated. Take the example of finding the sum of fourth powers of numbers from 1 to n. The data-directed solution is to

- build the list of numbers [1 .. n];
- take the power of each number, giving $[1, 16, \ldots, n^4]$; and
- find the sum of this list.

As a program, we have

```
sumFourthPowers n = sum (map (^4) [1 .. n])
```

How does the calculation proceed?

```
sumFourthPowers n
= sum (map (^4) [1 .. n])
= sum (map (^4) (1:[2 .. n]))
= sum ((^4) 1 : map (^4) [2 .. n])
= (1^4) + sum (map (^4) [2 .. n])
= 1 + sum (map (^4) [2 .. n]) = ...
= 1 + (16 + sum (map (^4) [3 .. n])) = ...
= 1 + (16 + (81 + ... + n^4))
```

As can be seen, none of the intermediate lists is created in this calculation. As soon as the head of the list is created, its fourth power is taken, and it becomes a part of the sum which produces the final result.

EXAMPLE: List minimum ───────────────────────────

A more striking example is given by the problem of finding the minimum of a list of numbers. One solution is to sort the list, and take its head! This would be ridiculous if the whole list were sorted in the process, but, in fact we have, using the definition of insertion sort from Chapter 4,

```
iSort [8,6,1,7,5]
= ins 8 (ins 6 (ins 1 (ins 7 (ins 5 []))))
= ins 8 (ins 6 (ins 1 (ins 7 [5])))
= ins 8 (ins 6 (ins 1 (5 : ins 7 [])))
= ins 8 (ins 6 (1 : (5 : ins 7 [])))
= ins 8 (1 : ins 6 (5 : ins 7 []))
= 1 : ins 8 (ins 6 (5 : ins 7 []))
```

As can be seen from the underlined parts of the calculation, each application of `ins` calculates the minimum of a larger part of the list, since the head of the result of `ins` is given in a single step. The head of the whole list is determined in this case without us working out the value of the tail, and this means that we have a sensible algorithm for minimum given by `(head . iSort)`.

EXAMPLE: Routes through a graph ――――――――――――――――

A graph can be seen as an object of type `Relation t`, as defined in Section 12.10. How can we find a route from one point in a graph to another? For example, in the graph

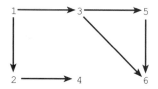

```
graphEx = makeSet [(1,2),(1,3),(2,4),(3,5),(5,6),(3,6)]
```

a route from 1 to 4 is the list `[1,2,4]`.

We solve a slightly different problem: find the list of *all* routes from a to b; our original problem is solved by taking the head of this list. Note that as a list is returned, the algorithm allows for the possibility of there being *no* route from a to b – the empty list of routes is the answer in such a case. This method, which is applicable in many different situations, is often called the **list of successes** technique: instead of returning one result, or an error if there is none, we return a list; the error case is signalled by the empty list. The method also allows for multiple results to be returned, as we shall see.

How do we solve the new problem? For the present we assume that the graph is *acyclic*: there is no circular path from any node back to itself.

- The only route from a to a is `[a]`.
- A route from a to b will start with a step to one of a's neighbours, c say. The remainder will be a path from c to b.

We therefore look for all paths from a to b going through c, for each neighbour c of a.

```
routes :: Ord t => Relation t -> t -> t -> [[t]]
routes rel a b
  | a==b        = [[a]]
  | otherwise   = [ a:r | c <- nbhrs rel a ,
                          r <- routes rel c b ]
```

The nbhrs function is defined by

```
nbhrs :: Ord t => Relation t -> t -> [t]
nbhrs rel a = flatten (image rel a)
```

where flatten turns a set into a list. Now consider the example, where we write routes' for routes graphEx and nbhrs' for nbhrs graphEx, to make the calculation more readable.

```
routes' 1 4
= [ 1:r | c <- nbhrs' 1 , r <- routes' c 4 ]
= [ 1:r | c <- [2,3] , r <- routes' c 4 ]
= [ 1:r | r <- routes' 2 4 ] ++
  [ 1:r | r <- routes' 3 4 ]                            (†)
= [ 1:r | r <- [ 2:s | d <- nbhrs' 2 ,
                       s <- routes' d 4 ]]++...
= [ 1:r | r <- [ 2:s | d <- [4] ,
                       s <- routes' d 4 ] ] ++ ...
= [ 1:r | r <- [ 2:s | s <- routes' 4 4 ] ] ++ ...      (‡)
= [ 1:r | r <- [ 2:s | s <- [[4]] ] ] ++ ...
= [ 1:r | r <- [ [2,4] ] ] ++ ...
= [[1,2,4]] ++ ...
```

The head of the list is given by exploring only the first neighbour of 1, namely 2, and its first neighbour, 4. In this case the search for a route leads directly to a result. This is not always so. Take the example of

```
routes' 1 6 = ...
= [ 1:r | r <- routes' 2 6 ] ++
  [ 1:r | r <- routes' 3 6 ]                            (†)
= ...
= [ 1:r | r <- [ 2:s | s <- routes' 4 6 ] ] ++
  [ 1:r | r <- routes' 3 6 ]                            (‡)
```

Corresponding points in the calculations are marked by (†) and (‡). The search for routes from 4 to 6 will *fail* though, as 4 has no neighbours – we therefore have

```
= [] ++ [ 1:r | r <- routes' 3 6 ] = ...
= [ 1:r | r <- [ 3:s | s <- routes' 5 6 ] ] ++ ...
= [[1,3,5,6]] ++ ...
```

The effect of this algorithm is to *backtrack* when a search has failed: there is no route from 1 to 6 via 2, so the other possibility of going through 3 is explored. This is *only* done when the first possibility is exhausted, though, so lazy evaluation ensures that this search through 'all' the paths turns out to be an efficient method of finding a single path.

We assumed at the start of this development that the graph was acyclic, so that we have no chance of a path looping back on itself, and so for a search to go into a loop. We can make a simple addition to the program to make sure that only paths without cycles are explored, and so that the program will work for an arbitrary graph. We add a list argument for the points not to be visited (again), and so have

```
routesC :: Ord t => Relation t -> t -> t -> [t] -> [[t]]
routesC rel a b l
  | a==b       = [[a]]
  | otherwise  = [ a:r | c <- nbhrs rel a \\ l ,
                         r <- routesC rel c b (a:l) ]
```

Two changes are made in the recursive case.

● In looking for neighbours of a we only look for those which are not in the list l.

● In looking for routes from c to b, we exclude visiting both the elements of l and the node a itself.

A search for a route from a to b in rel is given by routesC rel a b [].

EXERCISES

13.8 Defining graphEx2 to be

```
makeSet [(1,2),(2,1),(1,3),(2,4),(3,5),(5,6),(3,6)]
```

try calculating the effect of the original definition on

```
routes graphEx 1 4
```

Repeat the calculation with the revised definition which follows

```
routes rel a b
  | a==b       = [[a]]
  | otherwise  = [ a:r | c <- nbhrs rel a ,
                         r <- routes rel c b ,
                         not (elem a r) ]
```

and explain why this definition is not suitable for use on cyclic graphs. Finally, give a calculation of

```
routesC graphEx 1 4 []
```

13.5 Case study: parsing expressions

We have already seen the definition of `Expr`, the type of arithmetic expressions, in Section 10.2[1]

```
data Expr = Lit Int | Var Vars | Op Ops Expr Expr
data Ops  = Add | Sub | Mul | Div | Mod
```

and showed there how we could calculate the results of these expressions using the function `eval`. Chapter 12 began with a discussion of how to represent the values held in the variables using the abstract data type `Store`. Using these components, we can build a *calculator* for simple arithmetical expressions, but the input is unacceptably crude, as we have to enter members of the `Expr` type, so that to add 2 and 3, we are forced to type

```
Op Add (Lit 2) (Lit 3)                                      (†)
```

What we need to make the input reasonable is a function which performs the reverse of `show`: it will take the text `"(2+3)"` and return the expression (†).

Constructing a parser for a type like `Expr` gives a `read` function which effectively gives the functionality of the `Read` class, introduced in Section 8.3.

The type of parsers: `Parse`

In building a library of parsing functions, we first have to establish the type we shall use to represent parsers. The problem of parsing is to take a list of objects – of type `t`, characters in our example `"(2+3)"` – and from it to extract an object of some other type, `u`, in this case `Expr`. As a first attempt, we might define the type of parsers thus

```
type Parse1 t u = [t] -> u
```

Suppose that `bracket` and `number` are the parsers of this type which recognize brackets and numbers, then we have

```
bracket "(xyz" = '('
number  "234"  = 2 or 23 or 234?
bracket "234"  = no result?
```

[1] Note that here we use the revised version of the type given in the exercises on page 254, augmented with variables.

The problem evident here is that a parser can return more than one result – as in number "234" – or none at all, as seen in the final case. Instead of the original type, we suggest

```
type Parse2 t u = [t]->[u]
```

where a list of results is returned. In our examples,

```
bracket "(xyz" = [' ('] 
number  "234" = [2 , 23 , 234]
bracket "234" = []
```

In this case an empty list signals failure to find what was sought, while multiple results show that more than one successful parse was possible. We are using this 'list of successes' technique again, in fact.

Another problem presents itself. What if we look for a bracket *followed by* a number, which we have to do in parsing our expressions? We need to know the part of the input which remains after the successful parse. Hence we define

```
type Parse t u = [t] -> [(u,[t])]
```

and our example functions will give

```
bracket "(xyz" = [(' (' , "xyz")]
number  "234" = [(2,"34") , (23,"4") , (234,"")]
bracket "234" = []
```

Each item in the output list represents a successful parse. In number "234" we see three successful parses, each recognizing a number. In the first, the number 2 is recognized, leaving "34" unexamined, for instance.

The type ReadS u, which appears in the standard prelude and is used in defining the Read class, is a special case of Parse t u in which [t] is replaced by String.

Some basic parsers

Now we have established the type we shall use, we can begin to write some parsers. These and the parser-combining functions are illustrated in Figure 13.1; we go through the definitions now.

The first is a parser which always fails, so accepts nothing. There are no entries in its output list.

```
fail :: Parse t u
fail inp = []
```

```
type Parse t u = [t] -> [(u,[t])]

fail :: Parse t u
fail inp = []

succeed :: u -> Parse t u
succeed val inp = [(val,inp)]

token :: Eq t => t -> Parse t t
token t (a:x)
   | t==a         = [(t,x)]
   | otherwise    = []
token t []     = []

spot :: (t -> Bool) -> Parse t t
spot p (a:x)
   | p a          = [(a,x)]
   | otherwise    = []
spot p []      = []

alt :: Parse t u -> Parse t u -> Parse t u
alt p1 p2 inp = p1 inp ++ p2 inp

infixr 5 >*>
(>*>) :: Parse t u -> Parse t v -> Parse t (u,v)
(>*>) p1 p2 inp
  = [((y,z),rem2) | (y,rem1) <- p1 inp ,
                    (z,rem2) <- p2 rem1 ]

build :: Parse t u -> (u -> v) -> Parse t v
build p f inp = [ (f x,rem) | (x,rem) <- p inp ]

list :: Parse t u -> Parse t [u]
list p = (succeed []) `alt`
         ((p >*> list p) `build` convert)
         where
         convert (a,x) = (a:x)
```

Figure 13.1   The major parsing functions.

On the other hand, we can succeed immediately, without reading any input. The value recognized is a parameter of the function.

```
succeed :: u -> Parse t u
succeed val inp = [(val,inp)]
```

More useful is a parser to recognize a single object or token, t, say. We define

```
token :: Eq t => t -> Parse t t
token t (a:x)
  | t==a        = [(t,x)]
  | otherwise   = []
token t []   = []
```

More generally, we can recognize (or spot) objects with a particular property, as represented by a Boolean-valued function.

```
spot :: (t -> Bool) -> Parse t t
spot p (a:x)
  | p a         = [(a,x)]
  | otherwise   = []
spot p []    = []
```

These parsers allow us to recognize single characters like a left bracket, or a single digit

```
bracket = token '('
dig     = spot isDigit
```

but we need to be able to combine these simple parsers into more complicated ones, to recognize numbers consisting of lists of digits and expressions.

Combining parsers

Here we build a library of higher-order polymorphic functions which we then use to give our parser for expressions. First we have to think about the ways in which parsers need to be combined.

Looking at the expression example, an expression is *either* a literal, *or* a variable *or* an operator expression. From parsers for the three sorts of

expression, we want to build a single parser for expressions. For this we
use alt

```
alt :: Parse t u -> Parse t u -> Parse t u
```

```
alt p1 p2 inp = p1 inp ++ p2 inp
```

The parser combines the results of the parses given by parsers p1 and p2 into
a single list, so a success in either is a success of the combination. For
example,

```
(bracket `alt` dig) "234"
= [] ++ [(2,"34")]
```

the parse by bracket fails, but that by dig succeeds, so the combined parser
succeeds.

For our second function, we look again at the expression example. In
recognizing an operator expression we see a bracket *then* a number. How do
we put parsers together so that the second is applied to the input that
remains after the first has been applied?[2]

```
infixr 5 >*>
```

```
(>*>) :: Parse t u -> Parse t v -> Parse t (u,v)
```

```
(>*>) p1 p2 inp
    = [((y,z),rem2) | (y,rem1) <- p1 inp ,
                      (z,rem2) <- p2 rem1 ]
```

The values (y, rem1) run through the possible results of parsing inp using
p1. For each of these, we apply p2 to rem1, which is the input which is
unconsumed by p1 in that particular case. The results of the two successful
parses, y and z, are returned as a pair.

As an example, assume that number recognizes non-empty sequences
of digits, and look at (number >*> bracket) "24(". Applying number to
the string "24(" gives two results,

```
number "24)" = [(2,"4(") , (24,"(")]
```

---

[2] We make this function an operator, as we find that it is often used to combine a sequence of
parsers, and an infix form with defined associativity is most convenient for this. The do-it-
yourself infix notation using backquote can also have a defined associativity and binding
power, in fact.

and so (y, rem1) runs through two cases

```
(number >*> bracket) "24("
= [((y,z),rem2) | (y,rem1) <- [(2,"4(") , (24,"(")] ,
                 (z,rem2)   <- bracket rem1 ]
= [((2,z),rem2)  | (z,rem2)   <- bracket "4(" ] ++
  [((24,z),rem2) | (z,rem2)   <- bracket "(" ]
```

Now, bracket "4(" = [], so fails, giving

```
= [] ++ [((24,z),rem2) | (z,rem2)   <- bracket "(" ]
```

and

```
bracket "(" = [('(',"")]
```

which signals success, and finally gives

```
= [((24,z),rem2) | (z,rem2)   <- [('(',"")] ]
= [ ((24,'(') , "") ]
```

This shows we have one successful parse, in which we have recognized the number 24 followed by the left bracket '('.

Our final operation is to change the item returned by a parser, or to build something from it. Consider the case of a parser, digList, which returns a list of digits. Can we make it return the number which the list of digits represents? We apply conversion to the results, thus

```
build :: Parse t u -> (u -> v) -> Parse t v
```

```
build p f inp = [ (f x,rem) | (x,rem) <- p inp ]
```

so in an example, we have

```
(digList `build` digsToNum) "21a3"
= [ (digsToNum x,rem) | (x,rem) <- digList "21a3" ]
= [ (digsToNum x,rem)
        | (x,rem) <- [("2","1a3"),("21","a3")]]
= [ (digsToNum "2" , "1a3") , (digsToNum "21" , "a3") ]
= [ (2,"1a3") , (21,"a3")]
```

Using the three operations or *combinators* alt, >*> and build together with the primitives of the previous section we will be able to define all the parsers we require.

As an example, we show how to define a parser for a *list* of objects, when we are given a parser to recognize a single object. There are two sorts of list.

- A list can be empty, which will be recognized by the parser succeed [].
- Any other list is non-empty, and consists of an object followed by a list of objects. A pair like this is recognized by p >*> list p; we then have to turn this pair (a,x) into the list (a:x), for which we use build.

```
list :: Parse t u -> Parse t [u]

list p = (succeed []) 'alt'
         ((p >*> list p) 'build' convert)
         where
         convert (a,x) = (a:x)
```

EXERCISES

13.9 Define the functions

```
neList   :: Parse t u -> Parse t [u]
optional :: Parse t u -> Parse t [u]
```

so that neList p recognizes a non-empty list of the objects which are recognized by p, and optional p recognizes such an object *optionally* – it may recognize an object or succeed immediately.

13.10 Define the function

```
nTimes :: Int -> Parse t u -> Parse t [u]
```

so that nTimes n p recognizes n of the objects recognized by p.

A parser for expressions

Now we can describe our expressions and define the parser for them. Expressions have three forms.

- Literals: 67, ~89, where '~' is used for unary minus.

- Variables: 'a' to 'z'.
- Applications of the binary operations +, *, -, /, %, where % is used for mod, and / gives integer division. Expressions are fully bracketed, if compound, thus: (23+(34-45)), and white space not permitted.

The parser has three parts

```
parser :: Parse Char Expr
parser = litParse `alt` varParse `alt` opExpParse
```

corresponding to the three sorts of expression. The simplest to define is

```
varParse :: Parse Char Expr
varParse = spot isVar `build` Var

isVar :: Char -> Bool
isVar x = ('a' <= x && x <= 'z')
```

(Here the constructor Var is used as a function taking a character to the type Expr.)

An operator expression will consist of two expressions joined by an operator, the whole construct between two brackets.

```
opExpParse
  = (token '(' >*>
     parser     >*>
     spot isOp >*>
     parser     >*>
     token ')')
     `build` makeExpr
```

where the conversion function takes a nested sequence of pairs, like

```
('(',(Lit 23,('+',(Var 'x',')'))))
```

into the expression Op Add (Lit 23) (Var 'x'), thus

```
makeExpr (_,(e1,(bop,(e2,_)))) = Op (charToOp bop) e1 e2
```

Defining the functions isOp and charToOp is left as an exercise.

Finally, we look at the case of literals. A number consists of a non-empty list of digits, with an optional '~' at the front. We therefore use the functions from the exercises of the previous section to say

```
litParse
  = ((optional (token '~')) >*>
     (neList (spot isDigit))
     `build` (charlistToExpr.join)
     where
     join (l,m) = l++m
```

Left undefined here is the function `charlistToExpr` which should convert a list of characters to a literal integer; this is an exercise for the reader.

EXERCISES

13.11 Define the functions

```
isOp     :: Char -> Bool
charToOp :: Char -> Ops
```

used in the parsing of expressions.

13.12 Define the function

```
charlistToExpr :: [Char] -> Expr
```

so that

```
charlistToExpr "234" = Lit 234
charlistToExpr "~98" = Lit (-98)
```

which is used in parsing literal expressions.

13.13 A command to the calculator to assign the value of `expr` to the variable `var` can be represented thus

```
var:expr
```

Give a parser for these commands.

13.14 How would you change the parser for numbers if decimal fractions are to be allowed in addition to integers?

13.15 How would you change the parser for variables if names longer than a single character are to be allowed?

13.16 Explain how you would modify your parser so that the *whitespace* characters space and tab can be used in expressions, but would be ignored on parsing? (Hint: there is a simple pre-processor which does the trick!)

13.17 *Note:* this exercise is for those familiar with Backus–Naur notation for grammars.
Expressions without bracketing and allowing the multiplicative expressions
higher binding power are described by the grammar

```
Expr  ::= Int | Var | (Expr Ops Expr) |
          Lexpr Mop Mexpr | Mexpr Aop Expr
Lexpr ::= Int | Var | (Expr Ops Expr)
Mexpr ::= Int | Var | (Expr Ops Expr) | Lexpr Mop Mexpr
Mop   ::= '*' | '/' | '%'
Aop   ::= '+' | '-'
Ops   ::= Mop | Aop
```

Give a Haskell parser for this grammar. Discuss the associativity of the operator
'–' in this grammar.

The top-level parser

The parser defined in the last section, `parser` is of type

```
[Char] -> [ (Expr,[Char]) ]
```

yet what we need is to convert this to a function taking a string to the
expression it represents. We therefore define the function

```
topLevel :: Parse t u -> [t] -> u
topLevel p inp
  = case results of
        [] -> error "parse unsuccessful"
        _  -> head results
      where
      results = [ found | (found,[]) <- p inp ]
```

The parse p inp is successful if the result contains at least one parse (the
second case) in which all the input has been read (the test given by the
pattern match to `(found,[])`). If this happens, the first value `found` is
returned; otherwise we are in error.
We can define the type of commands thus

```
data Command = Eval Expr | Assign Var Expr | Null
```

which are intended to cause

- the evaluation of the expression,
- the assignment of the value of the expression to the variable, and
- no effect.

If the assignment command takes the form `var:expr`, then it is not difficult to design a parser for this type,

```
commandParse :: Parse Char Command
```

We will assume this has been built when we re-visit the calculator example below.

Conclusions

The type of parsers with the signature

```
type
  Parse t u = ....
  in
  fail     :: Parse t u
  succeed  :: u -> Parse t u
  token    :: Eq t => t -> Parse t t
  spot     :: (t -> Bool) -> Parse t t
  alt      :: Parse t u -> Parse t u -> Parse t u
  then     :: Parse t u -> Parse t v -> Parse t (u,v)
  build    :: Parse t u -> (u -> v) -> Parse t v
  topLevel :: Parse t u -> [t] -> u
```

allows us to construct so-called *recursive descent* parsers in a straightforward way. It is worth looking at the aspects of the language we have exploited.

- The type `Parse t u` is represented by a function type, so that all the parser combinators are higher-order functions.
- Because of polymorphism, we do not need to be specific about either the input or the output type of the parsers we build.

  In our example we have confined ourselves to inputs which are strings of characters, but they could have been *tokens* of any other type, if required: we might take the tokens to be *words* which are then parsed into sentences, for instance.

  More importantly in our example, we can return objects of any type using the same combinators, and in the example, we returned lists and pairs as well as simple characters and expressions.
- Lazy evaluation plays a role here also. The possible parses we build are generated *on demand* as the alternatives are tested. The parsers will backtrack through the different options until a successful one is found.

EXERCISES

13.18 Define a parser which recognizes strings representing Haskell lists of integers, like
`"[2,-3,45]"`.

13.19 Define a parser to recognize simple sentences of English, with a subject, verb and object. You will need to provide some vocabulary: `"cat"`, `"dog"`, and so on, and a parser to recognize a string. You will also need to define a function

```
tokenList :: Eq t => [t] -> Parse t [t]
```

so that, for instance,

```
tokenList "Hello" "Hello Sailor" = [ ("Hello"," Sailor") ]
```

13.20 Define the function

```
spotWhile :: (t -> Bool) -> Parse t [t]
```

whose parameter is a function which tests elements of the input type, and returns the longest initial part of the input all of whose elements have the required property. For instance

```
spotWhile digit "234abc"  = [ ("234","abc") ]
spotWhile digit "abc234"  = [ ([],"abc234") ]
```

13.6 Infinite lists

One important consequence of lazy evaluation is that it is possible for the language to describe **infinite** structures. These would require an infinite amount of time to evaluate fully, but under lazy evaluation, only parts of a data structure need to be examined. Any recursive type will contain infinite objects; we concentrate on lists here, as these are by far the most widely used infinite structures.

In this section we look at a variety of examples, starting with simple one-line definitions and moving to an examination of random numbers based on our simulation case study. The simplest examples of infinite lists are constant lists like

```
ones = 1 : ones
```

Evaluation of this in a Haskell system produces a list of ones, indefinitely. This can be *interrupted* under Unix by typing `Control-C`, which produces the result

```
[1, 1, 1, 1, 1, 1, 1^C{Interrupted!}
```

We can sensibly evaluate functions applied to ones. If we define

```
addFirstTwo (a:b:x) = a+b
```

then applied to ones we have

```
addFirstTwo ones
= addFirstTwo (1:ones)
= addFirstTwo (1:1:ones)
= 1+1
= 2
```

Built into the system we have the lists [n ..], [n,m ..], so that

```
[3 .. ]   = [3,4,5,6,...
[3,5 .. ] = [3,5,7,9,...
```

We can define these ourselves

```
from :: Int -> [Int]
from n        = n : from (n+1)

fromStep :: Int -> Int -> [Int]
fromStep n m = n : fromStep (n+m) m
```

and an example evaluation gives

```
fromStep 3 2
= 3 : fromStep 5 2
= 3 : 5 : fromStep 7 2
= ...
```

List comprehensions can also define infinite lists. The list of *all* Pythagorean triples is given by selecting c in [2 ..], and then selecting suitable values of a and b below that.

```
pythagTriples =
  [ (a,b,c) | c <- [2 .. ] , b <- [2 .. c-1] ,
              a <- [2 .. b-1] , a*a + b*b == c*c ]
pythagTriples
= [(3,4,5),(6,8,10),(5,12,13),(9,12,15),
   (8,15,17),(12,16,20),...
```

The powers of an integer are given by

```
powers :: Int -> [Int]
powers n = [ n^x | x <- [0 .. ] ]
```

and this is a special case of the iterate function, which gives the infinite list $[x, f x, .., f^n x, ...]$

```
iterate :: (t -> t) -> t -> [t]
iterate f x = x : iterate f (f x)
```

EXAMPLE: Generating prime numbers ————————————————

A positive integer greater than one is **prime** if it is divisible only by itself and one. The *Sieve of Eratosthenes* – an algorithm known for over two thousand years – works by cancelling out all the multiples of numbers, once they are established as prime. The primes are the only elements which remain in the list. The process is illustrated in Figure 13.2.

We begin with the list of numbers starting at 2. The head is 2, and we remove all the multiples of 2 from the list. The head of the remainder of the list, 3, is prime, since it was not removed in the sieve by 2. We therefore sieve the remainder of the list of multiples of 3, and repeat the process indefinitely. As a Haskell definition, we write

```
primes :: [Int]

primes      = sieve [2 .. ]
sieve (a:x) = a : sieve [ y | y <- x , y 'mod' a > 0]
```

where we test whether a divides y by evaluating y 'mod' a; y is a multiple of a if this is zero. Beginning the evaluation, we have

```
  primes
= sieve [2 .. ]
= 2 : sieve [ y | y <- [3 .. ] , y 'mod' 2 > 0]
= 2 : sieve (3 : [ y | y <- [4 .. ] , y 'mod' 2 > 0])
= 2 : 3 : sieve [ z | z <- [ y | y <- [4 .. ] ,
                    y 'mod' 2 > 0], z 'mod' 3 > 0]   = ...
= 2 : 3 : sieve [ z | z <- [5,7,9...] ,
                    z 'mod' 3 > 0]   = ...
= 2 : 3 : sieve [5,7,11,...]   = ...
```

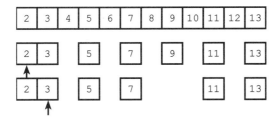

Figure 13.2 The Sieve of Eratosthenes.

Can we use `primes` to test for a number being a prime? If we evaluate
`member primes 7` we get the response `True`; while `member primes 6` gives no
answer. This is because an *infinite* number of elements have to be checked
before we conclude that 6 is not in the list. The problem is that `member` does
not use the fact that `primes` is ordered. This we do in `memberOrd`.

```
memberOrd :: Ord t => [t] -> t -> Bool
memberOrd (m:x) n
    | m<n        = memberOrd x n
    | m==n       = True
    | otherwise  = False
```

The difference here is in the final case: if the head of the list (m) is greater
than the element we seek (n), the element cannot be a member of the
(ordered) list. Evaluating the test again,

```
memberOrd [2,3,5,7,...] 6
= memberOrd [3,5,...] 6  = ...
= memberOrd [7,...] 6
= False
```

EXAMPLE: Generating random numbers —————————————————

Many computer systems require us to generate 'random' numbers, one after
another. Our queueing simulation is a particular example upon which we
focus here, after looking at the basics of the problem.

   Any Haskell program cannot produce a truly random sequence; after
all, we want to be able to predict the behaviour of our programs, and
randomness is inherently unpredictable. What we can do, however, is
generate a **pseudo-random** sequence of natural numbers, smaller than
`modulus`. This **linear congruential method** works by starting with a seed,
and then by getting the next element of the sequence from the previous value
thus

```
nextRand :: Int -> Int
nextRand n = (multiplier*n + increment) `mod` modulus
```

A (pseudo-)random sequence is given by iterating this function,

```
randomSequence :: Int -> [Int]
randomSequence = iterate nextRand
```

Given the values

```
seed       = 17489
multiplier = 25173
increment  = 13849
modulus    = 65536
```

the sequence produced by randomSequence seed begins

```
[17489,59134,9327,52468,43805,8378,...
```

The numbers in this sequence, which range from 0 to 65535, all occur with the same frequency. What are we to do if instead we want the numbers to come in the (integer) range a to b inclusive? We need to scale the sequence, which is achieved by a map:

```
scaleSequence :: Int -> Int -> [Int] -> [Int]
scaleSequence a b
  = map scale
    where
    scale n = n 'div' denom + a
    range   = b-a+1
    denom   = modulus 'div' range
```

The original range of numbers 0 to modulus−1 is split into range blocks, each of the same length. The number a is assigned to values in the first block, a+1 to values in the next, and so on.

In our simulation example, we want to generate for each arrival the length of service that person will need on being served. For illustration, we suppose that they range from 1 to 6 minutes, but that they are supposed to happen with different probabilities.

Waiting time	1	2	3	4	5	6
Probability	0.2	0.25	0.25	0.15	0.1	0.05

We need a function to turn such a distribution into a transformer of infinite lists. Once we have a function transforming individual values, we can map it along the list.

We can represent a distribution of objects of type t by a list of type [(t,Float)], where we assume that the numeric entries add up to one. Our function transforming individual values will be

```
makeFunction :: [(t,Float)] -> (Float -> t)
```

so that numbers in the range 0 to 65535 are transformed into items of type t. The idea of the function is to give the following ranges to the entries for the list above.

Waiting time	1	2	3	...
Range start	0	(m*0.2)+1	(m*0.45)+1	...
Range end	m*0.2	m*0.45	m*0.7	...

where m is used for modulus. The definition follows

```
makeFunction dist = makeFun dist 0.0

makeFun ((ob,p):dist) nLast rand
   | nNext >= rand && rand > nLast
         = ob
   | otherwise
         = makeFun dist nNext rand
           where
           nNext = p*fromInt modulus + nLast
```

The makeFun function has an extra argument, which carries the position in the range 0 to modulus-1 reached so far in the search; it is initially zero. The fromInt function used here converts an Int to an equivalent Float.

The transformation of a list of random numbers is given by

```
map (makeFunction dist . fromInt)
```

and the random distribution of waiting times we require begins thus

```
map (makeFunction dist . fromInt) (randomSequence seed)
= [2,5,1,4,3,1,2,5,4,2,2,2,1,3,2,5,...
```

with 6 first appearing at the 35th position.

Pitfall – infinite list generators

The list comprehension `pythagTriples2`, intended to produce the list of all Pythagorean triples, instead produces *no* output to the prompt.

```
pythagTriples2 =
    [ (a,b,c) | a <- [2 .. ] , b <- [a+1 .. ] ,
                c <- [b+1 .. ] , a*a + b*b == c*c ]
```

The problem is in the order of choice of the elements. The first choice for a is 2, and for b is 3; given this, there are an infinite number of values to try for c: 4, 5 and so on, indefinitely.

Two options present themselves. First we can re-define the solution, as in `pythagTriples`, so that it involves only one infinite list. Alternatively, we can try to write a function which returns all pairs of elements from two infinite lists:

```
infiniteProduct :: [t] -> [u] -> [(t,u)]
```

this is left as an exercise. Using such a function it is possible to adapt the definition of `pythagTriples2` to make it give all the Pythagorean triples.

EXERCISES

13.21 Define the infinite lists of factorial and Fibonacci numbers,

```
factorial = [1,1,2,6,24,120,720,...]
fibonacci = [0,1,1,2,3,5,8,13,21,...]
```

The corresponding functions were introduced in the exercises in Section 2.2.

13.22 Give a definition of the function

```
factors :: Int -> [Int]
```

which returns a list containing the factors of a positive integer. For instance,

```
factors 12 = [1,2,3,4,6,12]
```

Using this function or otherwise define the list of numbers whose only prime factors are 2, 3 and 5, the so-called **Hamming numbers**.

```
hamming = [1,2,3,4,5,6,8,9,10,12,15,...
```

13.23 Define the function

```
runningSums :: [Int] -> [Int]
```

which calculates the running sums

$[0, a_0, a_0+a_1, a_0+a_1+a_2, \ldots$

of a list

$[a_0, a_1, a_2, \ldots$

13.24 Define the function `infiniteProduct` specified above, and use it to correct the definition of `pythagTriples2`.

13.7 Why infinite lists?

Haskell supports infinite lists and other infinite structures, and we saw in the last section that we could define a number of quite complex lists, like the list of prime numbers, and lists of random numbers. The question remains, though, of whether these lists are anything other than a curiosity. There are two arguments which show their importance in functional programming.

First, an infinite version of a program can be more abstract, and so simpler to write. Consider the problem of finding the nth prime number, using the Sieve of Eratosthenes. If we work with finite lists, we need to know in advance how large a list is needed to accommodate the first n primes; if we work with an infinite list, this is not necessary: only that part of the list which is needed will be generated as computation proceeds.

Similarly, the random numbers given by `randomSequence seed` provided an unlimited resource: we can take as many random numbers from the list as we require. There needs to be no decision at the start of programming as to the size of sequence needed. (These arguments are rather like those for **virtual memory** in a computer. It is often the case that predicting the memory use of a program is possible, but tiresome; virtual memory makes this unnecessary, and so frees the programmer to proceed with other tasks.)

The second argument is of wider significance, and can be seen by re-examining the way in which we generated random numbers. We generated an infinite list by means of `iterate`, and we transformed the values using `map`; these operations are pictured in Figure 13.3 as a generator of and a transformer of lists of values. These values are shown in the dashed boxes. These components can then be linked together, giving more complex combinations, as in Figure 13.4. This approach **modularizes** the generation of values in a distribution in an interesting way. We have separated the

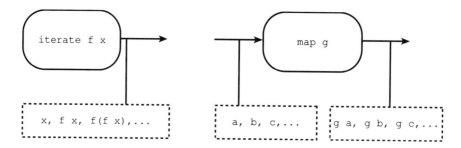

Figure 13.3 A generator and a transformer.

generation of the values from their transformation, and this means we can change each part independently of the other.

Once we have seen the view of infinite lists as the links between processes, other combinations suggest themselves, and in particular we can begin to write process-style programs which involve **recursion**.

Among the exercises in the previous section was the problem of finding the running sums

$$[0, a_0, a_0+a_1, a_0+a_1+a_2, \ldots$$

of the list $[a_0, a_1, a_2, \ldots$. Given the sum up to a_k, say, we get the next sum by adding the next value in the input, a_{k+1}. It is as if we *feed the sum back* into the process to have the value a_{k+1} added. This is precisely the effect of the network of processes in Figure 13.5, where the values passing along the links are shown in the dotted boxes.

The first value in the output `out` is 0, the remaining values are obtained by adding the next value in `iList` to the previous sum, appearing in the list `out`. This is translated into Haskell as follows. The output of the function on input `iList` is `out`. This is itself obtained by adding 0 to the front of the output from the `zipWith (+)`, which itself has inputs `iList` and `out`. In other words,

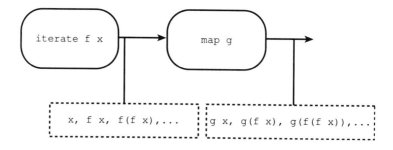

Figure 13.4 Linking processes together.

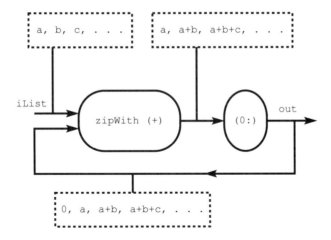

Figure 13.5   A process to compute the running sums of a list.

```
listSums :: [Int] -> [Int]

listSums iList = out
                 where
                 out = 0 : zipWith (+) iList out
```

where `zipWith` is defined by

```
zipWith f (a:x) (b:y) = f a b : zipWith f x y
zipWith f _      _     = []
```

and the operator section `(0:)` puts a zero on the front of a list. We give a calculation of an example now.

```
listSums [1 .. ]
= out
= 0 : zipWith (+) [1 .. ] out
= 0 : zipWith (+) [1 .. ] (0:...)          (1)
= 0 : 1+0 : zipWith [2 .. ] (1+0:...)      (2)
= 0 : 1 : 2+1 : zipWith [3 .. ] (2+1:...)  = ...
```

In making this calculation, we replace the occurrence of `out` in line `(1)` with the incomplete list `(0:...)`. In a similar way, we replace the tail of `out` by `(1+0:...)` in line `(2)`.

The definition of `listSums` is an example of the general function `scanl1'`, which combines values using the function `f`, and whose first output is `st`.

```
scanl1' :: (t -> u -> u) -> u -> [t] -> [u]
scanl1' f st iList
  = out
    where
    out = st : zipWith f iList out
```

The function listSums is given by scanl1' (+) 0, and a function which keeps a running sort of the initial parts of list is

```
sorts = scanl1' insert []
```

where insert inserts an element in the appropriate place in a sorted list. The list of factorial values, [1,1,2,6,...] is given by

```
scanl1' (*) 1 [1 .. ]
```

and taking this as a model, any primitive recursive function can be described in a similar way. (The function is called scanl1' because of its relation to the scanl1 function of the standard prelude, which is defined in a different way.)

EXERCISES

13.25 Give a definition of the list [2^n | n <- [0 ..]] using a process network based on scanl1'. (Hint: you can take the example of factorial as a guide.)

13.26 How would you select certain elements of an infinite list, for instance, how would you keep running sums of the *positive* numbers in a list of numbers?

13.27 How would you *merge* two infinite lists, assuming that they are sorted? How would you remove duplicates from the list which results? As an example, how would you merge the lists of powers of 2 and 3?

13.28 Give definitions of the lists of Fibonacci numbers [0,1,1,2,3,5,...] and Hamming numbers [1,2,3,4,5,6,8,9,...] using networks of processes. For the latter problem, you may find the merge function of the previous question useful.

13.8 Case study: simulation

We are now in a position to put together the ingredients of the queue simulation covered in

- Section 10.5, where we designed the algebraic types Inmess and Outmess;

- Section 12.6, where the abstract types `QueueState` and `ServerState` were introduced; and in

- Section 13.6, where we showed how to generate an infinite list of waiting times from a distribution over the times 1 to 6.

As we said in Section 10.5, our top-level simulation will be a function from a series of input messages to a series of output messages, so

```
doSimulation :: ServerState -> [Inmess] -> [Outmess]
```

where the first parameter is the state of the server at the start of the simulation. In Section 12.6 we presented the function performing one step of the simulation,

```
simulationStep :: ServerState ->
                  Inmess ->
                  (ServerState, [Outmess])
```

which takes the current server state, and the input message arriving at the current minute and returns the state after one minute's processing, paired with the output messages produced by the queues that minute (potentially every queue could release a customer at the same instant, just as no customers might be released.)

The output of the simulation will be given by the output messages generated in the first minute, and after those the results of a new simulation beginning with the updated state:

```
doSimulation servSt (im:messes)
  = outmesses ++ doSimulation servStNext messes
    where
    (servStNext , outmesses) = simulationStep servSt im
```

How do we generate an input sequence? From Section 13.6 we have the sequence of times given by

```
randomTimes
  = map (makeFunction dist . fromInt) (randomSequence seed)
  = [2,5,1,4,3,1,2,5,...
```

We are to have arrivals of one person per minute, so the input messages we generate are

```
simulationInput = zipWith Yes [1 .. ] randomTimes
= [ Yes 1 2 , Yes 2 5 , Yes 3 1 , Yes 4 4 , Yes 5 3 ,...
```

What are the outputs produced when we run the simulation on this input with four queues, by setting the constant numQueues to 4? The output begins

```
doSimulation serverStart simulationInput
= [Discharge 1 0 2, Discharge 3 0 1, Discharge 6 0 1,
    Discharge 2 0 5, Discharge 5 0 3, Discharge 4 0 4,
    Discharge 7 2 2,...
```

The first six inputs are processed without delay, but the seventh requires a waiting time of 2 before being served.

The infinite number of arrivals represented by simulationInput will obviously generate a corresponding infinite number of output messages. We can make a finite approximation by giving the input

```
simulationInput2 = take 50 simulationInput ++ noes
noes = No : noes
```

where after one arrival in each of the first fifty minutes, no further people arrive. Fifty output messages will be generated, and we define this list of outputs thus

```
take 50 (doSimulation serverStart simulationInput2)
```

Experimenting

We now have the facilities to begin experimenting with different data, such as the distribution and the number of queues. The total waiting time for a (finite) sequence of Outmess is given by

```
totalWait :: [Outmess] -> Int
totalWait = sum . map waitTime
        where
        waitTime (Discharge _ w _) = w
```

For simulationInput2 the total waiting time is 29, going up to 287 with three queues and down to zero with five. We leave it to the reader to experiment with the *round robin* simulation outlined in the exercises of Section 12.6.

A more substantial project is to model a set-up with a single queue feeding a number of bank clerks – one way to do this is to extend the serverState with an extra queue which feeds into the individual queues: an element leaves the feeder queue when one of the small queues is empty. This should avoid the unnecessary waiting time we face when making the wrong choice of queue, and the simulation shows that waiting times are reduced by this strategy, though by less than we might expect if service times are short.

13.9 Proof revisited

After summarizing the effect that lazy evaluation has on the types of Haskell, we examine the consequences for reasoning about programs. Taking lists as a representative example, we look at how we can prove properties of infinite lists, and of all lists, rather than simply the set of finite lists, which was the scope of the proofs we looked at in Chapter 5.

This section cannot give complete coverage of the issues of verification; we conclude with pointers to further reading.

Undefinedness

In nearly every programming language, it is possible to write a program which fails to terminate, and Haskell is no exception. We call the value of such programs the **undefined** value, as it gives no result to a computation.

The simplest expression which gives an undefined result is

```
undef :: t
undef = undef                                            (1)
```

which gives a non-terminating or undefined value of every type, but of course we can write an undefined program without intending to, as in

```
fac n = (n+1) * fac n
```

where we have confused the use of n and n+1 in defining factorial. The value of f n will be the same as undef, as they are both non-terminating.

We should remark that we are using the term 'undefined' in two different ways here. The *name* undef is given a definition by (1); the *value* that the definition gives it is the undefined value, which represents the result of a calculation or evaluation which fails to terminate (and therefore fails to define a result).

The existence of these undefined values has an effect on the type of lists. What if we define, for example, the list

```
list1 = 2:3:undef
```

The list has a well-defined head, 2, and tail 3:undef. Similarly, the tail has a head, 3, but its tail is undefined. The type [Int] therefore contains **partial** lists like `list1`, built from the undefined list, `undef`, parts of which are defined and parts of which are not.

Of course, there are also undefined integers, so we also include in `[Int]` lists like

```
list2 = undef:[2,3]
list3 = undef:4:undef
```

which contain undefined values, and might also be partial. Note that in `list3` the first occurrence of `undef` is at type `Int` while the second is at type `[Int]`.

What happens when a function is applied to `undef`? We use the rules for calculation we have seen already, so that the `const` function of the standard prelude satisfies

```
const 17 undef = 17
```

If the function applied to `undef` has to pattern match, then the result of the function will be `undef`, since the pattern match has to look at the structure of `undef`, which will never terminate. For instance, for the functions first defined in Section 5.2

```
sumList undef = undef                                    (1)
double  undef = undef                                    (2)
```

In writing proofs earlier in the book we were careful to state that in some cases the results only hold for *defined* values.

An integer is defined if it is not equal to `undef`; a list is defined if it is a finite list of defined values; using this as a model it is not difficult to give a definition of the defined values of any algebraic type.

A finite list as we have defined it may contain undefined values. Note that in some earlier proofs we stipulated that the results only hold for (finite) lists of defined values, that is for defined lists.

List induction revisited

As we said above, since there is an undefined list, `undef`, in each list type, lists can be built up from this; there will therefore be *two* base cases in the induction principle.

Proof by structural induction: fp-lists

To prove the property `P(x)` for all finite or partial lists (**fp-lists**) x we have to do three things.

Base cases   Prove P([]) and P(undef).
Induction step   Prove P(a:x) assuming that P(x) holds already.

Among the results we proved by structural induction in Section 5.2 were the equations

```
sumList (double x)    = 2 * sumList x                    (3)
x ++ (y ++ z)         = (x ++ y) ++ z                    (4)
member (x++y) b       = member x b || member y b         (5)
shunt (shunt x y) []  = shunt y x                        (6)
```

for all *finite* lists x, y and z. For these results to hold for all **fp-lists**, we need to show that

```
sumList (double undef)   = 2 * sumList undef                    (7)
undef ++ (y ++ z)        = (undef ++ y) ++ z                    (8)
member (undef++y) b      = member undef b || member y b  (9)
shunt (shunt undef y) [] = shunt y undef                       (10)
```

as well as being sure that the induction step is valid for all fp-lists. Now, by (1) and (2) the equation (7) holds, and so (3) holds for all fp-lists. In a similar way, we can show (8) and (9). More interesting is (10). Recall the definition of shunt:

```
shunt []     y = y
shunt (a:x) y = shunt x (a:y)
```

It is clear from this that since there is a pattern match on the first parameter, undef as the first parameter will give an undef result, so

```
shunt (shunt undef y) []
= shunt undef []
= undef
```

while an undef as second parameter is not problematic, and we have, for instance,

```
shunt [2,3] undef
= shunt [3] (2:undef)
= shunt [] (3:2:undef)
= (3:2:undef)
```

This is enough to show that (10) does not hold, and that we cannot infer that (6) holds for all fp-lists. Indeed the example above shows exactly that (6) is not valid.

Infinite lists

Beside the fp-lists, there are *infinite* members of the list types. How can we prove properties of infinite lists? A hint is given by our discussion of printing the results of evaluating an infinite list. In practice what happens is that we *interrupt* evaluation by hitting ^C after some period of time. We can think of what we see on the screen as an **approximation** to the infinite list.

If what we see are the elements $a_0, a_1, a_2, \ldots, a_n$, we can think of the approximation being the list

```
a₀:a₁:a₂:...:aₙ:undef
```

since we have no information about the list beyond the element a_n.

More formally, we say that the partial lists

```
undef, a₀:undef, a₀:a₁:undef, a₀:a₁:a₂:undef, ...
```

are approximations to the infinite list $[a_0, a_1, a_2, \ldots, a_n, \ldots]$.

Two lists l and m are equal if all their approximants are equal, that is for all natural numbers n, take n l = take n m. (The take function gives the defined portion of the nth approximant, and so it is enough to compare these parts.) A more usable version of this principle applies to infinite lists only:

Infinite list equality

A list l is infinite if for all natural numbers n, take n l ≠ take (n+1) l. Two infinite lists l and m are equal if for all natural numbers n, l!!n = m!!n.

EXAMPLE: Two factorial lists ————————————————————————

Our example here is inspired by the process-based programs of Section 13.7. If fac is the factorial function

```
fac :: Int -> Int
fac 0 = 1                                                    (1)
fac m = m * fac (m-1)                                        (2)
```

one way of defining the infinite list of factorials is

```
facMap = map fac [0 .. ]                                     (3)
```

while a process-based solution is

```
facs = 1 : zipWith (*) [1 .. ] facs                    (4)
```

Assuming these lists are infinite (which they clearly are), we have to prove for all natural numbers n that

```
facMap!!n = facs!!n                                    (5)
```

Proof. In our proof we will assume for all natural numbers n the results

```
(map f l)!!n       = f (l!!n)                          (6)
(zipWith g l m)!!n = g (l!!n) (m!!n)                   (7)
```

which we discuss again later in this section.

(5) is proved by mathematical induction, so we start by proving the result at zero. Examining the left-hand side first,

```
  facMap!!0
= (map fac [0 .. ])!!0                        by (3)
= fac ([0 .. ]!!0)                            by (6)
= fac 0                              by def of [0 .. ],!!
= 1                                           by (1)
```

The right-hand side is

```
  facs!!0
= (1 : zipWith (*) [1 .. ] facs)!!0           by (4)
= 1                                     by def of !!
```

establishing the base case. In the induction case we have to prove (5) using the induction hypothesis (8)

```
facMap!!(n-1) = facs!!(n-1)                            (8)
```

The left-hand side of (5) is

```
  facMap!!n
= (map fac [0 .. ])!!n                        by (3)
= fac ([0 .. ]!!n)                            by (6)
= fac n                              by def of [0 .. ],!!
= n * fac (n-1)                               by (2)
= n * (facMap!!(n-1))               by (5),[0 .. ],!!
```

The right-hand side of (5) is

```
facs!!n
= (1 : zipWith (*) [1 .. ] facs)!!n                    by (4)
= (zipWith (*) [1 .. ] facs)!!(n-1)                  by def of !!
= (*) ([1 .. ]!!(n-1)) (facs!!(n-1))                   by (7)
= ([1 .. ]!!(n-1)) * (facs!!(n-1))              by def of (*)
= n * (facs!!(n-1))                        by def of [1 .. ],!!
= n * (facMap!!(n-1))                                  by (8)
```

The final step of this proof is given by the induction hypothesis, and completes the proof of the induction step and the result itself.

∎

Proofs for infinite lists

When are results we prove for all fp-lists valid for *all* lists? If a result holds for all fp-lists, then it holds for all *approximations* to infinite lists. For some properties it is enough to know the property for all approximations to know that it will be valid for all infinite lists as well. In particular, this is true for all *equations*. This means that, for example, we can assert that for *all* lists l,

```
(map f . map g) l = map (f.g) l
```

and therefore by the principle of extensionality for functions,

```
map f . map g = map (f.g)
```

Many other of the equations we proved initially for finite lists can be extended to proof for the fp-lists, and therefore to *all* lists. Some of these are given in the exercises which follow.

Further reading

The techniques we have given here provide a flavour of how to write proofs for infinite lists and infinite data structures in general. We cannot give the breadth or depth of a full presentation, but refer the reader to Paulson (1987) for more details.

EXERCISES

13.29 Show that for all fp-lists y and z,

```
undef ++ (y ++ z)   = (undef ++ y) ++ z
member (undef++y) b = member undef b || member y b
```

to infer the results mentioned above.

13.30 Show that when rev x is defined to be shunt x [],

```
rev (rev undef) = undef                              (1)
```

In Chapter 5 we proved that

```
rev (rev x) = x                                      (2)
```

for all finite lists x.

Why can we not infer from (1) and (2) that rev (rev x) = x holds for all fp-lists x?

13.31 Prove for all natural numbers m, n and functions f :: Int->t that

```
(map f [m .. ])!!n = f (m+n)
```

[Hint: you will need to choose the right variable for the induction proof.]

13.32 Prove that the lists

```
facMap = map fac [0 .. ]
facs = 1 : zipWith (*) [1 .. ] facs
```

are infinite.

13.33 If we define indexing thus

```
(a:_)!!0 = a
(_:x)!!n = x!!(n-1)
[]!!n    = error "Indexing"
```

show that for all fp-lists l and natural numbers n,

```
(map f l)!!n = f (l!!n)
```

and therefore infer that the result is valid for all lists l.

13.34 Show that the following equations hold between functions.

```
filter p . map f    = map f . filter (p.f)
filter p . filter q = filter (q &&& p)
concat . map (map f) = map f . concat
```

where the operator `&&&` is defined by

```
(q &&& p) x = q x && p x
```

SUMMARY

Lazy evaluation of Haskell expressions means that we can write programs in a different style. A data structure created within a program execution will only be created on demand, as we saw with the example of finding the sum of fourth powers. In finding routes through a graph we saw that we could explore just that part of the graph which is needed to reveal a path. In these and many more cases the advantage of lazy evaluation is to give programs whose purpose is clear and whose execution is efficient.

We re-examined the list comprehension notation, which makes many list processing programs easier to express; we saw this in the particular examples of route finding and parsing.

Exploiting higher-order functions, polymorphism and list comprehensions we gave a library of parsing functions, which we saw applied to the type of arithmetical expressions, Expr. A design principle exploited here encourages the use of lazy lists: if a function can return multiple results it is possible to represent the result as a list; using lazy evaluation, the multiple results will only be generated one-by-one, as they are required. Also, we are able to represent 'no result' by the empty list, []. This 'list of successes' method is useful in a variety of contexts.

Rather than being simply a curiosity, this chapter has shown that we can exploit infinite lists for a variety of purposes.

- In giving an *infinite* list of prime or random numbers we provide an unlimited resource: we do not have to know how much of the resource we need while constructing the program; this *abstraction* makes programming simpler and clearer.

- Infinite lists provide a mechanism for process-based programming in Haskell.

The chapter concluded with a discussion of how proofs could be lifted to the partial and infinite elements of the list type: criteria were given in both cases, and we gave examples and counter-examples in illustration.

14 Input/output and interaction

The programs we have written so far in this book have been self-contained. However, most larger-scale programs have some interaction with the 'world outside'. This can take many forms.

- A program, like the Hugs or Gofer interpreter itself, can read from a terminal and write to a terminal.
- A mail system reads and writes from files as well as standard terminal channels.
- An operating system executes programs in parallel, as well as controlling devices like printers, CD-ROM readers and terminals.

This chapter explores how the simplest kinds of programs, reading and writing to a terminal, can be developed in Haskell. We look at two ways of doing this.

First we look at the **stream** model, where input and output are treated as lists. The advantages of this are that we are using a style of programming with which we are already familiar, and that we can re-use many of the programs we have developed so far. One disadvantage of this approach is that it can be difficult to predict exactly the behaviour of more complicated systems. The far more major problem is that it does not extend satisfactorily to problems like writing an operating system; our second approach does.

Monadic input/output is built from objects of type IO t, which do some input/output before returning an object of type t. We give a library of higher-order, polymorphic functions which combine these objects to give complex interactive systems. If we extend this set, we can bring in the kinds of operation we need to write an operating system, for example.

After discussing these two approaches, we compare their relative merits at the end of Section 14.2. We conclude the chapter by arguing that the monadic approach, in which computation is explicitly sequenced, is applicable in a variety of situations. We go on to define exactly what a monad is, and give a number of different examples of monads in functional programming.

14.1 Stream-based interactive programs

An interactive program transforms input into output thus

where the input and output are sequences of characters

```
type Input  = String
type Output = String
```

so in writing interactive programs, we can use all the resources of Haskell list processing. Under this view of input/output the channels are called **streams**, as we can think of the items as arriving or being written one after another in a stream of data.

As a first example we take a program to reverse lines of text: we can use this to recognize English words such as bard which are also words (drab) when reversed, or to spot palindromes, which are the same when reversed.

How do we write a program like this? The most straightforward approach is to think about how the data is transformed, in a number of steps. What are the steps here?

- First we have to split the input into lines;
- then we have to reverse each line, and
- finally we have to join the lines together.

When we have a sequence of transformations like this, we join them using '.' or >.>; recall that the operator >.> is 'forward' composition, where

```
f >.> g = g . f
```

so (f >.> g) can be read as 'do f then g'. Our program becomes

```
example1 :: Input -> Output
example1 = lines >.> map reverse >.> unlines
```

where the standard functions

```
lines   :: String -> [String]
unlines :: [String] -> String
```

split input into lines (at the newlines, '\n') and join a list of strings into a single string, separated by newlines, respectively. For example,

```
lines "hello\nbard\n"   = ["hello","bard"]
unlines ["hello","bard"] = "hello\nbard\n"
```

The effect of example1 is to return the lines of input, *reversed*, so that, if we apply example1 to the input

```
hello
bard
```

for instance, we get the output

```
olleh
drab
```

in which each line is reversed.

Reading values

Suppose we want to treat the input as representing something other than strings, and in particular suppose we want the input to consist of the representation of one integer per line. We can split the input into lines, and convert each line from a string into an integer, either writing a function ourselves, or using the built-in read. The example

```
example2 :: Input -> Output
example2 = lines >.> map read >.> map (+1) >.>
           map show >.> unlines
```

does this, adding one to each number before outputting the result. Output is in two stages: first the integer is converted into a string using show, and then the strings (or lines) are laid out using unlines. In the definition we have written three separate maps for emphasis; we could have equally well have written

```
example2 = lines >.> map (read >.> (+1) >.> show) >.>
           unlines
```

to emphasize that we are processing one line at a time.

As we have seen, there is a general mechanism for treating strings as values provided by Haskell. The function

```
read :: Read t => String -> t
```

will read a string and convert it to a value of the appropriate type, provided that that type belongs to the Read class. It is also necessary for the type at which read is being used to be evident from the context. In example2 that is so, because we apply (+1) to the result of the read.

Interactive programming

Given functions such as example1 and example2, how are they run **interactively**, with input coming from a terminal, say? We evaluate

```
interact example1
```

and so on; interact turns a String -> String function into an interactive program. As we said above, under example1 the input

```
hello
bard
```

gives rise to the output

```
olleh
drab
```

but there is another aspect we should look into: how are the input and output inter-related, or **interleaved**? An example interaction is given by

```
? interact example1
hello
olleh
bard
drab
Control-D
```

where as we did when we introduced the Haskell systems, our input is underlined; `Control-D` is used to signal the end of the input.

In this example the input and the output lines are *interleaved*, so that the reversed version of a line immediately follows its input – why is this?

Lazy evaluation and interleaving

This interleaving happens because we use lazy evaluation, which means that *part* of the output, a list, can be produced on the basis of *partial* information about the input. The effect of this is that after, say, one line of input we may see one line of output from a program and `interact` is implemented so that partial information about the output is printed as soon as it is available.

We can see this in action in a calculation, where we use the three dots '...' to mean 'not known yet'.

Taking `example1` on the input above, after the first '\n' in the input, we can produce the first line,

```
lines "hello\n..." = "hello" : lines "..."
```

Now, we have the head of the input to `map reverse`, so

```
map reverse ("hello" : ...) = "olleh" : map reverse ...
```

and we then have the start of the result string

```
unlines ("olleh" : ...) = "olleh\n..."
```

so that putting this together,

```
example1 "hello\n..." = "olleh\n..."
```

This shows how the first line of output can follow the first line of input. Given the definitions of `lines`, `map` and `unlines`, this behaviour will be repeated until the end of the file (that is the end of the input string to `example1`) is reached.

Prompts and messages

Our program to reverse strings can be made to **prompt** for further input, thus

```
example3 = lines >.> map reverse >.>
           map (++"\nAnother?") >.> unlines
```

since appended to each reversed string will be the message `"Another?"`. A sample interaction is

```
? interact example3
hello
olleh
Another?
   . . .
```

but observe that no output is produced until some input has been given. If we want to give some output before any input is read, then it must be done *outside* the loop involving `lines`, `map` and `unlines`, all of which examine their input before starting their output. If we write

```
example4 = example3 >.> ("Enter a string or Control-D\n"++)
```

then output of this program will begin with the `"Enter..D\n"` message, and this can be seen thus

```
example4 "..."
= (example3 >.> ("Enter..D\n"++)) "..."
= ("Enter..D\n"++) (example3 "...")
= "Enter..D\n" ++ (example3 "...")
```

where the output has its first part defined *without any information about the input being available*.

Scanning

The interactions we have seen so far are special, in that they have *no memory*: each piece of output is determined by the line of input, and nothing else. Many interactions have this form, but most have some sort of memory for what has gone before.

A simple example is an interaction which reads integers and outputs the total read so far. This form of list processing was given by our scanl1' of Section 13.7. As an interaction, we write

```
example5 = lines >.> map read >.>
           scanl1' (+) 0 >.>
           map show >.> unlines
```

The main processing is done by the scanl1'; the other functions achieve the conversion to and from strings.

Suppose now that we are asked to keep a running average of the integers typed in: at each stage we will have to know how many entries there have been, and their total, which we can keep as an (Int, Int) pair. Given a new value, we apply the function

```
oneStep :: Int -> (Int,Int) -> (Int,Int)
oneStep val (n,total) = (n+1,total+val)
```

and evaluating

```
example6 = lines >.> map read >.>
           scanl1' oneStep (0,0) >.>
           map show >.> unlines
```

will give an interaction of the form

```
?  interact example6
(0,0)
12
(1,12)
 . . .
```

Of course, this is not exactly what we are looking for – instead of printing the pair, we wanted to print the average, so we add an extra function to convert the pair to that.

```
aver (0,total) = 0
aver (n,total) = total 'div' n

example7 = lines >.> map read >.>
           scanl1' oneStep (0,0) >.> map aver >.>
           map show >.> unlines
```

which gives an interaction like

```
? interact example7
0
12
12
6
9
...
```

Related to the scanning interactions, we have the full calculator, which we look at now.

Case study: the calculator

The ingredients of the calculator are contained in three places in the text.

- In Section 10.2 we saw the introduction of the algebraic type of expressions, `Expr`, which we subsequently revised in Section 13.5, giving

```
data Expr = Lit Int | Var Vars | Op Ops Expr Expr
data Ops  = Add | Sub | Mul | Div | Mod
type Var  = Char
```

  We revise the evaluation of expressions after discussing the store below.

- In Chapter 12 we introduced the abstract type `Store`, which we use to model the values of the variables currently held. The signature of the abstract data type is

```
initial :: Store
lookup  :: Store -> Vars -> Int
update  :: Store -> Vars -> Int -> Store
```

- In Section 13.5 we looked at how to parse expressions and commands, and defined the ingredients of the function

```
commandParse :: String -> Command
```

  which is used to parse each line of input into a `Command`.

Expressions are evaluated by

```
eval :: Expr -> Store -> Int
eval (Lit n) st = n
eval (Var v) st = lookup st v
```

```
eval (Op op e1 e2) st
  = opValue op v1 v2
    where
    v1 = eval e1 st
    v2 = eval e2 st
```

where the `opValue` function, of type `Ops->Int->Int->Int` interprets each operator, such as `Add`, as the corresponding function, like `(+)`.

The list of commands to be interpreted is given by

```
commList :: String -> [Command]
commList = lines >.> map commandParse
```

and the interpretation itself is given by

```
calculate :: [Command] -> Store -> [String]
```

which has a clause for each kind of command. First, if we are to evaluate an expression,

```
calculate ((Eval e):cs) st
        = show (eval e st) : calculate cs st
```

the first line of output is the value of the expression; the remainder is given by calculating the effect of the remaining commands, `cs`, starting from the same store `st`. Next, if we have an assignment,

```
calculate ((Assign v e):cs) st
        = ([v] ++ " = " ++ show val) : calculate cs st'
          where
          val = eval e st
          st' = update st v val
```

we report the value assigned, and then `update` the store to `st'`, which is used to begin evaluation of the remaining commands. Finally, a null command has no effect,

```
calculate (Null:cs) st
        = "Null command" : calculate cs st
```

and at the end of the input, we reach the end of the output

```
calculate [] st = []
```

The definition which gives the calculator is

```
perform :: String -> String
perform inp = unlines (calculate (commList inp) initial)
```

where we begin calculation with the `initial` store.

Conclusion

The form of the interactions we have seen so far is *stylized* in that we can predict the form the output will take without knowing anything about the values which the program reads. In particular here we often have one line of `Output` per line of `Input`.

The approach we have taken has the advantage that we work at a high level: we primarily think about how to build the output from the input data. The issue of how the input and output are interleaved, or the interactive behaviour of the program is not programmed explicitly. Instead we rely on lazy evaluation to give an interleaving. Of course, this may have drawbacks; we may find that our programs have unintended interactive behaviour, and also discover that it is difficult to change this.

If we want to write more complex interactive systems where values can determine more explicitly the 'shape' of the interactions we will have to use a different approach. This is the subject of the next section.

EXERCISES

14.1 Modify `example4` so that the message `"Interaction over."` is printed after `Control-D` is typed. [Hint: this can be done in a similar way to the message at the start of the output.]

14.2 Write a program which checks interactively whether strings are palindromes. Example palindromes are

```
"abba"
"Madam I\'m Adam"
```

so that your check will need to remove punctuation and white space, and to be insensitive to the case of letters (capital or small). Your program should print suitable messages at the start and end of the interaction, as well as giving a prompt at each stage.

14.3 In order to understand some aspects of the implementation of Haskell, it is interesting to write an interactive calculator for expressions like

```
(2+(3%4))
(34*23)
```

not involving variables. These expressions can be parsed using the parser of Section 13.5, and the evaluation function of Section 10.2. The messages which your program outputs should provide enough information to make the program usable by a novice.

The exercises which follow give various extensions of the basic calculator, as well as looking at some of its drawbacks.

14.4 How would you add initial and final messages to the output of the calculator?

14.5 If the calculator is not given a valid command, then an error message will be generated by the function `topLevel`, and evaluation stops. Discuss how you would add an extra argument to `topLevel` to be used in the error case, so that evaluation with the calculator does not halt.

14.6 The form of definition of `calculate` is a generalization of `scanl1'`: at each stage we output a function of the current store and the value just read, as well as changing the store

```
oneStep :: InVal -> Store -> (Store,OutVal)
```

Define a function

```
mapSide :: (InVal -> Store -> (Store,OutVal)) ->
           Store ->
           [InVal] ->
           [OutVal]
```

which works like a `map` but changes the value of the `Store` at each step. Show how this can be used to define the `calculate` function, where the types `InVal` and `OutVal` are `Command` and `String`, respectively.

14.7 Discuss how you would have to modify the system to allow variables to have arbitrarily long names, consisting of letters and numbers, starting with a letter.

14.8 How would you extend the calculator to deal with decimal fractions as well as integers?

14.2 Using monads for I/O

We saw in the previous section how simple interactive programs could be written as functions from lists to lists, or streams to streams. The drawback to this simple and elegant approach is that it can be difficult to predict and control the precise interactive behaviour of these functions. In this section we see how a different, more explicit, model of interaction can help with this. This is the so-called **monadic**[1] approach.

After introducing the type IO t, we show how to build a library of higher-order, polymorphic functions which combine objects of this type to give complex interactive systems; their types are given in Figure 14.1. In doing this we make a particular point of illustrating the effect of the sequencing operator, >>=. We conclude by comparing the monadic and stream approaches to I/O.

The types IO t

Central to the monadic approach to I/O is the family of built-in types IO t. Objects belonging to this type will do some I/O and then return a value of type t. We first look at some simple examples informally.

- The operation which reads a line of text from a file does some I/O and returns the line, of type String. We therefore expect there to be an object

  ```
  getLine :: IO String
  ```

  which reads a line from the standard input.

- The operation which writes a line of text will just do some I/O, given the value that is to be printed. We therefore have a *function* which takes the string to be written, and gives back the I/O object which writes that string:

  ```
  putLine :: String -> IO ()
  ```

  The result of this interaction has type (). There is a single element of this type, which is also written (). This **one-element type** is used when some sort of value has to be returned, but what that particular value is has no importance.

  putLine is in fact a special case of the built-in

  ```
  putStr :: String -> IO ()
  ```

---

[1] The name comes from the *monads* which are a feature of category theory; the approach itself goes back to various people's research into taming I/O in a pure functional setting. A fascinating exposition of the history of this, and much more besides, can be found in Gordon (1994).

defined to add an end of line, thus

```
putLine st = putStr (st ++ "\n")
```

• Depending upon how much of a link we require between the Haskell system and the 'outside world' we can add various other primitives like getLine and putLine: in this way we can extend the monadic approach to embrace concurrency, device control and a host of other facilities.

Beyond these primitive operations, what we need are ways of **combining** these I/O objects to build complex systems. Here the monadic approach gives us *explicit* control of how interactions are put together.

How are these interactions actually performed in a Haskell implementation? An interaction which results in a value of type () will take place when an expression of type IO () is typed to an interpreted system prompt, or is made the main expression in a compiled version of the language. For instance, one of the simplest interactive programs is performed by typing

```
putLine "Hello World"
```

to the system prompt.

The 'then' operation

The central operation, which is often pronounced 'then', sequences two operations, one after the other. Its type is

```
(>>=) :: IO t -> (t -> IO u) -> IO u
```

What is the effect of this operation? It combines an IO t

with a *function* taking the result of this (of type t) into an IO u, that is an object of type t -> IO u,

We can join them together: passing the result of the first as an argument to the second, thus:

The result of putting them together is something which does some I/O before returning a value of type u:

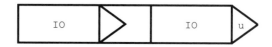

in other words, an object of type IO u.

Using the operation, we can build a number of simple interactions.

● One of the simplest operations is to read a line and then write out the result. We have

```
getLine  :: IO String
putLine  :: String -> IO ()
```

The getLine returns a value which can be passed into the putLine, so we can combine the two using >>= and writing

```
readWrite :: IO ()
readWrite = getLine >>= putLine
```

● Suppose we wish to write out the string, but reversed. One solution is to say

```
readRevWrite :: IO ()
readRevWrite = getLine >>= \st -> putLine (reverse st)
```

In this example we first read the line, then we pass the result to the function

```
\st -> putLine (reverse st)
```

We can think of this function as **naming** the string st for the remainder of the interaction: this consists of writing out the string reverse st.

This use of lambda expressions here is not accidental; we can think in general of the first half of

```
m >>= ....
```

as returning a value; we **name** this using a lambda, and then access it in the remainder of the interaction using this name:

```
m >>= \a -> ....a....
```

Next we turn to some more general combining forms for these interactions.

Other combinators and interactions

The type `IO t` carries some other standard functions which we look at now. First, we would like to be able to do some trivial interaction, simply returning a value without any I/O. The built-in function giving this is

```
return :: t -> IO t
```

It is quite often the case that when we do one interaction then another, we do not want to pass a result from the first to the second. For this we use

```
(>>) :: IO t -> IO u -> IO u
f >> g = f >>= const g
```

A third combinator allows us to change the result of an IO object or alternatively lift a function to a transformer of interactions:

```
apply :: (t -> u) -> t -> IO u
apply f a = return (f a)
```

Now, we can show a different way of building the example `readRevWrite` above. We have three stages in the interaction:

```
readRevWrite = getLine >>= apply reverse >>= putLine
```

First a line is read in, then it is reversed, and finally the result is written out. It is a matter of taste which style is preferable; in a simple case it is probably better not to name the variables, whereas in a larger example it is more straightforward to do that.
A final combinator is

```
interact :: (String -> String) -> IO ()
```

which we used in the previous section; it is this function which converts a `String` transforming function into a genuine interactive program. It is defined by the system so that the output `String` is produced incrementally from portions of the input data as they become available. This has the effect that input and output are interleaved in the customary fashion.

Conditions and iteration

One of the basic components we need to build more complex interactive systems is a **condition** which controls whether certain operations take place or not. We might, for instance, want to read the input until the end of file is

```
getLine   :: IO String
putStr    :: String -> IO ()
putLine   :: String -> IO ()
isEOF     :: IO Bool

(>>=)     :: IO t -> (t -> IO u) -> IO u
(>>)      :: IO t -> IO u -> IO u
return    :: t -> IO t

apply     :: (t -> u) -> t -> IO u
while     :: IO Bool -> IO () -> IO ()

interact :: (String -> String) -> IO ()
```

Figure 14.1 The functions over the interaction type IO t.

reached. A condition has the type IO Bool and an interaction which tests for the end of (standard) input is

```
isEOF :: IO Bool
```

Once we can see what a condition is, we can build up combinators to iterate interactions. For example, we can write a while combinator,

```
while :: IO Bool -> IO () -> IO ()
```

so that while test oper performs oper while test is True. Its definition is

```
while test oper
  = loop
     where
     loop = test >>= \res ->
              if res then (oper >> loop)
                      else return ()
```

What is the effect of the definition? It defines loop :: IO (), which is the loop we are trying to write. First we perform the test, whose result is named res in the remaining interaction. If res is True, we perform the operation and then loop; if not, we do no I/O and simply return the value ().

A summary of the operations we have discussed so far is given in Figure 14.1.

Using while we can now define some more complex examples, including those first examined in Section 14.1. Our first example simply copies Input to Output, a line at a time. In our case, we say

```
exampleIO :: IO ()
exampleIO = while (isEOF >>= apply not)
                  (getLine >>= putLine)
```

The command to be repeated is clear – we read then write – but it is worth explaining the condition. isEOF is in IO Bool; we want to apply the function not to its result to make a check for non-end of file. This is done by forming

```
apply not :: Bool -> IO Bool
```

which can then be sequenced with isEOF by means of >>=.

We could write the interaction in a different form, hiding the details in a where clause, thus:

```
exampleIO :: IO ()
exampleIO = while notEOF readWrite
              where
              notEOF    = isEOF >>= apply not
              readWrite = getLine >>= putLine
```

but clearly the effect of the two will be the same. In a similar way we can write

```
exampleIO1 :: IO ()
exampleIO1 = while notEOF readRevWrite
               where
               readRevWrite = (getLine >>=
                                   apply reverse >>=
                                   putLine)
```

and notEOF is defined earlier.

Conclusion: comparing the two approaches

It is instructive to compare the stream approach of Section 14.1 with the monadic style used here. In particular, we can compare example1 with exampleIO1, both of which are designed to reverse each line of input.

The stream-based solution, example1, stresses the *data*; in particular we are able to see an explicit description of the output as a String which results from applying a function to the input data. On the other hand, the way in which the input and output are interleaved is implicit, and it is not immediately obvious that they will be interleaved line by line.

In contrast, the monadic solution, `exampleIO1`, stresses the sequencing of the various operations. We see that a certain operation, `readRevWrite`, is repeated; within that operation we find a read then a write. From this description it is easy to see how the interleaving of I/O takes place; it is less clear how the output *data* depend upon the input.

This comparison shows that there is no clear 'right' answer. For small-scale interactions the stream approach seems more straightforward, but in larger examples the control given by the monadic combinators is essential. In the next section we give an overview of how the monadic approach affects other areas of functional programming.

EXERCISES

14.9 Repeat the examples and exercises of Section 14.1 using the monadic approach of this section.

14.10 Give a definition of the function

```
mapIO :: (t -> u) -> IO t -> IO u
```

whose effect is to transform an interaction by applying the function to its result. You can define it using `apply` if you wish; this is not necessary, however.

14.11 Define the function

```
repeat ::  IO Bool -> IO () -> IO ()
```

so that `repeat test oper` has the effect of repeating `oper` until the condition `test` is `True`.

14.12 Give a generalization of `while` in which the condition and the operation work over values of type `t`. Its new type is

```
whileG :: (t -> IO Bool) -> (t -> IO t) -> (t -> IO t)
```

14.13 Using the function `whileG` or otherwise, define an interaction which reads a number, `n` say, and then reads a further `n` numbers and finally returns their average.

14.14 Modify your answer to the previous exercise so that if the end of file is reached before `n` numbers have been read, a message to that effect is printed.

14.15 Define a function

```
accumulate :: [IO t] -> IO [t]
```

which performs a sequence of interactions and accumulates their result in a list. Also give a definition of the function

```
sequence :: [IO t] -> IO ()
```

which performs the interactions in turn, but discards their results. Finally, show how you would sequence a series, passing values from one to the next:

```
seqList :: [t -> IO t] -> t -> IO t
```

What will be the result on an empty list?

14.16 [Harder] We can think of implementing IO t as follows

```
type IO t = Input -> (Input,t,Output)
```

Each of these functions takes the Input, a String, and returns three things:

- the part of the input String which remains unread;
- the result of the interaction, of type t; and
- the Output produced by the interaction, another String.

Define the functions over IO t whose types are given in Figure 14.1. The difficult function to define is >>=; recall that if a function f returns a pair, then you can extract its components in a where clause, thus:

```
. . . . .
  where
  (a,b) = f e
```

14.3 Monads for functional programming

As research and experience in functional programming have increased, certain styles of programming have shown themselves to be particularly elegant and powerful. Among these is the *monadic* style, which extends beyond I/O to cover a number of fields. This section contains an introductory discussion of the approach; further details of this and other advanced techniques can be found in Jeuring and Meijer (1995).

As we saw in the conclusion to Section 14.2, a characteristic of monads is that they make explicit the sequence in which operations take place. It is the combinator >>= which sequences the operations of a general monad M.

```
(>>=) :: M t -> (t -> M u) -> M u
```

When is such a sequencing necessary? Consider the example of

```
e - f
```

The arguments to `-`, `e` and `f`, can be evaluated in any order, or indeed in parallel. Suppose, however, that the expressions `e` and `f` cause some I/O to take place, or cause some store to be changed. *Then* we need to say in which order the evaluation takes place, since different orders will give different results. A simple example, written in pseudo-Haskell, is

```
input e - input f
```

If the input is 7 followed by 4, evaluation left-to-right gives 3, while right-to-left gives -3; parallel evaluation has an unpredictable effect!
  How do we achieve an explicit sequence? The operation

```
readInt >>= \e ->
readInt >>= \f ->
return (e-f)
```

clearly inputs the left-hand value before the right, where `readInt :: IO Int` performs integer input.
  This sort of explicit sequencing is, as we said, a feature of many kinds of programming where **side-effects** accompany a computation. The novel feature of the monadic approach is that these side-effects can be incorporated into a **pure** functional programming language by means of monads.
  We should now say formally what a monad is.

What is a monad?

A monad is a family of types `M t`, based on a polymorphic type constructor `M`, with functions

```
return :: t -> M t
(>>=)  :: M t -> (t -> M u) -> M u
```

Formally, they should satisfy three equations

```
return a >>= f  =  f a                          (M1)
m >>= return    =  m                            (M2)
m >>= (\a -> (f a) >>= g)
   =  (m >>= f) >>= g                           (M3)
```

The first two rules show that `return` is like an identity for >>=, while (M3) states that >>= is an associative sequencing operation. Note that in (M3) the result of the lambda-defined function is (f a) >>= g, the lambda having lower binding power than the >>=.

SOME EXAMPLES

The identity monad

```
type I t  = t
return a  = a
(>>=) m f = f m
```

is the simplest example of a monad. We have already seen the example of the IO monad in Section 14.2, and in the exercises of that section we have shown one way of implementing such a family of types.

Other examples come from **collections** of objects. We can build a monad from lists

```
type L t  = [t]
return a  = [a]
(>>=) l f = concat (map f l)
```

or from the error type, `Err t`, whose values are members of t or errors – they *perhaps* contain a value of type t:

```
data Err t = OK t | Error
return a   = OK a
(>>=) v f  = case v of
                    (OK a) -> f a
                    Error  -> Error
```

Later in this section we will give an example of a **state** monad, `State t u`. An operation of this type can change the state before returning a value of type u.

The examples we have seen show that over each type family I, IO, L, Err we can build the same functions. This resembles the situation in which we can build a class, but there the definitions occur over different types, rather than different type families or type **constructors**. The Haskell language allows **constructor classes** to be built to model these, but we do not pursue the details of that here.

Some standard functions

We can define some standard functions over every monad. Their types should be familiar from the list case

```
map  :: (t -> u) -> M t -> M u
join :: M (M t) -> M t
```

and their definitions are

```
map f m = m >>= (\a -> return (f a))
join m  = m >>= (\a -> a)
```

(Over lists `join` is often called `concat`.) Many of the properties of `map` and `concat` over lists lift to these functions. For instance, we can show using properties (M1) to (M3) that for all f and g

```
map (f.g) = map f . map g
```
(M4)

EXAMPLE: Monadic computation over trees _____

We now illustrate how computations over the type of

```
data Tree t = Nil | Node t (Tree t) (Tree t)
```

can be given a monadic structure. We first look at a simple example, and in the following section we look at a rather more realistic one. We see that with a monadic approach their top-level structure is exactly the same. This structure guides the way that we build the implementation of the second example, as we shall see.

Suppose we are asked to give the sum of a tree of integers,

```
sTree :: Tree Int -> Int
```

A direct recursive solution is

```
sTree Nil            = 0
sTree (Node n t1 t2) = n + sTree t1 + sTree t2
```

In writing this we give no explicit sequence to the calculation of the sum: we could calculate `sTree t1` and `sTree t2` one after the other, or indeed in parallel. How might a monadic solution proceed?

```
sumTree :: Tree Int -> St Int
```

where St is a monad which we have yet to define. In the Nil case,

```
sumTree Nil = return 0
```

while in the case of a Node we calculate the parts in a given order:

```
sumTree (Node n t1 t2)
  = return n   >>= \num ->
     sumTree t1 >>= \s1  ->                                    (1)
     sumTree t2 >>= \s2  ->
     return (num + s1 + s2)
```

How is the definition structured? We put the operations in sequence, using >>=. First we return the value n, which is passed to the function \num -> ....; the effect of this is to give this value the name num. Next we calculate sumTree t1 and sumTree t2, naming their results s1 and s2. Finally we return the result, which is the sum num+s1+s2.

Now, since all we are doing here is calculating values and not trying to do any I/O or other side-effecting operation, we make the monad St the *identity* monad I which we saw above. This means that we could say

```
sumTree :: Tree Int -> Int
```

There is a remarkable similarity between the definition (1) and an imperative program, bearing in mind that >>= performs a sequencing and \j gives (or *assigns*) a value to j. In an imperative setting, we might well write

```
num := n ;
s1  := sumTree t1 ;
s2  := sumTree t2 ;
return (num + s1 + s2) ;
```

where 'num :=' corresponds to the '\num' and the semi-colon to >>=.

In the next section we tackle a more complex problem, but see the same monadic structure repeated.

Using a state monad in a tree calculation

Building on the experience of the previous section in defining sumTree we tackle here a rather more tricky problem. We want to write a function

```
numTree :: Eq t => Tree t -> Tree Int
```

so that given an arbitrary tree we transform it to a tree of integers in which the original elements are replaced by natural numbers, starting from 0. An example is given in Figure 14.2. The same element has to be replaced by the same number at every occurrence, and when we meet an as-yet-unvisited element we have to find a 'new' number to match it with.

How does our definition appear? We give the function a type,

```
numberTree :: Eq t => Tree t -> State t (Tree Int)
```

in which the monad State t will have to carry about enough information to allow us to replace the elements in the correct way. The structure of the program then is

```
numberTree Nil = return Nil
numberTree (Node x t1 t2)
  = numberNode x   >>= \num ->
    numberTree t1 >>= \nt1 ->                         (2)
    numberTree t2 >>= \nt2 ->
    return (Node num nt1 nt2)
```

The structure here is exactly the same as that of sumTree; we perform the operations on the components x, t1 and t2 (for the sub-trees we use recursion) and then combine them in the result (Node num nt1 nt2).

What else do we have to define to give the result? We need to identify the monad State t and to define the function which replaces an individual entry,

```
numberNode :: Eq t => t -> State t Int
```

We now have to think about the implementation of the monad. We have called it State since it keeps a record of the state, that is of which values are associated with which numbers. This we do in a table:

```
type Table t = [t]
```

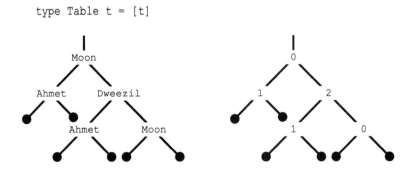

Figure 14.2 Replacing the elements of a tree with natural numbers.

where the table [True,False] indicates that True is associated with 0 and
False with 1.

What then is the state monad? It consists of functions

```
type State t u = Table t -> (Table t , u)
```

which we can think of as taking the state *before* doing the operation to the
state *after* the operation, together with its result. In other words, we return a
value of type u, but perhaps we change the value of the state of type Table t
as a side-effect.

Next we have to define the two monad operations. To return a value,
we leave the state unchanged:

```
return :: u -> State t u
return x = \tab -> (tab,x)
```

How do we sequence the operations?

```
(>>=) :: State t u -> (u -> State t v) -> State t v

st >>= f
  = \tab -> let
              (newTab,y) = st tab
            in
              f y newTab
```

The intended effect here is to do st, pass its result to f and then do the
resulting operation.

To perform st, we pass it the table tab; the output of this is a new
state, newTab, and a value y. This y is passed to f, giving an object of type
State t v; this is then performed starting with the *new* state newTab. Here
we can see that the operations are indeed done in sequence, leading from one
state value to the next.

This has given us the monad; all that remains is to define the function
numberNode. Our definition is

```
numberNode x table
  | elem x table      = (table      , lookup x table)
  | otherwise         = (table++[x] , length table)
```

If x is an element of table, we return its position in the table, given by
lookup; if it is not, we add it to the end of the table, and return its position

which is `length table`. The definition of

```
lookup :: Eq t => t -> Table t -> Int
```

is standard, and we leave it as an exercise for the reader.

Standing back, we can see that we have completed our definition of the function

```
numberTree :: Eq t => Tree t -> State t (Tree Int)
```

but one ingredient of the solution is still needed. If we form

```
numberTree exampleTree
```

for some `exampleTree` of the tree type, we have an object in

```
State t (Tree Int)
```

In order to `extract` the result, we have to write a function

```
extract :: State t u -> u
```

This has to perform the calculation, starting with some initial table, and return the resulting value of type `u`. The definition is

```
extract m = snd (m [])
```

where we see that `m` is applied to the initial state `[]`. The result of this is a pair, from which we select the second part, of type `u`. Now we can define our function

```
numTree :: Eq t => Tree t -> Tree Int
numTree = extract . numberTree
```

which has the effect we require.

To conclude, we have shown how a more complex calculation over a tree, (2) can be structured in exactly the same way as a simple one, (1). In the case of a tree type the advantage is tangible, but for more complex types a monadic structure becomes almost essential if we are to follow a computation with complicated side-effects.

The power of monadic programming

Looking at the examples we have covered, we can conclude that the advantages of structuring a computation using a monad are threefold:

- We follow a well-defined strategy for writing *sequential* programs, which has strong similarities with imperative programming.
- There is an advantage in *abstraction*: we can change the underlying monad yet retain the overall structure of the computation.
- Finally, we have seen that various properties can be inferred automatically once we have a monad. As we saw above, (M4) is a consequence of the monad properties (M1) to (M3).

This section can only give a taste of the monadic style; we urge readers who are interested to follow up Jeuring and Meijer (1995).

EXERCISES

14.17 Show that sets and binary trees can be given a monad structure, as can the type

```
data NewErr t = OK t | Error String
```

14.18 For the monads I , L and Err prove the rules (M1) to (M3). Also show that these rules hold for your implementations in the previous exercise.

14.19 Prove the property (M4) using the laws (M1) to (M3).

14.20 Prove the following property using the monad laws.

```
join.return = id
```

14.21 Can you define a different monad structure over lists from that given above? Check that your definition has properties (M1) to (M3).

14.22 Show how to lookup the position of an element in a list

```
lookup :: Eq t => t -> Table t -> Int
```

You might find it useful to define a function

```
look :: Eq t => t -> Table t -> Int -> Int
```

where the extra integer parameter carries the current 'offset' into the list.

14.23 Show how you can use a State-style monad in a computation to replace each element in a tree by a random integer, generated using the techniques of Section 13.6.

14.24 We can use monads to extend the case study of the calculator in a variety of ways. Consider how you would

- add exceptions or messages to be given on an attempt to divide by zero;
- count the number of steps taken in a calculation; and
- combine the two.

SUMMARY

This chapter has shown how interactive programs can be written in stream and monad form. The stream form has the advantage of giving a data-oriented view of the operation, while the monadic view gives explicit control of the sequencing of the input/output streams.

It is this sequencing property which makes a monadic approach suitable beyond I/O. In the final section of the chapter we gave a general definition of monads, a sequence of examples of various kinds of monad, and a brief discussion of the advantage of the monadic approach.

15 Program behaviour

This chapter explores not the values which programs compute, but the way in which those values are reached; we are interested here in program *efficiency* rather than program correctness.

We begin our discussion by asking how we can measure complexity in general, before asking how we measure the time and space behaviour of our functional programs. We work out the time complexity of a sequence of functions, leading up to looking at various implementations of the Set abstype.

The *space* behaviour of lazy programs is complex: we show that some programs use less space than we might predict, while others use more. This leads into a discussion of *folding* functions into lists, and we introduce the `foldl'` function, which folds from the left, and gives more space-efficient versions of folds of operators which need their arguments – the *strict* operations. In contrast to this, `foldr` gives better performance on lazy folds, in general.

In many algorithms, the naive implementation causes re-computation of parts of the solution, and thus poor performance. In the final section of the chapter we show how to exploit lazy evaluation to give more efficient implementations, by *memoizing* the partial results in a table.

15.1 Complexity of functions

If we are trying to measure the behaviour of functions, one approach is to ask how much time and space are consumed in evaluations for different input values. We might, for example, given a function `fred` over the natural numbers, count the number of steps taken in calculating the value of `fred n` for natural numbers n. This gives us a function, call it `stepsFred`, and then we can ask how complex that function is.

One way of estimating the complexity of a function is to look at how fast it grows for large values of its argument. The idea of this is that the essential behaviour of a function becomes clearer for large values. We examine this idea to start with through an example.

How fast does the function

```
f n = 2*n^2 + 4*n + 13
```

grow, as n gets large? The function has three components

- a constant 13,
- a term 4*n and
- a term 2*n^2

but as the values of n become large, how do these components behave?

- The constant 13 is unchanged;
- the term 4*n grows like a straight line; but
- a square term, 2*n^2, will grow the most quickly.

For 'large' values of n the square term is greater than the others, and so we say that f is of *order* 2, O(^2). In this case the square dominates for any n greater than or equal to 3; we shall say exactly what is meant by 'large' when we make the definition of order precise. As a rule of thumb we can say that order classifies how functions behave when all but the fastest growing components are removed, and constant multipliers are ignored; the remainder of the section makes this precise, but this rule should be sufficient for understanding the remainder of the chapter.

The notation (^2) is an example of an operator section, in which we partially apply a binary operator to one of its arguments. It gives a very compact notation for 'the function which takes n to n^2', and we shall use these notations in the rest of this chapter without comment. Note, however, the difference between the square function, (^2), and the power function, (2^), both of which are used here.

In the remainder of this section we make the idea of order precise, before examining various examples, and placing them on a scale for measuring complexity.

The big-Oh and theta notation – upper bounds

A function f :: Int -> Int is O(g), '*big-Oh* g', if there are positive integers m and d, so that for all n ⩾ m,

    f n ⩽ d*(g n)

The definition expresses the fact that when numbers are large enough (n⩾m) the value of f is no larger than a multiple of the function g, namely (d*).g.
    For example, f above is O(^2) since, taking m as 1 and d as 19,

    2*n^2 + 4*n + 13 ⩽ 2*n^2 + 4*n^2 + 13*n^2 = 19*n^2

Note that the measure gives an upper bound, which may be an over-estimate; by similar reasoning, f is O(^17) as well. In most cases we consider the bound will in fact be a tight one. One way of expressing that g is a tight bound on f is that in addition to f being O(g), g is O(f); we then say that f is Θ(g), '*theta* g'. Our example f is in fact Θ(^2).

A scale of measurement

We say that f ≪ g if f is O(g), but g is not O(f); we also use f ≡ g to mean that f is O(g) and simultaneously g is O(f).
    We now give a scale by which function complexity can be measured. Constants (O(^0)) grow more slowly than linear functions (O(^1)) which in turn grow more slowly than quadratic functions (O(^2)). This continues through the powers. All the powers (^n) are bounded by exponential functions, (O(2^)).

    (^0) ≪ (^1) ≪ (^2) ≪ ... ≪ (^n) ≪ ... ≪ (2^) ≪ ...

Two other points ought to be added to the scale. The logarithm function, log, grows more slowly than any positive power, and the product of the functions n and log n, nLog n = n * log n fits between linear and quadratic, thus

    (^0) ≪ log ≪ (^1) ≪ nLog ≪ (^2) ≪ ...

Counting

Many of the arguments we make will involve counting. In this section we look at some general examples which we will come across in examining the behaviour of functions.

The first question we ask is – given a list, how many times can we bisect it, before we cut it into pieces of length one? If the length is n, after the first cut, the length of each half is n/2, and after p cuts, the length of each piece is n/(2^p). This number will be smaller than or equal to one when

$$(2^p) \geqslant n > (2^{(p-1)})$$

which when we take log_2 of each side gives

$$p \geqslant log_2 n > p-1$$

The function giving the number of steps in terms of the length of the list will thus be $\Theta(log_2)$.

The second question concerns trees. A tree is called *balanced* if all its branches are the same length. Suppose we have a balanced binary tree, whose branches are of length n; how many nodes does the tree have? On the first level it has 1, on the second 2, on the kth it has $2^{(k-1)}$, so over all n+1 levels it has

$$1 + 2 + 4 + \ldots + 2^{(k-1)} + \ldots + 2^n = 2^{(n+1)} - 1$$

as can be seen from Figure 15.1.

We thus see that the size of a balanced tree is $\Theta(2^{\wedge})$ in the length of the branches; taking logarithms, a balanced tree will therefore have branches of length $\Theta(log_2)$ in the size of the tree. If a tree is *not* balanced, the length of its longest branch can be of the same order as the size of the tree itself; see Figure 15.1 for an example.

Our final counting question concerns taking sums. If we are given one object every day for n days, we have n at the end; if we are given n each day,

Figure 15.1   Counting the nodes of trees.

we have n^2, what if we are given 1 on the first day, 2 on the second, and so on? What is the sum of the list [1 .. n], in other words? Writing the list backwards, as well as forwards, we have

```
1       + 2      + 3      +   ...   + (n-1) + n +
n       + (n-1)  + (n-2)  +   ...   + 2      + 1      =
(n+1)   + (n+1)  + (n+1)  +   ...   + (n+1)  + (n+1)
```

adding *vertically* at each point we have a sum of (n+1), and this sum occurs n times, so

```
sum [1 .. n] = n*(n+1) 'div' 2
```

which makes it Θ(^2), or quadratic. In a similar way, the sum of the squares is Θ(^3), and so on.

EXERCISES

15.1 Show that the example

```
f n = 2*n^2 + 4*n + 13
```

is Θ(^2).

15.2 Give a table of the values of the functions (^0), log, (^1), nLog, (^2), (^3) and (2^) for the values

```
0 1 2 3 4 5 10 50 100 500 1000 10000 100000 10000000
```

15.3 By giving the values of d, m and c (when necessary), show that the following functions have the complexity indicated.

```
f1 n = 0.1*n^5 + 31*n^3 + 1000          O(^6)
f2 n = 0.7*n^5 + 13*n^2 + 1000          Θ(^5)
```

15.4 Show that (^n) $\ll$ (2^) for all positive n. By taking logarithms of both sides, show that log $\ll$ (^n) for all positive n.

15.5 Show that

```
log ≡ ln ≡ log₂
```

and in fact that all logarithms have the same rate of growth.

15.6 The function `fib` is defined by

```
fib 0 = 0
fib 1 = 1
fib n = fib (n-2) + fib (n-1)
```

Show that $(\wedge n) \ll \text{fib}$ for all n.

15.7 Show that $\ll$ is transitive – that is $f \ll g$ and $g \ll h$ together imply that $f \ll h$. Show also that $\equiv$ is an equivalence relation.

15.8 If `f` is `O(g)`, show that any constant multiple of `f` is also of the same order. If `f1` and `f2` are `O(g)`, show that their sum and difference are also `O(g)`.

15.9 If `f1` is `O(^k1)` and `f2` is `O(^k2)`, show that their product,

```
f n = f1 n * f2 n
```

is `O(^(k1+k2))`.

15.10 Prove by induction over n that

```
1 + 2 + 4 + ... + 2^n = 2^(n+1) - 1
1^2 + 2^2 + ... + n^2 = n*(n+1)*(2*n+1) `div` 6
1^3 + 2^3 + ... + n^3 = (n*(n+1) `div` 2)^2
```

15.2 The complexity of calculations

How can we measure the complexity of the functions we write? One answer is to use an implementation of Haskell, which can be expected to produce some diagnostic information about evaluation. In Hugs we use the command `:set +s` to achieve this. While this gives some information, we opt for a cleaner *model* of what is going on, and we choose to analyse the *calculations* we have been using. There are three principal measures we can use.

- The *time* taken to compute a result is given by the *number of steps* in a calculation which uses lazy evaluation.

- The *space* necessary for the computation can be measured in two ways. First, there is a lower limit on the amount of space we need for a calculation to complete successfully. During calculation, the expression being calculated grows and shrinks; obviously, we need enough space to hold the *largest* expression built during the calculation. This is often called the residency of the computation, we shall call it the *space complexity*.

- We can also make a measure of the *total space* used by a computation, which in some way reflects the total area of the calculation; it is of interest to implementors of functional languages, but for users (and for us) the first two are the crucial measures.

How then do we measure the complexity of a function?

Complexity measures

We measure the complexity of the function f by looking at the time and space complexity as described above, as *functions* of the *size* of the inputs to f. The size of a number is the number itself, while the size of a list is given by its length, and of a tree by the number of nodes it contains.

EXAMPLES

Let us start with the example of fac.

```
fac :: Int -> Int
fac 0 = 1
fac n = n * fac (n-1)
```

Working through the calculation, we have

```
fac n
= n * fac (n-1)
= ...
= n * (n-1) * ... * 2 * 1 * 1          (†)
= n * (n-1) * ... * 2 * 1
= n * (n-1) * ... * 2
= ...
= n!
```

The calculation contains 2*n+1 steps, and the largest expression, (†), contains n multiplication symbols. This makes the time and space complexity both Θ (^1), or linear.

Next we look at insertion sort. Recall that

```
iSort []    = []
iSort (a:x) = ins a (iSort x)

ins a [] = [a]
ins a (b:y)
    | (a<=b)      = a:b:y
    | otherwise   = b:ins a y
```

A general calculation will be

```
iSort [a₁,a₂,...,aₙ₋₁,aₙ]
= ins a₁ (iSort [a₂,...,aₙ₋₁,aₙ])
= ...
= ins a₁ (ins a₂ ( ... (ins aₙ₋₁ (ins aₙ []))...))
```

followed by the calculation of the n ins's. What sort of behaviour does ins have? Take the general example of

```
ins a [a₁,a₂,...,aₙ₋₁,aₙ]
```

where we assume that $[a_1, \ldots, a_n]$ is sorted. There are three possibilities

- In the *best* case, when $a<=a_1$, the calculation takes 1 step.
- In the *worst* case, when $a>a_n$, the calculation takes n steps.
- In an *average* case, the calculation will take $n/2$ steps.

What does this mean for iSort?

- In the *best* case, each ins will take one step, and the calculation will therefore take a further n steps, making it O(^1) in this case.
- On the other hand, in the *worst* case, the first ins will take one step, the second two, and so on. By our counting argument in Section 15.1 the calculation will take O(^2) steps.
- In an *average* case, the ins's will take a total of

  ```
  1/2 + 2/2 + ... + (n-1)/2 + n/2
  ```

  steps, whose sum is again O(^2).

We therefore see that in most cases, the algorithm takes quadratic time, but in some exceptional cases, when sorting an (almost) sorted list, the complexity is linear in the length of the list. In all cases the space usage will also be linear.

Before looking at another sorting algorithm, we look at the time taken to join together two lists, using ++.

```
[a₁,a₂,...,aₙ₋₁,aₙ] ++ x
= a₁ : ([a₂,...,aₙ₋₁,aₙ] ++ x)
= a₁ : (a₂ : [a₃,...,aₙ₋₁,aₙ] ++ x)
= ... n-3 steps ...
= a₁ : (a₂ : ... : (aₙ:x)...)
```

The time taken is *linear* in the length of the first list.

Our second sorting algorithm, quicksort, is given by

```
qSort []    = []
qSort (a:x)
    = qSort [y|y<-x,y<=a] ++[a]++ qSort [y|y<-x,y>a]
```

When the list is sorted and contains no duplicate elements, the calculation goes thus:

```
qSort [a₁,a₂,...,aₙ₋₁,aₙ]
= ... n steps ...
= [] ++ [a₁] ++ qSort [a₂,...,aₙ₋₁,aₙ]
= ... n-1 steps ...
= a₁ : ([] ++ [a₂] ++ qSort [a₃,...,aₙ])
= ... n-2 steps ...
= ...
= a₁ : (a₂ : (a₃ : ... aₙ:[]))
= [a₁,a₂,...,aₙ₋₁,aₙ]
```

Since the number of steps here is $1+2+...n$, we have *quadratic* behaviour in this sorted case. In the *average* case, we split thus

```
qSort [a₁,a₂,...,aₙ₋₁,aₙ]
= qSort [b₁,...,bₙ/₂] ++ [a₁] ++ qSort [c₁,...,cₙ/₂]
```

where the list has been bisected. Forming the two sublists will take $O(^1)$ steps, as will the joining together of the results. As we argued in Section 15.1, there can be $\log_2 n$ bisections before a list is reduced to one-element lists, so we have $O(^1)$ steps to perform $O(\log)$ many times; this makes quicksort take $O(nLog)$ steps, *on average*, although we saw that it can take quadratic steps in the worst (already sorted!) case.[1]

The logarithmic behaviour here is characteristic of a 'divide and conquer' algorithm: we split the problem into two smaller problems, solve these and then re-combine the results. The result is a comparatively efficient algorithm, which reaches its base cases in $O(\log_2)$ rather than $O(^1)$ steps.

[1] The explanation we have given here depends upon us re-arranging the order of the calculation steps; this is legitimate if we observe that lazy evaluation of combinators is *optimal*, in the sense of taking fewest steps to reach a result; any re-arrangement can only give more steps to our calculation, so the bound of nLog holds.

EXERCISES

15.11 Estimate the time complexity of the reverse functions

```
rev1 []    = []
rev1 (a:x) = rev1 x ++ [a]
```

and

```
rev2           = shunt []
shunt x []     = x
shunt x (a:y)  = shunt (a:x) y
```

15.12 We can define multiplication by repeated addition as follows

```
mult n 0 = 0
mult n m = mult n (m-1) + n
```

'Russian' multiplication is defined by

```
russ n 0 = 0
russ n m
   | (m 'mod' 2 == 0)   =  russ (n*n) (m 'div' 2)
   | otherwise          =  (russ (n*n) (m 'div' 2))*n
```

Estimate the time complexity of these two multiplication algorithms.

15.13 Estimate the time complexity of the Fibonacci function.

15.14 Show that the worst case time behaviour of the merge sort function below is
O(nLog).

```
mSort l
   | (len < 2)   = l
   | otherwise   = mer (mSort (take m l)) (mSort (drop m l))
       where
       len = length l
       m   = len 'div' 2

mer (a:x) (b:y)
   | (a<=b)      = a : mer x (b:y)
   | otherwise   = b : mer (a:x) y
mer (a:x) []     = (a:x)
mer []    y      = y
```

15.3 Implementations of sets

We first saw the Set abstract data type in Section 12.9, where we gave an implementation based on ordered lists without repetitions. Alternatively we can write an implementation based on arbitrary lists whose elements may occur in any order and be repeated.

```
type Set t = [t]

empty      = []
memSet     = member
inter x y  = filter (member x) y
union      = (++)
subSet x y = and (map (member y) x)
eqSet x y  = subSet x y && subSet y x
makeSet    = id
mapSet     = map
```

We can also write an implementation based on the search trees of Section 12.8. We now compare the time complexity of these implementations, and summarize the results in the table which follows:

	Lists	Ordered lists	Search trees (average)
memSet	O(^1)	O(^1)	O(log$_2$)
subSet	O(^2)	O(^1)	O(nLog)
inter	O(^2)	O(^1)	O(nLog)
makeSet	O(^0)	O(nLog)	O(nLog)
mapSet	O(^1)	O(nLog)	O(nLog)

As we can see from the table, there is no clear 'best' or 'worst' choice; depending upon the kind of set operation we intend to perform, different implementations make more sense. This is one more reason for providing the abstract data type boundary beneath which the implementation can change invisibly to suit the use to which the sets are being put.

EXERCISES

15.15 Confirm the time complexities given in the table above for the two list implementations of sets.

15.16 Implement the operations subSet, inter, makeSet and mapSet for the search tree implementation, and estimate the time complexity of your implementations.

15.17 Give an implementation of sets as lists without repetitions, and estimate the time complexity of the functions in your implementation.

15.4 Space behaviour

A rule of thumb for estimating the *space* needed to calculate a result is to measure the largest expression produced during the calculation. This is accurate if the result being computed is a number or a Boolean, but it is *not* when the result is a data structure, like a list.

Lazy evaluation

Recall the explanation of lazy evaluation in Section 14.1, where we explained that parts of results are printed as soon as possible. Once part of a result is printed, it need no longer occupy any space. In estimating space complexity, we must be aware of this.

Take the example of the lists [m .. n], defined thus

```
[m .. n]
   | n>=m        = m:[m+1 .. n]
   | otherwise   = []
```

Calculating [1 .. n] gives

```
  [1 .. n]
= 1:[1+1 .. n]
       ??  n>=2
= 1:[2 .. n]
= 1:2:[2+1 .. n]
= ...
= 1:2:3:...:n:[]
```

where we have underlined those parts of the result which can be output. To measure the space complexity we look at the non-underlined part, which is of constant size, so the space complexity is $O(\char`\^0)$. The calculation has approximately $2*n$ steps, giving it linear time complexity, as expected.

Saving values in `where` clauses

Consider the example of

```
exam1 = [1 .. n]++[1 .. n]
```

The time taken to calculate this will be O(^1), and the space used will be O(^0), but we will have to calculate the expression [1 .. n] *twice*. Suppose instead that we compute

```
exam2 = list++list
          where
          list=[1 .. n]
```

The effect here is to compute the list [1 .. n] *once*, so that we *save* its value after calculating it in order to be able to use it again. Unfortunately, this means that after evaluating `list`, the whole of the list is stored, giving an O(^1) space complexity.

    This is a general phenomenon: if we save something by referring to it in a `where` clause we have to pay the penalty of the space that it occupies; if the space is available, fair enough; if not, we have turned a working computation into one which fails for lack of space.

    This problem can be worse! Take the examples

```
exam3 = [1 .. n]++[last [1 .. n]]
exam4 = list ++[last list]
          where
          list=[1 .. n]
```

in which `last` returns the last element of a non-empty list. The space required by exam3 is O(^0), while in exam4 it is O(^1), since we hold on to the calculated value of `list`, even though we only require one value from it, the last. This feature, of keeping hold of a large structure when we only need part of it is called a *dragging problem*. In the example here, the problem is clear, but in a larger system the source of a dragging problem can be most difficult to find.

    The lesson of these examples must be that while it is *always* sensible not to repeat the calculation of a simple value, saving a compound value like a list or a tuple can increase the space usage of a program.

Saving space?

As we saw in Section 15.2, the naive factorial function has O(^1) space complexity, as it forms the expression

```
n * ((n-1) * ... * (1 * 1)...)
```

before it is evaluated. Instead, we can perform the multiplications as we go along, using

```
aFac 0 p = p
aFac n p = aFac (n-1) (p*n)
```

and compute the factorial of n using aFac n 1. Now, we examine the calculation

```
aFac n 1
= aFac (n-1) (1*n)
    ??  (n-1)==0 = False
= aFac (n-2) (1*n*(n-1))
= ...
= aFac 0 (1*n*(n-1)*(n-2)*...*2*1)
= (1*n*(n-1)*(n-2)*...*2*1)                                    (†)
```

so that the effect of this program is exactly the same: it still forms a large *unevaluated* expression! The reason that the expression is unevaluated is that it is not clear that its value is needed until the step (†).

How can we overcome this? We need to make the intermediate values *needed*, so that they are calculated earlier. We do this by adding a test; another method is given in Section 15.5.

```
aFac n p
 | p==p           = aFac (n-1) (p*n)
```

Now the calculation of the factorial of 4, say, is

```
aFac 4 1
= aFac (4-1) (1*4)
    ??  (4-1)==0     = False
    ??  (1*4)==(1*4) = True                                    (‡)
= aFac (3-1) (4*3)
    ??  (3-1)==0     = False
    ??  (4*3)==(4*3) = True                                    (‡)
= aFac (2-1) (12*2)
= ...
= aFac 0 (24*1)
= (24*1) = 24
```

The lines (‡) show where the guard p==p is tested, and so where the intermediate multiplications take place. From this we can conclude that this more *strict* version has better (constant) space behaviour.

EXERCISES

15.18 Estimate the space complexity of the function

```
sumSquares :: Int -> Int
sumSquares n = sumList (map sq [1 .. n])
```

where

```
sumList = foldr (+) 0
sq n    = n*n
```

and `map` and `[1 .. n]` have their standard definitions.

15.19 Give an informal estimate of the complexity of the text processing functions in Chapter 4.

15.5 Folding revisited

One of the patterns of computation which we identified in Chapter 4 is *folding* an operator or function into a list. This section examines the complexity of the two standard folding functions, and discusses how we can choose between them in program design. Before this we make a definition which expresses the fact of a function needing to evaluate an argument. This distinction will be crucial to our full understanding of folding.

Strictness

A function is *strict* in an argument if the result is undefined whenever an undefined value is passed to this argument. For instance, (+) is strict in both arguments, while (&&) is strict in its first only. Recall that it is defined by

```
True  && x = x
False && x = False                                        (1)
```

The pattern match in the first argument forces it to be strict there, but equation (1) shows that it is possible to get an answer from (&&) when the second argument is `undef`, so it is therefore not strict in the second.

If a function is not strict in an argument, we say that it is **non-strict** or **lazy** in that argument.

Folding from the right

Our definition of folding was given by

```
foldr :: (t -> u -> u) -> u -> [t] -> u

foldr f st []    = st
foldr f st (a:x) = f a (foldr f st x)
```

which we saw was of general application. Sorting a list, by insertion sort, was given by

```
iSort = foldr ins []
```

and indeed any primitive recursive definition over lists can be given by applying `foldr`.

Writing the function applications as infix operations gives

```
foldr f st [a₁,a₂,...,aₙ₋₁,aₙ]
= a₁ `f` (a₂ `f` ... `f` (aₙ₋₁ `f` (aₙ `f` st))...)          (2)
```

and shows why the 'r' is added to the name: bracketing is to the right, with the starting value `st` appearing to the right of the elements also. If f is lazy in its second argument, we can see from (2) that given the head of the list, output may be possible. For instance, `map` can be defined thus

```
map f = foldr ((:).f) []
```

and in calculating `map (+2) [1 .. n]` we see

```
foldr ((:).(+2)) [] [1 .. n]
= ((:).(+2)) 1 (foldr ((:).(+2)) [] [2 .. n])
= 1+2 : (foldr ((:).(+2)) [] [2 .. n])
= 3 : (foldr ((:).(+2)) [] [2 .. n])
= ...
```

As in Section 15.4, we see that this will be $O(^0)$, since the elements of the list will be output as they are calculated. What happens when we fold a strict operator into a list? The definition of `fac` is Section 15.2 can be re-written

```
fac n = foldr (*) 1 [1 .. n]
```

and we saw there that the effect was to give O(^1) space behaviour, since the multiplications in equation (2) cannot be performed until the whole expression is formed, as they are bracketed to the right. We therefore define the function to fold from the *left* now.

Folding from the left

Instead of folding from the right, we can define

```
foldl :: (u -> t -> u) -> u -> [t] -> u
foldl f st []    = st
foldl f st (a:x) = foldl f (f st a) x
```

which gives

$$\text{foldl f st } [a_1, a_2, \dots, a_{n-1}, a_n]$$
$$= (\dots((\text{st } `f` a_1) `f` a_2) `f` \dots `f` a_{n-1}) `f` a_n \qquad (3)$$

We can calculate this in the factorial example, the effect being

```
  foldl (*) 1 [1 .. n]
= foldl (*) (1*1) [2 .. n]
= ...
= foldl (*) (...((1*1)*2)*...*n) []
= (...((1*1)*2)*...*n)
```

As in Section 15.2, the difficulty is that foldl as we have defined it is not strict in its second argument. Using the standard function seq it is possible to make it strict in the second argument.

```
seq :: Eval t => t -> u -> u
```

The effect of seq x y is to evaluate x before returning y. We cannot use seq over every type; we can only force evaluation of values in types belonging to the built-in Eval class. This class includes all types, but the presence of Eval t in the context of a type documents the fact that we force a function to evaluate something of type t.
     If we write

```
strict :: Eval t => (t -> u) -> t -> u
strict f x = seq x (f x)
```

then `strict f` is a *strict* version of the function `f` which evaluates its argument x before computing the result `f x`. We can therefore write as a strict version of `foldl` the function `foldl'`,

```
foldl' :: Eval u => (u -> t -> u) -> u -> [t] -> u
foldl' f st []    = st
foldl' f st (a:x) = strict (foldl' f) (f st a) x
```

Now, evaluating the example again,

```
foldl' (*) 1 [1 .. n]
= foldl' (*) 1 [2 .. n]
= foldl' (*) 2 [3 .. n]
= foldl' (*) 6 [4 .. n]
= ...
```

Clearly, this evaluation is in constant space, $O(^0)$. Can we draw any conclusions from these examples?

Designing folds

When we fold in a *strict* function, we will form a list-sized expression with `foldr`, so it will always be worth using `foldl'`. This covers the examples of `(+)`, `(*)` and so on.

We saw earlier that when `map` was defined using `foldr` we could begin to give output before the whole of the list argument was constructed. If we use `foldl'` instead, we will have to traverse the whole list before giving any output, since any `foldl'` computation follows the pattern

```
foldl' f st₁ l₁
= foldl' f st₂ l₂
= ...
= foldl' f stₖ lₖ
= ...
= foldl' f stₙ []
= stₙ
```

so in the case of `map`, `foldr` is the clear choice of the two.

A more interesting example is given by the function which is `True` only if a list of Booleans consists of `True` throughout. We fold in `(&&)`, of course, but should we use `foldr` or `foldl'`? The latter will give a constant-space version, but will examine the *entire* list. Since `(&&)` is lazy in its second argument, we might not need to examine the value returned from the remainder of the list. For instance,

```
foldr (&&) True (map (==2) [2 .. n])
= (2==2) && (foldr (&&) True (map (==2) [3 .. n]))
= True && (foldr (&&) True (map (==2) [3 .. n]))
= foldr (&&) True (map (==2) [3 .. n])
= (3==2) && (foldr (&&) True (map (==2) [4 .. n]))
= False && (foldr (&&) True (map (==2) [4 .. n]))
= False
```

This version uses constant space, *and* may not examine the whole list; foldr is therefore the best choice.

Beside the examples of (+) and (*), there are many other examples where foldl' is preferable, including:

- Reversing a list. To use foldr we have to add an element a to the end of a list, x. The operation x++[a] is strict in x, while the 'cons' operation (:) is lazy in its list argument.
- Converting a list of digits "7364" into a number is strict in both the conversion of the front, 736 and the final character, '4'.

Since foldl' consumes an entire list before giving any output, it will be of no use in defining functions to work over infinite lists or the partial lists we looked at while writing interactive systems.

EXERCISES

15.20 Define the functions to reverse a list and to convert a digit list into a number using both foldr and foldl' and compare their behaviour by means of calculation.

15.21 Is it better to define insertion sort using foldr or foldl'? Justify your answer.

15.22 How are the results of foldr and foldl' related? You may find it useful to use the functions reverse and

```
flip :: (t -> u -> v) -> (u -> t -> v)
flip f a b = f b a
```

in your answers.

15.23 What is the relationship between `foldr` and `foldl'` when the function to be folded is

associative:	a `'f'` (b `'f'` c) = (a `'f'` b) `'f'` c;
has st as an identity:	st `'f'` a = a = a `'f'` st;
commutative:	a `'f'` b = b `'f'` a;

and what is the relationship when all three hold?

15.6 Avoiding re-computation: memoization

In this section we look at general strategies which allow us to avoid having to re-compute results during the course of evaluating an expression. This happens particularly in some recursive solutions of problems, where the solutions to sub-problems can be used repeatedly.

We begin the discussion by looking again at the Fibonacci function.

```
fib :: Int -> Int
fib 0 = 0
fib 1 = 1
fib n = fib (n-2) + fib (n-1)
```

This definition is remarkably inefficient. Computing `fib n` calls `fib (n-2)` and `fib (n-1)` – the latter will call `fib (n-2)` again, and within *each* call of `fib (n-2)` there will be two calls to `fib (n-3)`. The time complexity of `fib` is greater than any power. How might we avoid this recomputation? We explore two ways of augmenting the definition to make it efficient; in the first we return a complex data structure from each call, and in the second we define an infinite list to hold all the values of the function.

First we observe that to get the value at n we need the two previous values; we could therefore return *both* these values in the result.

```
fibP :: Int -> (Int,Int)
fibP 0 = (0,1)
fibP n = (b,a+b)
            where
            (a,b) = fibP (n-1)
```

A calculation is given in Figure 15.2, where different variables a_1, a_2 etc. have been used for the different occurrences of the local variables a and b; this is not necessary, but does make the different occurrences clearer.

```
fibP 3
= (b,a+b)
  where
  (a,b) = fibP 2
        = (b₁,a₁+b₁)
          where
          (a₁,b₁) = fibP 1
                  = (b₂,a₂+b₂)
                    where
                    (a₂,b₂) = fibP 0
                            = (0,1)
                  = (1,1)
        = (1,2)
= (2,3)
```

Figure 15.2 Calculating `fibP 3`.

As an alternative strategy, we can try to define the list of Fibonacci values, `fibs`, directly. The values of the function given above now become values at particular indices:

```
fibs        :: [Int]
fibs!!0     = 0
fibs!!1     = 1
fibs!!(n+2) = fibs!!n + fibs!!(n+1)
```

This gives a *description* of the list, but it is not executable in this form. The first two lines tell us that `fibs = 0 : 1 : rest`, while the third equation tells us what the `rest` is. The `(n+2)`nd element of `fibs` is the nth element of `rest`; similarly, the `(n+1)`st element is the nth element of `(tail fibs)`. We therefore have, for every n,

```
rest!!n = fibs!!n + (tail fibs)!!n
```

which says that each element is obtained by adding the corresponding elements of two lists, that is

```
rest = zipWith (+) fibs (tail fibs)
```

so that putting the parts together, we have

```
fibs = 0 : 1 : zipWith (+) fibs (tail fibs)
```

a **process network** computing the Fibonacci numbers. This gives a linear time, constant space algorithm for the problem, in contrast to the pair solution which is linear in both time and space, since all the nested calls to `fibP` are built before any result can be given.

Dynamic programming

The example in this section illustrates a general method of solving problems by what has become known as **dynamic programming**. Dynamic programming solutions work by breaking a problem into subproblems, but as in the Fibonacci example, the subproblems will not be independent, in general. A naive solution therefore will contain massive redundancy, which we remove by building a *table* of solutions to subproblems.

The example we consider is to find the length of a maximal common subsequence of two lists – the subsequences need not have all their elements adjacent. In the examples of

[2,1,4,5,2,3,5,2,4,3]   [1,7,5,3,2]

the length of 4 is given by the subsequence [1,5,3,2]. This problem is not simply a 'toy'; a solution to this can be used to find the common lines in two files, which gives the basis of the Unix `diff` program, which is used, for instance, for comparing different versions of programs stored in separate files.

The naive solution is given by `mLen` in Figure 15.3. The interesting part of the definition is given by the third equation. In the case that the lists have equal first elements, these elements must be in a maximal common subsequence, so we find the overall solution by looking in the tails, and adding one to the result. More problematic is the case when the heads are distinct; we have a choice of excluding either a or b; in this algorithm we try both possibilities, and take the maximal result. There, of course, is the source of the redundant computations; each of these may well give rise to a computation of `mLen x y`. How are we to avoid this situation? We shall store these results in a *table*, which will be represented by a list of lists. Once a result appears in the table, we have no need to recompute it.

As an intermediate step, we rewrite the solution as `maxLen` which uses list indexing, so that

```
maxLen l m u v
```

is the longest common subsequence in the lists `take u l` and `take v m`. The function is given in Figure 15.3, and the definition is a straightforward adaptation of `mLen`.

```
mLen :: Eq t => [t] -> [t] -> Int

mLen x []        = 0
mLen [] y        = 0
mLen (a:x) (b:y)
   | a==b         = 1 + mLen x y
   | otherwise   = max (mLen x (b:y)) (mLen (a:x) y)

maxLen :: Eq t => [t] -> [t] -> Int -> Int -> Int

maxLen l m 0 j = 0                                          (1)
maxLen l m i 0 = 0                                          (2)
maxLen l m i j
   | l!!(i-1) == m!!(j-1)  = (maxLen l m (i-1) (j-1)) + 1   (3)
   | otherwise             = max (maxLen l m i (j-1))
                                 (maxLen l m (i-1) j)       (4)

maxTab ::  Eq t => [t] -> [t] -> [[Int]]

maxTab l m
  = result
     where
     result = [0,0 .. ] : zipWith f [0 .. ] result
     f i prev
         = ans
           where
           ans  = 0 : zipWith g [0 .. ] ans
           g j v
              | l!!i == m!!j       = prev!!j +1
              | otherwise          = max v (prev!!(j+1))
```

Figure 15.3   Maximum common subsequence – three algorithms.

Now we aim to define the table maxTab l m so that

```
(maxTab l m)!!u!!v = maxLen l m u v
```

This requirement is made specific by equations (1) to (4). The base case is
given by (1), stating that

```
(maxTab l m)!!0!!v = 0
```

for all v. In other words,

```
(maxTab l m)!!0 = [0,0 .. ]
```

so,

```
result = [0,0 .. ] :  ...
```

The equations (2) to (4) tell us how to define the list `maxTab!!i+1` from the list `maxTab!!i`, and `i`, so we can define

```
maxTab l m = result
              where
              result = [0,0 .. ] : zipWith f [0 .. ] result
```

where `f :: Int -> [Int] -> [Int]` is the function taking `i` and the previous value, `maxTab!!i` to `maxTab!!i+1`. Now we have to define this list, which appears in the solution as `ans`.

Equation (2) tells us that it starts with 0, and `g` is the function taking `maxTab!!i+1!!j` and `j` to `maxTab!!i+1!!j+1`, where we are also able to use the values of `maxTab!!i`, named by `prev`. Using these insights, the definition of `g` is a straightforward transliteration of (3) and (4):

```
ans   = 0 : zipWith g [0 .. ] ans
g j v
  | l!!i == m!!j         = prev!!j +1
  | otherwise            = max v (prev!!(j+1))
```

The top-level result is given by calling

```
maxTab l m !! (length l) !! (length m)
```

and this is computed in linear time and space.

Haskell provides an **array** facility which has the advantage of providing more efficient storage allocation when accessed in a sequential way, in other words through a monadic interface. Arrays can be used to give a more efficient implementation of a number of algorithms, including this one here, effectively in an imperative style. Further details can be found in Hudak *et al.* (1992) and Peterson *et al.* (1996).

Greedy algorithms

A greedy solution to a dynamic programming problem works by building up the optimal solution by making *local* choices of what appear to be the best solutions of subproblems. In the common subsequence problem, we can think of searching along the two lists in a single sweep, looking successively for the first points of agreement; we search all pairs of indices smaller than n before looking at n. In an example, the greedy solution gives

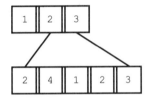

which is *not* optimal: the subsequence [1,2,3] has been missed, since we make the choice of 2 as the first element, as it is the first point of agreement. This local choice is not part of an optimal global solution, but the algorithm gives reasonable performance.

In many situations, where local choices are always part of a global solution, a greedy solution will work. Examples we have seen thus far include:

- the line splitting algorithm we gave in Chapter 4 is optimal in minimizing the sum of the inter-word spaces included when the lines are justified;

- the Huffman codes described in Chapter 11 are optimal in the sense of giving the shortest possible codings of files. We did not search all possible sets of codes in giving the Huffman code, rather we built it up from locally sensible choices.

EXERCISES

15.24 Give an implementation of the greedy solution to the maximal common subsequence problem, and show that it behaves as explained above on the lists [1,2,3] and [2,4,1,2,3] above.

15.25 Can you give an improvement of the maximal common subsequence solution along the lines of fibP, returning a complex (finite) data structure as the result of a function call, rather than simply one value?

15.26 Finding the 'edit distance' between two strings was first discussed in Section 10.5 where we gave a dynamic programming solution to the problem. Show how you can give an efficient implementation of this algorithm using the techniques of this section, and also how you give a greedy solution to the problem. How do the two solutions compare?

15.27 Based on the examples of this section, give a program which gives the difference between two files, matching the corresponding lines, and giving the output in a suitable form, such as a list of the pairs of matching line numbers, or a form copied from the Unix diff program.

SUMMARY

In this chapter we have examined the efficiency of lazy functional programs. We saw that we are able to analyse the time complexity of many of our more straightforward functions without too much difficulty. To analyse the *space* behaviour is more difficult, but we have shown how the space consumption of lazy programs can be estimated from our calculations.

The introduction of foldl brings the space issue into focus, and the distinction we made between *strict* and lazy functions allows us to analyse the different behaviour of the two folds.

We concluded the discussion with an application of lazy infinite lists to *memoizing* results for re-use; the transition from naive to efficient versions was done in a systematic way, which can be carried over to other application areas.

APPENDIX A

Functional and imperative programming

Values and states

Consider the example of finding the sum of squares of natural numbers up to a particular number.

A functional program describes the values that are to be calculated, directly.

```
sumSquares :: Int -> Int
sumSquares 0 = 0
sumSquares n = n*n + sumSquares (n-1)
```

These equations state what the sum of squares is for a natural number argument. In the first case it is a direct description; in the second it states that the sum to non-zero n is obtained by finding the sum to n-1 and adding the square of n.

A typical imperative program might solve the problem thus

```
s := 0 ;
i := 0 ;
while i<n do begin
    i := i+1 ;
    s := i*i + s ;
end {while}
```

The sum is the final value of the variable s which is changed repeatedly during program execution, as is the 'count' variable, i. The effect of the program can only be seen by following the sequence of changes made to these variables by the commands in the program, while the functional program can be read as a series of equations defining the sum of squares. This meaning is *explicit* in the functional program, whereas the imperative program has an overall effect which is not obvious from the program itself.

A more striking algorithm still is one which is completely explicit.

> To find the sum of squares, build the list of numbers 1
> to n, square each of them, and sum the result.

This program, which uses neither complex control flow, as does the imperative example, nor recursion as seen in the function sumSquares, can be written in a functional style, thus:

```
newSumSq :: Int -> Int
newSumSq n = sum (map square [1 .. n])
```

where square x = x*x, the operation map applies its first argument to every member of a list, and sum finds the sum of a list of numbers. More examples of this sort of *data-directed* programming can be seen in the body of the text.

Functions and variables

An important difference between the two styles is what is meant by some of the terminology. Both 'function' and 'variable' have different interpretations.

As was explained earlier, a function in a functional program is simply something which returns a value which depends upon some inputs. In an imperative language like Pascal a function is rather different. It will return a value depending upon its arguments, but in general it will also change the values of variables. Rather than being a pure function it is really a procedure which returns a value when it terminates.

In a functional program a variable stands for an *arbitrary* or *unknown* value. Every occurrence of a variable in an equation is interpreted in the same way. They are just like variables in logical formulas, or the mathematical variables familiar from equations like

$$a^2 - b^2 = (a-b)(a+b)$$

In any particular case, the value of all three occurrences of a will be the same. In exactly the same way, in

```
sumSquares n = n*n + sumSquares (n-1)
```

all occurrences of n will be interpreted by the same value. For example

```
sumSquares 7 = 7*7 + sumSquares (7-1)
```

The crucial motto is 'variables in functional programs *do not vary*'.

On the other hand, the value of a variable in an imperative program changes throughout its lifetime. In the sum of squares program above, the variable s will take the values 0,1,5,... successively. Variables in imperative programs *do* vary over time.

Program verification

Probably the most important difference between functional and imperative programs is logical. As well as being a program, a functional definition is a logical equation describing a *property* of the function. Functional programs are *self-describing*, as it were. Using the definitions, other properties of the functions can be deduced.

To take a simple example, for all n>0, it is the case that

```
sumSquares n > 0
```

To start with,

```
sumSquares 1
= 1*1 + sumSquares 0
= 1*1 + 0
= 1
```

which is greater than 0. In general, for n greater than zero,

```
sumSquares n = n*n + sumSquares (n-1)
```

Now, n*n is positive, and if sumSquares (n-1) is positive, their sum, sumSquares n, must be. This proof can be formalized using *mathematical induction*; see Chapter 3 for further details and examples.

Program verification is possible for imperative programs as well, but imperative programs are not self-describing in the way functional ones are. To describe the effect of an imperative program, like the 'sum of squares' program above, we need to add to the program logical formulas or assertions which describe the state of the program at various points in its execution. These methods are both more indirect and more difficult, and verification seems very difficult indeed for 'real' languages like Pascal and C. Another aspect of program verification is *program transformation* in which programs are transformed to other programs which have the same effect but better performance, for example. Again, this is difficult for traditional imperative languages.

Records and tuples

In Section 2.10 the tuple types of Haskell are introduced. In particular we saw the definition

```
type Person = (String,String,Int)
```

This compares with a Pascal declaration of a record

```
type Person = record
   name  : String;
   phone : String;
    age   : Integer
end;
```

which has three fields which have to be named. In Haskell the fields of a tuple can be accessed by pattern matching, but it is possible to define functions called *selectors* which behave in a similar way, if required:

```
name   :: Person -> String
name (n,p,a) = n
```

and so on. If `per :: Person` then `name per :: String`, similarly to `r.name` being a string variable if `r` is a variable of type `Person` in Pascal.

Haskell 1.3 also contains records with named fields, rather more like those of Pascal. For further details, see Peterson *et al.* (1996).

Lists and pointers

Haskell contains the type of lists built in, and other recursive types such as trees can be defined directly. We can think of the type of linked lists given by pointers in Pascal as an *implementation* of lists, since in Haskell it is not necessary to think of pointer values, or of storage allocation (new and dispose) as it is in Pascal. Indeed, we can think of Haskell programs as *designs* for Pascal list programs. If we define

```
type list = ^node;
type node = record
    head : value;
    tail : list
end;
```

then we have the following correspondence, where the Haskell `head` and `tail` functions give the head and tail of a list:

```
[]                nil
head l            x^.head
tail l            x^.tail
(a:x)             cons(a,x)
```

The function cons in Pascal has the definition

```
function cons(b:value;y:list):list;
  var l:list;
  begin
    new(l);
    l^.head := b;
    l^.tail := y;
    cons := l
  end;
```

Functions such as

```
sumList []    = 0
sumList (a:x) = a + sumList x
```

can then be transferred to Pascal in a straightforward way:

```
function sumList(l:list):integer;
  begin
    if l=nil
      then sumList := 0
      else sumList := l^.head + sumList(l^.tail)
  end;
```

A second example is

```
double []    = []
double (a:x) = (2*a) : double x
```

where we use cons in the Pascal definition of the function

```
function double(l:list):list;
  begin
    if l=nil
    then double := nil
    else double := cons( 2*l^.head , double(l^.tail) )
  end;
```

If we define the functions

```
function head(l:list):value;        function tail(l:list):list;
  begin                               begin
    head := l^.head                     tail := l^.tail
  end;                                end;
```

then the correspondence is even clearer

```
function double(l:list):list;
  begin
    if l=nil
    then double := nil
    else double := cons( 2*head(l) , double( tail(l) ) )
  end;
```

This is strong evidence that a functional approach can be useful even if we are writing in an imperative language: the functional language can be the high-level *design* language for the imperative implementation. Making this separation can give us substantial help in finding imperative programs – we can think about the design and the lower-level implementation *separately*, which makes each problem smaller, simpler and therefore easier to solve.

Higher-order functions

Traditional imperative languages give little scope for higher-order programming; Pascal allows functions as arguments, so long as those functions are not themselves higher-order, but has no facility for returning functions as results.

Control structures like `if-then-else` bear some resemblance to higher-order functions, as they take commands, c_1, c_2 etc. into other commands,

```
if b then c₁ else c₂      while b do c₁
```

just as `map` takes one function to another. Turning the analogy around, we can think of higher-order functions in Haskell as *control structures* which we can define ourselves. This perhaps explains why we form libraries of polymorphic functions: they are the control structures we use in programming particular sorts of system. Examples in the text include libraries for building parsers (Section 13.5) and interactive programs (Section 14.2), as well as the built-in list-processing functions.

Polymorphism

Again, this aspect is poorly represented in many imperative languages; the best we can do in Pascal, say, is to use a text editor to copy and modify the list processing code from one type of lists for use with another. Of course, we then run the risk that the different versions of the programs are not modified in step, unless we are very careful to keep track of modifications, and so on.

As is argued in the text, polymorphism is one of the mechanisms which helps to make programs *re-usable* in Haskell; it remains to be seen whether this will also be true of advanced imperative languages.

Defining types and classes

The algebraic type mechanism of Haskell, explained in Chapter 10, subsumes various traditional type definitions. Enumerated types are given by algebraic types all of whose constructors are 0-ary (take no arguments); variant records can be implemented as algebraic types with more then one constructor, and *recursive* types usually implemented by means of pointers become recursive algebraic types.

Just as we explained for lists, Haskell programs over trees and so on can be seen as *designs* for programs in imperative languages manipulating the pointer implementations of the types.

The abstract data types, introduced in Chapter 12, are very like the abstract data types of Modula-2 and so on; the design methods we suggest for use of abstract data types mirror aspects of the *object-based* approach advocated for modern imperative languages such as Ada.

The Haskell class system also has object-oriented aspects, as we saw in Section 10.6. It is important to note that Haskell classes are in some ways quite different from the classes of, for instance, C++. In Haskell classes are made up of types, which themselves have members; in C++ a class is like a type, in that it contains objects. Because of this many of the aspects of object-oriented design in C++ are seen as issues of type design in Haskell.

List comprehensions

List comprehensions provide a convenient notation for *iteration* along lists; the analogue of a for loop, which can be used to run through the indices of an array. For instance, to sum all pairs of elements of l and m, we write

```
[ a+b | a <- l , b <- m ]
```

The order of the iteration is for a value a from the list l to be fixed and then for b to run through the possible values from m; this is then repeated with the next value from 1, until the list is exhausted. Just the same happens for a *nested* for loop

```
for i:=0 to lLen-1 do
  for j:=0 to mLen-1 do                                    (†)
    write( l[i]+m[j] )
```

where we fix a value for i while running through all values for j.

In the for loop, we have to run through the indices; a list generator runs through the values directly. The indices of the list l are given by

```
[0 .. length l - 1]
```

and so a Haskell analogue of (†) can be written thus:

```
[ l!!i + m!!j | i <- [0 .. length l - 1] ,
                j <- [0 .. length m - 1] ]
```

if we so wish.

Lazy evaluation

Lazy evaluation and imperative languages do not mix well. In Pascal, for instance, we can write the function definition

```
function succ(x : integer):integer;
begin
  y    := y+1;
  succ := x+1
end;
```

This function adds one to its argument, but also has the *side-effect* of increasing y by one. If we evaluate f(y,succ(z)) we cannot predict the effect it will have.

- If f evaluates its second argument first, y will be increased before being passed to f; on the other hand,
- if f needs its first argument first (and perhaps its second argument not at all), the value passed to f will not be increased, even if it is increased before the function call terminates.

In general, it will not be possible to predict the behaviour of even the simplest programs. Since evaluating an expression can cause a change of the state, the order of expression evaluation determines the overall effect of a program, and so a lazy implementation can behave differently (in unforeseen ways) from the norm.

State, infinite lists and monads

Section 13.6 introduces infinite lists, and one of the first examples given there was an infinite list of random numbers. This list could be supplied to a function requiring a supply of random numbers; because of lazy evaluation, these numbers will only be generated on demand.

If we were to implement this imperatively, we would probably keep in a variable the last random number generated, and at each request for a number we would update this store. We can see the infinite list as supplying *all the values that the variable will take* as a single structure; we therefore do not need to keep the state, and hence have an *abstraction* from the imperative view.

We have seen in Section 14.3 that there has been recent important work on integrating side-effecting programs into a functional system by a monadic approach.

Conclusion

Clearly there are parallels between the functional and the imperative, as well as clear differences. The functional view of a system is often higher-level, and so even if we ultimately aim for an imperative solution, a functional *design* or *prototype* can be most useful.

We have seen that monads can be used to give an interface to imperative features within a functional framework. Many of the Haskell implementations offer these facilities, and so give a method of uniting the best features of two important programming paradigms without compromising the purity of the language. Other languages, including Standard ML (Milner *et al.*, 1990), combine the functional and the imperative, but in ways that compromise their pure functional properties in the process.

APPENDIX B

Further reading

This textbook introduces the fundamentals of lazy functional programming, and from here we can set off in many different directions. This appendix gives some signposts; others are to be found on the World Wide Web page

    http://www.ukc.ac.uk/computer_science/Haskell_craft/

Two other very useful Web sites are Mark Jones' Functional Programming FAQ,

    http://www.cs.nott.ac.uk/Department/Staff/mpj/faq.html

and the archive of functional programming papers at

    http://www.lpac.ac.uk/SEL-HPC/Articles/FuncArchive.html

which is classified according to subject and can be searched for keywords.

Haskell

Haskell is described in Hudak *et al.* (1992) and Peterson *et al.* (1996), and a tutorial for those familiar with functional ideas can be found in Hudak and Fasel (1992). A number of articles about applications of Haskell can be found in the functional archive whose URL is given above. The language report itself can be found at the URL

    http://haskell.cs.yale.edu/haskell-report/
    haskell-report.html

Other functional programming languages

One of Haskell's predecessors which has been widely used is Miranda; introductory material and an overview of Miranda can be found in Turner (1985, 1990a). Thompson (1995) is an introductory functional programming text which uses Miranda.

A functional language is *strict* if arguments are evaluated before being passed to functions. The most widely used strict but strongly typed functional programming language is Standard ML (Milner *et al.*, 1990), for which Wikström (1987) and Paulson (1991) provide an introduction.

A different style of functional programming, eschewing variables as much as possible, was introduced in Backus (1978). An imperative language, used for telephone switching and other real-time applications, with functionally-inspired features is ERLANG (Armstrong *et al.*, 1993).

Two recent surveys of applications of functional programming languages in large-scale projects are Runciman and Wakeling (1995) and Hartel and Plasmeijer (1995b).

More advanced topics

A recent tutorial on these topics is the *Proceedings of the First International Spring School on Functional Programming* (Jeuring and Meijer, 1995). Turner (1990b) is a useful survey of research topics in functional programming. In that volume Bird (1990) gives examples in the 'Bird-Meertens' style of program transformation, Hughes (1990) argues powerfully for the advantages of a lazy programming style and Thompson (1990) explores the foundations of interactive programming as discussed in this text. Another source of program transformation examples is Darlington (1982), which is also a part of a useful collection of papers.

As we have seen in the text, monads provide a useful way of structuring interactive and other programs. How programs like these can be verified is a topic of Gordon (1994), which also contains a useful survey of the field, showing its tortuous history. A general reference on verification of functional programs is provided by Paulson (1987), while Sanella (1986) investigates how functional programs can best have their properties specified.

If some background reading for logic is required, two serviceable texts on logic for computer scientists are Galton (1990) and Reeves and Clarke (1990), each of which provides sufficient background to make sense of the logical rendering of Haskell found in this text.

Foundations and future developments

The polymorphic type system upon which Haskell polymorphism is based is Milner (1978), and the field of more advanced type systems is surveyed in the useful Cardelli and Wegner (1985). The lambda calculus is one of the historical roots of functional programming; Barendregt (1993) gives an overview of the foundations of the typed lambda calculus, as well as of more recent innovations, which are also surveyed in Huet (1990). Constructive type theories can be seen as simultaneously functional languages and logics; Thompson (1991), Girard *et al.* (1989) and Luo (1994) give three complementary perspectives.

Functional programming in education

A special edition of the *Journal of Functional Programming* (Thompson and Wadler, 1993), explores ways in which functional programming can be taught. The first *Conference in Functional Programming Languages in Education* (Hartel and Plasmeijer, 1995a), contains a wealth of material on various different approaches to educational use of functional languages. Out of this conference has come a Web page

```
http://www.cs.kun.nl/fple/
```

carrying references to teaching resources for using functional programming languages in teaching.

Implementation techniques

In the last ten years, powerful techniques of implementation of especially lazy functional languages have been developed. The twin texts Peyton Jones (1987) and Peyton Jones and Lester (1992) describe these in lucid detail.

APPENDIX C

Glossary

We include this glossary to give a quick reference to the most widely-used terminology in the book. Words appearing in **bold** in the descriptions have their own entries. Further references and examples are to be found by consulting the index.

Abstract type An abstract type definition consists of the type name, the **signature** of the type, and the implementation equations for the names in the signature.

Algebraic type An algebraic type definition states what are the **constructors** of the type. For instance, the declaration

```
data Tree = Leaf Int |
           Node Tree Tree
```

says that the two constructors of the `Tree` type are `Leaf` and `Node`, and that their types are, respectively,

```
Leaf :: Int->Tree
Node :: Tree->Tree->Tree
```

Application This means giving values to (some of) the arguments of a function. If an n-argument function is given fewer than n arguments, this is called a **partial application**. Application is written using **juxtaposition**.

Argument A **function** takes one or more arguments into an **output**. Arguments are also known as **inputs** and **parameters**.

Associativity The way in which an expression involving two applications of an operator is interpreted. If x#y#z is interpreted as (x#y)#z then # is left associative, if as

x#(y#z) it is right associative; if both bracketings give the same result then # is called associative.

Base types The types of numbers, including `Int` and `Float`, **Booleans**, `Bool`, and **characters**, `Char`.

Binding power The 'stickiness' of an operator, expressed as an integer; the higher the number the stickier the operator. For example, 2+3*4 is interpreted as 2+(3*4) as '*' has higher binding power – binds more tightly – than '+'.

Booleans The type containing the two 'truth values' `True` and `False`.

Calculation A calculation is a line-by-line **evaluation** of a Haskell **expression** on paper. Calculations use the **definitions** which are contained in a **script** as well as the built-in definitions.

Cancellation The rule for finding the type of a partial application.

Character A single letter, such as `'s'` or `'\t'`, the tab character. They form the `Char` type.

Class A collection of types. A class is defined by specifying a **signature**; a type is made an **instance** of the class by supplying an implementation of the definitions of the signature over the particular type.

Clause A clause is one of the alternatives making up a **conditional equation**. A clause consists of a **guard** followed by an **expression**. When evaluating a function application, the first clause whose guard evaluates to `True` is chosen.

Combinator Another name for a **function**.

Comment Part of a **script** which plays no computational role; it is there for the reader to read and observe. Comments are specified in two ways: the part of the line to the right is made a comment by the symbol `- -`; a comment of arbitrary length is enclosed by `{-` and `-}`.

Complexity A measurement of the time or space behaviour of a function.

Composition The combination of two functions by passing the **output** of one to the **input** of the other.

Concatenate To put together a number of lists into a single list.

Conditional equation A conditional equation consists of a left-hand side followed by a number of **clauses**. Each clause consists of a **guard** followed by an expression which is to be equated with the left-hand side of the **equation** if that particular clause is chosen during evaluation. The clause chosen is the first whose guard evaluates to `True`.

Conformal pattern match An equation in which a pattern appears on the left-hand side of an equation, as in

```
(a,b) = ....
```

Constructor An **algebraic type** is specified by its constructors, which are the functions which build elements of the algebraic type.

In the example in the entry for algebraic types, elements of the type are constructed using `Leaf` and `Node`; the elements are `Leaf n` where `n::Int` and `Node s t` where `s` and `t` are trees.

Context The hypotheses which appear before `=>` in type and class declarations. A context `M t` means that the type `t` must belong to the class `M` for the function or class definition to apply. For instance, to apply a function of type

```
Eq t => [t] -> t -> Bool
```

to a list and an object, these must come from types over which equality is defined.

Curried function A function of at least two arguments which takes its arguments one at a time, so having the type

```
t1 -> t2 -> ... -> t
```

in contrast to the *uncurried* version

```
(t1,t2,...) -> t
```

The name is in honour of Haskell B. Curry, after whom the Haskell language is also named.

Declaration A **definition** can be accompanied by a statement of the **type** of the object defined; these are often called type declarations.

Default A default holds in the absence of any other definition. Used in `class` definitions to give definitions of some of the operations in terms of others; an example is the definition of `/=` in the `Eq` class.

Definition A definition associates a **value** or a **type** with a **name**.

Derived class instance An instance of a standard class which is derived by the system, rather than put in explicitly by the programmer.

Design In writing a system, the effort expended *before* implementation is started.

Enumerated type An **algebraic type** with each constructor having no arguments.

Equation A **definition** in Haskell consists of a number of equations. On the left-hand side of the equation is a **name** applied to zero or more **patterns**; on the right-hand side is a value. In many cases the equation is **conditional** and has two or more **clauses**.

Where the meaning is clear we shall sometimes take 'equation' as shorthand for 'equation or conditional equation'.

Evaluation Every **expression** in Haskell has a value; evaluation is the process of finding that value. A **calculation** evaluates an expression, as does an interactive Haskell system when that expression is typed to the prompt.

Export The process of defining which definitions will be visible when a module is **imported** by another module.

Expression An expression is formed by applying a **function** or **operator** to its arguments; these arguments can be **literal** values, or expressions themselves. A simple numerical expression is

```
(2+8)-10
```

in which the operator '-' is applied to two arguments.

Extensionality The principle of proof which says that two functions are equal if they give equal results for every input.

Filter To pick out those elements of a list which have a particular property, represented by a **Boolean**-valued function.

Floating point number A number which is given in decimal (e.g. `456.23`) or exponent (e.g. `4.5623e+2`) form; these numbers form the type `Float`.

Fold To combine the elements of a list using a binary **operation**.

Forward composition Used for the operator '>.>' with the definition

```
f >.> g = g . f
```

`f >.> g` can be read 'f then g'.

Function A function is an object which returns a **value**, called the **output** or **result** when it is applied to its **inputs**. The inputs are also known as its **parameters** or **arguments**.

Examples include the square root function, whose input and output are numbers, and the function which returns the borrowers (output) of a book (input) in a database (input).

Function types The type of a **function** is a function type, so that, for instance, the function which checks whether its integer argument is even has type `Int->Bool`. This is the type of functions with **input** type `Int` and **output** type `Bool`.

Generalization Replacing an object by something of which the original object is an instance.

This might be the replacement of a function by a polymorphic function from which the original is obtained by passing the appropriate parameter, or replacing a logical formula by one which implies the original.

Guard The **Boolean** expression appearing to the right of '|' and to the left of '=' in a **clause** of a **conditional equation** in a Haskell **definition**.

Higher-order function A **function** is higher-order if either one of its **arguments** or its **result**, or both, are functions.

Identifier Another word for **name**.

Implementation The particular **definitions** which make a design concrete; for an **abstract data type**, the definitions of the objects named in the **signature**.

Import The process of including the **exported** definitions of one module in another module.

Induction The name for a collection of methods of proof, by which statements of the form 'for all x ...' are proved.

Infix An **operation** which appears between its **arguments**. Infix functions are called **operators**.

Inheritance One **class** inherits the operations of another if the first class is in the **context** of the definition of the second. For instance, of the standard classes, `Ord` inherits (in)equality from `Eq`.

Input A **function** takes one or more inputs into an **output**. Inputs are also known as **arguments** and **parameters**. The 'square' function takes a single numerical input, for instance.

Instance The term 'instance' is used in two different ways in Haskell.

An instance of a **type** is a type which is given by **substituting** a type expression for a type **variable**. For example, `[(Bool,u)]` is an instance of `[t]`, given by substituting the type `(Bool,u)` for the variable t.

An instance of a **class**, for example `Eq (t,u)`, is given by declaring how the function(s) of the class, in this case `==`, are defined over the given type (here `(t,u)`). Here we would say

```
(a,b) == (c,d) = (a==c) && (b==d)
```

Integers The positive and negative whole numbers. In Haskell the type `Int` represents the integers in a fixed size, whilst the type `Integer` represents them exactly, so that evaluating 2 to the power 1000 will give a result consisting of some three hundred digits.

Interactive program A program which reads from and writes to the terminal; reading and writing will be *interleaved*, in general.

Interface The common information which is shared between two program modules.

Juxtaposition Putting one thing next to another; this is the way in which function application is written down in Haskell.

Lambda expression An **expression** which denotes a **function**. After a '\' we list the arguments of the function, then an '->' and then the result. For instance, to add a number to the length of a list we could write

```
\l n -> length l + n
```

The term 'lambda' is used since '\' is close to the Greek letter 'λ', or lambda, which is used in a similar way in Church's lambda calculus.

Lazy evaluation The sort of expression **evaluation** in Haskell. In a function application only those arguments whose values are *needed* will be evaluated, and moreover, only the parts of structures which are needed will be examined.

Linear complexity Order 1, O(^1), behaviour.

Lists A list consists of a collection of elements of a particular type, given in some order, potentially containing a particular item more than once. The list [2,1,3,2] is of type [Int], for example.

Literal Something that is 'literally' a value: it needs no **evaluation**. Examples include 34, [23] and "string".

Local definitions The definitions appearing in a where clause or a let expression. Their **scope** is the equation or expression to which the clause or let is attached.

Map To apply an operation to every element of a list.

Mathematical induction A method of proof for statements of the form 'for all natural numbers n, the statement P(n) holds'.

   The proof is in two parts: the base case, at zero, and the induction step, at which P(n) is proved on the assumption that P(n-1) holds.

Memoization Keeping the value of a sub-computation (in a list, say) so that it can be re-used rather than re-computed, when it is needed.

Module Another name for a **script**; used particularly when more than one script is used to build a program.

Monad A monad consists of a type with (at least) two functions, return and >>=. Informally, a monad can be seen as performing some sorts of action before returning an object. The two monad functions respectively return a value without any action, and sequence two monadic operations.

Monomorphic A type is **monomorphic** if it is not **polymorphic**.

Most general type The most general type of an expression is the type t with the property that every other type for the expression is an **instance** of t.

Mutual recursion Two definitions, each of which depends upon the other.

Name A **definition** associates a name or **identifier** with a value. Names of **classes**, **constructors** and **types** must begin with capital letters; names of **values**, **variables** and **type variables** begin with small letters. After the first letter, any letter, digit, ''' or '_' can be used.

Natural numbers The non-negative whole numbers: 0, 1, 2,....

Offside rule The way in which the end of a part of a definition is expressed using the *layout* of a **script**, rather than an explicit symbol for the end.

Operation Another name for **function**.

Operator A **function** which is written in infix form, between its **arguments**. The function f is made infix thus: `f`.

Operator section A partially applied operator.

Output When a **function** is applied to one or more **inputs**, the resulting value is called the output, or **result**. Applying the 'square' function to (-2) gives the output 4, for example.

Overloading The use of the same **name** to mean two (or more) different things, at different types. The equality operation, ==, is an example. Overloading is supported in Haskell by the **class** mechanism.

Parameter A **function** takes one or more parameters into an **output**. Parameters are also known as **arguments** and **inputs**, and applying a function to its inputs is sometimes known as 'passing its parameters'.

Parsing Revealing the structure of a sentence in a formal language.

Partial application A **function** of type $t_1 -> t_2 -> \ldots -> t_n -> t$ can be applied to n arguments, or less. In the latter case, the **application** is partial, since the result can itself be passed further parameters.

Pattern A pattern is either a **variable**, a **literal**, a **wild card** or the application of a **constructor** to other patterns.

Polymorphism A type is polymorphic if it contains type **variables**; such a type will have many **instances**.

Prefix An **operation** which appears before its **arguments**.

Primitive recursion Over the natural numbers, defining the values of a function outright at zero, and at n greater than zero using the value at n-1.

Over an **algebraic type** defining the function by cases over the constructors; recursion is permitted at arguments to a constructor which are of the type in question.

Proof A logical argument which leads us to accept a logical statement as being valid.

Pure programming language A functional programming language is pure if it does not allow **side-effects**.

Quadratic complexity Order two, O(^2), behaviour.

Recursion Using the name of a value or type in its own **definition**.

Result When a **function** is applied to one or more **inputs**, the resulting value is called the result, or **output**.

Scope The area of a program in which a **definition** or definitions are applicable.

In Haskell the scope of top-level definitions is by default the whole **script** in which they appear; it may be extended by importing the module into another. More limited scopes are given by **local definitions**.

Script A script is a file containing **definitions**, **declarations** and module statements.

Set A collection of objects for which the order of elements and the number of occurrences of each element are irrelevant.

Side-effect In a language like Pascal, evaluating an expression can cause other things to happen besides a value being computed. These might be I/O operations, or changes in values stored. In Haskell this does not happen, but a **monad** can be used to give a similar effect, without compromising the simple model of evaluation underlying the language. Examples are IO and State.

Signature A sequence of type **declarations**. These declarations state what are the types of the operations (or functions) over an **abstract type** or a **class** which can be used to manipulate elements of that type.

Stream A stream is a channel upon which items arrive in sequence; in Haskell we can think of **lazy** lists in this way, so it becomes a synonym for lazy list.

String The type String is a **synonym** for lists of characters, [Char].

Structural induction A method of proof for statements of the form 'for all lists l, the statement P(l) holds of l'. The proof is in two parts: the base case, at [], and the induction step, at which P(a:x) is proved on the assumption that P(x) holds.

Also used of the related principle for any algebraic type.

Substitution The replacement of a **variable** by an **expression**. For example, (9+12) is given by substituting 12 for n in (9+n). Types can also be substituted for type variables; see the entry for **instance**.

Synonym Naming a type is called a type synonym. The keyword type is used for synonyms.

Syntax The description of the properly formed programs (or sentences) of a language.

Transformation Turning one program into another program which computes identical results, but with different behaviour in other respects such as time or space efficiency.

Tuples A tuple type is built up from a number of component types. Elements of the type consist of tuples of elements of the component types, so that

```
(2,True,3) :: (Int,Bool,Int)
```

for instance.

Type A collection of values. Types can be built from the **base** types using **tuple**, **list** and **function types**. New types can be defined using the **algebraic** and **abstract** type mechanisms, and types can be named using the type **synonym** mechanism.

Type variable A **variable** which appears in a **polymorphic type**. An **identifier** beginning with a small letter can be used as a type variable; in this text we use the letters t, u, v and so on.

Undefinedness The result of an expression whose evaluation continues forever, rather than giving a *defined* result.

Unification The process of finding a common **instance** of two (type) expressions containing (type) variables.

Value A value is a member of some **type**; the value of an **expression** is the result of **evaluating** the expression.

APPENDIX D

Understanding programs

This appendix is included to offer help to readers confronted with an unfamiliar function definition. There are various things we can do with the definition, and these are examined in turn here. Given a functional program like

```
mapWhile :: (t -> u) -> (t -> Bool) -> [t] -> [u]

mapWhile f p []     = []                              (1)
mapWhile f p (a:x)
    | p a           = f a : mapWhile f p x            (2)
    | otherwise     = []                              (3)
```

we can understand what it means in various complementary ways. We can read the program itself, we can write *calculations* of examples using the program, we can *prove* properties of the program, and we can estimate its space and time complexity,

Reading the program

Besides any comments which might accompany a program, the program itself is its most important documentation.

The type declaration gives information about the input and output types: for mapWhile, we have to supply three arguments:

- a function, f say, of arbitrary type, t -> u;
- a *property* of objects of type t; that is a function taking a t to a Boolean value; and
- a list of items of type t.

The output is a list of elements of type u – the output type of f.

The function definition itself is used to give values of mapWhile, but also can be read directly as a description of the program.

- On [], the result is [].
- On a non-empty list, if the head a has property p, then according to (2), we have f a as the first element of the result, with the remainder given by a recursive call on x.
- If the property p fails of a, the result is terminated, as it were, by returning the empty list [].

In the definition we have a complete description of how the program behaves, but we can animate this by trying specific examples.

Calculating with the program

A more concrete view of what the program does is given by calculating particular examples. For instance,

```
mapWhile (2+) (>7) [8,12,7,13,16]
= 2+8 : mapWhile (2+) (>7) [12,7,13,16]            by (2)
= 10 : 2+12 : mapWhile (2+) (>7) [7,13,16]         by (2)
= 10 : 14 : []                                     by (3)
= [10,14]
```

Other examples include

```
mapWhile (2+) (>2) [8,12,7,13,16] = [10,14,9,15,18]
mapWhile (2+) (>2) [] = []
```

Note that in these examples we use mapWhile at the instance

```
(Int -> Int) -> (Int -> Bool) -> [Int] -> [Int]
```

of its polymorphic type, given by replacing the type variables t and u by the type Int.

Reasoning about the program

We can get a deeper understanding about a program by *proving* properties that the program might have. For mapWhile, we might prove that for all f, p and finite lists x,

```
mapWhile f p x                 = map f (takeWhile p x)      (4)
mapWhile f (const True) x = map f x                         (5)
mapWhile id p x                = takeWhile p x              (6)
```

where we can, in fact, see (5) and (6) as consequences of the characterization of mapWhile given by property (4).

Program behaviour

It is not hard to see that the program will at worst take time linear (that is $O(^\wedge 1)$) in the length of the list argument assuming $O(^\wedge 0)$ behaviour of f and p, as it runs through the elements of the list once, if at all.

The *space* behaviour is more interesting; because we can output the head of a list once produced, the space required will be constant, as suggested by underlining the parts which can be output in the calculation above.

```
mapWhile (2+) (>7) [8,12,7,13,16]
= 2+8 : mapWhile (2+) (>7) [12,7,13,16]
= 10 : 2+12 : mapWhile (2+) (>7) [7,13,16]
= 10 : 14 : [] = [10,14]
```

Getting started

Each view of the program gives us a different understanding of its behaviour, but when we are presented with an unfamiliar definition we can begin to understand what its effect is by calculating various small examples. If we are given a collection of functions, we can test out the functions from the bottom up, building one calculation on top of another.

The important thing is to realize that rather than being stuck, we can get started by calculating representative examples to show us the way.

Haskell operators

The Haskell operators are listed below in decreasing order of binding power: see Section 2.4 for a discussion of associativity and binding power.

	Left associative	*Non-associative*	*Right associative*
9	!, !!, //		.
8			**, ^, ^^
7		*, %, /, `div`, `mod`, `rem`, `quot`	
6	+, -	:+	
5		\\	:, ++
4		/=, <, <=, ==, >, >=, `elem`, `notElem`	
3			&&
2			||
1		:=	
0			$

Also defined in this text are the operators

		>>=	
9	>.>		
5			>*>

The restrictions on names of operators, which are formed using the characters

> ! # $ % & * + . / < = > ? @ \ ^ | : - ~

are that operators must not start with a colon; this character starts an infix constructor. Operators can contain - and ~, but only as their first character.

Finally, certain combinations of symbols are reserved, and cannot be used:
`:: => = @ \ | ^ <- ->`.

To change the associativity or binding power of an operator, `&&&` say, we make a declaration like

```
infixl 7 &&&
```

which states that `&&&` has binding power 7, and is a left associative operator. We can also declare operators as non-associative (`infix`) and right associative (`infixr`). Omitting the binding power gives a default of 9. These declarations can also be used for back-quoted function names, as in

```
infix 0 `poodle`
```

APPENDIX F

Implementations of Haskell

Implementations of Haskell have been built at various sites around the world. In this text we have discussed Gofer and Hugs, which are written by Mark Jones, at the University of Nottingham. These interpreters (and a simple Gofer compiler) are available by FTP from

```
ftp://ftp.cs.nott.ac.uk/nott-fp/languages/gofer
ftp://ftp.cs.nott.ac.uk/haskell/hugs
```

Production-quality compilers have been built at Glasgow University, Yale University and Chalmers. These systems are available from a number of FTP sites

```
ftp://ftp.cs.chalmers.se/pub/haskell
ftp://ftp.dcs.glasgow.ac.uk/pub/haskell
ftp://nebula.cs.yale.edu/pub/haskell
ftp://src.doc.ic.ac.uk/pub/computing/programming/languages/
haskell
```

The last site, at Imperial College London, is a mirror of the Glasgow site. Other implementations are also being developed. For up-to-date information, see the functional programming FAQ, at

```
http://www.cs.nott.ac.uk/Department/Staff/mpj/faq.html
```

or the document `papers/Haskell.status` available from the FTP sites above.

Gofer and Hugs errors

This appendix examines some of the more common programming errors in Haskell, and shows the error messages to which they give rise in Gofer and Hugs.

The programs we write all too often contain errors. On encountering an error, the system either halts, and gives an *error message*, or continues, but gives a *warning message* to tell us that something unusual has happened, which might signal that we have made an error. In this appendix, we look at a selection of the messages output by Gofer and Hugs; we have chosen the messages which are both common and require some explanation; messages like

```
Program error: {head []}
```

are self-explanatory. The messages are classified into roughly distinct areas. Syntax errors show up malformed programs, while type errors show well-formed programs in which objects are used at the wrong types. In fact, an ill-formed expression can often show itself as a type error and not as a syntax error, so the boundaries are not clear.

Syntax errors

A Haskell system attempts to match the input we give to the syntax of the language. Commonly, when something goes wrong, we type something *unexpected*. Typing '2==3)' will provoke the error message

```
ERROR: Syntax error in input (unexpected ')')
```

If a part of a definition is missing, as in

```
fun x
fun 2 = 34
```

we receive the message

```
Syntax error in declaration (unexpected ';')
```

The ';' here is an indication of the end of a definition – the error message therefore tells us that a definition has been ended unexpectedly, as there is no right-hand side corresponding to the fun x.

The inclusion of a type definition in a where clause are signalled by

```
Syntax error in declaration (unexpected keyword "type")
```

The syntax of patterns is more restricted than the full expression syntax, and so we get error messages like

```
Repeated variable "x" in pattern
```

when we use the same variable more than once within a pattern.

In specifying constants, we can make errors: floating point numbers can be too large, and characters specified by an out of range ASCII code:

```
Inf.0
ERROR: Decimal character escape out of range
```

Not every string can be used as a name; some words in Haskell are **keywords** or **reserved identifiers**, and will give an error if used as an identifier. The keywords are

```
case class data default deriving else hiding if import in
infix infixl infixr instance interface let module of
qualified then to type where
```

The final restriction on names is that names of constructors and types must begin with a capital letter; nothing else can do so, and hence we get error messages like

```
Undefined constructor function "Montana"
```

if we try to define a function called Montana.

Type errors

As we have seen in the body of the text, the main type error we meet is exemplified by the response to typing True + 4 to the Gofer prompt:

```
ERROR: Type error in application
*** expression    : True + 4
*** term          : True
*** type          : Bool
*** does not match : Int
```

which is provoked by using a Bool where an Int is expected.

In Hugs (and other Haskell systems) a different message is given

```
ERROR: Cannot construct instance Num Bool in expression
```

This comes from the class mechanism: the system attempts to make Bool an instance of the class Num of numeric types over which '+' is defined. The error results since there is no such instance declaration making Bool belong to the class Num.

As we said before, we can get type errors from syntax errors. For example, writing abs -2 instead of abs (-2) gives the error message

```
ERROR: Type error in application
*** expression    : abs - 2
*** term          : abs
*** type          : a -> a
*** does not match : Int
```

because it is parsed as 2 subtracted from abs::a->a, and the operator '-' expects an Int, rather than a function of type a->a. Other common type errors come from confusing the roles of ':' and '++' as in 2++[2] and [2]:[2].

We always give type declarations for our definitions; one advantage of this is to spot when our definition does not conform to its declared type. For example,

```
myCheck :: Int -> Bool
myCheck n = n+0
```

gives the error message

```
ERROR "error.hs" (line 8): Type error in function binding
*** term          : myCheck
*** type          : Int -> Int
*** does not match : Int -> Bool
```

Without the type declaration the definition would be accepted, only to give an error (presumably) when it is used. A final error related to types is given by definitions like

```
type Fred = (Fred, Int)                                    (†)
```

a *recursive* type synonym; these are signalled by

```
ERROR "error.hs" (line 11): Recursive type synonym "Fred"
```

The effect of (†) can be modelled by the algebraic type definition

```
data Fred = Node Fred Int
```

which introduces the *constructor* Node to identify objects of this type.

Program errors

Once we have written a syntactically and type correct script, and asked for the value of an expression which is itself acceptable, other errors can be produced during the *evaluation* of the expression.

The first class of errors comes from missing cases in definitions. If we have written a definition like

```
bat [] = 45
```

and applied it to [45] we get the response

```
Program error: {bat [45]}
```

which shows the point at which evaluation can go no further, since there is no case in the definition of bat to cover a non-empty list. Similar errors come from built-in functions, such as head.

Other errors happen because an *arithmetical constraint* has been broken. These include an out-of-range list index, division by zero, using a fraction where an integer is expected and floating point calculations which go out of range; the error messages all have the same form:

```
Program error: {[] !! 22}
Program error: {3 'div' 0}
```

If we make a conformal definition, like

```
[a,b] = [1 .. 10]
```

this will fail with a lengthy message

```
Program error: {v134 [1, 2, 3] ++ takeWhile (v4 {dict} 10)
(iterate (primPlusInt 1) (primPlusInt 1 3))}
```

which reveals the implementation of this sort of definition.

Evaluation in Haskell is by need, and so a script which uses a name with no corresponding definition for the name will not be in error; only if the value of that name is required will we get the message

```
ERROR: Undefined variable "cat"
```

Module errors

The module and import statements can provoke a variety of error messages: files may not be present, or may contain errors; names may be included more than once, or an alias on inclusion may cause a name clash. The error messages for these and other errors are self-explanatory.

System messages

In response to some commands and interrupts, the system generates messages, including

```
^C{Interrupted!}
```

signalling the interruption of the current task,

```
ERROR: Garbage collection fails to reclaim sufficient space
```

which shows that the space consumption of the evaluation exceeds that available. One way around this is to increase the size of the heap. To see the current size of the heap and the other settings of the system type

```
:set
```

The message given there shows how the heap size can be changed, as well as how to affect other system parameters.

If the option +s is set, the system prints diagnostic information of the form

```
(2 reductions, 8 cells)
```

The number of reductions corresponds to the number of steps in our calculations and the cells to the total space usage.

A measure of the space complexity of a function, as described in Chapter 15 is given by the size of the smallest heap in which the evaluation can take place; there is no direct measure of this given by the system.

Some useful functions

Haskell systems contain a substantial number of function and class definitions, many of which have been explored in this text. For the standard functions over Booleans, characters and numbers, see Chapter 2. In particular for integers and floats see the tables of standard functions in Sections 2.1 and 2.8.

Many of the standard functions involve the list type; we review these here. They provide useful examples of programming style, as well as functions which can be re-used.

This section is loosely based on parts of the standard preludes of Haskell (Hudak *et al.*, 1992; Peterson *et al.*, 1996); the full preludes contain definitions of functions which we mention but do not define, as well as many more besides.

Basic polymorphic functions

To extract components of lists we have

```
head :: [t] -> t          tail :: [t] -> [t]
head (a:_) = a            tail (_:x) = x
```

with

```
last :: [t] -> t          init :: [t] -> [t]
```

performing similar functions at the other end of the list.

To join two lists we have

```
(++) :: [t] -> [t] -> [t]
[]      ++ y = y
(a:x)   ++ y = a:(x++y)
```

and to join (or concatenate) a list of lists we fold ++ into the list:

```
concat :: [[t]] -> [t]
concat = foldr (++) []
```

To remove the elements of one list from another (if they occur) we have

```
(\\) :: Eq t => [t] -> [t] -> [t]
```

The built in `length` gives the length of a list, as an `Int`, and `!!` gives list indexing:

```
(!!) :: (Integral t) => [u] -> t -> u
(a:_) !! 0 = a
(_:x) !! n = x !! (n-1)
```

The functions `map` and `filter` are familiar from Chapter 6; a variant of `filter` is

```
partition :: (t -> Bool) -> [t] -> ([t],[t])
partition p = foldr select ([],[])
              where
              select a (t,f)
                 | p a       = (a:t,f)
                 | otherwise = (t,a:f)
```

so that a list is split into two lists, consisting of those elements having and failing to have the required property. For example,

```
partition isDigit "there are 2 fish at number 27"
 = ("227","there are  fish at number ")
```

Using `filter` we can remove all duplicates from a list, leaving its 'nub'

```
nub :: Eq t => [t] -> [t]
nub []    = []
nub (a:x) = a : nub (filter (a/=) x)
```

To generate an infinite list we can apply a function repeatedly:

```
iterate :: (t -> t) -> t -> [t]
iterate f a = a : iterate f (f a)
```

and finally we can reverse a list:

```
reverse :: [t] -> [t]
reverse = foldl (flip (:)) []
```

where a function has its two arguments 'flipped' by

```
flip :: (t -> u -> v) -> (u -> t -> v)
flip f a b = f b a
```

Fold functions

To combine elements of lists we use the fold functions, which fold from the left and the right:

```
foldl :: (t -> u -> t) -> t -> [u] -> t
foldl f a []     = a
foldl f a (b:x)  = foldl f (f a b) x

foldr :: (u -> t -> t) -> t -> [u] -> t
foldr f a []     = a
foldr f a (b:x)  = f b (foldr f a x)
```

A variant of foldl is more efficient:

```
foldl' :: Eval t => (t -> u -> t) -> t -> [u] -> t
foldl' f a []     = a
foldl' f a (b:x)  = strict (foldl' f) (f a b) x
```

and another works over non-empty lists:

```
foldl1 :: (t -> t -> t) -> [t] -> t
foldl1 f (a:x)   = foldl f a x
```

There is a similar definition of the function foldr1.

Splitting up lists

Here we look at some functions which allow us to split lists. take and drop split a list after a certain number of elements:

```
take :: Integral t => t -> [u] -> [u]
take 0 _    = []
take _ []   = []
take n (a:x) = a : take (n-1) x

drop :: Integral t => t -> [u] -> [u]
drop 0 x    = x
drop _ []   = []
drop n (_:x) = drop (n-1) x
```

while

```
splitAt :: Integral t => t -> [u] -> ([u], [u])
```

combines the two, returning a pair, thus

```
splitAt 4 "fishcake" = ("fish","cake")
```

Instead of specifying an index at which to split, we can take or drop *while* a property (of type t -> Bool) holds of the elements:

```
takeWhile :: (u -> Bool) -> [u] -> [u]
takeWhile p [] = []
takeWhile p (a:x)
  | p a       = a : takeWhile p x
  | otherwise = []
```

with similar definitions for dropWhile and span, so that

```
span isDigit "234henry67" = ("234","henry67")
```

We can also split into lines (that is, at newlines) or words (at white space):

```
lines    :: String -> [String]
lines "" = []
lines s  = l : (if null s' then [] else lines (tail s'))
              where (l, s') = splitAt ('\n'==) s
                                Span
words    :: String -> [String]
```

and these functions have inverses to join the words or lines together:

```
unlines   :: [String] -> String
unlines    = concat . map (++ "\n")


unwords   :: [String] -> String
```

Functions of specific types

There are various standard functions over Boolean and numerical lists:

```
and, or :: [Bool] -> Bool
and = foldr (&&) True
or  = foldr (||) False


any, all :: (t -> Bool) -> [t] -> Bool
any p = or  . map p
all p = and . map p
```

To test for elementhood, we have

```
elem, notElem    :: Eq t => t -> [t] -> Bool
elem    = any . (==)
notElem = all . (/=)
```

Over numerical lists we can find the sum and product:

```
sum, product :: Num t => [t] -> t
sum     = foldl' (+) 0
product = foldl' (*) 1
```

and accumulate the partial sums and products:

```
sums, products :: Num t => [t] -> [t]
sums     = scanl (+) 0
products = scanl (*) 1
```

In a similar way we calculate the maximum or minimum of non-empty lists of elements from types with an ordering, that is types lying in the Ord class.

```
maximum, minimum :: Ord t => [t] -> t
maximum = foldl1 max
minimum = foldl1 min
```

Lists and tuples

We can `zip` two lists into a list of pairs

```
zip  :: [t] -> [u] -> [(t,u)]
zip  = zipWith  (\a b -> (a,b))
```

with functions `zip3` and so on taking three lists into a list of triples. A `zip` is reversed by

```
unzip :: [(t,u)] -> ([t],[u])
```

In defining `zip` we use the more general `zipWith` which combines the corresponding elements of the two lists using the function supplied:

```
zipWith :: (t->u->v) -> [t]->[u]->[v]
zipWith f (a:x) (b:y) = f a b : zipWith f x y
zipWith _ _      _    = []
```

Bibliography

Armstrong J., Virding R. and Williams M.
(1993). *Concurrent Programming in
ERLANG*. Prentice-Hall

Backus J. (1978). Can programming be
liberated from the Von Neumann style?
Communications of the ACM, **21**(8)

Barendregt H. (1993). Lambda calculi with
types. In Abramsky S. *et al.*, eds, *Handbook
of Logic and Computer Science*, Vol. 2.
Oxford University Press

Bird R.S. (1990). A calculus of functions for
program derivation. In Turner D.A., ed.,
Research Topics in Functional Programming.
Addison-Wesley

Cardelli L. and Wegner P. (1985). On
understanding types, data abstraction and
polymorphism. *Computing Surveys*, **17**

Cormen T.H., Leiserson C.E. and Rivest R.L.
(1990). *Introduction to Algorithms*. MIT Press

Darlington J. (1982). Program transformation.
In Darlington J., Henderson P. and Turner
D.A., eds, *Functional Programming and its
Applications*. Cambridge University Press

Galton A. (1990). *Logic for Information
Technology*. Wiley

Girard J.-Y., Lafont Y. and Taylor P. (1989).
*Proofs and Types, Cambridge Tracts in
Theoretical Computer Science*, Vol. 7.
Cambridge University Press

Gordon A.J. (1994). *Functional Programming
and Input/Output*. British Computer Society
Distinguished Dissertations in Computer
Science. Cambridge University Press

Hartel P. and Plasmeijer R., eds (1995a).
*Functional Programming Languages in
Education (FPLE)*. Springer-Verlag, Lecture
Notes in Computer Science, 1022

Hartel P. and Plasmeijer R. (1995b). Special
issue on state-of-the-art applications of pure
functional programming languages. *Journal
of Functional Programming*, **5**

Hudak P. and Fasel J.H. (1992). A gentle
introduction to Haskell. *ACM SIGPLAN
Notices*, **27**(5)

Hudak P., Peyton Jones S. and Wadler P., eds
(1992). Report on the Programming
Language Haskell, version 1.2. *ACM
SIGPLAN Notices*, **27**(5)

Huet G., ed. (1990). *Logical Foundations of
Functional Programming*. Addison-Wesley

Hughes J. (1990). Why Functional
Programming Matters. In Turner D.A., ed.,
Research Topics in Functional Programming.
Addison-Wesley

Jeuring J. and Meijer E., eds (1995). *Advanced
Functional Programming*. Springer-Verlag,
Lecture Notes in Computer Science, 925

Jones M. (1995a). *Gofer functional programming
enviroment; release notes* 2.20, 2.21, 2.28, 2.30

Jones M. (1995b). A system of constructor
classes: overloading and implicit higher-order
polymorphism. *Journal of Functional
Programming*, **5**

Laufer K. (1994). Combining type classes and
existential types. In *Proceedings of the Latin
American Informatics Conference*, Mexico

Luo Z. (1994). *Computation and Reasoning: a
Type Theory for Computer Science*. Oxford
University Press

Milner R. (1978). A theory of type polymorphism in programming. *Journal of Computer and System Sciences*, **17**

Milner R., Tofte M. and Harper R. (1990). *The Definition of Standard ML*. MIT Press

Okasaki C. (1994). Simple and efficient purely functional queues and deques. *Journal of Functional Programming*, **4**

Paulson L.C. (1987). *Logic and Computation – Interactive Proof with Cambridge LCF*. Cambridge University Press

Paulson L.C. (1991). *ML for the Working Programmer*. Cambridge University Press

Peterson J. and Hammond K., eds (1996). Report on the Programming Language Haskell, version 1.3. *Technical Report* Department of Computer Science Yale University. Also available via http://haskell.cs.yale.edu/haskell-report/haskell-report.html

Peyton Jones S. (1987). *The Implementation of Functional Programming Languages*. Prentice-Hall

Peyton Jones S. and Lester D. (1992). *Implementing Functional Languages*. Prentice-Hall

Reeves S. and Clarke M. (1990). *Logic for Computer Science*. Addison-Wesley

Runciman C. and Wakeling D., eds (1995). *Applications of Functional Programming*. UCL Press

Sanella D. (1986). Formal specification of ML programs. *Technical Report ECS-LFCS-86-15*, Laboratory for Foundations of Computer Science, Edinburgh University

Thompson S.J. (1990). Interactive functional programs: a method and a formal semantics. In Turner D.A., ed., *Research Topics in Functional Programming*. Addison-Wesley

Thompson S.J. (1991). *Type Theory and Functional Programming*. Addison-Wesley

Thompson S.J. (1995). *Miranda: The Craft of Functional Programming*. Addison-Wesley

Thompson S.J. and Wadler P. (1993). Functional programming in education – introduction. *Journal of Functional Programming*, **3**

Turner D.A. (1985). Miranda: a non-strict functional language with polymorphic types. In Jouannaud J.P., ed., *Functional Programming Languages and Computer Architecture*. Springer-Verlag

Turner D.A. (1990a). An overview of Miranda. In Turner D.A., ed., *Research Topics in Functional Programming*. Addison-Wesley

Turner D.A. (1990b). *Research Topics in Functional Programming*. Addison-Wesley

Wikström Å. (1987). *Functional Programming in Standard ML*. Prentice-Hall

Index